Intel® Xeon Phi™ Coprocessor High-Performance Programming

Intel® Xeon Phi™ Coprocessor High-Performance Programming

Jim Jeffers

James Reinders

AMSTERDAM • BOSTON • HEIDELBERG • LONDON
NEW YORK • OXFORD • PARIS • SAN DIEGO
SAN FRANCISCO • SINGAPORE • SYDNEY • TOKYO
Morgan Kaufmann is an imprint of Elsevier

Acquiring Editor: Todd Green
Development Editor: Lindsay Lawrence
Project Manager: Mohanambal Natarajan
Designer: Mark Rogers

Morgan Kaufmann is an imprint of Elsevier
225 Wyman Street, Waltham, MA 02451, USA

Library of Congress Cataloging-in-Publication Data
Application submitted

British Library Cataloguing-in-Publication Data
A catalogue record for this book is available from the British Library

ISBN: 978-0-12-410414-3

For information on all Morgan Kaufmann publications
visit our website at www.mkp.com

Printed in the United States of America

13 14 15 16 17 10 9 8 7 6 5 4 3 2

Contents

Foreword

I cannot think of a more exciting (that is to say, tumultuous) era in high performance computing since the introduction in the mid-80s of massively parallel computers such as the Intel iPSC and nCUBE, followed by the IBM SP and Beowulf clusters. But now, instead of benefiting only high-performance applications parallelized with MPI or other distributed memory models, the revolution is happening within a node and is benefiting everyone, whether running a laptop or multi-petaFLOP/s supercomputer. In sharp contrast to the GPGPUs that fired our collective imagination in the last decade, the Intel®Xeon Phi™ product family (its first product version already being one teraFLOP/s double-precision peak speed!) brings supercomputer performance right into everyone's office while employing standard programing tools fully compatible with the desktop environment including a full suite of numerical software and the entire GNU/Linux stack. With both architectural and software unity from multi-core Intel® Architecture processors to many-core Intel Xeon Phi products we have for the first time a holistic path for portable, high-performance computing that is based upon a familiar and proven threaded, scalar-vector programming model. And Intel's vision for Intel® Many Integrated Core (Intel® MIC) architecture takes us from the early petaFLOP era in 2012 into the exaFLOP era in 2020–indeed, the Intel Xeon Phi coprocessor based on Intel MIC architecture is credibly a glimpse into that future.

So what's the catch? There's actually no new news here—sequential (more specifically singled-threaded and non-vectorized) computation is dead even in the desktop. Long dead. Pipelined functional units, multiple instruction issue, SIMD extensions, and multi-core architectures killed that years ago. But if you have one of the 99 percent of applications that are not yet both multi-threaded and vectorized, then on multicore Intel Xeon with AVX SIMD units you could be missing a factor of up to 100x in performance, and the highly-threaded Intel MIC architecture implies a factor of up to 1000x. Yes, you are reading those numbers correctly. A scalar, single-threaded application, depending on what is limiting its performance, could be leaving several orders of magnitude in single-socket performance on the table. All modern processors, whether CPU or GPGPU, require very large amounts of parallelism to attain high performance. Some good news on Intel Xeon Phi coprocessors is that with your application running out of the box thanks to the standard programming environment (again in contrast to GPGPUs that require recoding even to run), you can use familiar tools to analyze performance and have a robust path for incremental transformations to optimize the code, and those optimizations will carry directly over to mainstream processors. But how to optimize the code? Which algorithms, data structures, numerical representations, loop constructs, languages, compilers, and so on, are a good match for Intel Xeon Phi products? And how to do all of this in a way that is not necessarily specific to the current Intel MIC architecture but instead positions you for future and even non-Intel architectures? This book generously and accessibly puts the answer to all of these questions and more into your hands.

A critical point is that early in the "killer-micro" revolution that replaced custom vector processors with commodity CPUs, application developers ceased to develop vectorized algorithms because the first generations of these CPUs could indeed attain a good fraction of peak performance on operation-rich sequential code. Fast forward two decades and this is now far from true but the passage of time has erased from our collective memory much of the wisdom and folklore of the vectorized algorithms so successful on Cray and other vector computers. However, the success of that era should give us great confidence that a multi-threaded, scalar-vector programming model supported by a rich vector instruction set is a great match for a very broad range of algorithms and disciplines. Needless to say, there are new challenges such as the deeper and more complex memory hierarchy of modern processors, an order of magnitude more threads, the lack of true hardware gather/scatter, and compilers still catching up with (rediscovering?) what was possible 25 years ago.

In October 2010, I gave a talk entitled "DSLs, Vectors, and Amnesia," at an excellent workshop on language tools in Houston organized by John Mellor-Crummey. Amnesia referred to the loss of vectorization capabilities mentioned above. I used the example of rationalizing the bizarrely large speedups[1] claimed in the early days of using GPGPUs as a platform to identify successes and failures in mainstream programming. Inconsistent optimization of applications on the two platforms is the trivial explanation, with the GPGPU realizing a much higher fraction of its peak speed. But why was this so, and what was to learn from this about writing code with portable performance? There were two reasons underlying the performance discrepancy. First, the data-parallel programming languages such as OpenCL and NVidia's CUDA† forced programmers to write massively data-parallel code that, with a good compiler and some tuning of vector lengths and data layout, perfectly matched the underlying hardware and realized high performance. Second, the comparison was usually made against a scalar, non-threaded x86 code that we now understand to be far from optimal. The universal solution was to back-port the GPGPU code to the multi-core CPU with retuning for the different numbers of cores and vector/cache sizes—indeed with care and some luck the same code base could serve on both platforms (and certainly so if programming with OpenCL). All of the optimizations for locality, bandwidth, concurrency, and vectorization carry straight over, and the cleaner, simplified, dependency-free code is more readily analyzed by compilers. Thus, there is every reason to expect that nearly all algorithms that work well on current GPGPUs can with a minimal amount of restructuring execute equally well on the Intel Xeon Phi coprocessor, and that algorithms requiring fine-grain concurrent control should be significantly easier to express on the coprocessor than on GPGPU.

In reading this book you will come to know its authors. Through the Intel MIC architecture early customer enabling program, I have worked with Jim Jeffers who in addition to being articulate, clear thinking, and genial, is an expert well worth your time and the price of this book. Moreover, he and the other leaders of the Intel Xeon Phi product development program truly sense that they are doing something significant and transformative that will shape the future of computing and is worth the huge commitment of their professional and personal life.

This book belongs on the bookshelf of every HPC professional. Not only does it successfully and accessibly teach us how to use and obtain high performance on the Intel MIC architecture, it

[1]Factors of over 100x in performance compared to conventional x86 CPUs that according to hardware metrics such as bandwidth and floating point speed were just 4–12x slower.

is about much more than that. It takes us back to the universal fundamentals of high-performance computing including how to think and reason about the performance of algorithms mapped to modern architectures, and it puts into your hands powerful tools that will be useful for years to come.

Robert J. Harrison
Institute for Advanced Computational Science
Stony Brook University
October 2012

Preface

We have both spent two years helping educate customers about the prototype and preproduction hardware before Intel introduced the first Intel® Xeon Phi™ coprocessor. During those two years, we have learned much as we endeavored to teach and assist customers in programming for the Intel® Many Integrated Core (Intel® MIC) architecture.

While we offer many tips specific to getting the most from an Intel Xeon Phi coprocessor, we hope that you will find, at the heart of this book, the keys to general parallel programming. These keys are not specifically for Intel Xeon Phi coprocessors but for any general-purpose parallel computer. The challenges of parallel computing are simple to enumerate: expose lots of parallelism and minimize communication (said another way: maximize locality). In the course of extolling the need to address these challenges, we provide guidance and motivation that will enhance any parallel program. Every programmer we have talked with who has optimized for Intel Xeon Phi coprocessors has told us that their code also now runs faster on Intel Xeon processors as well as parallel systems with non-Intel microprocessors because of their optimization work.

We were certainly inspired to write this book by the insights and success many have had with this highly parallel programming. But we have been equally inspired by the frustrations and difficulties associated with highly parallel programming. Sometimes these stem from insufficient appreciation for the magnitude of parallelism such a device needs to consume to stay busy and the techniques needed to do so. Our desire to share the successful methods to better teach and prepare a broad range of programmers has been the key inspiration for this book.

We have distilled the hard earned knowledge gained in these first couple of years by ourselves, customers, and many engineers at Intel. We share the critical concepts and practical advice on how to program for the Intel Xeon Phi coprocessor and its Intel MIC architecture.

We have endeavored to provide guidance on what matters most in programming, so that the reader can best approach the products available today and those we anticipate as this new architecture continues to grow in capabilities in the future.

Organization

This book is organized to get started programming quickly. We dive into programming after a brief introduction to motivate through programming examples that illustrate methods for achieving performance.

We organized Chapters 1–5 to build upon each other, and Chapters 6–14 to be self-contained to support reading in any order. Chapters 6 and later more completely explain individual elements of the system with the hope that the programming examples have motivated the reader to explore these chapters as well.

No one book can cover everything. This book presents the essentials that will enable you to program effectively. Even though this book covers the key concepts along with all the essential concepts needed to program effectively, there is only so much detail you can have in four hundred pages. We are already soliciting ideas for a Volume 2, which will expand upon the essential information in this book by providing valuable items that we were not able to fit into Volume 1.

Lots-of-cores.com

We will make available downloads, examples, errata, supplemental information, and excerpts from Volume 2 as they become available, at our Web site (http://lotsofcores.com) for this multivolume project to teach programming of the Intel® Xeon Phi™ coprocessor.

We hope this book enables you to share our excitement in the opening of the new chapter in parallel computing that comes from Intel MIC architecture and Intel Xeon Phi coprocessors.

James L. Jeffers and James R. Reinders
Intel Corporation
January 2013

Acknowledgements

We are grateful to customers and Intel engineers who have helped us in our quest to make this book happen.

Thank you, Scott McMillan, for writing the chapter on MPI. Your insights and writing skills are greatly appreciated.

Thank you to Robert Harrison, Director, Institute for Advanced Computational Science at Stony Brook University, for his support, expertise, and passion, and for sharing his unique insights in the preface.

We wish to thank several people for the documentation or white papers that they had written which we used as source material. The quality and quantity of material we had to start with was a big help in writing this book in a timely manner: Ron Te and Mike Casscles for the System Software Developers Guide; Clayton Craft for the Instruction Set Architecture document; Robert Reed and Shannon Cepeda for the stencil code in Chapter 4; Shannon Cepeda and Wendy Doerner for vectorization training and papers; Martyn Corden for his articles about vectorization; Shannon Cepeda, Larry Meadows, and David Mackay for tuning papers; Johnnie Peters with Alexandra Yates on Linux configuration information in Chapter 10; Rakesh Krishnaiyer for advice on prefetching; Taylor Kidd for countless training documents that highlighted the key points and many items worth special mention; Raymundo Vazquez for information regarding timers; information regarding cluster configurations from Michael Hebenstreit, Romain Dolbeau, Jeremy C. Siadal, Andreas Hirstius, Andres More, Clem Cole, Matias Cabral, and Werner Krotz-Vogel.

We want to extend our gratitude to the great work done by the Intel SSG Information Development team, who has written outstanding product documentation that was both educational for us and useful source material. Our apologies if we fail to mention everyone who contributed; we thank the whole team, which included efforts from Mitch Bodart, Ivan De Cesaris, Kevin Davis, Rajiv Deodhar, Karen Dickinson, Wendy Doerner, Stephen Goodman, Ronald Green, Elena Indrupskaya, Irina Kosareva, Rakesh Krishnaiyer, Lorri Menard, Sabrina Mesters-Woell, Ravi Narayanaswamy, Sunil Pandey, Christopher Raleigh, Premanand M Rao, Amanda Sharp, Michael Sturm, Michael Toguchi, Miwako Tokugawa, Stan Whitlock, and Anatoly Zvezdin.

Many people associated with the Knights Corner project gave input and feedback that was especially valuable to the first chapter, including Mani Anandan, Andrew Brownsword, George Chrysos, William Clifford, Kim Colosimo, Charles Congdon, Joe Curley, Ervin Dehmlow, Pradeep Dubey, Gus Esponosa, Robert Geva, Milind Girkar, Ron Green, Michael Greenfield, John Hengeveld, Scott Huck, Jim Jeffers, Mike Julier, Rakesh Krishnaiyer, Belinda Liverio, David Mackay, Bill Magro, Larry Meadows, Chris Newburn, Brian Nickerson, Beth Reinders, Frances Roth, Bill Savage, Elizabeth Schneider, Gregg Skinner, Sanjiv Shah, Lance Shuler, Dancil Strickland, Brock Taylor, Philippe Thierry, Xinmin Tian, Matt Walsh, and Joe Wolf.

Many of people named thus far helped review parts of the book. We are grateful to them and others who gave their time to help improve this book, including Rob Fowler of RENCI/University of North Carolina, Neil Stringfellow and Jeff Poznanovic of CSCS/Swiss National Supercomputing Centre, Kevin Thomas and James L. Schwarzmeier of Cray Inc. and Clayton Craft, Jeanette

Feldhousen, Michael Hebenstreit, Elena Indrupskaya, Hans Pabst, Steve Lionel, Susan Meredith, Xinmin Tian, Zhang Zhang, and Georg Zitzlsberger of Intel, and James A. Ang of Sandia National Laboratories.

Heinrich Bockhorst, Kathy Carver, Jim Cownie, Loc Nguyen, Klaus-Dieter Oertel, Dmitry Sivkov, Alexander Supalov, and James Tullos provided valuable feedback on Chapter 12.

Andrey Vladimirov of Colfax Corporation is an inspiration with his insights and training materials and has provided valued feedback for this book including some code examples used in Chapter 7.

To the team at the Texas Advance Computing Center (TACC) for valuable feedback on the book and the Intel Manycore program, plus elements of the stencil algorithm used in Chapter 3, including Kent Milfeld, Dan Stanzione, Bill Barth, Karl Schultz, Tommy Minyard, Jim Brown, John McCalpin, Lars Koesterke, and TACC Director, Jay Boisseau.

Glenn Brook, Ryan Braby, Ryan Hulguin, Vince Betro, and many others at the National Institute of Computational Science (NICS) for their feedback on the book and their excellent work and feedback using coprocessors for science.

Special thanks from James Reinders to his wife Elizabeth and daughter Katie who were supportive of the long hours writing. Beth Reinders was the notable talent behind guiding Chapter 1 to make sense and her insights into the critical points that needed to be crisp for a broader audience especially for challenges that we had with Chapters 1 and 8. Finally, my coauthor and friend, Jim Jeffers, who was the perfect partner to getting this book out with his talents for teaching, understanding, questioning, and hard work always with a sense of humor even the midst of customer crisis and a major product launch (why did we agree to write this book in our spare time?).

Special thanks from Jim Jeffers to his wife Laura and his children Tim, Patrick, Colleen, Sarah, and Jon for their support, encouragement, and consideration over weekends, evenings, and absences while traveling and working on the book. Also, to my longtime friend and colleague, Joe Curley, for bringing me back to Intel to contribute to this ambitious and exciting program. To Nathan Schultz for his support and encouragement, especially during the final push to complete this book. Finally, to James Reinders for his guidance, expertise, focus, and friendship in driving this book to completion.

For their time, support, and expertise we would like to thank George Chrysos, Joe Curley, Stuart Douglas, Herb Hinstorff, Michael Julier, Michael McCool, Chris Newburn, Elizabeth Reinders, Nathan Schultz, and Arch Robison.

The Intel Press team, in particular David Clark and Stuart Douglas, did a tremendous job helping us complete this book. Dan Mandish for his fine artwork. We appreciate the hard work by the entire Morgan Kaufmann team including the three people we worked with directly: Todd Green, Lindsay Lawrence, and Mohanambal Natarajan.

Numerous colleagues offered information, advice, and vision. Many students took classes from us and their feedback improved the quality of our teaching material that in turn fed into this book. There are certainly many people who have helped directly and indirectly and we failed to mention. We thank *all* those who helped and we apologize for any who helped us and we failed to mention.

Thank you all,

James L. Jeffers & James R. Reinders

CHAPTER

Introduction

1

In this book, we bring together the essentials to high performance programming for a Intel® Xeon Phi™ coprocessor. As we'll see, programming for the Intel Xeon Phi coprocessors is mostly about programming in the same way as you would for an Intel® Xeon® processor-based system, but with extra attention on exploiting lots of parallelism. This extra attention pays off for processor-based systems as well. You'll see this "Double Advantage of Transforming-and-Tuning" to be a key aspect of why programming for the Intel Xeon Phi coprocessor is particularly rewarding and helps protect investments in programming.

The Intel Xeon Phi coprocessor is both generally programmable and tailored to tackle highly parallel problems. As such, it is ready to consume very demanding parallel applications. We explain how to make sure your application is constructed to take advantage of such a large parallel capability. As a natural side effect, these techniques generally improve performance on less parallel machines and prepare applications better for computers of the future as well. The overall concept can be thought of as "Portable High Performance Programming."

Sports cars are not designed for a superior experience driving around on slow-moving congested highways. As we'll see, the similarities between an Intel Xeon Phi coprocessor and a sports car will give us opportunities to mention sports cars a few more times in the next few chapters.

Sports Car in Two Situations: Left in Traffic, Right on Race Course.

Trend: more parallelism

To squeeze more performance out of new designs, computer designers rely on the strategy of adding more transistors to do multiple things at once. This represents a shift away from relying on higher speeds, which demanded higher power consumption, to a more power-efficient parallel approach. Hardware performance derived from parallel hardware is more disruptive for software design than speeding up the hardware because it benefits parallel applications to the exclusion of nonparallel programs.

It is interesting to look at a few graphs that quantify the factors behind this trend. Figure 1.1 shows the end of the "era of higher processor speeds," which gives way to the "era of higher processor parallelism" shown by the trends graphed in Figures 1.2 and 1.3. This switch is possible because, while both eras required a steady rise in the number of transistors available for a computer design, trends in transistor density continue to follow Moore's law as shown in Figure 1.4. A continued rise in transistor density will continue to drive more parallelism in computer design and result in more performance for programs that can consume it.

Why Intel® Xeon Phi™ coprocessors are needed

Intel Xeon Phi coprocessors are designed to extend the reach of applications that have demonstrated the ability to fully utilize the scaling capabilities of Intel Xeon processor-based systems and fully exploit available processor vector capabilities or memory bandwidth. For such applications, the Intel Xeon Phi coprocessors offer additional power-efficient scaling, vector support, and local memory bandwidth, while maintaining the programmability and support associated with Intel Xeon processors.

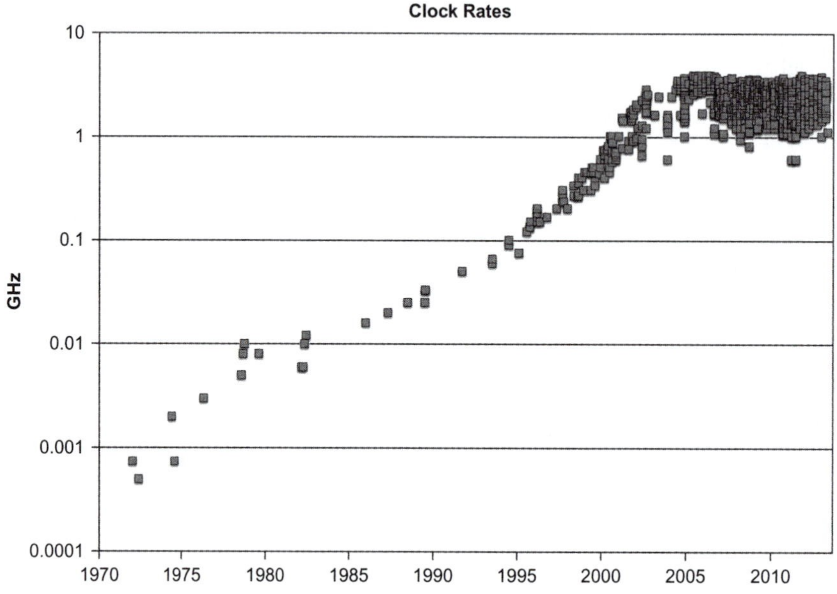

FIGURE 1.1

Processor/Coprocessor Speed Era [Log Scale].

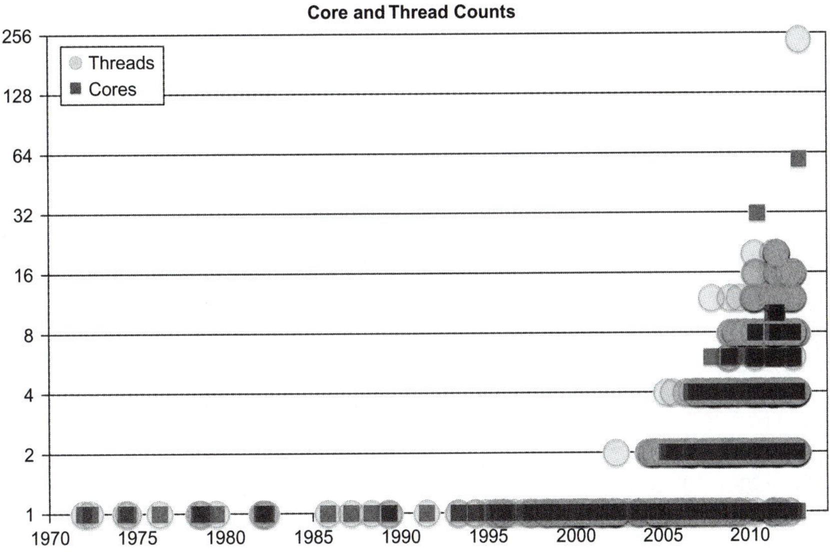

FIGURE 1.2

Processor/Coprocessor Core/Thread Parallelism [Log Scale].

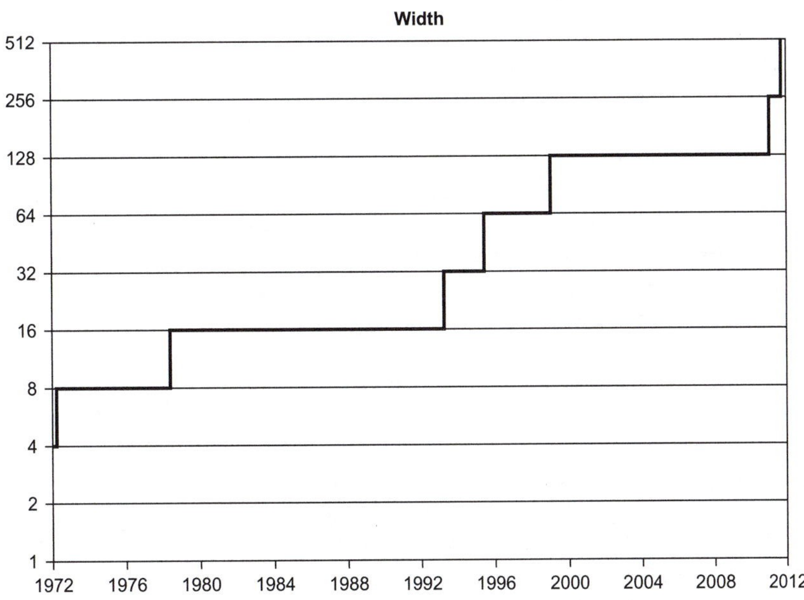

FIGURE 1.3

Processor/Coprocessor Vector Parallelism [Log Scale].

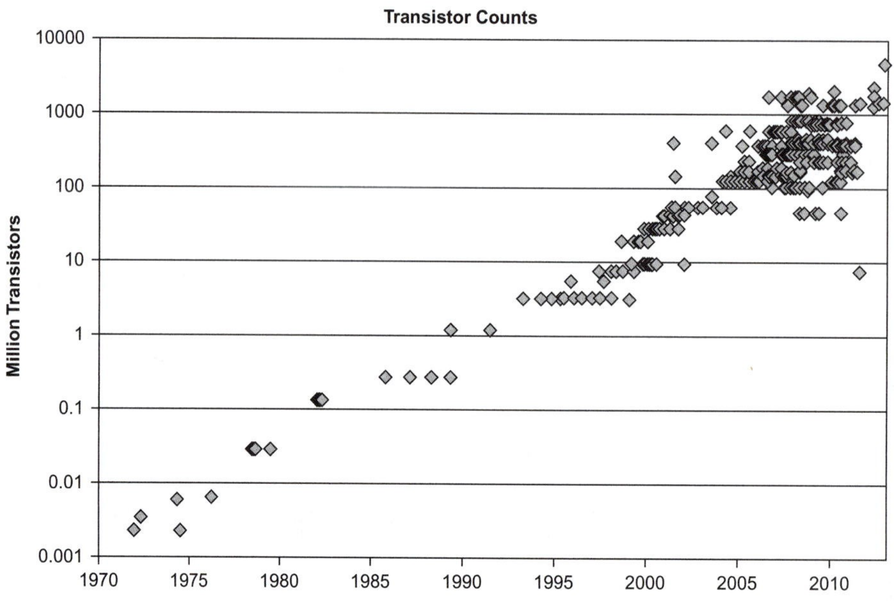

FIGURE 1.4

Moore's Law Continues, Processor/Coprocessor Transistor Count [Log Scale].

Most applications in the world have not been structured to exploit parallelism. This leaves a wealth of capabilities untapped on nearly every computer system. Such applications can be extended in performance by a highly parallel device only when the application expresses a need for parallelism through parallel programming.

Advice for successful parallel programming can be summarized as "Program with lots of threads that use vectors with your preferred programming languages and parallelism models." Since most applications have not yet been structured to take advantage of the full magnitude of parallelism available in any processor, understanding how to restructure to expose more parallelism is critically important to enable the best performance for Intel Xeon processors or Intel Xeon Phi coprocessors. This restructuring itself will generally yield benefits on most general-purpose computing systems, a bonus due to the emphasis on common programming languages, models, and tools across the processors and coprocessors. We refer to this bonus as the dual-transforming-tuning advantage.

It has been said that a single picture can speak a thousand words; for understanding Intel Xeon Phi coprocessors (or any highly parallel device) it is Figure 1.5 that speaks a thousand words. We should not dwell on the exact numbers as they are based on some models that may be as typical as applications can be. The picture speaks to this principle: Intel Xeon Phi coprocessors offer the ability to make a system that can potentially offer exceptional performance while still being buildable and power efficient. Intel Xeon processors deliver performance much more readily for a broad range of applications but do reach a practical limit on peak performance as indicated by the end of

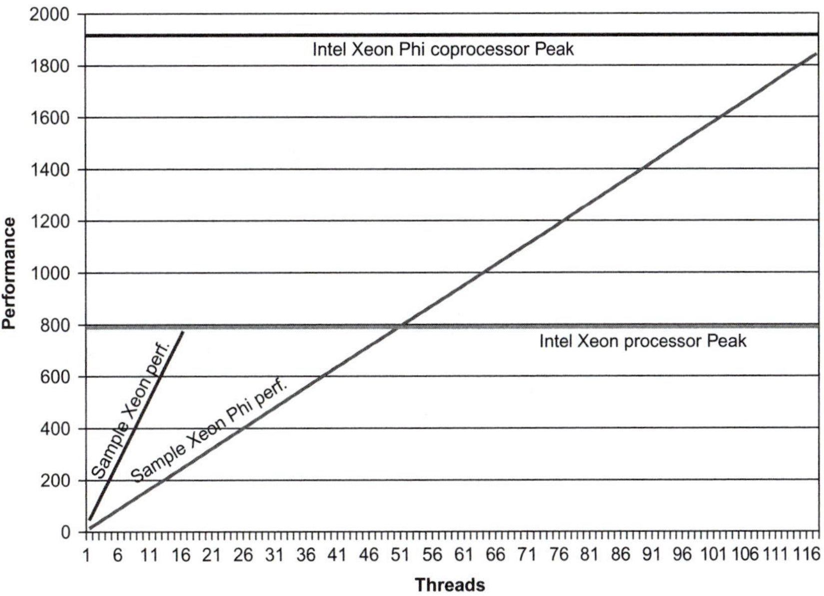

FIGURE 1.5

This Picture Speaks a Thousand Words.

the line in Figure 1.5. The key is "ready to use parallelism." Note from the picture that more parallelism is needed to make the Intel Xeon Phi coprocessor reach the same performance level, and that requires programming adapted to deliver that higher level of parallelism required. In exchange for the programming investment, we may reach otherwise unobtainable performance. The transforming-and-tuning double advantage of these Intel products is that the use of the same parallel programming models, programming languages, and familiar tools to greatly enhance preservation of programming investments. We'll revisit this picture later.

Platforms with coprocessors

A typical platform is diagrammed in Figure 1.6. Multiple such platforms may be interconnected to form a cluster or supercomputer. A platform cannot consist of only coprocessors. Processors are cache coherent and share access to main memory with other processors. Coprocessors are cache-coherent SMP-on-a-chip[1] devices that connect to other devices via the PCIe bus, and are not hardware cache coherent with other processors or coprocessors in the node or the system.

The Intel Xeon Phi coprocessor runs Linux. It really is an x86 SMP-on-a-chip running Linux. Every card has its own IP address. We logged onto one of our pre-production systems in a terminal window. We first got a shell on the host (an Intel Xeon processor), and then we did "ssh mic0", which

[1]SMP: symmetric multiprocessor, a multiprocessor system with shared memory and running a single operating system.

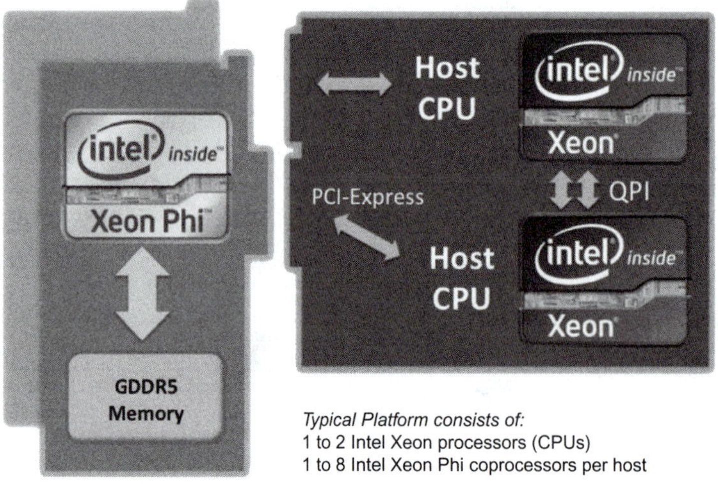

FIGURE 1.6

Processors and Coprocessors in a Platform Together.

logged me into the first coprocessor card in the system. Once we had this window, we listed /proc/cpuinfo. The result is 6100 lines long, so we're showing the first 5 and last 26 lines in Figure 1.7.

In some ways, for me, this really makes the Intel Xeon Phi coprocessor feel very familiar. From this window, we can "ssh" to the world. We can run "emacs" (you can run "vi" if that is your thing). We can run "awk" scripts or "perl." We can start up an MPI program to run across the cores of this card, or to connect with any other computer in the world.

If you are wondering how many cores are in an Intel Xeon Phi coprocessor, the answer is "it depends." It turns out there are, and will be, a variety of configurations available from Intel, all with more than 50 cores. Preserving programming investments is greatly enhanced by the transforming-and-tuning double advantage. For years, we have been able to buy processors in a variety of clock speeds. More recently, an additional variation in offerings is based on the number of cores. The results in Figure 1.7 are from a 61-core pre-production Intel Xeon Phi coprocessor that is a precursor to the production parts known as an Intel Xeon Phi coprocessor SE10x. It reports a processor number 243 because the threads are enumerated 0..243 meaning there are 244 threads (61 cores times 4 threads per core).

The first Intel® Xeon Phi™ coprocessor

The first Intel® Xeon Phi™ coprocessor was known by the code name Knights Corner early in development. While programming does not require deep knowledge of the implementation of the device, it is definitely useful to know some attributes of the coprocessor. From a programming standpoint, treating it as an x86-based SMP-on-a-chip with over fifty cores, with multiple hardware threads per core, and 512-bit SIMD instructions, is the key. It is not critical to completely absorb

```
root@dpdknf01:/KNC — ssh — 100x35
% cat /proc/cpuinfo | head -5
processor       : 0
vendor_id       : GenuineIntel
cpu family      : 11
model           : 1
model name      : 0b/01
%
% cat /proc/cpuinfo | tail -26

processor       : 243
vendor_id       : GenuineIntel
cpu family      : 11
model           : 1
model name      : 0b/01
stepping        : 1
cpu MHz         : 1090.908
cache size      : 512 KB
physical id     : 0
siblings        : 244
core id         : 60
cpu cores       : 61
apicid          : 243
initial apicid  : 243
fpu             : yes
fpu_exception   : yes
cpuid level     : 4
wp              : yes
flags           : fpu vme de pse tsc msr pae mce cx8 apic mtrr mca pat fxsr ht syscall lm lahf_lm
bogomips        : 2192.10
clflush size    : 64
cache_alignment : 64
address sizes   : 40 bits physical, 48 bits virtual
power management:

%
```

FIGURE 1.7

Preproduction Intel® Xeon Phi™ Coprocessor "cat /proc/cpuinfo".

everything else in this part of the chapter, including the microarchitectural diagrams in Figures 1.8 and 1.9 that we chose to include for those who enjoy such things as we do.

The cores are in-order dual issue x86 processor cores, which trace some history to the original Pentium® design, but with the addition of 64-bit support, four hardware threads per core, power management, ring interconnect support, 512-bit SIMD capabilities, and other enhancements, these are hardly the Pentium cores of 20 years ago. The x86-specific logic (excluding L2 caches) makes up less than 2 percent of the die area for an Intel Xeon Phi coprocessor.

Here are key facts about the first Intel Xeon Phi coprocessor product:

- A coprocessor (requires at least one processor in the system), in production in 2012.
- Runs Linux (source code available http://intel.com/software/mic).
- Manufactured using Intel's 22 nm process technology with 3-D Trigate transistors.
- Supported by standard tools including Intel® Parallel Studio XE 2013. A list of additional tools available can be found online (http://intel.com/software/mic).
- Many cores:
  - More than 50 cores (it will vary within a generation of products, and between generations; it is good advice to avoid hard-coding applications to a particular number).
  - In-order cores support 64-bit x86 instructions with uniquely wide SIMD capabilities.
  - Four hardware threads on each core (resulting in more than 200 hardware threads available on a single device) are primarily used to hide latencies implicit in an in-order

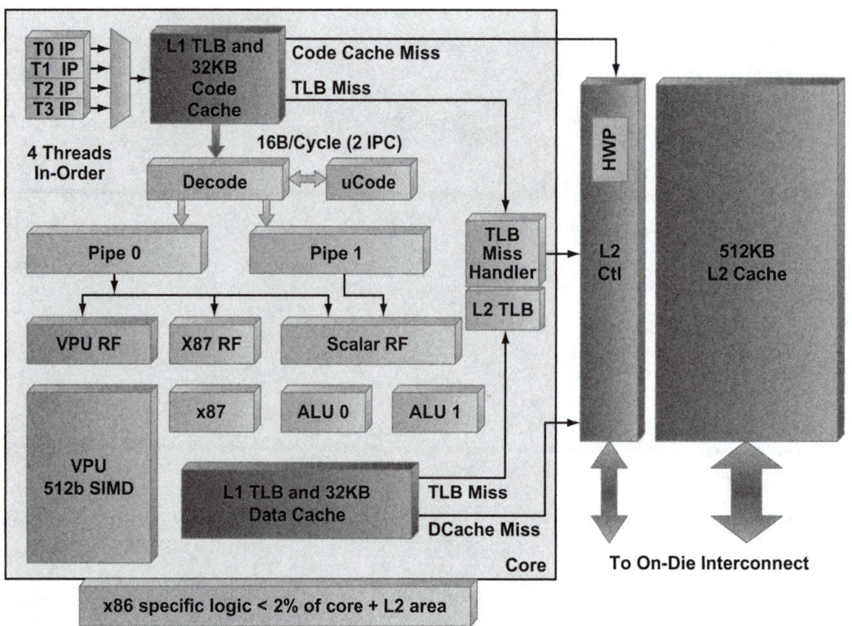

FIGURE 1.8

Architecture of a Single Intel® Xeon Phi™ Coprocessor Core.

microarchitecture. In practice, use of at least two threads per core is nearly always beneficial. As such, it is much more important that applications use these multiple hardware threads on Intel Xeon Phi coprocessors than they use hyper-threads on Intel Xeon processors.

- Cores interconnected by a high-speed bidirectional ring.
- Cores clocked at 1 GHz or more.
- Cache coherent across the entire coprocessor.
- Each core has a 512-KB L2 cache locally with high-speed access to all other L2 caches (making the collective L2 cache size over 25 MB).
- Caches deliver highly efficient power utilization while offering high bandwidth memory.

• Special instructions in addition to 64-bit x86:
  - Uniquely wide SIMD capability via 512-bit wide vectors instead of the narrower MMX™, Intel® SSE, or Intel® AVX capabilities.
  - High performance support for reciprocal, square root, power, and exponent operations.
  - Scatter/gather and streaming store capabilities to achieve higher effective memory bandwidth.

• Special features:
  - On package memory controller supports up to 8 GB GDDR5 (varies based on part).
  - PCIe connect logic is on-chip.

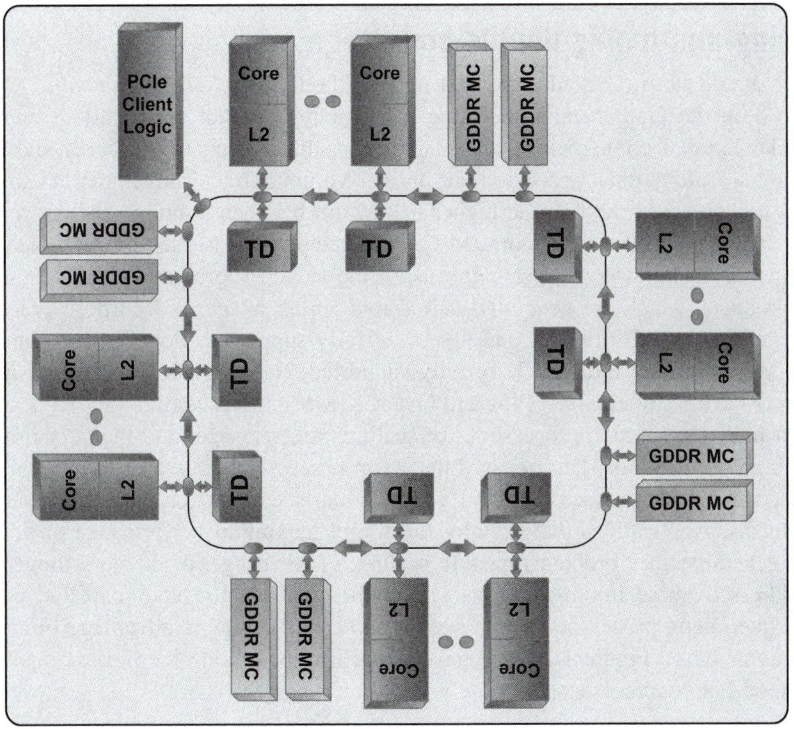

FIGURE 1.9

Microarchitecture of the Entire Coprocessor.

- Power management capabilities.
- Performance monitoring capabilities for tools like Intel VTune™ Amplifier XE 2013.

Keeping the "Ninja Gap" under control

On the premise that parallel programming can require Ninja (expert) programmers, the gaps in knowledge and experience needed between expert programmers and the rest of us have been referred to as the "ninja gap." Optimization for performance is never easy on any machine, but it is possible to control the level of complexity to manageable levels to avoid a high ninja gap. To understand more about how this ninja gap can be quantified, you might read "Can Traditional Programming Bridge the Ninja Performance Gap for Parallel Computing Applications?" (Satish et al. 2012). The paper shares measurements of the challenges and shows how Intel Xeon Phi coprocessors offer the advantage of controlling the ninja gap to levels akin to general-purpose processors. This approach is able to rely on the same industry standard methods as general-purpose processors and the paper helps show how that benefit can be measured and shown to be similar to general-purpose processors.

Transforming-and-tuning double advantage

Programming should not be called easy, and neither should *parallel programming*. We can however, work to keep the fundamentals the same: maximizing parallel computations and minimizing data movement. Parallel computations are enabled through scaling (more cores and threads) and vector processing (more data processed at once). Minimal data movement is an algorithmic endeavor, but can be eased through the higher bandwidth between memory and cores that is available with the Intel Many Integrated Core (MIC) Architecture that is used by Intel Xeon Phi coprocessors. This leads to *parallel programming* using the same programming languages and models across Intel products, which are generally also shared across all general-purpose processors in the industry. Languages such Fortran, C, and C++ are fully supported. Popular programming models such as OpenMP, MPI, and Intel TBB are fully supported. Newer models with widespread support such as Coarray Fortran, Intel Cilk™ Plus and OpenCL can apply as well.

Tuning on Intel Xeon Phi coprocessors, for scaling, vector usage, and memory usage, all stand to also benefit an application when run on Intel Xeon processors. This protection of investment by maintaining a value across processors and coprocessor is critical for helping preserve past and future investments. Applications that initially fail to get maximum performance on Intel Xeon Phi coprocessors generally trace problems back to scaling, vector usage, or memory usage. When these issues are addressed, these improvements to an application usually have a related positive effect when run on Intel Xeon processors. Some people call this the double advantage of "transforming-and-tuning," as shown in Figure 1.10, and have found it to be among the most compelling features of the Intel Xeon Phi coprocessors.

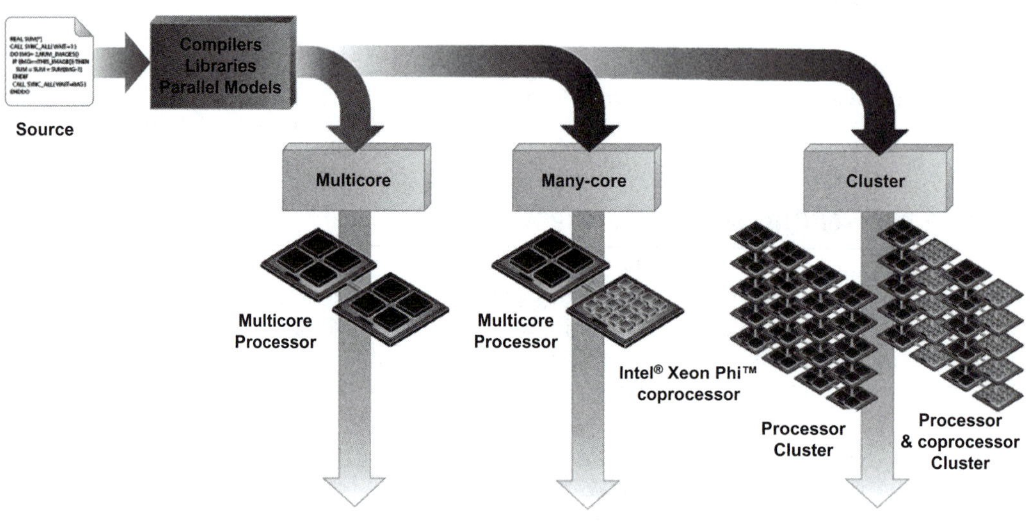

FIGURE 1.10

Double Advantage of Transforming-and-Tuning.

When to use an Intel® Xeon Phi™ coprocessor

Applications can use both Intel Xeon processors and Intel Xeon Phi coprocessors to simultaneously contribute to application performance. Applications should utilize a coprocessor for processing when it can contribute to the performance of a node. Generally speaking that will be during the portions of an application that can exploit high degrees of parallelism. For some workloads, the coprocessor(s) may contribute significantly more performance than the processor(s) while on others it may be less. System designs that include Intel Xeon Phi coprocessor(s) extend the range of node performance beyond what is possible with processors only. Because of the sophisticated power management in both Intel Xeon processors and Intel Xeon Phi coprocessors, the power efficiency of a node can be maintained across a broad range of applications by consuming power only when needed to contribute to node performance.

Maximizing performance on processors first

We have often seen that the single most important lesson from working with Intel Xeon Phi coprocessors is this: the best way to prepare for Intel Xeon Phi coprocessors is to fully exploit the performance that an application can get on Intel Xeon processors first. Trying to use an Intel Xeon Phi coprocessor without having maximized the use of parallelism on Intel Xeon processor will almost certainly be a disappointment.

Figure 1.11 illustrates a key point: higher performance comes from pairing parallel software with parallel hardware because it takes parallel applications to access the potential of parallel hardware. Intel Xeon Phi coprocessors offer a corollary to this: higher performance comes from pairing

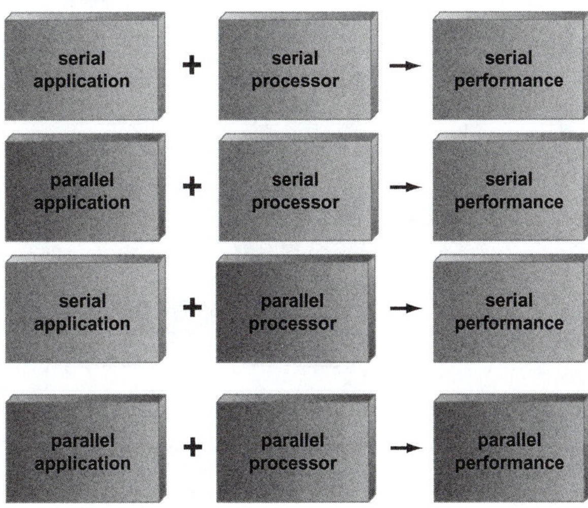

FIGURE 1.11

High Performance Comes from Parallel Software + Parallel Hardware.

highly parallel software with highly parallel hardware. The best place to start is to make sure your application is maximizing the capabilities of an Intel Xeon processor.

Why scaling past one hundred threads is so important

In getting an application ready for utilizing an Intel Xeon Phi coprocessor, nothing is more important than scaling. An application must scale well past one hundred threads to qualify as highly parallel. Efficient use of vectors and/or memory bandwidth is also essential. Applications that have not been created or modified to utilize high degrees of parallelism (task, threads, vectors, and so on) will be more limited in the benefit they derive from hardware that is designed to offer high degrees of parallelism.

Figures 1.12 and 1.13 show examples of how application types can behave on Intel Xeon processors versus Intel Xeon Phi coprocessors in two key cases: computationally bound and memory bound applications. Note that a logarithmic scale is employed in the graph, therefore the performance bars at the bottom represent substantial gains over bars above; results will vary by application. Measuring the current usage of vectors, threads, and aggregate bandwidth by an application can help understand where an application stands in being ready for highly parallel hardware. Notice that "more parallel" enhances both the processor and coprocessor performance. A push for "more parallel" applications will benefit Intel Xeon processors and Intel Xeon Phi coprocessors because both are general-purpose programmable devices.

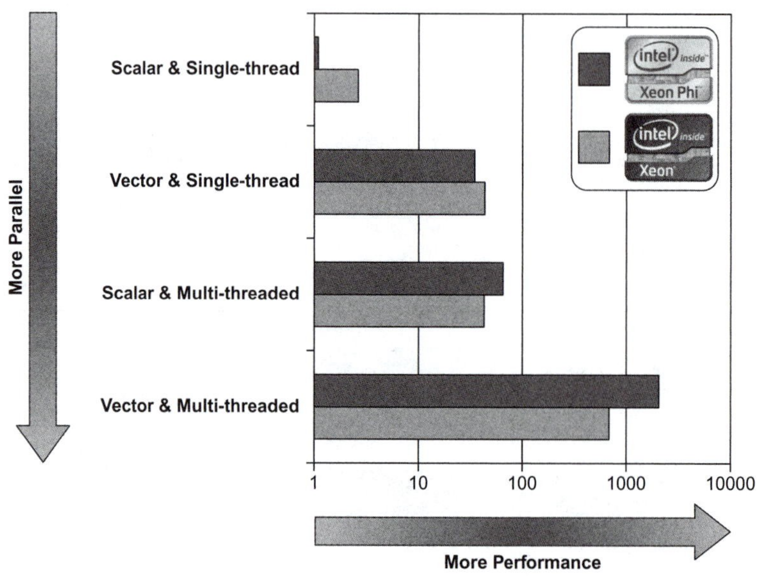

FIGURE 1.12

Combining Threads and Vectors Works Best. Coprocessors Extend.

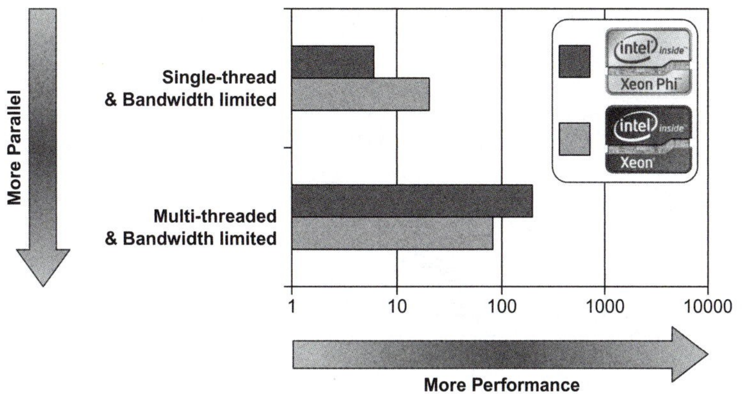

FIGURE 1.13

High Memory Needs Can Benefit From Threading. Coprocessors Extend.

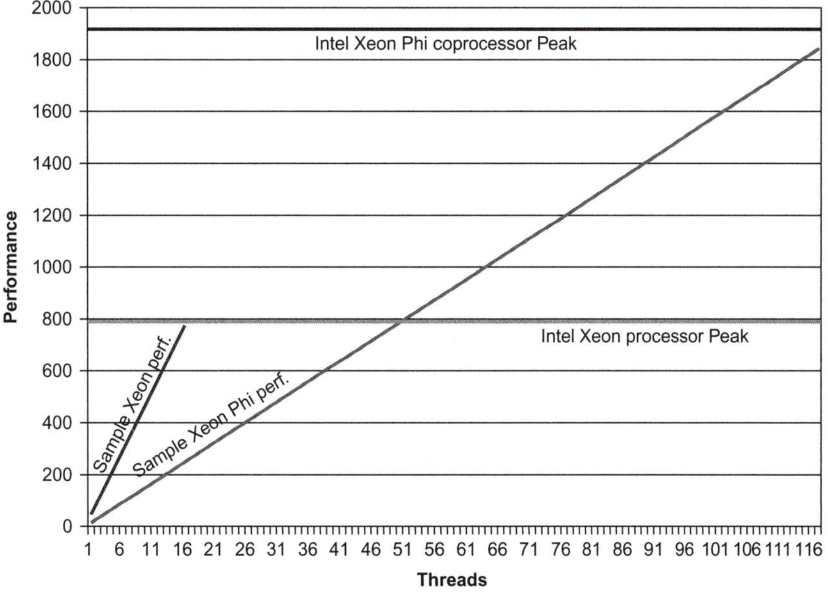

FIGURE 1.14

The Potential is Higher, But So is the Parallelism Needed to Get There.

Thinking back to the picture that speaks a thousand words, Figures 1.14, 1.15, and 1.16 offer a view to illustrate the same need for constructing to use lots of threads and vectors. Figure 1.14 illustrates model data to make a point: Intel Xeon Phi coprocessors can reach heights in beyond performance that of an Intel Xeon processor, but it requires more parallelism to do so. Figures 1.15

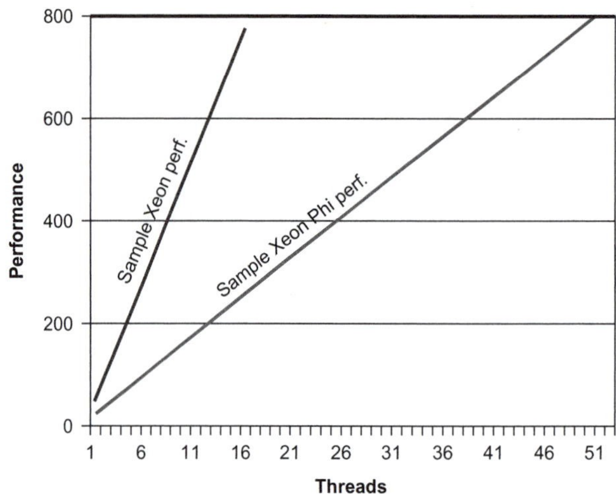

FIGURE 1.15

Within the Range of a Processor, the Processor Needs Fewer Threads.

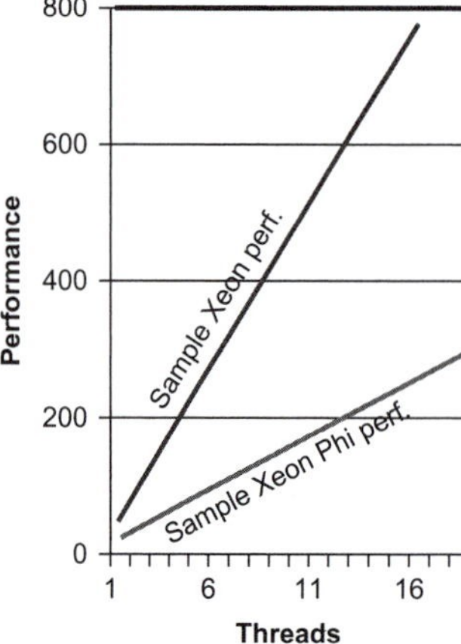

FIGURE 1.16

Limiting Threads Is Not Highly Parallel.

and 1.16 are simply close-ups of parts of Figure 1.14 to make a couple of points. Figure 1.15 illustrates the universal need for more parallelism to reach the same performance level on a device optimized for high degrees of parallelism (in this case, an Intel Xeon Phi coprocessor). Figure 1.16 illustrates that limiting "highly parallel" to the levels of parallelism that peak an Intel Xeon processor are insufficient to be interesting on an Intel Xeon Phi coprocessor. These close-up looks drive home the point of Figure 1.14: to go faster, you need more parallelism, while adding the less obvious "to go the same speed, you need more parallelism."

Maximizing parallel program performance

Whether making a choice to run an application on Intel Xeon processors or Intel Xeon Phi coprocessors, we can start with two fundamental considerations to achieve high performance:

1. Scaling: Is the scaling of an application ready to utilize the highly parallel capabilities of an Intel Xeon Phi coprocessor? The strongest evidence of this is generally demonstrated scaling on Intel Xeon processors.
2. Vectorization and memory usage: Is the application either:
   a. Making strong use of vector units?
   b. Able to utilize more local memory bandwidth than available with Intel Xeon processors?

If these two fundamentals (both #1 and #2) are true for an application, then the highly parallel and power-efficient Intel Xeon Phi coprocessor is most likely to be worth evaluating.

Measuring readiness for highly parallel execution

To know if your application is maximized on an Intel Xeon processor-based system, you should examine how your application scales, uses vectors, and uses memory. Assuming you have a working application, you can get some impression of where you are with regards to scaling and vectorization by doing a few simple tests.

To check scaling, create a simple graph of performance as you run with various numbers of threads (from one up to the number of cores, with attention to thread affinity) on an Intel Xeon processor-based system. This can be done with settings for OpenMP, Intel® Threading Building Blocks (Intel TBB) or Intel Cilk Plus (for example, OMP_NUM_THREADS for OpenMP). If the performance graph indicates any significant trailing off of performance, you have tuning work you can do to improve your application scaling before trying an Intel Xeon Phi coprocessor.

To check vectorization, compile your application with and without vectorization. For instance, if you are using Intel compilers auto-vectorization: disable vectorization via compiler switches: -no-vec -no-simd, use at least −O2 -xhost for vectorization. Compare the performance you see. If the performance difference is insufficient you should examine opportunities to increase vectorization. Look again at the dramatic benefits vectorization may offer as illustrated in Figure 1.13. If you are using libraries, like the Intel Math Kernel Library (Intel MKL), you should consider that math routines would remain vectorized no matter how you compile the application itself. Therefore, time spent in the math routines may be considered as vector time. Unless your application is bandwidth limited, the most effective use of Intel Xeon Phi coprocessors will be when most cycles executing are vector instructions[2]. While some may tell you that "most cycles" needs to be over 90 percent, we have found this number to vary widely based on the application and whether the Intel Xeon Phi coprocessor needs to be the top performance source in a node or just needs to contribute performance.

[2]In other words, Vector Processing Unit (VPU) instructions being used on vector (not scalar) data.

Intel VTune Amplifier XE 2013 can help measure computations on Intel Xeon processors and Intel Xeon Phi coprocessors to assist in your evaluations.

Aside from vectorization, being limited by memory bandwidth on Intel Xeon processors can indicate an opportunity to improve performance with an Intel Xeon Phi coprocessor. For this to be most efficient, an application needs to exhibit good locality of reference and must utilize caches well in its core computations.

The Intel VTune Amplifier XE product can be utilized to measure various aspects of a program, and among the most critical is *L1 compute density*. This is greatly expanded upon in a paper titled "Optimization and Performance Tuning for Intel® Xeon Phi™ Coprocessors, Part 2: Understanding and Using Hardware Events" (Intel 2012) available at http://tinyurl.com/phicount.

When using MPI, it is desirable to see a communication versus computation ratio that is not excessively high in terms of communication. The ratio of computation to communication will be a key factor in deciding between using offload versus native model for programming for an application. Programs are also most effective using a strategy of overlapping communication and I/O with computation. Intel® Trace Analyzer and Collector, part of Intel® Cluster Studio XE 2013, is very useful for profiling MPI communications to help visualize bottlenecks and understand the effectiveness of overlapping with computation.

What about GPUs?

While GPUs cannot offer the programmability of an Intel Xeon Phi coprocessor, they do share a subset of what can be accelerated by scaling combined with vectorization or bandwidth. In other words, applications that show positive results with GPUs should always benefit from Intel Xeon Phi coprocessors because the same fundamentals of vectorization or bandwidth must be present. The opposite is not true. The flexibility of an Intel Xeon Phi coprocessor includes support for applications that cannot run on GPUs. This is one reason that a system built including Intel Xeon Phi coprocessors will have broader applicability than a system using GPUs. Additionally, tuning for GPU is generally too different from a processor to have the dual-transforming-tuning benefit we see in programming for Intel Xeon Phi coprocessors. This can lead to a substantial rise in investments to be portable across many machines now and into the future.

Beyond the ease of porting to increased performance

Because an Intel Xeon Phi coprocessor is an x86 SMP-on-a-chip, it is true that a port to an Intel Xeon Phi coprocessor is often trivial. However, the high degree of parallelism of Intel Xeon Phi coprocessors are best suited to applications that are structured to use the parallelism. Almost all applications will benefit from some tuning beyond the initial base performance to achieve maximum performance. This can range from minor work to major restructuring to expose and exploit parallelism through multiple tasks and use of vectors. The experiences of users of Intel Xeon Phi coprocessors and the "forgiving nature" of this approach are generally promising but point out one challenge: the temptation to stop tuning before the best performance is reached. This can be a good thing if the return on investment of further tuning is insufficient and the results are good enough. It can be a bad thing if expectations were that working code would always be high performance. There ain't no such thing as a free lunch! The hidden bonus is the "transforming-and-tuning" double advantage of programming investments for Intel Xeon Phi coprocessors that generally applies directly to any general-purpose processor as well. This greatly enhances the preservation of any investment to tune working code by applying to other processors and offering more *forward scaling* to future systems.

Transformation for performance

There are a number of possible user-level optimizations that have been found effective for ultimate performance. These advanced techniques are not essential. They are possible ways to extract additional performance for your application. The "forgiving nature" of the Intel Xeon Phi coprocessor makes transformations optional but should be kept in mind when looking for the highest performance. It is unlikely that peak performance will be achieved without considering some of these optimizations:

- Memory access and loop transformations (for example: cache blocking, loop unrolling, prefetching, tiling, loop interchange, alignment, affinity)
- Vectorization works best on unit-stride vectors (the data being consumed is contiguous in memory). Data structure transformations can increase the amount of data accessed with unit-strides (such as AoS[3] to SoA[4] transformations or recoding to use packed arrays instead of indirect accesses).
- Use of full (not partial) vectors is best, and data transformations to accomplish this should be considered.
- Vectorization is best with properly aligned data.
- Large page considerations (we recommend the widely used Linux libhugetlbfs library)
- Algorithm selection (change) to favor those that are parallelization and vectorization friendly.

Hyper-threading versus multithreading

The Intel Xeon Phi coprocessor utilizes multithreading on each core as a key to masking the latencies inherent in an in-order microarchitecture. This should not be confused with hyper-threading on Intel Xeon processors that exists primarily to more fully feed a dynamic execution engine. In HPC workloads, very often hyper-threading may be ignored or even turned off without degrading effects on performance. This is not true of Intel Xeon Phi coprocessor hardware threads, where multithreading of programs should not be ignored and hardware threads cannot be turned off.

[3]Array of Structures (AoS)
[4]Structure of Arrays (SoA)

The Intel Xeon Phi coprocessor offers four hardware threads per core with sufficient memory capabilities and floating-point capabilities to make it generally impossible for a single thread per core to approach either limit. Highly tuned kernels of code may reach saturation with two threads, but generally applications need a minimum of three or four active threads per core to access all that the coprocessor can offer. For this reason, the number of threads per core utilized should be a tunable parameter in an application and be set based on experience in running the application. This characteristic of programming for Intel products will continue into the future, even though the "hyper-threading versus hardware threading" and the number of hardware threads may vary. Programs should parameterize the number of cores and the number of threads per core in order to easily run well on a variety of current and future processors and coprocessors.

Coprocessor major usage model: MPI versus offload

Given that we know how to program the Intel Xeon processors in the host system, the question that arises is how to involve the Intel Xeon Phi coprocessors in an application. There are two major approaches:

1. A processor-centric "offload" model where the program is viewed as running on processors and offloading select work to coprocessors.
2. A "native" model where the program runs natively on processors and coprocessors and may communicate with each other by various methods.

The choice between offload and native models is certain to be one of considerable debate for years to come. Applications that already utilize MPI can actually use either method by either limiting MPI ranks to Intel Xeon processors and use offload to the coprocessors, or distribute MPI ranks across the coprocessors natively. It is possible that the only real MPI ranks be established on the coprocessor cores, but if this leaves the Intel Xeon processors unutilized then this approach is likely to give up too much performance in the system.

Being separate and on a PCIe bus creates two additional considerations. One is the need to fit problems or subproblems into the more limited memory on the coprocessor card, and the other is the overhead of data transfers that favor minimization of communication to and from the card. It is worth noting also that the number of MPI ranks used on an Intel Xeon Phi coprocessor should be substantially fewer than the number of cores in no small part because of limited memory on the coprocessor. Consistent with parallel programs in general, the advantages of overlapping communication (MPI messages or offload data movement) with computation are important to consider as well as techniques to load-balance work across all the cores available. Of course, involving Intel Xeon processor cores and Intel Xeon Phi coprocessor cores adds the dimension of "big cores" and "little cores" to the balancing work even though they share x86 instructions and programming models. While MPI programs often already tackle the overlap of communication and computation, the placement of ranks on coprocessor cores still have to deal with the highly parallel programming needs and limited memory. This is why an offload model can be attractive, even within an MPI program where ranks are on the processors.

The offload model for Intel Xeon Phi coprocessors is quite rich. The syntax and semantics of the Intel Language Extensions for Offload are generally a superset of other offload models including nVidia's OpenACC. This provides for greater interoperability with OpenMP, ability to manage multiple coprocessors (cards), and the ability to offload complex program components that an Intel Xeon Phi coprocessor can process but that a GPU could not (hence nVidia's OpenACC does not allow). We expect that OpenMP 4.0 (standard to be finalized in 2013) will include offload directives that provide support for these needs, and Intel supports the draft (TR1) from OpenMP and plans to support OpenMP 4.0 after it is finalized. Intel Xeon Phi coprocessors as part of our commitment to providing OpenMP capabilities. Intel Language Extensions for Offload also provides for an implicit sharing model that is beyond what OpenMP 4.0 will support. It rests on a shared memory model supported by Intel Xeon Phi coprocessors that allow a shared memory-programming model (Intel calls "MYO") between Intel Xeon processors and Intel Xeon Phi coprocessors. This bears some similarity to PGAS (partitioned global address space) programming models and is not an extension provided by OpenMP 4.0. The Intel "MYO" capability offers a global address space within the node allowing sharing of virtual addresses, for select data, between processors and coprocessor on the same node. It is offered in C and C++, but not Fortran since future support of Coarray will be a standard solution to the same basic problem. Offloading is available as Fortran offloading via pragmas, C/C++ offloading with pragmas and optionally shared (MYO) data. Use of MPI can distribute applications across the system as well.

Compiler and programming models

No popular programming language was designed for parallelism. In many ways, Fortran has done the best job adding new features, such as DO CONCURRENT, to address parallel programming needs as well as benefiting from OpenMP. C users have OpenMP as well as Intel Cilk Plus. C++ users have embraced Intel Threading Building Blocks and more recently have Intel Cilk Plus to utilize as well. C++ users can use OpenMP as well.

Intel Xeon Phi coprocessors offer the full capability to use the same tools, programming languages and programming models as an Intel Xeon processor. However, as a coprocessor designed for high degrees of parallelism, some models are more interesting than others.

In a way, it is quite simple: an application needs to deal with having lots of tasks, and deal with vector data efficiently (also known as vectorization).

There are some recommendations we can make based on what has been working well for developers. For Fortran programmers, use OpenMP, DO CONCURRENT, and MPI. For C++ programmers, use Intel TBB, Intel Cilk Plus, and OpenMP. For C programmers, use OpenMP and Intel Cilk Plus. Intel TBB is a C++ template library that offers excellent support for task oriented load balancing. While Intel TBB does not offer vectorization solutions, it does not interfere with any choice of solution for vectorization. Intel TBB is open source and available on a wide variety of platforms supporting most operating systems and processors. Intel Cilk Plus is a bit more complex in that it offers both tasking and vectorization solutions. Fortunately, Intel Cilk Plus fully interoperates with Intel TBB. Intel Cilk Plus offers a simpler set of tasking capabilities than Intel TBB but by using keywords in the language so as to have full compiler support for optimizing.

Intel Cilk Plus also offers elemental functions, array syntax and "#pragma SIMD" to help with vectorization. Best use of array syntax is done along with blocking for caches, which unfortunately means naïve use of constructs such as A[:] = B[:] + C[:]; for large arrays may yield poor performance. Best use of array syntax ensures the vector length of single statements is short (some small multiple of the native vector length, perhaps only 1X). Finally, and perhaps most important to programmers today, Intel Cilk Plus offers mandatory vectorization pragmas for the compiler called "#pragma SIMD." The intent of "#pragma SIMD" is to do for vectorization what OpenMP has done for parallelization. Intel Cilk Plus requires compiler support. It is currently available from Intel for Windows, Linux, and Apple OS X. It is also available in a branch of gcc.

If you are happy with OpenMP and MPI, you have a great start to using Intel Xeon Phi coprocessors. Additional options may be interesting to you over time, but OpenMP and MPI are enough to get great results when used with an effective vectorization method. Auto-vectorization may be enough for you especially if you code in Fortran with the possible additional considerations for efficient vectorization such as alignment and unit-stride accesses. The "#pragma SIMD" capability of Intel Cilk Plus (available in Fortran too) is worth a look. The SIMD pragmas/directives are expected to be part of OpenMP 4.0 (standard to be finalized in 2013).

Dealing with tasks means specification of task, and load balancing among them. MPI has provided this capability for decades with full flexibility and responsibility given to the programmer. Shared memory programmers have Intel TBB and Intel Cilk Plus to assist them. Intel TBB has widespread usage in the C++ community, and Intel Cilk Plus extends Intel TBB to offer C programmers a solution as well as help with vectorization in C and C++ programs.

Cache optimizations

The most effective use of caches comes by paying attention to maximizing the locality of references, blocking to fit in L2 cache, and ensuring that prefetching is utilized (by hardware, by compiler, by library or by explicit program controls).

Organizing data locality to fit 512 K or less L2 cache usage per core generally gives best usage of the L2 cache. All four hardware threads per core share their "per core" local L2 cache but have high-speed access to the caches associated with other cores. Any data used by a particular core will occupy space in that local L2 cache (it can be in multiple L2 caches around the chip). While Intel Xeon processors have a penalty for "cross-socket" sharing, which occurs after about 16 threads (assuming 8 cores, two hyper-threads each), the Intel Xeon Phi coprocessors have a lower penalty across more than 200 threads. There is a benefit to having locality first organized around the threads being used on a core (up to four) first, and then around all the threads across the coprocessor. While the defaults and automatic behavior can be quite good, ensuring that code designed for locality performs best will likely include programmatic specification of affinity such as the use of KMP_AFFINITY when using OpenMP and I_MPI_PIN_DOMAIN with MPI. Note that while there is a strong benefit to sharing for threads on the same core, beyond that you should not expect to see performance variations based on how close a core is to another core on coprocessor. While this may seem surprising, the hardware design is so good in this respect we have yet to see any appreciable performance benefit based on adjacency of cores within the coprocessor so I would not advise spending time trying to optimize placement beyond locality to a core and then load balancing across the cores (for instance using KMP_AFFINITY = scatter to round-robin work allocation).

The coprocessor has hardware prefetching into L2 that is initiated by the first cache miss within a page. The Intel compilers issue software prefetches aggressively for memory references inside loops by default (-O2 and above, report on compiler decisions available with -opt-report3 -opt-report-phase hlo). Typically, the compiler issues two prefetches per memory reference: one from memory into L2 and a second one for prefetching from L2 into L1. The prefetch distance is computed by the compiler based on the amount of work inside the loop. Explicit prefetching can be added either with prefetch pragmas (#pragma prefetch in C/C++ or CDEC$ prefetch in Fortran) or prefetch intrinsics (_mm_prefetch in C/C++, or mm_prefetch in Fortran); you may want to explicitly turn off compiler prefetching (-opt-prefetch = 0 to turn off all compiler prefetches *or* -opt-prefetch-distance = 0,2 to turn off compiler prefetches into L2) when you are adding prefetch intrinsics manually. Software prefetches do not get counted as cache misses by the performance counters. This means that "cache misses" can truly be studied with performance tools with a goal of driving them to essentially zero (aim for low single-digit percentages of memory accesses counted as misses) inside loops when you can successfully fetch all data streams with prefetches. Prefetching needs to be from memory to L2 and separately from L2 to L1. Utilizing prefetches from memory to L1 directly should not be expected to yield great performance because the latency of such will generally lead to more outstanding L1 prefetches than are available in the hardware. Such limits mean that organizing data streams is best when the number of streams of data per thread is less than eight and prefetching is actively used on each stream of data. As a rule of thumb, the number of active prefetches per core should be managed to about 30 or 40 and be divided across the active data streams.

Beyond the caches, certain memory transforms can be employed for additional tuning for TLBs including the ability to use large or small pages, organizing data streams, and to organizing data to avoid hot spots in the TLBs.

Examples, then details

We use the next three chapters to dive into a number of instructive examples in order to learn the essentials of high performance parallel programming. We'll ponder the similarities between an Intel Xeon Phi coprocessor and a sports car. In this chapter, we made the case that a sports car is not designed for a superior experience driving around on slow-moving congested highways. In the next few chapters, we'll move the sports car to more favorable roads where the opportunity is there to open up the performance. In this way, the information in this chapter, combined with that in the subsequent three chapters, is sufficient to learn the programming. The remaining chapters of this book provide more in-depth explanation of many details these first four chapters have only touched upon. Documentation and additional information is also available at http://intel.com/software/mic.

For more information

Some additional reading worth considering includes:

- "Optimization and Performance Tuning for Intel® Xeon Phi™ Coprocessors, Part 2: Understanding and Using Hardware Events" (Intel 2012) available at http://tinyurl.com/phicount.

- "An Overview of Programming for Intel® Xeon® processors and Intel® Xeon Phi™ coprocessors" (Intel 2012) available at http://tinyurl.com/xeonphisum.
- Satish, N., C. Kim, J. Chhugani, H. Saito, R. Krishnaiyer, M. Smelyanskiy, M. Girkar, and P. Dubey. "Can traditional programming bridge the Ninja performance gap for parallel computing applications?" Computer Architecture (ISCA), 2012 39th Annual International Symposium on, vol. no. 9–13 June 2012, pp. 440–451.
- Documentation and additional information is also available at http://intel.com/software/mic.

CHAPTER

High Performance Closed Track Test Drive!

2

Imagine you were given free access to a high performance sports car for an afternoon, a day, a week, or longer. Your first thought probably would not be to drive it to the grocery store, or any specific place for that matter. You are not going to spend lots of time reading the owner's manual. At first, you would simply want to drive it really fast! The best way to do that without getting hurt (or arrested!), would be try it out on a safe, closed test track with long straightaways, no other cars, and maybe a few curves to add some fun and challenge as you get more comfortable with driving the car. In the next few chapters, we will familiarize you with the high performance capabilities of the Intel® Xeon Phi™ coprocessor using the analogy of learning how to drive a sports car in more and more challenging and real circumstances. We want you to have a bit of early fun and thrills. Stuff you can tell your friends and family like, "Hey, I drove at 200 mph!"[1] or "Hey, I just made a computer do 2 trillion calculations a second!" We will use some simple code examples that tap specific performance elements of the coprocessor, pointing out the keys to writing code that leverages the incredible performance available.

[1]The abbreviation *mph* stands for miles per hour or about 322 kilometers per hour (kph).

We will build on our knowledge over several chapters until we come to a real world example application that takes the key concepts and applies them, even when a few bumps are in the road. In other words, we finally want to find the fastest, most efficient way to do something useful like actually getting to the grocery store. So, let's hop in and start driving our sleek shiny sports car. In this chapter, we'll focus on accessing two of the key performance features on our "car," namely the many processing cores with floating point vector processing units (the cylinders) and the high speed memory (the fuel injection system).

Looking under the hood: coprocessor specifications

We want to get on the road right away, but like most with a new car, we will at least take a quick glance under the hood at our "engine." Similar to other Intel processing products, like the Intel® Xeon® processor, there will be several available models of Intel® Xeon Phi™ coprocessors. As PCI Express coprocessor cards they deliver peak calculation performance greater than 1 teraFLOP/s (10^{12} floating point operations per second) for double precision floating point (DP) calculations and greater than 2 teraFLOP/s for single precision floating point (SP) calculations. Differing characteristics between models will be the instruction clock rate, the number of processing cores, and the speed and amount of random access memory available. We will describe these key architectural elements in more detail in Chapter 8, Coprocessor Architecture.

Throughout the book, you will note that we will occasionally repeat a core mantra for achieving the high performance potential available with the Intel Xeon Phi coprocessor. That mantra is *vectorize and scale*. These will be the topics of Chapters 5 and 6, respectively. The mantra also happens to apply quite well to Intel Xeon processors. That is, the code needs to both vectorize and scale to achieve the best performance results. *Vectorizing* refers to using the fundamental data parallel engines that support single instruction, multiple data (SIMD) usage available in Intel architecture processors with the SSE and AVX instruction extensions and the Intel Xeon Phi instruction set architecture. Scaling refers to enabling the code to run across the many cores and hardware threads as independent parallel tasks. On the Intel Xeon Phi coprocessors, the vector engine, known as the vector processing unit (VPU), supports 512-bit vector width. A *vector* is a group of data items of the same data type that can be processed in parallel by a single instruction. A vector is typically generated by a compiler, when possible, by converting array expressions into the vector format supported by the underlying processing architecture. There are also instructions to quickly *broadcast* or replicate scalar variables into vector form to support multiplying or adding the same value to the group of values that form a vector. As shown in Figure 2.1, for 32-bit wide single precision floating point (SP) format numbers, 16 values or *lanes* can be processed simultaneously. For 64-bit wide double precision floating point (DP) format numbers, eight lanes can be processed simultaneously. Furthermore, the coprocessor supports a key performance enhancing capability of executing both a multiplication and an addition, known as fused multiply and add (FMA) in a single instruction without precision loss, enabling two floating point operations in one instruction.

We have run our code examples on preproduction coprocessors with the key specifications listed in Table 2.1. We will also be referencing "relative" performance, such as percentage of peak, so you can get a sense of the actual performance of the code on various Intel Xeon Phi coprocessor models.

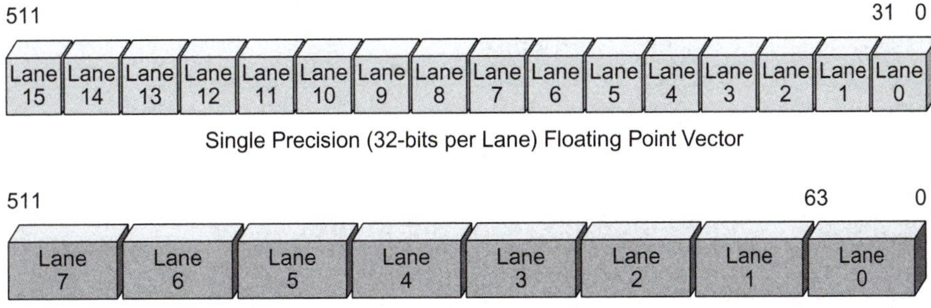

FIGURE 2.1

Vector Floating Point Formats on Intel® Xeon Phi™ Coprocessor.

Table 2.1 Our Intel® Xeon Phi™ Coprocessor Test Card Specs

Clock Frequency	1.091 GHz
Number of Cores	61
Memory Size/Type	8 GB/GDDR5
Memory Speed	5.5 GT/sec
Peak DP/SP FLOPs	1.065/2.130 TeraFLOP/s
Peak Memory Bandwidth	352 GB/s

Note: *Specifications for the multiple available production models will vary*

The method to determine the peak single precision floating point capability of an Intel Xeon Phi coprocessor is:

$$\text{Clock Frequency} \times \text{Number of Cores} \times 16 \text{ lanes} \times 2(\text{FMA}) \text{ FLOPs/cycle}$$

For the coprocessor model we are using that becomes:

$$1.091\text{GHz} \times 61 \text{ cores} \times 16 \text{ lanes} \times 2 = 2129.6 \text{ gigaFLOP/s}$$

For double precision peak FLOPs it becomes half that since 8 lanes are available:

$$1.091\text{GHz} \times 61 \text{ cores} \times 8 \text{ lanes} \times 2 = 1064.8 \text{ gigaFLOP/s}$$

The other key high performance area we'll be looking at in this chapter is the memory subsystem bandwidth. As you can see in Table 1.1, the GDDR5 memory on the coprocessor we will be testing has a peak "electrical" bandwidth of 352 gigabytes per second (GB/s). Unlike the FLOP/s peak performance, for which code can be written to achieve a high percentage, the true achievable maximum bandwidth for memory is limited to about 50 to 60 percent of the specified peak memory bandwidth by other factors in the hardware implementation. However, this still provides for very high throughput to allow extraordinary performance.

Okay, let's close the hood, hop in, start up our sports car and start experiencing some high performance thrills!

Starting the car: communicating with the coprocessor

While there are small differences in starting the engine in different models of automobiles, we usually are not presented with something so unusual that extensive instructions with many steps are required to get the car started. Similarly, a key goal of the design for the Intel Xeon Phi coprocessor is that its operation be virtually the same as a typical high performance computing node or workstation. As will be discussed in much more detail in Chapters 9 and 10, the coprocessor software environment is configured to behave exactly like a remotely accessible Linux-based computer on a network.

As with any networked computer, there are important setup and configuration elements required to match the target environment. For the purposes of this book, we will assume a system administrator (who may be you) has already gone through the installation process and instructions as provided with the coprocessor model being deployed. There are likely two primary categories our readers will use to gain access to run code on an Intel Xeon Phi coprocessor: Category 1 have direct control of a personal workstation or dedicated cluster of computing nodes with one or more coprocessors or Category 2 will request and receive a time allocation to access a large supercomputing cluster such as Stampede, at the Texas Advanced Computing Center.

Most installations in Category 2 will have their own procedures in place to successfully compile and launch applications and receive results. Some installations may provide the ability to use an *interactive session,* which may then provide operation similar to Category 1.

Category 1 will have a standard Linux usage. You will have login access to a node or workstation that hosts one or more installed coprocessors and the coprocessor operating software environment, known as the Intel® Manycore Platform Software Stack (MPSS), as well as compilers, libraries, and development tools that support Intel Xeon Phi coprocessors such as Intel® Composer XE 2013. For developing and running the code in the remainder of this book, we will assume you are operating in Category 1. That is, you are logged into a computer (the host) with at least one Intel Xeon Phi coprocessor installed. You should be able to adapt to Category 2 usage by following the instructions from your provider.

If your system administrator did not configure the host bootstrap process to automatically startup the Intel Xeon Phi coprocessor, you will start the card with the following command:

```
$ sudo service mpss start
```

As the service starts and bootstraps the coprocessor (it may take several seconds to a minute or more) you should see messages similar to:

```
Starting MPSS Stack:        [  OK  ]
mic0: online (...   )
$
```

You will need sudo privileges to run the service. If you do not have sudo privileges for your machine, speak to your system administrator. Why did it take a while before the command completed? Because, as a Linux-based computing platform in its own right, the coprocessor must go through a similar bootstrap process as any Linux machine must, including hardware and software initialization and network configuration. Chapter 10 describes the configuration and system administration of the Linux environment on the coprocessor in more detail.

Now that the coprocessor is up and running, you can access it with standard methods such as SSH, SCP, telnet, or FTP. The most typical method is to log on with SSH. We will assume your username is *pat* and your system administrator has followed the standard installation procedures that enable the same login credentials on the coprocessor as the host system. To get a command prompt on the first Intel Xeon Phi Coprocessor in the system you can enter:

```
[pat@localhost pat] $ ssh pat@mic0
```

This will result in a command prompt similar to this:

```
[pat@mic0 pat] %
```

NOTE

For the remainder of the book we will use $ to represent the host command prompt and % to represent the coprocessor command prompt. Your actual prompts may vary.

You can type most Linux commands at the command prompt for instance:

```
% pwd
/home/pat
```

To copy or "upload" a file such as a binary executable file built on the host that targets execution on the coprocessor you can use the standard secure copy command *scp* as follows:

```
$ scp helloxeonphi pat@mic0:/home/pat
```

Then on the coprocessor command prompt:

```
% cd /home/pat
% ls
helloxeonphi
```

That is pretty much all you need to know to get started with the coprocessor. Once the service that boots and manages communication with the card is launched on the host, you access it very much like a standard Linux-based computer. So, we know how to start our sports car and the controls are familiar. Time to strap on our seat belts and try it out on our closed track course!

Taking it out easy: running our first code

No car goes from standstill to 200 mph instantly, and if it did, you would pretty surely crash. For our first example code, we'll get a feel for our engine as we shift into first gear and start moving. One key speed measure, equivalent to miles per hour, for the Intel Xeon Phi coprocessor is floating point operations per second (FLOP/s). In the first example code, we will use only one core of the Intel Xeon Phi coprocessor to just get "warmed up." Take a look at the helloflops1.c code in Figure 2.2. After initialization and setup, the code boils down to an inner loop with a single line that performs what is commonly referred to as the SAXPY calculation.

The key line of code in the inner loop is:

```
fa[k] = a * fa[k] + fb[k];
```

This code also expresses a primary compute capability of the Intel Xeon Phi coprocessor we mentioned in the previous section, the availability of fused multiply and add (FMA) in a single instruction. The coprocessor vector unit supports up to three operands. In the key line of code, they are the variable *a*, and array values *fa*[*k*] and *fb*[*k*]. This syntax enables the two floating point operations, multiplication and addition, executed in one cycle without loss of precision during the calculation (fused). The primary target use for FMA is high performance linear algebra calculations, especially matrix math that can be used to solve systems of linear equations. Matrix operations are the foundation for many scientific codes.

To compile the helloflops1.c code under the Linux operating system using the Intel C compiler, ensure your compiler is installed and the environment is set up per the installation instructions, and then use the following command line:

```
$ icc -mmic -vec -report=3 -O3 helloflops1.c -o helloflops1
```

This invocation of the C compiler requests the code to be generated for an Intel® Many Integrated Core (MIC) architecture coprocessor (`-mmic`), also known as the Intel Xeon Phi coprocessor, generates a vector report (`-vec-report=3`), uses standard optimization techniques (`-O3`), and writes the resulting executable file to `helloflops1`. We'll discuss the impact of these option settings after running the code.

Before giving it a first run, it is good practice to understand what we might ideally expect in performance from our code so we can determine if the results we get are good or poor. Because the single line of inner loop code directly expresses the highest performing single clock calculation and because our data type is float, ideally, this code should approach the single precision peak performance of the Intel Xeon Phi coprocessor. If we look back at our prior discussion of the peak FLOP/s available, we might be thinking we should get something approaching 2+ TeraFLOP/s! That would be great!

However, that would put us a little bit ahead of ourselves. The helloflops1.c code hasn't expressed anything about scaling the code across cores and threads. So, this code will run on just one core and one thread of the coprocessor. Remembering the peak FLOP/s calculation and substituting one for the number of cores, we end up with something around 34.9 gigaFLOP/s as the maximum peak we might expect. Don't worry; we'll soon have a chance to add the scaling to take full advantage of the coprocessor's very high performance.

```
//
// helloflops1
//
// A simple example to try
// to get lots of Flops on
// Intel(r) Xeon Phi(tm) coprocessors.
//

#include <stdio.h>
#include <stdlib.h>
#include <string.h>
#include <sys/time.h>
//
// dtime -
//
// utility routine to return
// the current wall clock time
//
double dtime()
{
    double tseconds = 0.0;
    struct timeval mytime;
    gettimeofday(&mytime,(struct timezone*)0);
    tseconds = (double)(mytime.tv_sec +
                        mytime.tv_usec*1.0e-6);
    return( tseconds );
}


#define FLOPS_ARRAY_SIZE (1024*1024)
#define MAXFLOPS_ITERS 100000000
#define LOOP_COUNT 128
// Floating pt ops per inner loop iteration
#define FLOPSPERCALC 2
// define some arrays - 64 byte aligned for fast cache access
float fa[FLOPS_ARRAY_SIZE] __attribute__((align(64)));
float fb[FLOPS_ARRAY_SIZE] __attribute__((align(64)));
```

FIGURE 2.2

Code Listing of helloflops1.c.

```
//
// Main program - pedal to the metal.
// ..calculate tons o'flops!
//
int main(int argc, char *argv[] )
{
    int i,j,k;
    double tstart, tstop, ttime;
    double gflops = 0.0;
    float a=1.1;

    //
    // initialize the compute arrays
    //

    printf("Initializing\r\n");
    for(i=0; i<FLOPS_ARRAY_SIZE; i++)
    {
        fa[i] = (float)i + 0.1;
        fb[i] = (float)i + 0.2;
    }

    printf("Starting Compute");

    tstart = dtime();
    // loop many times to really get lots of
    // calculations
    for(j=0; j<MAXFLOPS_ITERS; j++)
    {
    //
    // scale 1st array and add in the 2nd array
    //
        for(k=0; k<LOOP_COUNT; k++)
        {
            fa[k] = a * fa[k] + fb[k];
        }
     }
     tstop = dtime();
```

FIGURE 2.2

(Continued)

```
    // # of gigaflops we just calculated
    gflops = (double)( 1.0e-9 * LOOP_COUNT *
                       MAXFLOPS_ITERS * FLOPSPERCALC);

    // elasped time
    ttime = tstop - tstart;

    //
    // Print the results
    //
    if ((ttime) > 0.0)
    {
        printf("GFlops = %10.3lf, Secs = %10.3lf,
                   GFlops per sec = %10.3lf\r\n",
                   gflops, ttime, gflops/ttime);
    }
    return( 0 );
}
```

FIGURE 2.2

(Continued)

Okay, assuming your system administrator (who could be you!) has the coprocessor up, running and accessible, you can execute `./helloflops1` on the coprocessor by using standard Linux methods such as `scp` to upload the executable to a directory such as /home/pat on the coprocessor and run it:

```
% ./helloflops1
```

Here is an example of expected output:

```
Initializing
Starting Compute
GFlops = 25.600, Secs = 1.488, GFlops per sec = 17.206
```

So the first thing we notice is that we get "pretty good" results but it appears to be about half of what we predicted getting 49.3 percent of one core's peak efficiency. Did we consider all the factors? Do the resulting instructions generated by the compiler for the loop setup and control overhead reduce the performance? Actually, we failed to account for a piece of important and subtle information about how the coprocessor executes in single threaded mode. Since the coprocessor targets highly parallel, scalable applications, its instruction scheduling mechanism is built to assume that more than one thread will be applied to a compute-heavy problem. It is designed to always schedule a new thread to execute each clock cycle. In the special case when you invoke only one thread on a core, the scheduler effectively switches to a special "null thread" that does nothing but let a cycle pass before looking to reschedule an available thread. Essentially, we skip every other cycle when only one thread is active, reducing our expected performance in half. So, given that, our example code achieved quite close to the theoretical peak performance for a single thread.

Before we move on, let's review the power and importance of vectorizing in the code. Run the compilation command again or look back at the output when you ran it. It should look something like this:

```
helloflops1.c(54): (col. 9) remark: LOOP WAS VECTORIZED
helloflops1.c(70): (col. 13) remark: LOOP WAS VECTORIZED
helloflops1.c(64): (col. 9) remark: loop was not vectorized: not inner loop
```

This output was generated because we used the option `-vec-report=3` to give us information about the compiler's choices for vectorizing portions of the code (note: the equals sign (=) is optional in this compiler option). Loop and array processing are usually required for successful vector code generation. In the case of helloflops1.c, the compiler was able to successfully arrange for chunks of our arrays to be loaded into machine registers or directly from memory via caches, and in this case, use up to 16 SP floating point lanes for simultaneous calculation. Two loops were vectorized. The initialization loop was vectorized, and the key calculation inner loop that we are timing was also vectorized. Generally outer loops cannot be effectively vectorized, hence the message for line 64 (for "j" loop).

To determine the performance benefit of vectorizing, recompile the code as follows:

```
$ icc -mmic -no-vec -vec-report=3 -O3 helloflops1.c -o helloflops1novec
```

We asked the compiler not to vectorize the code with the `-no-vec` option. Now upload the executable file to the coprocessor and run it again. You might have to wait a bit longer for the results this time. When completed, the output will look something like this:

```
% ./helloflops1novec
Initializing
Starting Compute
GFlops = 25.600, Secs = 131.322, GFlops per sec = 0.195
```

When we remove vectorization, we get dramatically less performance. We can't overstate the importance of ensuring your key inner loops and longer running code can be vectorized to take advantage of the performance potential of the Intel Xeon Phi coprocessor. You can immediately lose the ability to increase performance by 8 to 16 times or even more due to instruction scheduling differences.

Now, let's take the next step to ramp up our speed and see how we can scale our code to use multiple threads achieving closer to the performance potential available.

Starting to accelerate: running more than one thread

Now that we are getting a feel for the reaction of the gas pedal on our high performance vehicle, let's step it up a bit and push a little harder on the pedal to get a bit more speed.

As mentioned in the prior section, for a single core, we could expect a highly vectorized code using FMA calculations to achieve greater than 34 gigaFLOP/s. However, to ensure maximum performance, we need the core to execute the FMA calculation on every clock cycle. To do that, it must be running more than one thread.

In this section, we'll look at how we can modify the code to use more threads, allowing us to achieve the next important facet of parallel programing, scaling; that is, enabling our code to execute on multiple threads, and eventually multiple cores. There are a number of available methods to support scaling using threads. Several of these will be discussed in more detail in later chapters. In our current case, we are going to use OpenMP, a widely used standard supported by compilers for Intel Xeon Phi coprocessors. OpenMP is the prevalent standard API and programming model for shared memory multiprocessing written in Fortran and C/C++ for High Performance Computing. Given that all the Intel Xeon Phi coprocessor cores share the same random access memory, OpenMP fits well for our current use. While this book is not intended to be a tutorial on OpenMP, we will be explaining the use of some of the more simple constructs because it is important to understand how the code will execute and scale. More information is covered in Chapter 6.

Our current goal is to enable at least one more thread on a single core to enable our code to run closer to the core's peak performance. Since we achieved quite close to the theoretical peak in our first run with helloflops1.c, our approach will be to try to use the same code, but add an additional thread that will execute the same number of calculations in parallel by processing a second block of array values. Figure 2.3 depicts what we will try to achieve with our code.

To see how we will achieve adding another thread, look at Figure 2.4, which highlights in boldface type where in helloflops2.c a few OpenMP directives and API calls are added to change the program from primarily serial execution to one that scales using OpenMP threads. Effectively, OpenMP will run another instance of the code, but in parallel and on a different set of data. Our goal will be to double the amount of data processed in the same time period. Read the code carefully, focusing on the additions highlighted in boldface type that have been made over helloflops1.c. The OpenMP header file, `omp.h` allows the compiler to process the OpenMP constructs we will be including. We will use the simple and powerful OpenMP `parallel for` directive to enable the desired threading. The `parallel for` directive is placed just before a C `for` loop and will cause the loop iterations to be performed via a work division algorithm. The loop iterations are divided among the available threads and run in parallel.

Since we want each thread to perform the same amount of computation, we have added an additional outer loop that is bounded by the number of threads available. We have added an OpenMP `parallel for` loop pragma before this outer loop. Given the number of threads, the `parallel for` work division processing will simultaneously launch the number of threads specified and each will perform the original computation loop with one slight modification. Each thread will work on a separate set of array elements as set by the offset variable added to the code.

To achieve our goal of running two threads to see if we can achieve close to the peak SP floating point performance for a core, two other OpenMP setup calls are used:

```
omp_set_num_threads(2);
kmp_set_defaults("KMP_AFFINITY=compact");
```

The first call sets the number of threads we will use when running OpenMP code. We'll describe the notion of *affinity* in more detail in the next section, but in this case setting `AFFINITY` to `compact` will ensure we run our two requested threads on the same core.

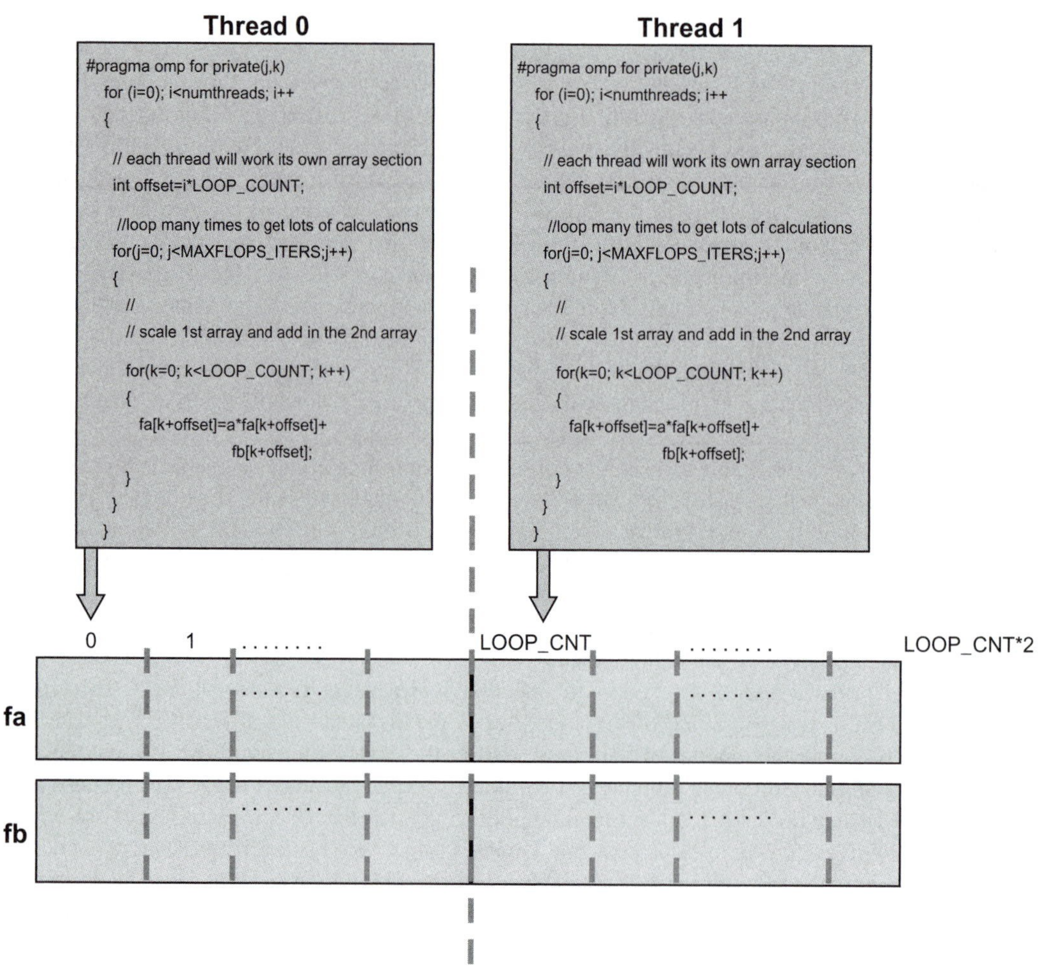
Thread 0
#pragma omp for private(j,k)
for (i=0); i<numthreads; i++
{
// each thread will work its own array section
int offset=i*LOOP_COUNT;
//loop many times to get lots of calculations
for(j=0; j<MAXFLOPS_ITERS;j++)
{
//
// scale 1st array and add in the 2nd array
for(k=0; k<LOOP_COUNT; k++)
{
fa[k+offset]=a*fa[k+offset]+
fb[k+offset];
}
}
}
Thread 1
#pragma omp for private(j,k)
for (i=0); i<numthreads; i++
{
// each thread will work its own array section
int offset=i*LOOP_COUNT;
//loop many times to get lots of calculations
for(j=0; j<MAXFLOPS_ITERS;j++)
{
//
// scale 1st array and add in the 2nd array
for(k=0; k<LOOP_COUNT; k++)
{
fa[k+offset]=a*fa[k+offset]+
fb[k+offset];
}
}
}
0
1
LOOP_CNT
LOOP_CNT*2
fa
fb

FIGURE 2.3

Partitioning Array *fa*[] and *fb*[] Using OpenMP across Two Threads.

Now it's time to run the code and see if we achieve the desired speedup of twice what we saw when running one thread. Compile the code with the following command:

```
$ icc –openmp –mmic –vec–report=3 –O3 helloflops2.c –o helloflops2
```

Note that we should still get the vectorization information specifying the key inner loop is vectorized. If not, make sure you no longer are using the `–no-vec` option in the command line. Upload

```
//
// helloflops2
//
// A simple example that gets lots of Flops on
// Intel(r) Xeon Phi(tm) coprocessors
// using openmp to scale
//
#include <stdio.h>
#include <stdlib.h>
#include <string.h>
#include <omp.h>
#include <sys/time.h>

// dtime -
// utility routine to returns the current wall clock time
double dtime()
{
    double tseconds = 0.0;
    struct timeval mytime;
    gettimeofday(&mytime,(struct timezone*)0);
    tseconds = (double)(mytime.tv_sec +
                        mytime.tv_usec*1.0e-6);
    return( tseconds );
}

#define FLOPS_ARRAY_SIZE (1024*1024)
#define MAXFLOPS_ITERS 100000000
#define LOOP_COUNT 128
// number of float pt ops per calculation
#define FLOPSPERCALC 2

// define some arrays - make sure they are 64 byte
// aligned - for fastest cache access
float fa[FLOPS_ARRAY_SIZE] __attribute__((align(64)));
float fb[FLOPS_ARRAY_SIZE] __attribute__((align(64)));
//
// Main program - pedal to the metal...
// ...calculate using tons o'flops!
//
int main(int argc, char *argv[] )
{
```

FIGURE 2.4

Code Listing of helloflops2.c with OpenMP Directives Added to Support Scaling to Two Threads.

```
int i,j,k;
    int numthreads;
    double tstart, tstop, ttime;
    double gflops = 0.0;
    float a=1.1;
    //
    // initialize the compute arrays
    //
    printf("Initializing\r\n");
    omp_set_num_threads(2);
    kmp_set_defaults("KMP_AFFINITY=compact");
#pragma omp parallel for
    for(i=0; i<FLOPS_ARRAY_SIZE; i++)
    {
        if (i==0) numthreads = omp_get_num_threads();
        fa[i] = (float)i + 0.1;
        fb[i] = (float)i + 0.2;
    }
    printf("Starting Compute on %d
                    threads\r\n", numthreads);

    tstart = dtime();

    // use omp to scale the calculation
    // across the threads requested
    // need to set environment variables
    // OMP_NUM_THREADS and KMP_AFFINITY

#pragma omp parallel for private(j,k)
    for (i=0; i<numthreads; i++)
    {
        // each thread will work its own array section
        int offset = i*LOOP_COUNT;

        // loop many times to get lots of calculations
        for(j=0; j<MAXFLOPS_ITERS; j++)
        {
            //
            // scale 1st array and add in the 2nd array
```

FIGURE 2.4

(Continued)

```
                for(k=0; k<LOOP_COUNT; k++)
                {
                    fa[k+offset]=a*fa[k+offset]+
                                        fb[k+offset];
                }
            }
        }
        tstop = dtime();
        // # of gigaflops we just calculated
        gflops = (double)( 1.0e-9 * numthreads *
                    LOOP_COUNT* MAXFLOPS_ITERS* FLOPSPERCALC);

        // elasped time
        ttime = tstop - tstart;
        //
        // Print the results
        //
        if ((ttime) > 0.0)
        {
            printf("GFlops = %10.3lf, Secs = %10.3lf,
                    GFlops per sec = %10.3lf\r\n",
                        gflops, ttime, gflops/ttime);
        }
        return( 0 );
    }
```

FIGURE 2.4

(Continued)

the compiled program as before to the Intel Xeon Phi coprocessor and execute it. The output should like something like this:

```
% ./helloflops2
Initializing
Starting Compute on 2 threads
GFlops = 51.200, Secs = 1.486, GFlops per sec = 34.453
```

Excellent! Now we're starting to get somewhere. As expected, we should have gotten a performance number somewhere above 34 gigaFLOP/s on our test coprocessor. With the two threads operating, computation happens on every cycle. We now have code that gets close to the full computation potential of one core of the coprocessor achieving a whopping 98.7 percent of the single core efficiency. Before moving on, feel free to try setting three or four threads in `omp_set_num_threads()`. The maximum number of threads the Intel Xeon Phi coprocessor can directly manage per core is four. The overall performance in gigaFLOP/s should remain roughly the same with two, three, or four threads. We've arranged this code to extract the maximum performance with just two threads. That won't always be the case with all code. We will discuss optimizing the number of threads to use in later chapters. Now, let's move on, have a little fun going full throttle and touching the full computational potential of our coprocessor in the next section.

Petal to the metal: hitting full speed using all cores

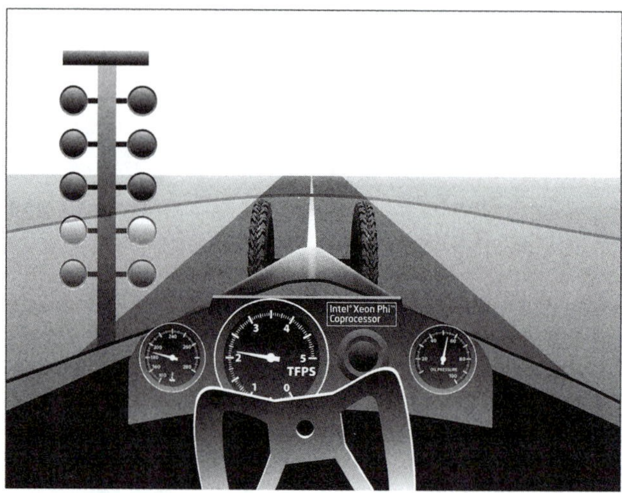

Finally, we are at the head of the straightaway and ready to push our car to close to maximum speed. In fact, instead of adding code to do it we are going to remove a few lines! Looking closely at the OpenMP portions of the code, notice that only a few lines specify the number of threads, and how they should be distributed using the `KMP_AFFINITY` value. We could keep these lines and simply increase the number of threads in the call to `omp_set_num_threads()` to be twice the number of cores. However, we will need a new affinity setting in `kmp_set_defaults()`, because the `compact` setting will distribute by setting all four threads to a single core before moving onto the next core. For instance, if we call `omp_set_num_threads(8)`, the first four threads will all be assigned to core 0 and the next four threads will be assigned to core 1. Since our code operates best with two threads per core, we won't see the maximum performance we expect because we'd only be accessing two cores. Furthermore, editing and recompiling the code over and over again with different settings can get time consuming and tedious. The good news is that we can set the number of threads and the affinity using environment variables OMP_NUM_THREADS and KMP_AFFINITY in the coprocessor's Linux operating environment. Since we already have a call to `omp_get_num_threads()` to retrieve the how many threads are desired, we can simply delete the lines calling `omp_set_num_threads() and kmp_set_defaults()` create an updated file helloflops3.c. To build helloflops3:

```
$ icc -openmp -mmic -vec-report=3 -O3 helloflops3.c -o helloflops3
```

Before running `helloflops3`, we can use the following at the coprocessor command prompt:

```
% export OMP_NUM_THREADS=2
% export KMP_AFFINITY=compact
```

Note, with these settings we'll end up with the same results for one core in the last section. However, after running the code to verify that expectation, we can make a change such as this:

```
% export OMP_NUM_THREADS=122
% export KMP_AFFINITY=scatter
```

In this case we are asking for 122 threads (2×61 cores) and specifying that threads be "scattered" across the cores. So, the OpenMP runtime will assign threads such that they are spread among the cores first and then subsequent threads greater than the number of cores will then be assigned starting again at the first core. Figure 2.5 depicts the impact of setting `KMP_AFFINITY` to `compact` and `scatter`. There are a number of ways to set `KMP_AFFINITY` to control the thread to core assignments. Please read the compiler documentation to learn more about this important but somewhat complex subject.

In our case, with a 61-core coprocessor, our assignments will result in exactly two threads per core across all the available cores. If your coprocessor has a different number of cores, simply set the number of threads to two times the number of cores available. Now, given these settings, Figure 2.6 shows how the *fa*[ ] and *fb*[ ] arrays will be portioned and processed.

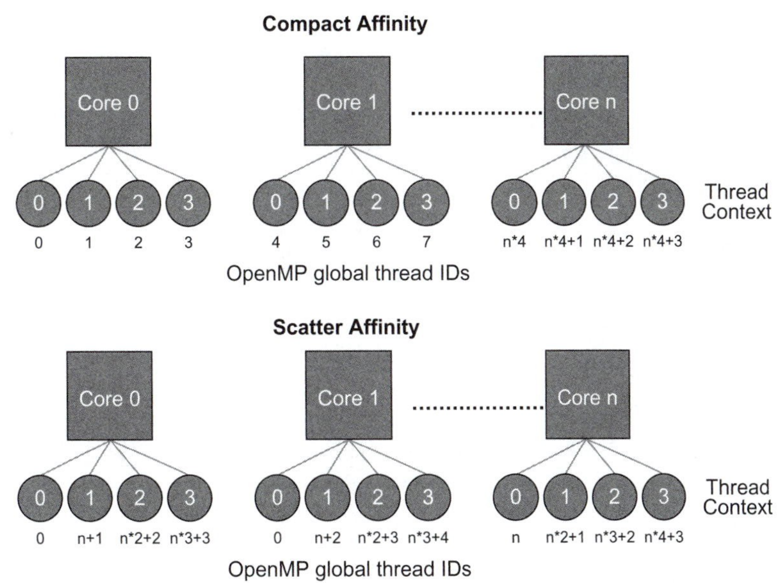

FIGURE 2.5

How helloflops3.c Scales Across All the Cores of the Intel® Xeon Phi™ Coprocessor.

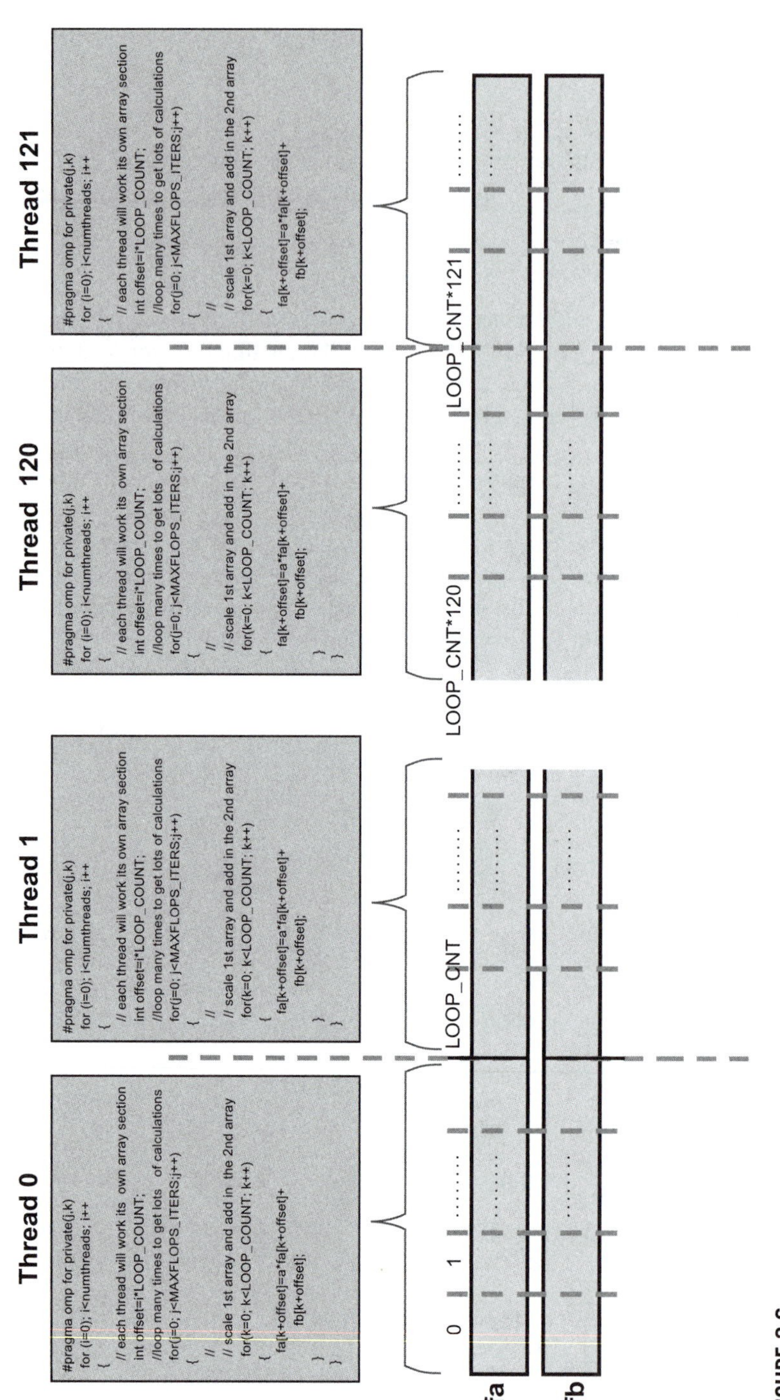

FIGURE 2.6

How helloflops3.c Scales Across All the Cores of the Intel® Xeon Phi™ Coprocessor.

We're now ready for our "pedal to the metal" moment. Upload the output file, helloflops3, to your working directory on the coprocessor. Enter the following:

```
% export OMP_NUM_THREADS=122  [or 2 times the number of cores]
% export KMP_AFFINITY=scatter
% ./helloflops3
Initializing
Starting Compute on 122 threads
GFlops =   3123.200, Secs = 1.530, GFlops per sec = 2041.090
```

On our 61-core test platform we get over 2 teraFLOP/s on the computation! We also achieved over 95.8 percent total efficiency. Now that's fun and exciting (in 2013 at least!). Take a moment to revel in the accomplishment. Tell your colleagues, friends, neighbors, and family members you just did over 2 trillion calculations per second. They are sure to be impressed! (Or they'll call you the world's biggest geek!) Experiment a little and change OMP_NUM_THREADS and KMP_AFFINITY to different settings and predict the results. For instance, if you set OMP_NUM_THREADS to the number of available cores, leaving KMP_AFFINITY at scatter you should end up with about half the performance because you'll be back to running at one thread per core. Set KMP_AFFINITY to compact leaving the number of threads at two times the cores, you'll also end up at roughly half the maximum performance because you'll be running full out at up to four threads per core, but only on about half the cores.

Now, let's take a brief look at the flexibility and breadth of the development options and programming models offered with the Intel Xeon Phi coprocessor. So far we have been working with standard C code. However, Fortran is the language of choice for many high performance computing developers and for much existing application code. Figure 2.7 shows helloflops3f.f90, the Fortran equivalent of our helloflops3.c code.

Assuming the Intel Composer XE 2013 Fortran compiler is installed you can use the following command line to compile helloflops3f.f90:

```
$ ifort -align array64byte -openmp -mmic -vec-report=3 -O3 helloflops3.f90 -o helloflops3f
```

The -align array64byte option indicates that all static array data should be aligned to 64 memory address boundaries ensuring the array data can be loaded from memory to cache optimally. Next, upload helloflops3f to your working directory and enter the following at the coprocessor command prompt:

```
% export OMP_NUM_THREADS=122 [or 2 times the number of cores]
% export KMP_AFFINITY=scatter
% ./helloflops3f
Initializing
Starting Compute on 122 threads
GFlops =   3123.200 Secs = 1.535, GFlops per sec = 2034.045
```

As you can see, the Fortran version also gets virtually the same performance as our C code. Intel Xeon Phi coprocessors offer you the flexibility to use the programming language that suits you needs.

Finally, we will show you the same helloflops code using a new programming model being introduced with Intel Xeon Phi coprocessors. So far, we have been using the coprocessor as a

```
! A simple fortran example that gets lots of
! Flops (Floating Point Operations) on Intel®
! Xeon Phi(tm) coprocessors using openmp to scale

! Main program - pedal to the metal...calculate
! using tons o'flops!

program helloflops
  use ISO_FORTRAN_ENV
  use omp_lib
  implicit none
  integer, parameter :: sp = REAL32
  integer, parameter :: dp = REAL64
  integer, parameter :: FLOPS_ARRAY_SIZE = 1024*512
  integer, parameter :: MAXFLOPS_ITERS = 100000000
  integer, parameter :: LOOP_COUNT = 128
  integer, parameter :: FLOPSPERCALC = 2

  real (sp), allocatable :: fa(:)
  real (sp), allocatable :: fb(:)

  integer   :: i,j,k
  integer   :: numthreads, offset
  real (dp) :: tstart, tstop, ttime
  real (dp) :: gflops = 0.0_dp
  real (sp) :: a = 1.1_sp

  allocate( fa(FLOPS_ARRAY_SIZE) )
  allocate( fb(FLOPS_ARRAY_SIZE) )

  ! initialize the compute arrays

  !$OMP PARALLEL
  !$OMP MASTER
  numthreads = omp_get_num_threads()
  !$OMP end MASTER
  !$OMP end PARALLEL

  write(*,*) "Initializing"

  !$OMP PARALLEL DO
  do i = 1, FLOPS_ARRAY_SIZE
     fa(i) = i + 0.1_sp;
     fb(i) = i + 0.2_sp;
  end do

  write(*,*) 'Starting Compute on ', numthreads, ' threads'
  tstart = mytime()
```

FIGURE 2.7

Fortran Listing of helloflops3 Code with OpenMP Directives for Scaling.

```
! scale the calculation across threads requested
! need to set environment variables OMP_NUM_THREADS
! and KMP_AFFINITY

!$OMP PARALLEL do PRIVATE(j,k,offset)
 do i=1, numthreads
    ! each thread will work its own array section
    ! calc offset into the right section
    offset = i*LOOP_COUNT

    ! loop many times to get lots of calculations
    do j=1, MAXFLOPS_ITERS
        ! scale 1st array and add in the 2nd array
        !dir$ vector aligned
        do k=1, LOOP_COUNT
            fa(k+offset) = a * fa(k+offset) +
            fb(k+offset)
        end do
    end do
end do

tstop = mytime()

! # of gigaflops we just calculated
gflops = 1.0e-9 * numthreads * LOOP_COUNT *
         MAXFLOPS_ITERS * FLOPSPERCALC

!elasped time
ttime = tstop - tstart

! Print the results

if (ttime > 0.0) THEN
    write (*,'(A,F10.3,A,F10.3,A,F10.3)')
              'GFlops = ',gflops, &
              ' Secs = ',ttime,' GFlops per sec =
              ',gflops/ttime
end if
contains
  ! ---------------------------------------------------
  ! mytime: returns the current wall clock time
  ! ---------------------------------------------------

  function mytime()  result (tseconds)
    real (dp)        :: tseconds
    integer (INT64) ::  count, count_rate, count_max
    real (dp)        :: tsec, rate

    CALL SYSTEM_CLOCK(count, count_rate, count_max)
    tsec = count
    rate = count_rate
    tseconds = tsec / rate
  end function mytime

end program helloflops
```

FIGURE 2.7

(Continued)

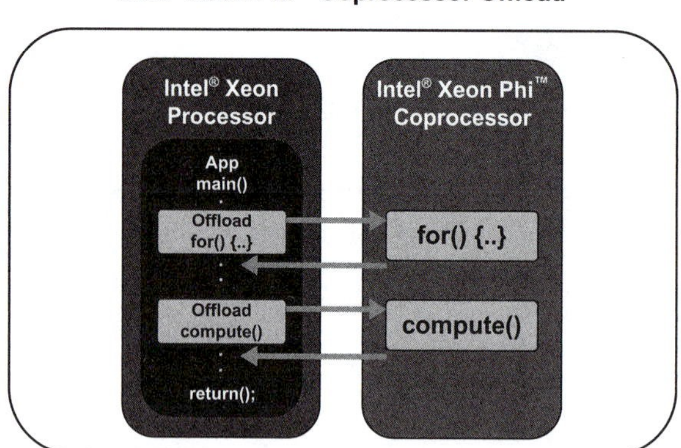

FIGURE 2.8

Simple Offload Flow Between a Host Processor and One Intel® Xeon Phi™ Coprocessor on the Same Platform.

traditional Linux-based networked compute node using a standard network access model and a *native* Linux command prompt. We compiled programs with the `–mmic` switch to target launch and execution directly on the coprocessors. Another usage offered is the *offload* programming model. In the offload model, a program running on the host can optionally launch or "offload" portions of code to a coprocessor on the same platform. The developer identifies lines or sections of code that are best suited for the coprocessor's wide vector processing and many cores by inserting directives similar to those used to invoke OpenMP capability. Chapter 7 describes offload usage in more depth but Figure 2.8 provides a conceptual view of offload.

The code is compiled for the host processor, and when offload directives are encountered and the coprocessor is running and available, the required data and code is automatically transferred between the host and coprocessor as needed. If no coprocessor is running or available, the line or block of code executes on the host. For now, we will give you a taste of using offload by converting helloflops3.c to use offload. Figure 2.9 shows helloflops3offload.c.

The key additions for offload are the two `#pragma offload target (mic)` directives just before the code we want to run on the Intel Xeon Phi coprocessor. Notice we didn't change the OpenMP directives. These still work as expected when using offload. We also made required modifications to our global array definitions of *fa*[] and *fb*[] to indicate they would be part of the offload use. Chapter 7 explains the required data definition usage in more detail. The two blocks of code we will offload are 1) the `omp_get_num_threads()` call so we get the number of threads running on the coprocessor, not on the host processor, and 2) our full processing loop that performs all calculations. To compile the code we enter:

```
$ icc –openmp –vec–report=3 –O3 helloflops3offload.c –o helloflops3offload
```

First you will see we no longer are using the `–mmic` option; this code targets the host processor. The #pragma offload directives we added indicate the specific places that code for the coprocessor

```
//
//
// helloflops3offload
//
// A simple example that gets lots of
// Flops (Floating Point Operations) on
// Intel(r) Xeon Phi(tm) coprocessors using offload
// with openmp to scale
//

#include <stdio.h>
#include <stdlib.h>
#include <string.h>
#include <omp.h>
#include <sys/time.h>

// dtime
//
// returns the current wall clock time
//
double dtime()
{
    double tseconds = 0.0;
    struct timeval mytime;
    gettimeofday(&mytime,(struct timezone*)0);
    tseconds = (double)(mytime.tv_sec +
                mytime.tv_usec*1.0e-6);
    return( tseconds );
}

#define FLOPS_ARRAY_SIZE (1024*512)
#define MAXFLOPS_ITERS 100000000
#define LOOP_COUNT 128

// number of float pt ops per calculation
#define FLOPSPERCALC 2
// define some arrays -
// make sure they are 64 byte aligned
// for best cache access
__declspec ( target (mic)) float fa[FLOPS_ARRAY_SIZE]
            __attribute__((align(64)));
__declspec ( target (mic)) float fb[FLOPS_ARRAY_SIZE]
            __attribute__((align(64)));
```

FIGURE 2.9

Code Listing of helloflops3offload.c with Offload Directives Added for Offloading from Host to the Intel® Xeon Phi™ Coprocessor.

```
//
// Main program - pedal to the metal...
// ..calculate using tons o'flops!
//
int main(int argc, char *argv[] )
{
    int i,j,k;
    int numthreads;
    double tstart, tstop, ttime;
    double gflops = 0.0;
    float a=1.1;

    //
    // initialize the compute arrays
    //
    //

#pragma offload target (mic)
#pragma omp parallel
#pragma omp master
    numthreads = omp_get_num_threads();

    printf("Initializing\n");

#pragma omp parallel for
    for(i=0; i<FLOPS_ARRAY_SIZE; i++)
    {
        fa[i] = (float)i + 0.1;
        fb[i] = (float)i + 0.2;
    }
    printf("Starting Compute on %d
            threads\n",numthreads);

    tstart = dtime();

    // scale the calculation across threads requested
    // need to set environment variables
    // OMP_NUM_THREADS and KMP_AFFINITY

#pragma offload target (mic)
#pragma omp parallel for private(j,k)
    for (i=0; i<numthreads; i++)
    {
```

FIGURE 2.9

(Continued)

```
        // each thread will work its own array section
        // calc offset into the right section
        int offset = i*LOOP_COUNT;

        // loop many times to get lots of calculations
        for(j=0; j<MAXFLOPS_ITERS; j++)
        {
            // scale 1st array and add in the 2nd array
            #pragma vector aligned
            for(k=0; k<LOOP_COUNT; k++)
            {
                fa[k+offset] = a * fa[k+offset] +
                               fb[k+offset];
            }
        }
    }
    tstop = dtime();
    // # of gigaflops we just calculated
    gflops = (double)( 1.0e-9*numthreads*LOOP_COUNT*
                    MAXFLOPS_ITERS*FLOPSPERCALC);

    //elasped time
    ttime = tstop - tstart;
    //
    // Print the results
    //
    if ((ttime) > 0.0)
    {
        printf("GFlops = %10.3lf, Secs = %10.3lf,
                GFlops per sec = %10.3lf\n",
                   gflops, ttime, gflops/ttime);
    }
    return( 0 );
}
```

FIGURE 2.9

(Continued)

should be generated. You should also see the vector report results, but this time the compiler will also distinguish whether the portion of code targeting the coprocessor was vectorized with a *MIC* indication in the output.

NOTE

The vec-report option, when used with offloading, can be easier to read if the reports for the host and the coprocessor are not interspersed. The section "Vec-report Option Used with Offloads" in Chapter 7 explains how to do this.

Now let's set up to run the code. Because we are going to run only from the host processor side and have no interaction with the coprocessor command prompt, we need some environment setup on the host to ensure the run goes as expected. Enter the following on the host prompt:

```
$ export MIC_ENV_PREFIX=MIC
$ export MIC_OMP_NUM_THREADS=120
$ export MIC_KMP_AFFINITY=scatter
```

This setup is used by the offload runtime system to understand what we desire on the coprocessor versus the local processor. `MIC_ENV_PREFIX=MIC` triggers the runtime to override default parameters and to use the `MIC_` OpenMP parameters for the run. Another thing to note for offload usage is that it is best to leave one coprocessor core free to handle the control and data interactions done at runtime. That's why for this run we are using 120 threads or 60 cores, leaving one core free for management and control between the processor and the coprocessor. Okay, let's run it. Execute the program from the host command prompt; no need to upload to the coprocessor this time:

```
$ ./helloflops3offload
Initializing
Starting Compute on 120 threads
GFlops = 3072.200 Secs = 1.524, GFlops per sec = 2016.219
```

The code is still able to achieve over 2 teraFLOP/s. The overhead includes the time to launch the code and transfer the data arrays between the host and the coprocessor. Of course, we did quite a bit of computation on those arrays so we minimized the overhead impact. In fact, the amount of computation versus the overhead to handle data transfers will become an important consideration in your choices for programming models and what should be done on the host processor versus on the coprocessor. What we have shown briefly so far in this chapter is, with Intel Xeon Phi coprocessors and Intel Xeon processors, you indeed have a variety of choices and some new programming models but mostly familiar ones, to find the best fit for your scientific and computational needs.

Now we will "switch gears" and take a look in the next section at another key high performance area available on the Intel Xeon Phi coprocessor, the high bandwidth memory subsystem that ultimately provides the fuel (data) for our computation engine.

Easing in to the first curve: accessing memory bandwidth

We've seen what it's like to rush down a straightaway at blistering speed; it is now time to work on the next, somewhat more challenging aspect of our driving skills. Similar to navigating a curve at relatively high speed; efficiently accessing the high speed memory on the Intel Xeon Phi coprocessor is another key to achieving good results and high performing applications.

The memory subsystem is comprised of high speed GDDR5 memory. As will be discussed further in Chapter 8, different models of coprocessors will have slightly different memory size and speed characteristics. Looking back at the specifications of our coprocessor version, it has an 8-gigabyte capacity and a memory channel interface speed of 5.5 gigatransfers per second (GT/s). As depicted in Figure 2.10, there are eight memory controllers each accessing two memory channels used on our coprocessor. Each memory transaction to GDDR5 memory is 4 bytes of data, resulting in 5.5 GT/s × 4 bytes or 22 GB/s per channel. 16 total channels provide a maximum transfer rate of 352 GB/s.

Unlike the on-chip processing elements like the VPU that have fairly predictable behavior and performance characteristics, the memory subsystem performance is affected by the hardware implementation, electromagnetic noise on the "wires," and a variety of other complex system factors. We can only expect to achieve an effective peak on the order of 50 to 60 percent of the specified maximum transfer rate in even ideal circumstances.

In this section, we will pursue a similar path to extracting high bandwidth, as we did to drive to achieve a very high rate of computation. The need to use all the cores and the right threading was somewhat obvious for our helloflops code. That need is not quite as obvious for the highest speed memory transfer. So, we will step back, as we did before, and see what we can achieve with a single core accessing the memory subsystem. Then we will look at what happens when we use more and more cores. We will learn the key considerations to best maximize memory flow for use in real applications.

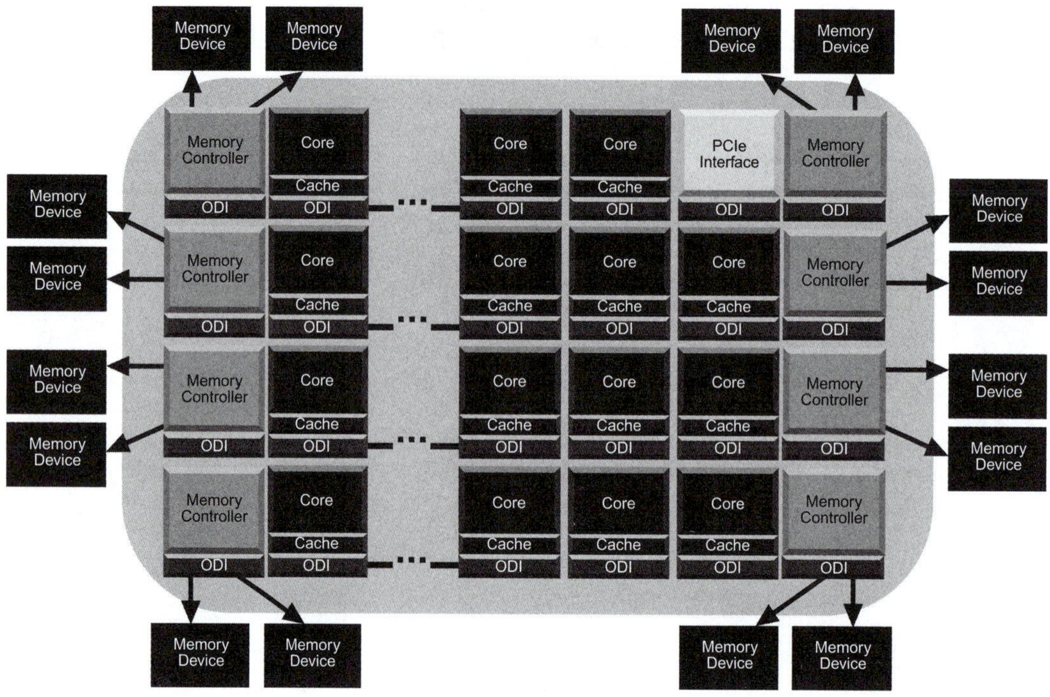

FIGURE 2.10

Memory Architecture on the Intel® Xeon Phi™ Coprocessor.

The hellomem.c code shown in Figure 2.11 will be used to measure and maximize our memory bandwidth usage. We are just going to copy one large array into another several times, performing a simple read/write memory access pattern in the main inner loop. There should be no possible cache reuse because the cache will not retain any portion of the array without evicting it to load new array data from memory. Therefore, the code will become limited by the memory transfer rate available. Vectorizing will remain important, because we do want to ensure we read and write contiguous blocks of data, minimizing access requests and thereby enabling very high throughput.

We are again using OpenMP to support scaling the code with threads and cores. We are now ready to compile using the following:

```
$ icc -openmp -mmic -vec-report=3 -O3 hellomem.c -o hellomem
```

We could run the code all out, but we are going to ease into our curve this first time. Upload `hellomem` to the coprocessor and then enter the following on the coprocessor command prompt:

```
% export OMP_NUM_THREADS=1
% ./hellomem
```

```
//
//
// hellomem
//
// A simple example that measures copy  memory bandwidth on
// Intel(r) Xeon Phi(tm) coprocessors using openmp to scale
//

#include <stdio.h>
#include <stdlib.h>
#include <string.h>
#include <omp.h>
#include <sys/time.h>

// dtime - utility routine that returns the current wall clock time

double dtime()
{
    double tseconds = 0.0;
    struct timeval mytime;
    gettimeofday(&mytime,(struct timezone*)0);
    tseconds = (double)(mytime.tv_sec + mytime.tv_usec*1.0e-6);
    return( tseconds );
}

// Set to float or double
#define REAL double

#define BW_ARRAY_SIZE (1000*1000*64)
#define BW_ITERS 1000

// number of mem ops each iteration
// 1 read  + 1 write
#define OPS_PERITER 2

// define some arrays
// make sure they are 64 byte aligned - for fastest cache
// access
REAL fa[BW_ARRAY_SIZE] __attribute__((align(64)));
REAL fb[BW_ARRAY_SIZE] __attribute__((align(64)));
REAL fc[BW_ARRAY_SIZE] __attribute__((align(64)));
```

FIGURE 2.11

Code Listing of hellomem.c.

```
//
// Main program - array copy
//
int main(int argc, char *argv[] )
{
    int i,j,k;
    double tstart, tstop, ttime;
    double gbytes = 0.0;
    REAL a=1.1;
    //
    // initialize the compute arrays
    //

    printf("Initializing\r\n");
#pragma omp parallel for
    for(i=0; i<BW_ARRAY_SIZE; i++)
    {
        fa[i] = (REAL)i + 0.1;
        fb[i] = (REAL)i + 0.2;
        fc[i] = (REAL)i + 0.3;
    }

// print the # of threads to be used
// Just display from 1 thread - the "master"
#pragma omp parallel
#pragma omp master
    printf("Starting BW Test on %d
threads\r\n",omp_get_num_threads());

    tstart = dtime();

    // use omp to scale the test across
    // the threads requested. Need to set environment
    // variables OMP_NUM_THREADS and KMP_AFFINITY
    for (i=0; i<BW_ITERS; i++)
    {
```

FIGURE 2.11

(Continued)

```
        //
        // copy the arrays to/from memory (2 bw ops)
        // use openmp to scale and get aggregate bw
        //
#pragma omp parallel for
            for(k=0; k<BW_ARRAY_SIZE; k++)
            {
               fa[k] = fb[k];
            }
        }

        tstop = dtime();
        // # of gigabytes we just moved

        gbytes = (double)( 1.0e-9 * OPS_PERITER * BW_ITERS *
                           BW_ARRAY_SIZE*sizeof(REAL));
        // elasped time
        ttime = tstop - tstart;
        //
        // Print the results
        //
        if ((ttime) > 0.0)
        {
            printf("Gbytes = %10.3lf, Secs = %10.3lf,"
                   "Gbytes per sec - %10.3lf\r\n",
                   gbytes, ttime, gbytes/time);
        }
        return( 0 );
    }
```

FIGURE 2.11

(Continued)

You should see output similar to this:

```
Initializing
Starting BW Test on 1 threads
Gbytes = 1024.000, Secs = 207.403, GBytes per sec = 4.937
```

As we saw with our helloflops code running on one core and one thread, the result does not come very close to achieving the maximum bandwidth. However, for this case, the use of just one thread, given the coprocessor's thread scheduler skipping every other cycle as described earlier, isn't a factor. That is because the delivery of data "streamed" directly from memory is significantly slower than the raw computational speed of the coprocessor. A memory request for data not in the cache will take significantly longer than two clock cycles. On the other hand, the available bandwidth is significantly higher than traditional DDR3 memory used on CPU platforms using a Intel Xeon processor. The higher speed memory is needed to provide a reasonable balance between the impressive computational speed available and the data flow from memory. In fact, understanding and managing that balance is a critical component of writing successful high performance code. We will be looking at ways to achieve that balance in subsequent chapters.

So, if it is not the thread scheduling, why do we only get a portion of the available bandwidth? Basically it falls back to the expected usage and design target of the Intel Xeon Phi coprocessor. The design target is highly parallel codes utilizing both vectorization and scaling across cores. Each core has a set of 32 internal buffers for managing outstanding memory requests. No more requests can be made when all those buffers are in use. On a per-core basis, the maximum bandwidth available is no more than 8 to 10 GB/s in ideal circumstances. So, when the only thing our code is doing is requesting more memory accesses and we are only running on one core, we are limited by those internal buffers. To truly reach the full throughput of the memory subsystem, we have to use more cores and gain access to many more of those memory management buffers aggregating the memory requests across more cores on the coprocessor. This matches the expected parallel application uses that will benefit from more cores, more threads, and wide vectors. In the next section, we'll look at what it takes to get close to the maximum effective bandwidth on our coprocessor.

High speed banked curved: maximizing memory bandwidth

Now that we know a bit more about the feel of an easy curve, we will keep increasing the "gas" through a series of banked curves leading up to achieving a very high memory transfer speed.

The good news is that we actually have our code set up to go without recompiling. We'll cover some additional special features and opportunities to ramp up the speed even more, later in this section.

Since we now know a little bit about how each core on the Intel Xeon Phi coprocessor will access memory and the memory subsystem characteristics, we can make some educated guesses about how we might get the most performance along the way. The first thing to note is that we probably are not going to get more bandwidth out of the memory with multiple threads per core. All that will occur in that case is that the threads will compete and stall waiting to access one or more of the 32 internal memory management buffers. While the overhead should be very small, OpenMP thread management will either add no benefit or give us slightly less performance. We can test this theory out soon. However, unlike the helloflops code, which called for a minimum of two threads, these factors indicate one thread per core is all we need. To most easily achieve that with no code changes we can simply set the affinity as follows:

```
% export KMP_AFFINITY=scatter
```

As mentioned in prior sections, this will cause the threads to be scattered and each placed on the next core with least number of threads assigned. The result for any number of threads equal or less then available cores will be one thread per core. Figure 2.12 shows how OpenMP will split up the data processing of the array copying.

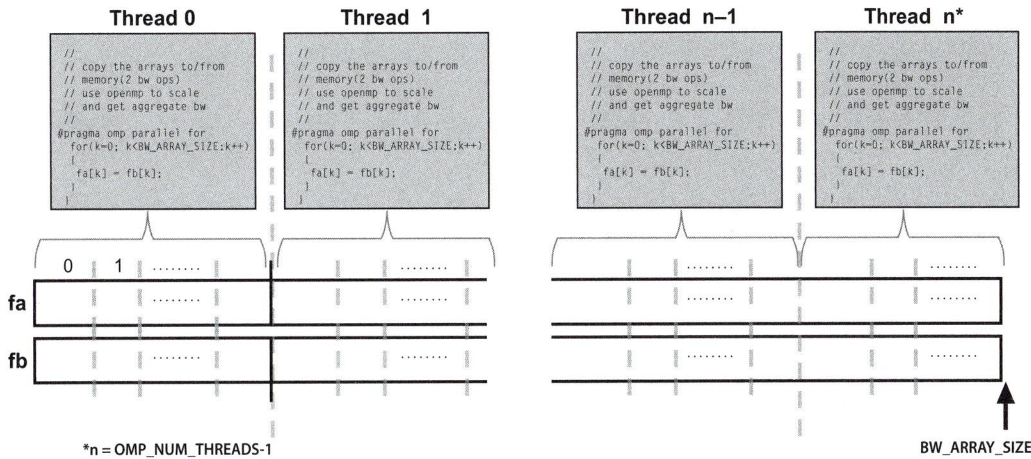

FIGURE 2.12

How hellomem.c Uses OpenMP to Scale and Access the Aggregate Bandwidth across the Intel® Xeon Phi™ Coprocessor.

Now let's rerun the hellomem code several times increasing the number of threads methodically from two threads to the maximum number of cores we have available, as shown below:

```
% export OMP_NUM_THREADS=2
% ./hellomem
Initializing
Starting BW Test on 2 threads
Gbytes = 1024.000, Secs = 104.381, GBytes per sec = 9.810
% export OMP_NUM_THREADS=10
% ./hellomem
Initializing
Starting BW Test on 10 threads
Gbytes = 1024.000, Secs = 21.991, GBytes per sec = 46.565
% export OMP_NUM_THREADS=20
% ./hellomem
Initializing
Starting BW Test on 20 threads
Gbytes = 1024.000, Secs = 13.198, GBytes per sec = 77.585
% export OMP_NUM_THREADS=30
% ./hellomem
Initializing
Starting BW Test on 30 threads
Gbytes = 1024.000, Secs = 10.246, GBytes per sec = 99.938
% export OMP_NUM_THREADS=40
% ./hellomem
```

```
Initializing
Starting BW Test on 40 threads
Gbytes = 1024.000, Secs = 8.545, GBytes per sec = 119.841
% export OMP_NUM_THREADS=50
% ./hellomem
Initializing
Starting BW Test on 50 threads
Gbytes = 1024.000, Secs = 7.712, GBytes per sec = 132.778
% export OMP_NUM_THREADS=60
% ./hellomem
Initializing
Starting BW Test on 60 threads
Gbytes = 1024.000, Secs = 7.461, GBytes per sec = 137.249
% export OMP_NUM_THREADS=61
% ./hellomem
Initializing
Starting BW Test on 61 threads
Gbytes = 1024.000, Secs = 7.386, GBytes per sec = 138.637
```

Figure 2.13 is a chart showing the data we get on our test coprocessor. You'll notice that somewhere around 30 to 40 cores, the curve begins to flatten out. We continue to get incremental benefit when using most of the available cores.

So, when using most of the cores we achieved bandwidth approaching 40 percent of the peak gigabytes per second. There are additional compiler switches available that can provide further improvements depending on the application and usage. Also, the Intel Xeon Phi coprocessor and

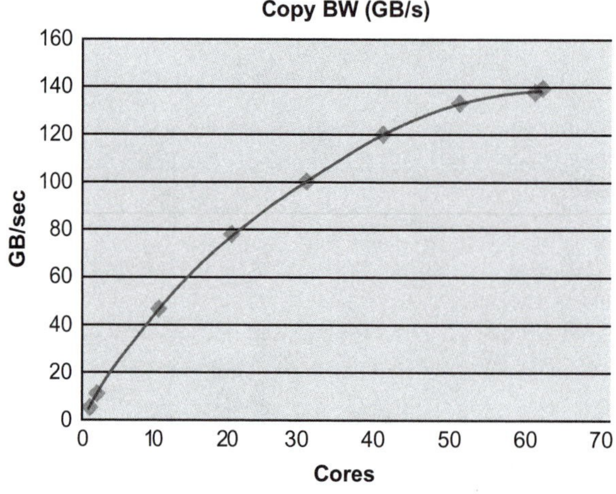

FIGURE 2.13

Effect of Using Multiple Cores to Aggregate Memory Bandwidth on the Intel® Xeon Phi™ Coprocessor.

the coprocessor's Linux operating system support 2-MB memory pages. These topics are beyond our current scope but the compiler documentation and Chapter 8 discuss these uses further. We now have the knowledge how to tap the memory bandwidth, another key performance capability of the Intel Xeon Phi coprocessor.

Back to the pit: a summary

We have now introduced you to the impressive performance and several of the programming options available with the Intel Xeon Phi coprocessor using a simple baseline code example. We are sorry if you were disappointed that we bypassed the traditional "Hello World" (and several hundred threads' worth of repeated printouts!) in favor of what seems a much more appropriate starter application for a high performance coprocessor, "Hello Flops!" Now that we have spent some time safely learning the key touch points of performance of our "sports car" on our closed test track, let's review the key points we learned in this chapter.

To achieve the highest computational performance available with the Intel Xeon Phi coprocessor, it's critical to ensure the code vectorizes to take advantage of the local data parallelism provided by the vector processing unit. Also, scaling using one of the available thread-based libraries to enable the computational power of the many available cores is the other important element. The development environment available for the coprocessor provides access to many well-known threading libraries, programming languages and models, like OpenMP, Fortran and Offload.

When performing multiplication and addition in one calculation, the Intel Xeon Phi coprocessor has the ability to use fused multiply and add (FMA) instructions that support prevalent linear algebra and matrix multiplication based math and science. When used extensively in the code, the coprocessor can reach close to its computational peak performance in those sections.

Also, we mentioned the design of the coprocessor requires at least two threads per core to achieve the full computational throughput of each core. Another key to higher performance is the consistent availability of the input data in the cache. For our helloflops series of example programs, we ensured this by using a data set size that would fit in the cache.

We used OpenMP, one of the most used parallel coding standards, to extend our code to support scaling our code to run parallel tasks or threads on every core.

We created versions of our high-speed floating point code in Fortran and with the offload model while maintaining high performance showing some of the breadth of usages available with Intel Xeon Phi coprocessors.

After successfully getting our example code to execute at over 2 SP teraFLOP/s, very close to the Intel Xeon Phi coprocessor's peak performance, we also looked at the high speed memory subsystem of the coprocessor. Using GDDR5 memory devices, the coprocessor has a peak electrical bandwidth well over 300 GB/s. We noted that effective accessible bandwidth is about 50 to 60 percent of the peak memory bandwidth. Each core has 32 internal memory request buffers that limit any single core to no more than 8 to 10 GB/s.

Using this knowledge and a simple memory copy example code we were able to achieve about 40 percent of the peak memory bandwidth.

In our next chapter, we'll hit the open road as we move on to still somewhat simple, but more realistic, scenarios that use both computation and a larger flow of input and output data from memory.

CHAPTER

A Friendly Country Road Race

3

Now that we've experienced some of the thrills of pushing our high performance sports car toward its peak performance in a synthetic, limited risk environment of a closed course, let's move on in our learning. Let's see what it's like to operate it in a still somewhat simple, but more realistic environment. We want to begin to understand the ways we can utilize the coprocessor's top performing features versus what is available on the processor. In this case, think of it as a friendly race between vehicles with different strengths on open country roads of different types. We'll encounter some bumps and obstacles that our competitor car can better navigate, as well as straightaways and turns optimal for our sports car. You have to be more attentive to your driving and the environment, but there are still few obstacles to prevent you from successfully navigating to your destination at optimum speeds.

Preparing for our country road trip: chapter focus

In this chapter, we are going to continue our examination of highly parallel programming with Intel® Xeon Phi™ coprocessors by using a more substantial yet still relatively simple code example that includes both computation and more complex memory access. This will allow us to consider some of the additional benefits and considerations for creating high performing parallel code for the coprocessor and also the Intel® Xeon™ processor. We will also do comparisons of running code on the processor and coprocessor as we improve the code. This should illustrate some of the points brought out in Chapter 1 on the benefits of general code enhancements for improved parallelization on both the processor and coprocessor.

We will work to ensure our code both vectorizes and scales to make the best use of the inherent parallel computational capabilities of both the coprocessor and the processor, as well as, demonstrate the advantages of the coprocessor's features for highly parallel applications. Finally, we will look at a few possibilities for fine-tuning on the coprocessor.

Getting a feel for the road: the 9-point stencil algorithm

The application we use for our analysis in this chapter implements a nine-point stencil algorithm for calculating partial differential equations, and for processing and filtering image data. See "For more information" at the end of this chapter for references on stencil codes and their usage. As depicted in Figure 3.1, our primary input data is a large two-dimension array of floating point values. We will perform processing and transformation on those data to create a new resulting two-dimensional array by passing a 3×3 data grid (nine points) centered on each array location.

In our implementation, we are going to apply the stencil as a blurring filter over an image. At each point, we will calculate a new value applying a weighted average of the center point and the eight surrounding points. Figure 3.2 shows a conceptual C implementation of the primary calculation loops. Note that the code does not attempt to fully process the boundaries at top, left, bottom, or right side of the images. This is generally referred to as the "halo" and there are various techniques to manage it. For simplicity and part of our notion of a "country road," we are going to assume the values have been initialized to reasonable values for the subsequent calculations, and we will concentrate on the bulk of the processing inside the halo. In Chapter 4, we will encounter another more complex stencil type code where we specifically deal with the boundary conditions.

For this imaging-based implementation, we have chosen to further simplify the stencil calculation by assuming that we are really interested in applying just three constant weighted averaging values in the stencil, `diag`, `next`, and `ctr`. The expectation is that the neighboring pixel values that are equidistant from the center should have equal weight with each other. Figure 3.3 provides a view of how the core of the stencil calculation takes the four values diagonal from the current center point of interest, directionally, northwest, northeast, southwest, and southeast; then the adjacent values "next" to the center, north, south, east, west; and finally applying the center value weight. If a more general implementation is desired that allows for different weights at each of the 9 stencil locations, it would be fairly straightforward to enhance the implementation to use nine independent values.

Finally, we have an outer loop that allows multiple passes of the same stencil calculation across the image. Each pass will reapply the filtering making the resulting image more blurry with each pass. You might note that it is possible with the proper setting of the stencil weights that we could approach the same blurring result in one pass. For our purposes, we want to ensure we can fully exercise the coprocessor and processor compute and memory subsystems and this behavior simulates other stencil applications where multiple passes are desired.

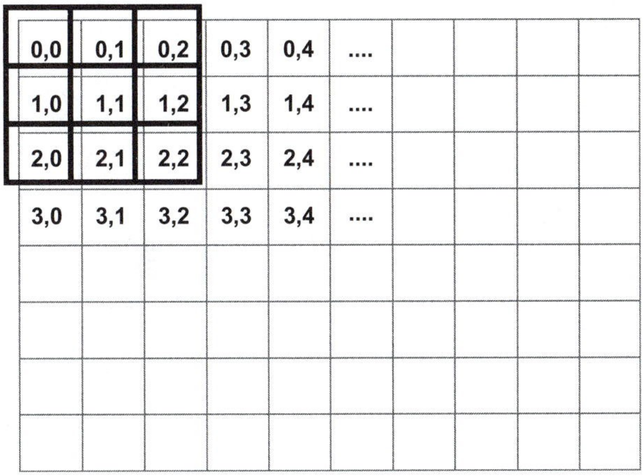

0,0	0,1	0,2	0,3	0,4	....				
1,0	1,1	1,2	1,3	1,4	....				
2,0	2,1	2,2	2,3	2,4	....				
3,0	3,1	3,2	3,3	3,4	....				

FIGURE 3.1

9-Point Stencil Operation over a Two-Dimensional Array.

```
for (i=0; i<iter_count; i++) {
  for (y=1; y < height-1; y++) {
    for (x=1; x < width-1; x++) {
      fout[y][x] = diag *  fin[y-1][x-1] +
                   diag *  fin[y-1][x+1] +
                   diag *  fin[y+1][x-1] +
                   diag *  fin[y+1][x+1] +
                   next *  fin[y-0][x-1] +
                   next *  fin[y-0][x+1] +
                   next *  fin[y-1][x-0] +
                   next *  fin[y+1][x+0] +
                   ctr  *  fin[y][x];
      }
    }
    tmp = fout; fout = fin; fin = tmp;
  }
```

FIGURE 3.2

Baseline 9 Point Stencil Image Blurring Algorithm Code.

At the starting line: the baseline 9-point stencil implementation

We are now ready to line up and have a friendly competition between our two different style "cars." Of course, we will continue to use our "sports car" the Intel Xeon Phi coprocessor with the specifications in Table 2.1. Our competition will be an Intel Xeon dual processor platform with the basic specifications in Table 3.1.

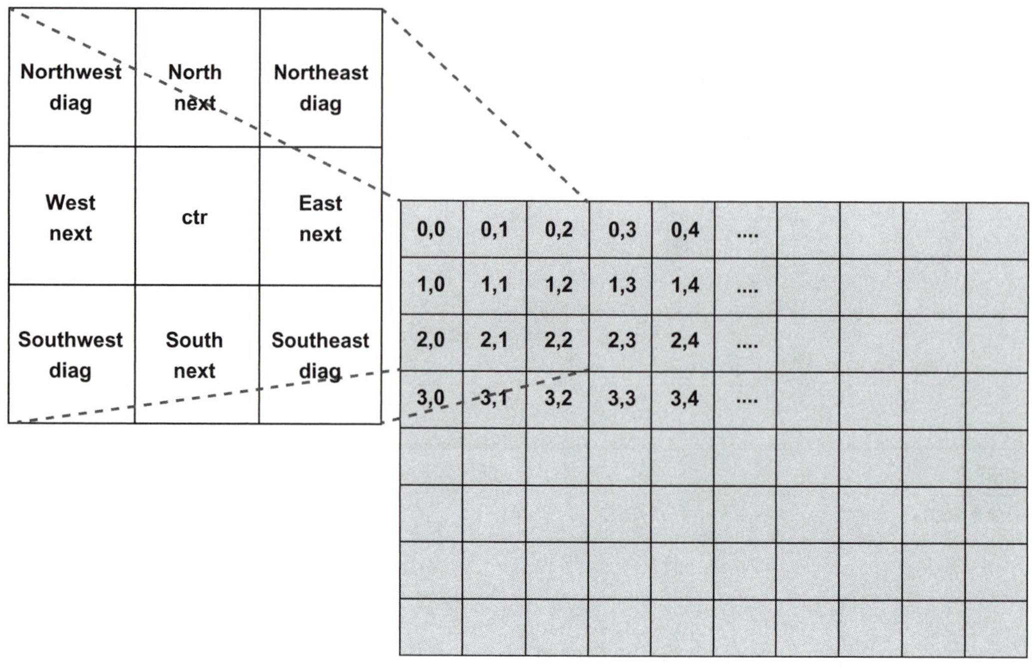

FIGURE 3.3

Applying the Stencil Values Based on Direction and Distance from the Center.

Table 3.1 Our Intel® Xeon® Processor Platform Specifications

Clock Frequency	2.6 GHz
Number of Cores	16 (8 × 2 CPUs)
Memory Size/Type	64 GB / DDR3
Memory Speed	1333
Peak DP/SP FLOPs	345.6 / 691.2 GigaFLOP/s
Peak Memory Bandwidth	85.3 GB/s

The processor is like a solid, general purpose, high-powered all-terrain SUV. It does most things very well, has a much faster clock frequency, stronger serial code performance per thread and a larger memory capacity than the coprocessor. Like the coprocessor, parallel vector-based code is needed to maximize its performance. However, the coprocessor, with its many more cores and threads, and higher speed memory, should have an advantage on code that scales across the higher core count, fits into its memory, and may benefit from increased memory speed.

We will evaluate the results of a series of "races" on different "terrain" as we walk through the key steps to enable the code to vectorize and scale, much like we did with our helloflops code examples in Chapter 2. Before reading on, you may want to consider some of the key comparison points made in Chapter 1, particularly the principle captured in Figure 1.5 describing the potential performance balance between processor and the coprocessor. Take a moment to flip back to Chapter 1 and review Figure 1.5 before proceeding here.

Figure 3.4 lists the file sten2d9pt_base.c, our full initial baseline implementation of the 9-point two-dimensional stencil processing in C language. The key function `stencil9pt_base()` implements the algorithm already described in Figure 3.2. To further generalize the code, we have linearized the array accesses into one dimension, calculating the correct starting index `c` at the start of each `y` "row." We have also implemented the notion of adding padding or extra unused data at the end of each row with the `WIDTHP` constant. In some circumstances, padding enables a performance benefit by aligning heavily utilized memory addresses for efficient cache line accesses. In the case of the processor and coprocessor, 64-byte alignment matches the cache structure. We will work more with alignment and padding later in the chapter.

NOTE

You may recall from Chapter 2 that the coprocessor vector registers are 64 bytes wide and loading them with 64-byte aligned addresses is crucial to achieving high performance. Chapters 5 and 8 discuss the benefits of alignment and the cache structure in more detail.

We are also calculating 8 stencil "direction" variables `n`, `s`, `e`, `w`, `nw`, `ne`, `sw`, and `se` to locate the correct linear indices to access and calculate the result in the two-dimensional "image." These

```
#include <stdio.h>
#include <stdlib.h>
#include <string.h>
#include <math.h>
#include <time.h>
#include <sys/time.h>
#include <omp.h>
#include <assert.h>
#include <sys/mman.h>
#define SAVEFILES 0 // 1 if saving results
#define DBG 0       // Print out results
#define REAL double
#define PAD64 0
#define WIDTH 5900
#if PAD64
#define WIDTHP ((((WIDTH*sizeof(REAL))+63)/64)*(64/sizeof(REAL)))
#else
#define WIDTHP WIDTH
#endif
#define HEIGHT 10000

void initbuf(REAL *fbuf, const int width,
             const int height)
{
  REAL val;
  int x,y;

  for (y=0; y < height; y++) {
    val = (y % 10) ? 0 : 1.0;
    for (x=0; x < width; x++) {
      fbuf[x+y*WIDTHP] = val;
    }
  }
  return;
}
void
stencil9pt_base(REAL *finp, REAL *foutp,
            int width, int height,
                REAL ctr, REAL next, REAL diag,int count)
{
  REAL *fin = finp;
  REAL *fout = foutp;
  int i,x,y;
  for (i=0; i<count; i++) {
    for (y=1; y < height-1; y++) {
       // starting center pt (avoid halo)
      int c = 1 + y*WIDTHP+1;
      // offsets from center pt.
      int n = c-WIDTHP;
      int s = c+WIDTHP;
      int e = c+1;
      int w = c-1;
      int nw = n-1;
```

FIGURE 3.4

The sten2d9pt_base.c Listing.

```
        int ne = n+1;
        int sw = s-1;
        int se = s+1;
        for (x=1; x < width-1; x++) {
          fout[c] = diag * fin[nw] +
                    diag * fin[ne] +
                    diag * fin[sw] +
                    diag * fin[se] +
                    next * fin[w] +
                    next * fin[e] +
                    next * fin[n] +
                    next * fin[s] +
                    ctr  * fin[c];
          // increment to next location
          c++;n++;s++;e++;w++;nw++;ne++;sw++;se++;
        }
      }
      REAL *ftmp = fin;
      fin = fout;
      fout = ftmp;
    }
    return;
  }
  static double dtime() {
    double tseconds = 0.0;
    struct timeval mytime;
    gettimeofday(&mytime,(struct timezone *) 0);
    tseconds = (double) (mytime.tv_sec +
               (double)mytime.tv_usec * 1.0e-6);
    return (tseconds) ;
  }
  #if DBG
  dbgprint(REAL *fbuf,int width, int height)
  {
    // print out a chunk for review of calc..
    //
    int x, y, offset;
    // Head left
    for (y=0; y<20; y++)
    {
          offset = y*width;
          for (x=0; x<10; x++)
          {
                printf("%10.3f", fbuf[offset+x]);
          }
          printf("\n");
    }
    printf("Tail Left\n");
    for (y=height-20; y<height; y++)
    {
    offset = y*width;
          for (x=0; x<10; x++)
          {
```

FIGURE 3.4

(Continued)

```
                printf("%10.3f", fbuf[offset+x]);
            }
            printf("\n");
    }

    printf("Tail Right\n");
    for (y=height-20; y<height; y++)
    {
            offset = y*width;
            for (x=width-10; x<width; x++)
            {
                printf("%10.3f", fbuf[offset+x]);
            }
            printf("\n");
    }


    printf("\n\n");
}
#endif

void savetofile(char *filename, REAL *fbuf, int width, int height) {
  FILE *fp = fopen(filename, "w");
  assert(fp);
  size_t numitems = width * height;
  fwrite(fbuf, sizeof(REAL), numitems, fp);

  fclose(fp);
}

int main(int argc, char *argv[])
{
  double t_begin, t_end;
  int    i;
  int    width    = WIDTH;
  int    height   = HEIGHT;
  REAL   *fout, *fin, *ftmp;

  REAL *fa = (REAL *)malloc(sizeof(REAL)*WIDTHP*HEIGHT);
  REAL *fb = (REAL *)malloc(sizeof(REAL)*WIDTHP*HEIGHT);

  REAL   time  = 0.0;
  int    count = 1000;

  REAL stendiag, stennext, stenctr;

  fin = fa;
  fout = fb;

  printf("Initializing..%d Threads, %d x %d,
          PAD=%d..\n\n",omp_get_num_threads(),
          WIDTH, HEIGHT, WIDTHP);
```

FIGURE 3.4

(Continued)

```
  initbuf(fin, width, height);
  initbuf(fout, width, height);

#if DBG
  dbgprint(fin, WIDTHP, height);
#endif

#if SAVEFILES
  savetofile("stencil9pt_init.dat", fin, WIDTHP, HEIGHT);
#endif
  // stencil params: slowly blurring...

  stendiag = 0.00125;
  stennext = 0.00125;
  stenctr = 0.99;

  printf("Running stencil kernel %d times\n", count);

  t_begin = dtime();

  stencil9pt_base(fin, fout, width, height,
                  stenctr, stennext, stendiag,count);

  t_end = dtime();

#if DBG
  dbgprint(fout, WIDTHP, height);
#endif
#if SAVEFILES
  savetofile("stencil9pt_result.dat",fb, WIDTHP, HEIGHT);
#endif

  double elapsed_time = t_end - t_begin;
  REAL mflops = (width*height)*17.0*count/elapsed_time *
                1.0e-06;

  printf("Elapsed time : %.3f (s)\n", elapsed_time);
  printf("FLOPS        : %.3f (MFlops)\n", mflops);


  free(fa);
  free(fb);

  return 0;
}
```

FIGURE 3.4

(Continued)

variables are incremented for each step in x, moving the stencil over each 3 × 3 pixel block from left to right. We skip direct processing of the "halo" at top, left, bottom, and right edges. We have implemented a "ping pong" double buffering scheme for swapping the input and output image arrays on each outer loop iteration. You will notice that we have defined a few control capabilities for compiling the code with different aspects with #define. A notable one is the definition of REAL, which can easily be changed between float (single precision) and double (double precision).

Read through main() to get familiar with the flow of the code. Unlike Chapter 2 where we statically allocated our arrays through a global declaration, we allocate our two image buffers with malloc(). We then initialize our buffers with the initbuf() function. For our purposes, we are effectively using a grayscale image format where 0.0 represents the darkest pixel value (black) and 1.0 is the brightest pixel value (white). For simplicity and easily confirming we have a correct implementation, we simply choose to create an initial image that has a single pixel high white horizontal line every tenth row. Feel free to create other patterns or even read in an image from a file and give it a try. Defining DBG as 1 will print out a representative portion of the image data at the start and end of the run. Next, note the values set in the key stencil blurring filter variables, stendiag, stennext, and stenctr. For proper image results, the values when added together should equal 1.0 such that stendiag*4 + stennext*4 + stenctr = 1.0. Because we are going to iterate the stencil count times (default = 1000), we chose a large value for the weight of the center pixel, and therefore for simplicity we also use identical values for stendiag and stennext. It may typically be more logical to have stendiag be proportionally larger (for example sqrt(2)*stennext) based on distance from the center pixel. Given the input image of a solid horizontal line every tenth row, each iteration will further blur the image around the solid lines until the line definition is completely lost.

It's time to put our code to the test and see how each of our proverbial "cars" handles it as we review and improve the code. First we are going to try the code as is, using the equivalent of a bumpy dirt road as our track.

Rough road ahead: running the baseline stencil code

We are ready for our first in the series of head-to-head competitions between the coprocessor and the processor. We have our stencil baseline code as our target "road." You probably noticed that, other than including the OpenMP header file (omp.h), there are no explicit attempts to make the code parallel. Therefore it will be executing on a single thread of processor and coprocessor with no scaling. Can you guess which one will win this first round? We are going to use the Intel Composer XE Compiler suite with a simple command line to compile the code. We will assume you have already installed and are set up with the compiler and the coprocessor as was done in Chapter 2. We use the following command line to compile the code for the coprocessor:

```
$ icc –openmp –mmic –O3 –vec–report=3 sten2d9pt_base.c –o sten2d9pt_xphi
```

Even though we used the –openmp compiler option, we already know we haven't written any OpenMP pragmas into the code yet so we can't expect it to scale; that will come in another racing round. However, we would want the compiler to vectorize the key loop in sten2d9pt_base() to at least get a first level of parallel performance. Take a look at the vector report output. Did the key inner for loop vectorize? On our version of the compiler here is a portion of the vector report output related to our target loop:

```
sten2d9pt_base.c(67): (col. 7) remark: loop was not vectorized: existence of vector dependence.
sten2d9pt_base.c(68): (col. 9) remark: vector dependence: assumed ANTI dependence between fin line 68 and fout line 68.
sten2d9pt_base.c(68): (col. 9) remark: vector dependence: assumed FLOW dependence between fout line 68 and fin line 68.
sten2d9pt_base.c(68): (col. 9) remark: vector dependence: assumed FLOW dependence between fout line 68 and fin line 68.
sten2d9pt_base.c(68): (col. 9) remark: vector dependence: assumed ANTI dependence between fin line 68 and fout line 68.
sten2d9pt_base.c(68): (col. 9) remark: vector dependence: assumed ANTI dependence between fin line 68 and fout line 68.
sten2d9pt_base.c(68): (col. 9) remark: vector dependence: assumed FLOW dependence between fout line 68 and fin line 68.
sten2d9pt_base.c(68): (col. 9) remark: vector dependence: assumed FLOW dependence between fout line 68 and fin line 68.
sten2d9pt_base.c(68): (col. 9) remark: vector dependence: assumed ANTI dependence between fin line 68 and fout line 68.
sten2d9pt_base.c(68): (col. 9) remark: vector dependence: assumed ANTI dependence between fin line 68 and fout line 68.
```

Needless to say that does not seem like a good sign. Without going into the deep details of the messages, the compiler has found an assumed dependence between the `fin` and `fout` pointers. The loop is not vectorized. We agreed to this race so we are going to go ahead with it anyway! First, we still need to compile the code for the processor. Here is the command line:

```
$ icc –openmp –O3 –vec-report=3 sten2d9pt_base.c –o sten2d9pt_xeon
```

All we really did was remove the `–mmic` switch that was targeting the coprocessor native execution. The vector report, naturally, still indicates the assumed dependency between fin and fout so no vectorized code on the processor either.

Now, it is time run the first race and get the results. However, be forewarned these runs will take quite a long time. Unless you are ready for a cup of coffee or two, you may want to skip it this time and just look at our results!

To run on the coprocessor, you can copy the file to a working directory with scp or other method based on your setup. We assume you already have a command prompt terminal session to execute the code:

```
% ./sten2d9pt_xphi
Initializing..1 Threads, 5900 x 10000, PAD=5900...
Running stencil kernel 1000 times
Elapsed time : 2838.342 (s)
FLOPS   : 353.375 (MFlops)
```

Wow, it took over 47 minutes to run on the coprocessor! Now, to run the code on the processor:

```
$ ./sten2d9pt_xeon
Initializing..1 Threads, 5900 x 10000, PAD=5900...
Running stencil kernel 1000 times
Elapsed time : 244.178 (s)
FLOPS   : 4107.658 (MFlops)
```

The processor was able to run the non-vectorized, single-threaded code in just over 4 minutes. That is over 11 times faster than the coprocessor. Round one goes to the processor in a rout. Did you expect that result? Given the lower clock speed and the hardware optimization to favor parallel performance it's pretty clear that, with neither vectorization nor scaling of the code, the processor has a strong advantage over the coprocessor in pure serial execution (just like Figure 1.5 indicates).

The next step is to move towards parallelizing the code by helping the compiler to vectorize that inner loop.

Cobblestone street ride: vectors but not yet scaling

For a compiler, automatically vectorizing C code that uses pointers is difficult. Code correctness is paramount for a compiler. In the absence of additional information, the compiler cannot usually determine if two pointers point at the same memory. That's the problem with our baseline stencil code inner loop. The compiler cannot determine if our `fin` and `fout` array pointers are truly pointing to separate memory blocks. Chapter 5 delves into a lot of information and guidance on several ways a developer can arm the compiler with more information to support vectorizing.

In our case, we know for sure that `fin` and `fout` always access distinct and separate blocks of memory. A compiler directive, #pragma ivdep, tells the compiler it can ignore non-obvious dependencies. This is one of the techniques we cover in Chapter 5 on how to help the compiler vectorize code often by overcoming the limits of the C/C++ languages. Figure 3.5 shows the `sten2d9pt_vect()` function in the updated code file sten2d9pt_vect.c with an #pragma ivdep included.

We will compile it for the coprocessor with the same command line options as before:

```
$ icc -openmp -mmic -O3 -vec-report=3 sten2d9pt_vect.c -o sten2d9pt_xphi
```

This time the vector report indicates that the loop was now indeed vectorized. Let's compile for the processor:

```
$ icc -openmp -O3 -vec-report=3 sten2d9pt_vect.c -o sten2d9pt_xeon
```

As expected, the processor code compile reports the inner loop is vectorized as well. We still haven't looked at scaling the code across cores or threads so we should anticipate that we will remain far from the fastest performance, but we should see a boost from vectorization. Time to

```
void
stencil9pt_vect(REAL *finp, REAL *foutp,
            int width, int height,
                REAL ctr, REAL next, REAL diag,int count)
{
  REAL *fin = finp;
  REAL *fout = foutp;
  int i,x,y;

  for (i=0; i<count; i++) {
    for (y=1; y < height-1; y++) {
       // starting center pt (avoid halo)
      int c = 1 + y*WIDTHP+1;
      // offsets from center pt.
      int n = c-WIDTHP;
      int s = c+WIDTHP;
      int e = c+1;
      int w = c-1;
      int nw = n-1;
      int ne = n+1;
      int sw = s-1;
      int se = s+1;
#pragma ivdep
      for (x=1; x < width-1; x++) {
        fout[c] = diag * fin[nw] +
                  diag * fin[ne] +
                  diag * fin[sw] +
                  diag * fin[se] +
                  next * fin[w] +
                  next * fin[e] +
                  next * fin[n] +
                  next * fin[s] +
                  ctr  * fin[c];

        // increment to next location
        c++;n++;s++;e++;w++;nw++;ne++;sw++;se++;
      }
    }
    REAL *ftmp = fin;
    fin = fout;
    fout = ftmp;
  }
  return;
}
```

FIGURE 3.5

The sten2d9pt_vect Function.

hit the road and compete on this still slightly bumpy but improved “road.” Execute both on the coprocessor and processor:

```
% ./sten2d9pt_xphi
Initializing..1 Threads, 5900 x 10000, PAD=5900...
```

```
Running stencil kernel 1000 times
Elapsed time : 623.302 (s)
FLOPS   : 1609.171 (MFlops)

% ./sten2d9pt_xeon
Initializing..1 Threads, 5900 x 10000, PAD = 5900...

Running stencil kernel 1000 times
Elapsed time : 186.585 (s)
FLOPS   : 5375.572 (MFlops)
```

The vectorization of the code gives close to a 4.5x improvement on the coprocessor and almost 1.3x improvement on the processor. The processor still far outpaces the coprocessor on non-scaling code but the wider vectors had a strong showing on the coprocessor and narrowed the performance gap from over 11x to under 4x.

We have delayed going all out so far, but it is time to get much more out of these two parallel computation engines.

Open road all-out race: vectors plus scaling

Now that our primary processing inner loop is vectorizing, we want to try to parallelize further by scaling the computation across the cores and threads available to enable much greater performance and approach the potential of the code and computation platforms. As we did in Chapter 2, we will use the prevalent OpenMP standard to enable scaling across the cores. Figure 3.6 has an updated listing of the principal sten2d9pt_omp() call in our updated file sten2d9pt_omp.c. Also, a modified section of `main()` with some minor changes is also shown.

We add the line `#pragma omp parallel for private(x)` before the y processing loop to enable the OpenMP `parallel for` loop work division mechanism. Essentially, OpenMP will divide and balance the computation into sets of rows for each available thread to process independently and in parallel. It should dramatically speed up the computation on both the coprocessor and the processor.

In `main()`, we simply added a few lines during the initialization to support properly retrieving and printing the number of threads that will be used. The #pragma omp master indicates that just the single master thread should execute the line. We certainly don't need hundreds of lines of the same information printed on the screen.

This change should allow all out highly parallel code execution on both the processor and coprocessor. So it is time to line up our two cars and see who wins the ultimate speed test. To compile the code we execute the following command lines:

```
$ icc –openmp –mmic –O3 –vec-report = 3 sten2d9pt_omp.c –o sten2d9pt_xphi
$ icc –openmp –O3 –vec-report = 3 sten2d9pt_omp.c –o sten2d9pt_xeon
```

Since we will now be running with OpenMP, we need to set each platform's OpenMP parameters and test out the various numbers of threads per core to find the optimal use.

```
void
stencil9pt_omp(REAL *finp, REAL *foutp,
               int width, int height,
               REAL ctr, REAL next, REAL diag, int count)
{
  REAL *fin = finp;
  REAL *fout = foutp;
  int i,x,y;

  for (i=0; i<count; i++) {
#pragma omp parallel for private(x)
    for (y=1; y < height-1; y++) {
      // starting center pt (avoid halo)
      int c = 1 + y*WIDTHP+1;
      // offsets from center pt.
      int n = c-WIDTHP;
      int s = c+WIDTHP;
      int e = c+1;
      int w = c-1;
      int nw = n-1;
      int ne = n+1;
      int sw = s-1;
      int se = s+1;
#pragma ivdep
      for (x=1; x < width-1; x++) {
        fout[c] = diag * fin[nw] +
                  diag * fin[ne] +
                  diag * fin[sw] +
                  diag * fin[se] +
                  next * fin[w] +
                  next * fin[e] +
                  next * fin[n] +
                  next * fin[s] +
                  ctr  * fin[c];

        // increment to next location
        c++;n++;s++;e++;w++;nw++;ne++;sw++;se++;
      }
    }
    REAL *ftmp = fin;
    fin = fout;
    fout = ftmp;
  }
  return;
}

main()
.
.
.

#pragma omp parallel
#pragma omp master
  printf("Initializing..%d Threads, %d x %d,
          PAD=%d..\n\n", omp_get_num_threads(),
          WIDTH, HEIGHT, WIDTHP);
.
.
.
.
```

FIGURE 3.6

The sten2d9pt_omp Function and Updated Portion of main().

```
% export KMP_AFFINITY=scatter
% export OMP_NUM_THREADS=244
% ./sten2d9pt_xphi
Initializing..244 Threads, 5900 x 10000, PAD=5900...

Running stencil kernel 1000 times

Elapsed time : 12.696 (s)
FLOPS   : 78999.44 (MFlops)

% export OMP_NUM_THREADS=183
% ./sten2d9pt_xphi
Initializing..183 Threads, 5900 x 10000, PAD=5900...

Running stencil kernel 1000 times

Elapsed time : 10.564 (s)
FLOPS   : 94946.364 (MFlops)

% export OMP_NUM_THREADS=122
% ./sten2d9pt_xphi
Initializing..122 Threads, 5900 x 10000, PAD=5900...

Running stencil kernel 1000 times

Elapsed time : 8.772 (s)
FLOPS   : 114338.399 (MFlops)

% export OMP_NUM_THREADS=61
% ./sten2d9pt_xphi
Initializing..61 Threads, 5900 x 10000, PAD=5900...

Running stencil kernel 1000 times

Elapsed time : 11.366 (s)
FLOPS   : 88246.452 (MFlops)
```

On the processor execute:

```
$ export KMP_AFFINITY=scatter
$ export OMP_NUM_THREADS=32
$ ./sten2d9pt_xeon
Initializing..32 Threads, 5900 x 10000, PAD=5900...
Running stencil kernel 1000 times
Elapsed time : 46.247 (s)
FLOPS   : 21688.103 (MFlops)

$ OMP_NUM_THREADS=16
$ ./sten2d9pt_xeon
Initializing..16 Threads, 5900 x 10000, PAD=5900...
Running stencil kernel 1000 times
Elapsed time : 43.862 (s)
FLOPS   : 22867.185 (MFlops)
```

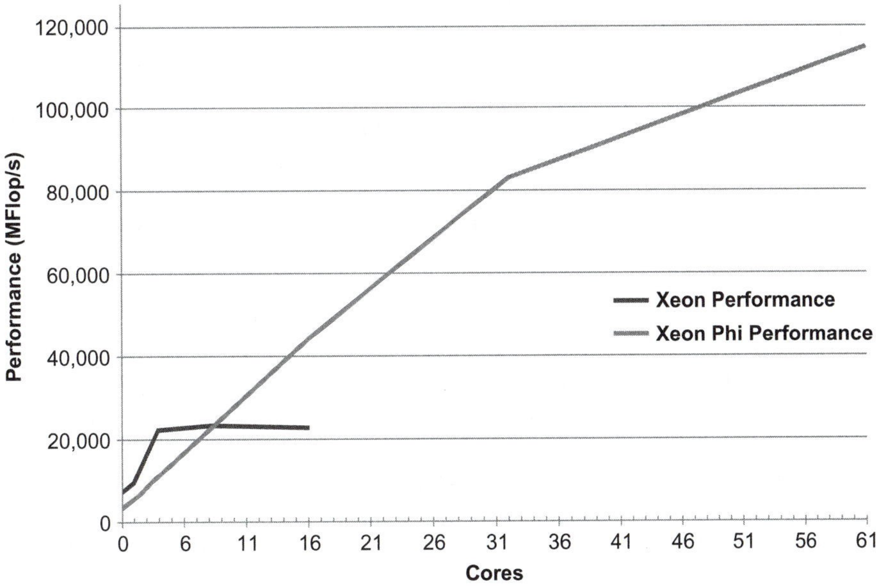

FIGURE 3.7

Processor and Coprocessor Performance on the Highly Parallel 9-Point 2D Stencil Code.

Well, quite a dramatic turnaround for the coprocessor and the processor when using straightforward parallel constructs to fully enable scaling on a highly parallel code. The coprocessor increased performance over 300x from the non-vectorized, unscaled baseline. The processor increased over 5.5x from the baseline. The coprocessor was able to run the scalable code about 5x faster than the processor. Figure 3.7 shows a graph of the performance of the `sten2d9pt_omp()` function vectorized and scaled code over increasing numbers of cores on the processor platform and the coprocessor. Is there anything familiar about the graph? It matches fairly well with the conceptual "picture speaks a thousand words" graph in Figure 1.5 in Chapter 1. The main difference is the flattening of performance on the processor after initial scaling due to the memory-bound nature of the problem.

Some grease and wrenches!: a bit of tuning

This code has some opportunities for further, more advanced optimization and tuning targeting both algorithmic and architecture level enhancements. Stencil code by its nature lends itself to memory and cache tuning since data locality and reuse are inherent. Optimizing memory access plus data retention in the caches present interesting opportunities for improvement. Next, we will look at a few of these optimizations with a focus on the architecture level of the coprocessor. We also will switch focus from competing with our processor to working specifically with the coprocessor. This further tuning generally will continue to benefit the processor code as well. Chapter 5 on improving vectorization will give some further insight into these methods from a compiler perspective, and Chapter 8 describes the architectural elements that can make these "tweaks" beneficial.

Adjusting the "Alignment"

If your car does not have optimal alignment in all four wheels, it causes drag on the tires and an overall loss in driving efficiency and performance. The analogous situation for the coprocessor and processor occurs if the memory access pattern, particularly for memory data intended for vector processing, is not aligned to the caching architecture.

When dealing with data formatted as multidimensional arrays, this misalignment can easily be present. In our case we will look at the alignment considerations with our two-dimensional image data arrays. Similar to a car where front-end and rear-end alignment are sometimes required, for our two-dimensional array we need to consider the cache alignment on the "front" or leftmost column of data and the "rear" or rightmost column. In fact they work in concert with each other. As we saw in Chapter 2, we made some effort in the code to align the "statically" defined single dimension arrays to 64-byte address boundaries (aligned to cache line access for the coprocessor) through directives in the array definition or through compiler switches to ensure optimal performance. In many cases, such as our stencil code, to be more flexible, arrays are dynamically allocated based on the input problem size. That changes some of the methods and considerations to achieve the desired alignment.

The first step is to ensure the "front end" is aligned. This can be done by substituting the call to `malloc()` with `_mm_malloc()`, which takes an additional 'byte address alignment parameter ensuring the base address of the array is aligned as requested. The second step is ensuring that the address of the first element on each row in our two-dimension array is also aligned. This can be done through a "rear-end" alignment technique known as *padding*. In fact, you may have noticed that we already have written the code with padding in mind, but we did not enable it yet. Using padding, we allocate a bit of extra unused space at the end of each row, if needed, which can be thought of as a thin "strip" of data columns on the right-hand side of the two-dimensional array. We allocate exactly enough space to ensure that the first element of each new row is on the desired address boundary, in our case, 64 bytes. This padding will avoid the need for the coprocessor to do unaligned accesses to load data into the cache and into the 64-byte–wide vector registers, which can cause performance loss. Look closely at the definition of `WIDTHP` when `PAD64` is enabled in code listing in Figure 3.4. It will calculate the total number of columns needed to ensure the desired 64 byte alignment.

Now we will modify our code slightly to create a new code file sten2d9pt_pad.c to create more beneficial memory address alignments to determine if we can see an advantage. The changes to the original code in Figure 3.4 are quite simple, 1) set `PAD64` to `1`; 2) replace the `malloc()` calls with `_mm_malloc()` with a second parameter of 64 specifying the byte alignment desired; 3) replace `free()` calls with `_mm_free()`. To compile the code we execute the following command line:

```
$ icc –openmp –mmic –O3 –vec-report=3 sten2d9pt_pad.c –o sten2d9pt_xphi
```

On the coprocessor execute:

```
% export KMP_AFFINITY=scatter
% export OMP_NUM_THREADS=244
% ./sten2d9pt_xphi
Initializing..244 Threads, 5900 x 10000, PAD=5904...
Running stencil kernel 1000 times
Elapsed time : 11.469 (s)
```

```
FLOPS   : 87452.707 (MFlops)

% export OMP_NUM_THREADS=183
% ./sten2d9pt_xphi
Initializing..183 Threads, 5900 x 10000, PAD=5904...

Running stencil kernel 1000 times

Elapsed time : 10.326 (s)
FLOPS : 97132.546 (MFlops)

% export OMP_NUM_THREADS=122
% ./sten2d9pt_xphi
Initializing..122 Threads, 5900 x 10000, PAD=5904...

Running stencil kernel 1000 times

Elapsed time : 8.973 (s)
FLOPS   : 111774.803 (MFlops)

% export OMP_NUM_THREADS=61
% ./sten2d9pt_xphi
Initializing..61 Threads, 5900 x 10000, PAD=5904...

Running stencil kernel 1000 times

Elapsed time : 11.644 (s)
FLOPS   : 86138.371 (MFlops)
```

Note that the output line that includes `PAD=5904` indicates that we indeed are padding the rows by an extra 4 elements. Also, the results are a bit mixed. For 244 threads a clear improvement of over 1 second from the 244 thread case in sten2d9pt_omp.c without the alignment changes. For 183, 122, and 61 threads, there is very little change with 183 threads indicating a slight improvement, and 122 and 61 threads indicate slightly poorer performance. A lot of factors can play a role in whether a particular optimization makes a difference and where, including the algorithm, problem size, runtime overhead, and the compiler. Sometimes, it takes a few combinations to get a breakthrough. Let's try some other common optimizations and see if we can continue to see some sort of improvement.

Using streaming stores

Let us try adding some proverbial "grease" to our axles to see if that provides any benefit. There is one fairly simple way to streamline the memory accesses for architectures that support it; using what is known as *streaming stores* to memory. Streaming stores are memory writes that do not require a read operation before writing to memory. A read before writing is typically the default behavior, but in cases it is not needed, the read takes additional bandwidth and time. The Intel Xeon Phi coprocessor supports streaming stores at the instruction level so the compiler must determine when it can use this optimization. However, the programmer can aid the compiler by indicating where it is known to be useful.

First, consider the key line of code in our inner loop of our stencil code:

```
fout[c] = diag * fin[nw] +
          diag * fin[ne] +
          diag * fin[sw] +
          diag * fin[se] +
          next * fin[w] +
          next * fin[e] +
          next * fin[n] +
          next * fin[s] +
          ctr * fin[c];
```

Since the result of the calculation is written independently to `fout[c]` without using its data as part of the calculation, a streaming store is appropriate. We can help ensure the compiler will generate streaming store instructions using either the compiler switch `-opt-streaming-stores always` or more finely in the code with the directive `#pragma vector nontemporal` (see the compiler documentation for more details on usage).

In our case, we create another version of the code, sten2d9pt_sstores.c, that includes the previous alignment changes, and we add `#pragma vector nontemporal` just after the `#pragma ivdep` before the calculation loop. This will indicate to the compiler that we want it use streaming stores for this upcoming loop. We will compile the code and run it as follows:

```
$ icc -openmp -mmic -O3 -vec-report=3 sten2d9pt_sstores.c -o sten2d9pt_xphi
On the coprocessor execute:
% export KMP_AFFINITY=scatter
% export OMP_NUM_THREADS=244
% ./sten2d9pt_xphi
Initializing..244 Threads, 5900 x 10000, PAD=5904...

Running stencil kernel 1000 times

Elapsed time : 9.507 (s)
FLOPS   : 105498.781 (MFlops)

% export OMP_NUM_THREADS=183
% ./sten2d9pt_xphi
Initializing..183 Threads, 5900 x 10000, PAD=5904...

Running stencil kernel 1000 times

Elapsed time : 8.663 (s)
FLOPS   : 115773.405 (MFlops)

% export OMP_NUM_THREADS=122
% ./sten2d9pt_xphi
Initializing..122 Threads, 5900 x 10000, PAD=5904...

Running stencil kernel 1000 times

Elapsed time : 8.491 (s)
```

```
FLOPS   : 118112.822 (MFlops)

% export OMP_NUM_THREADS=61
% ./sten2d9pt_xphi
Initializing..61 Threads, 5900 x 10000, PAD=5904...

Running stencil kernel 1000 times

Elapsed time : 13.588 (s)
FLOPS   : 73978.915 (MFlops)
```

The streaming store request in conjunction with the alignment optimizations measurably improved the 244, 183, and 122 thread cases. We now have the fastest case we have seen thus at 8.491 seconds for our stencil code. We will try one more common memory optimization before moving on.

Using huge 2-MB memory pages

Memory is the primary fuel for our stencil code so, like ensuring our car's fuel injectors are clean, using "huge" 2-MB pages can many times improve performance. 4-KB pages are the traditional size used by `malloc()` and `_mm_malloc()` in the coprocessor Linux OS version we are using to run our examples. These pages are used to map virtual to physical addresses with the relatively time consuming translations cached in the coprocessor's Translation Lookaside Buffer (TLB) discussed further in Chapter 8. Depending on the access pattern for large arrays of data, using huge pages can significantly minimize the number of TLB misses requiring the coprocessor to spend time doing full translations.

Future planned coprocessor versions will likely add "transparent" huge page support for `malloc()` that will allow 2-MB pages to be allocated if they are available. However, to ensure allocated memory uses huge pages, the `mmap()` function can be used, and it will fail if huge pages are requested but unavailable.

We will add one final modification to our stencil code creating sten2d9pt_huge.c to see the performance impact of huge pages. We will replace our `_mm_malloc()` calls with calls to `mmap()` as follows:

```
REAL *fa = (REAL *)mmap(0, WIDTHP*HEIGHT*sizeof(REAL),

        PROT_READ|PROT_WRITE,
        MAP_ANONYMOUS|MAP_PRIVATE|MAP_HUGETLB,
        -1,0);
```

The `MAP_HUGETLB` is the key to the 2-MB page request. We will compile and run the code as follows:

```
$ icc –openmp –mmic –O3 –vec-report=3 sten2d9pt_huge.c –o sten2d9pt_xphi
```

On the coprocessor execute:

```
% export KMP_AFFINITY=scatter
% export OMP_NUM_THREADS=244
% ./sten2d9pt_xphi
```

```
Initializing..244 Threads, 5900 x 10000, PAD=5904...

Running stencil kernel 1000 times

Elapsed time : 9.466 (s)
FLOPS    : 105955.358 (MFlops)

% export OMP_NUM_THREADS=183
% ./sten2d9pt_xphi
Initializing..183 Threads, 5900 x 10000, PAD=5904...

Running stencil kernel 1000 times

Elapsed time : 8.749 (s)
FLOPS    : 114636.799 (MFlops)

% export OMP_NUM_THREADS=122
% ./sten2d9pt_xphi
Initializing..122 Threads, 5900 x 10000, PAD=5904...

Running stencil kernel 1000 times

Elapsed time : 8.226 (s)
FLOPS    : 121924.389 (MFlops)

% export OMP_NUM_THREADS=61
% ./sten2d9pt_xphi
Initializing..61 Threads, 5900 x 10000, PAD=5904...

Running stencil kernel 1000 times

Elapsed time : 14.486 (s)
FLOPS    : 69239.365 (MFlops)
```

Again, as with the other optimizations we tried, we see mixed results for adding huge page support depending on the number of threads used, but we ultimately see a measureable benefit in our fastest performing 122 thread case. The combination of tuning methods results in an additional almost 7 percent improvement from our best pre-tuning performance.

Our goal here was to show some of the steps you can consider for improving the performance of code on the coprocessor. We have also seen that any tuning techniques have tradeoffs and the benefit depends on a number of factors including the number of threads, the memory access pattern and the problem size. Using profiling tools like Intel VTune Amplifier can provide further insights and guidance to identify focus areas in the code, especially when it is more complex than the stencil code here which has only one primary inner calculation loop.

In the next chapter, we will be looking at a similar but more complex real-world stencil-based code and diving a little bit deeper into other optimization considerations and techniques. Chapters 5 and 6 provide some more information on possible tuning areas and compiler options that can enable optimization on key sections of code. Following your review of the next several chapters, it might be interesting to pursue further optimizations with this stencil code. Let us know how you make out on http://lotsofcores.com.

Summary

In this chapter, we continued our "driving lessons" with a little more challenge using a highly parallel, but still relatively simple two dimensional 9-point (3 × 3) stencil code to implement an image blurring filter. Again, this demonstrated the critical importance of tapping the vector capabilities and multiple cores and threads for both the processor and, particularly for, the Intel Xeon Phi coprocessor. As we saw with this code, a naïve implementation with no effort to consider the parallel elements left over 300x performance on the table for the coprocessor, yet we accessed it with just a bit of thought and a few lines of code. On the other hand, we saw dramatic improvements on the processor are possible as well. Furthermore, it was shown that if you have do have code that is not currently parallelized, or is limited in the ability to be parallelized, the processor may be the platform of choice.

We also did some initial fine-tuning of the code on the coprocessor attempting to tap some of the architectural elements including cache-oriented memory address alignment, streaming stores, and huge pages. We saw that each tuning attempt can have mixed results depending on a number of factors, especially the threading selected. Ultimately we did see a small improvement for our stencil code with this added tuning.

In the next chapter, we will continue and complete our hands-on "high speed driving course" with some real-world fluid dynamics simulation code.

For more information

Here are some additional reading materials we recommend related to this chapter.

- Stencil Code, a chapter on how to approach for parallel programming, in *Structured Parallel Programming: Patterns for Efficient Computation,* Michael McCool, Arch Robison, James Reinders; Morgan Kaufmann Publishers Inc., San Francisco, CA, USA, 2012.
- Excellent paper on stencils: Fredrik Berg Kjolstad and Marc Snir. *Ghost cell pattern.* In Proceedings of the 2010 Workshop on Parallel Programming Patterns, ParaPLoP '10, pages 4:1–4:9, New York, NY, USA, 2010. ACM.
- Stencil Code, http://wikipedia.org/wiki/Stencil_code
- Stencil computation optimization and auto-tuning on state-of-the-art multicore architectures, http://dl.acm.org/citation.cfm?id=1413375
- Download the code from this, and other chapters, http://lotsofcores.com

CHAPTER

Driving Around Town: Optimizing A Real-World Code Example

4

Now that we have taken our sports car on the open road and experienced some easier-to-navigate challenges, we will increase the difficulty and deal with some real-world circumstances, similar to what might be experienced in general driving around a city or town. To drive around town to someplace like the grocery store, you must navigate through intersections, stop signs, traffic signals, and sometimes unexpected detours. Rules of the road constrain your speed and direction. Changing circumstances require using the information at hand, and the knowledge of how the car will respond to drive safely and most efficiently to your destination.

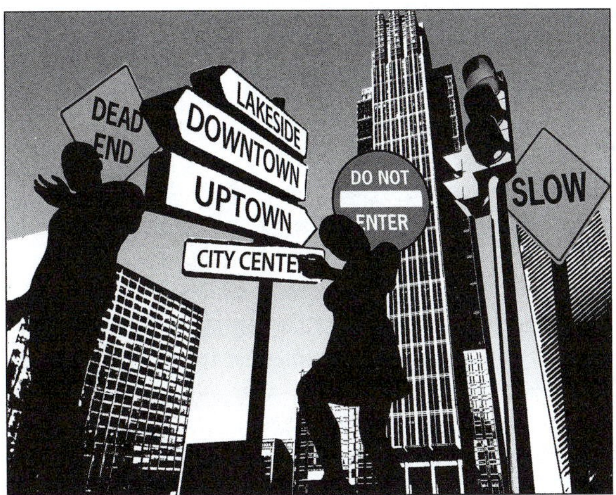

In this chapter, we will extend our sports car analogy to a real scientific code example that comes from Naoya Maruyama of Riken Advanced Institute for Computational Science in Japan. The purpose of the code is to simulate diffusion of a solute through a volume of liquid over time within a 3D container such as a cube, as depicted in Figure 4.1. A three-dimensional seven-point stencil operation is used to calculate the effects on the neighboring sub-volume sections on each

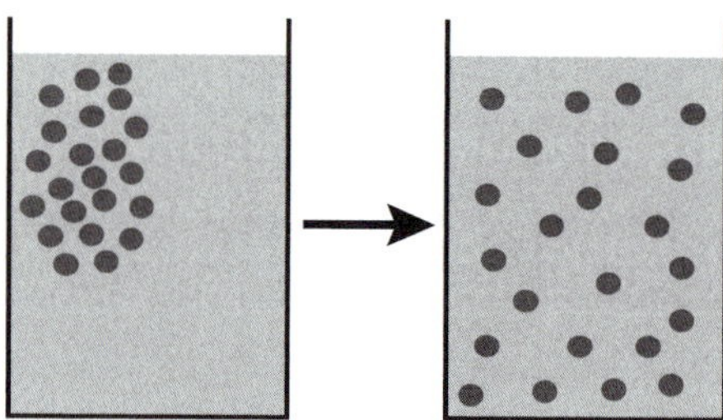

FIGURE 4.1

Diffusion of a Compound over Time through an Enclosed Volume.

other over time. So, if there is no food on our shelves, we need to head out to the street and learn the best paths get to the grocery store as quickly as we can!

Choosing the direction: the basic diffusion calculation

Before we start driving on the road, we should know which direction goes towards our destination. Similarly, we need to understand enough about the algorithm being used to ensure we perform correct and complete calculations. A shown in Figure 4.2, we are going to apply a seven-point stencil to calculate a new density in the volume using weighted values in the stencil applied to the current target sub-volume and its neighbors.

We will repeat this calculation for every section of the volume creating a new baseline volume. The code then iterates over the number of time steps selected to create the final diffused volume state.

The baseline C code that shows the primary diffusion algorithm implementation is shown in Figure 4.3. The `f1[]` array contains the current volume data and the `f2[]` array is used to store the results of the current time step iteration. Four loops, one for each dimension and one for the number of time steps requested, are implemented. The inner loop applies the stencil calculations using the target center sub-volume section and its neighboring north, south, east, west, top, and bottom sections. Once all the sub-volumes for the current time step are processed, the `f1[]` and `f2[]` array pointers are swapped, setting the new reference state. While easy to read, this implementation is equivalent to a straight road with no turns available; it will not take us to our desired destination.

Turn ahead: accounting for boundary effects

Like approaching a T intersection where we must make a turn or drive off the road, we must account for a structural issue with our diffusion simulation; the three-dimensional container has boundary walls. Since our stencil operates on each sub-volume section that comprises the whole,

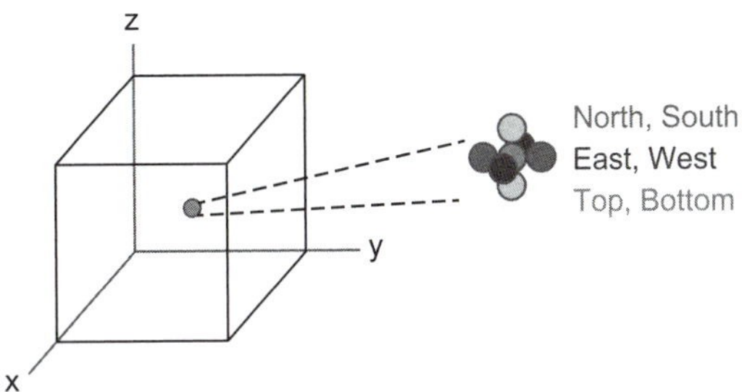

FIGURE 4.2

3D Stencil Used to Calculate the Diffusion of a Solute through a Liquid Volume.

```
for (i = 0; i < niter; i++) {
 for (z = 0; z < nz; z++)
  for (y = 0; y < ny; y++)
   for (x = 0; x < nx; x++)
     f2[z,y,x] = cc*f1[z,y,x] + cw*f1[z,y,x-1] + ce*f1[z,y,x+1] +
                 cn*f1[z,y-1,x] + cs*f1[z,y+1,x] +
                 cb*f1[z-1,y,x] + ct*f1[z+1,y,x]
 temp = f2; f2 = f1; f1 = temp;
}
```

FIGURE 4.3

Baseline Stencil Diffusion Algorithm Code, No Consideration for Boundary Conditions.

we need to consider how to properly calculate the molecular density for sub-volumes that sit next to the edges of our container. At a minimum, we need to avoid calculating array index values that go outside our allocated memory space representing the volume.

Figure 4.4 shows an evolved implementation that accounts for the boundary conditions. The implementation also simplifies the `f1[]` array access by linearizing the stencil indices by adding the `w, e, n, s, b, t` (west, east, north, south, bottom, top) variables. The boundary conditions occur for any sub-volume that has an x, y, or z value of zero or x, y, or z value at the full width, height, or depth of the volume as represented by the variables nx, ny, and nz. In these cases, we simply replace the value of the neighbor volume with the target central density value to get a reasonable approximation of the diffusion at that point. Now, we have reached the first important stage of implementing a real-world algorithm; it will provide the complete and correct results when run.

Figure 4.5 shows the complete code listing. The function `diffusion_baseline()` implements the key computational processing.

Looking at the `main()` function, we see that two arrays of equal size, `f1[]` and `f2[]`, are allocated to support the double buffering used in the primary calculation function. The double buffering is required to ensure the stencil processing is completed without modifying the in-place target volume data, which will be used in subsequent calculations when its neighboring sub-volumes are calculated.

```
for (int i = 0; i < count; ++i) {
 for (int z = 0; z < nz; z++) {
  for (int y = 0; y < ny; y++) {
   for (int x = 0; x < nx; x++) {
      int c, w, e, n, s, b, t;
      c = x + y * nx + z * nx * ny;
      w = (x == 0) ? c : c - 1;         e = (x == nx-1) ? c : c + 1;
      n = (y == 0) ? c : c - nx;        s = (y == ny-1) ? c : c + nx;
      b = (z == 0) ? c : c - nx * ny; t = (z == nz-1) ? c : c + nx * ny;
      f2_t[c] = cc * f1_t[c] + cw * f1_t[w] + ce * f1_t[e]
          + cs * f1_t[s] + cn * f1_t[n] + cb * f1_t[b] + ct * f1_t[t];
   }
  }
 }
 REAL *t = f1_t; f1_t = f2_t; f2_t = t;
}
```

FIGURE 4.4

Working Diffusion Calculation with Boundary Processing.

After initializing that `f1[]` array, and the east, west, north, south, top, bottom, stencil diffusion weights, `ce, cw, cn, cs, ct, cb`, and the time step *dt*, based on the size of the volume, the time step is used to determine the iteration *count*. Next, a time stamp is taken and the diffusion calculation function is called to perform *count* time steps. Upon completion of the function, the resulting floating-point performance is calculated based on the thirteen floating-point operations per inner loop iteration, and the memory bandwidth (in GB/s) is determined, using number of bytes of volume data read and written during the call.

Since we have not applied any optimizations, such as scaling across cores, when compiled and run we can expect this single-threaded code to perform quite slowly. If you take our word for it, you can skip compiling and running this baseline code yourself; it will indeed take well over an hour for the run to complete. You will have several more opportunities to follow along and study the improvements where the code runs much faster. However, to establish an initial baseline performance we will show you our results as below.

To compile the code to run natively on the Intel® Xeon Phi™ coprocessor use the following command:

```
$ icc –openmp –mmic –std=c99 –O3 –vect-report=3 diffusion_base.c -O diffusion_base
```

Upload the executable program `diffusion_base` to the coprocessor and then on the coprocessor command prompt in your working directory execute the code as follows:

```
% ./diffusion_base
```

On our test system we get the following output:

```
Running diffusion kernel 6553 times
Elapsed time : 5699.550 (s)
FLOPS        : 250.763 (MFlops)
Throughput   : 0.231 (GB/s)
Accuracy     : 1.592295e-05
```

```
/***************************************************
Copyright (c) 2011-2012, Naoya Maruyama

All rights reserved.

Redistribution and use in source and binary forms, with or without modification,
are permitted provided that the following conditions are met:

* Redistributions of source code must retain the above copyright notice, this
list of conditions and the following disclaimer.
* Redistributions in binary form must reproduce the above copyright notice, this
list of conditions and the following disclaimer in the documentation and/or
other materials provided with the distribution.
* Neither the name of RIKEN AICS nor the names of its contributors may be used
to endorse or promote products derived from this software without specific prior
written permission.

THIS SOFTWARE IS PROVIDED BY THE COPYRIGHT HOLDERS AND CONTRIBUTORS "AS IS" AND
ANY EXPRESS OR IMPLIED WARRANTIES, INCLUDING, BUT NOT LIMITED TO, THE IMPLIED
WARRANTIES OF MERCHANTABILITY AND FITNESS FOR A PARTICULAR PURPOSE ARE
DISCLAIMED. IN NO EVENT SHALL THE COPYRIGHT HOLDER OR CONTRIBUTORS BE LIABLE FOR
ANY DIRECT, INDIRECT, INCIDENTAL,

SPECIAL, EXEMPLARY, OR CONSEQUENTIAL DAMAGES (INCLUDING, BUT NOT LIMITED TO,
PROCUREMENT OF SUBSTITUTE GOODS OR SERVICES; LOSS OF USE, DATA, OR PROFITS; OR
BUSINESS INTERRUPTION) HOWEVER CAUSED AND ON ANY THEORY OF LIABILITY, WHETHER IN
CONTRACT, STRICT LIABILITY, OR TORT(INCLUDING NEGLIGENCE OR OTHERWISE) ARISING
IN ANY WAY OUT OF THE USE OF THIS SOFTWARE, EVEN IF ADVISED OF THE POSSIBILITY
OF SUCH DAMAGE.
*************************************************************/

#include <stdio.h>
#include <stdlib.h>
#include <string.h>
#include <math.h>
#include <time.h>
#include <sys/time.h>
#include <omp.h>
#include <assert.h>
#include <sys/mman.h>

#define REAL float
#define NX (256)
#define NXP nx

#ifndef M_PI
#define M_PI (3.1415926535897932384626)
#endif


void init(REAL *buff, const int nx, const int ny, const int nz,
          const REAL kx, const REAL ky, const REAL kz,
```

FIGURE 4.5

The `diffusion_baseline.c` Listing.

```
  REAL ax, ay, az;
  int jz, jy, jx;
  ax = exp(-kappa*time*(kx*kx));
  ay = exp(-kappa*time*(ky*ky));
  az = exp(-kappa*time*(kz*kz));
  for (jz = 0; jz < nz; jz++) {
    for (jy = 0; jy < ny; jy++) {
      for (jx = 0; jx < nx; jx++) {
        int j = jz*NXP*ny + jy*NXP + jx;
        REAL x = dx*((REAL)(jx + 0.5));
        REAL y = dy*((REAL)(jy + 0.5));
        REAL z = dz*((REAL)(jz + 0.5));
        REAL f0 = (REAL)0.125
          *(1.0 - ax*cos(kx*x))
          *(1.0 - ay*cos(ky*y))
          *(1.0 - az*cos(kz*z));
        buff[j] = f0;
      }
    }
  }
}

REAL accuracy(const REAL *b1, REAL *b2, const int len) {
  REAL err = 0.0;
  int i;
  for (i = 0; i < len; i++) {
    err += (b1[i] - b2[i]) * (b1[i] - b2[i]);
  }
  return (REAL)sqrt(err/len);
}

void
diffusion_baseline(REAL *f1, REAL *f2, int nx, int ny,
                   int nz,REAL ce, REAL cw, REAL cn,
                   REAL cs, REAL ct,REAL cb, REAL cc,
                   REAL dt, int count) {
  int i;
  for (i = 0; i < count; ++i) {
    for (int z = 0; z < nz; z++) {
      for (int y = 0; y < ny; y++) {
        for (int x = 0; x < nx; x++) {
          int c, w, e, n, s, b, t;
          c =  x + y * NXP + z * NXP * ny;
          w = (x == 0)    ? c : c - 1;
          e = (x == NXP-1) ? c : c + 1;
          n = (y == 0)    ? c : c - NXP;
          s = (y == ny-1) ? c : c + NXP;
          b = (z == 0)    ? c : c - NXP * ny;
          t = (z == nz-1) ? c : c + NXP * ny;
          f2[c] = cc * f1[c] + cw * f1[w] + ce * f1[e]
              + cs * f1[s] + cn * f1[n] + cb * f1[b]
              + ct * f1[t];
```

FIGURE 4.5

(Continued)

```
        }
      }
    }
    REAL *t = f1;
    f1 = f2;
    f2 = t;
  }
  return;
}

static double cur_second(void) {
  struct timeval tv;
  gettimeofday(&tv, NULL);
  return (double)tv.tv_sec + (double)tv.tv_usec
                / 1000000.0;
}


void dump_result(REAL *f, int nx, int ny, int nz,
                 char *out_path) {
  FILE *out = fopen(out_path, "w");
  assert(out);
  size_t nitems = nx * ny * nz;
  fwrite(f, sizeof(REAL), nitems, out);
  fclose(out);
}

int main(int argc, char *argv[])
{

  struct timeval time_begin, time_end;

  int    nx    = NX;
  int    ny    = NX;
  int    nz    = NX;

  REAL *f1 = (REAL *)malloc(sizeof(REAL)*NX*NX*NX);
  REAL *f2 = (REAL *)malloc(sizeof(REAL)*NX*NX*NX);
  assert(f1 != MAP_FAILED);
  assert(f2 != MAP_FAILED);
  REAL *answer = (REAL *)malloc(sizeof(REAL) *
                               NXP*ny*nz);
  REAL *f_final = NULL;

  REAL   time  = 0.0;
  int    count = 0;
  int    nthreads;

  REAL l, dx, dy, dz, kx, ky, kz, kappa, dt;
  REAL ce, cw, cn, cs, ct, cb, cc;

    #pragma omp parallel
```

FIGURE 4.5

(Continued)

```
  #pragma omp master
    nthreads = omp_get_num_threads();

  l = 1.0;
  kappa = 0.1;
  dx = dy = dz = l / nx;
  kx = ky = kz = 2.0 * M_PI;
  dt = 0.1*dx*dx / kappa;
  count = 0.1 / dt;
  f_final = (count % 2)? f2 : f1;

  init(f1, nx, ny, nz, kx, ky, kz, dx, dy, dz,
        kappa, time);

  ce = cw = kappa*dt/(dx*dx);
  cn = cs = kappa*dt/(dy*dy);
  ct = cb = kappa*dt/(dz*dz);
  cc = 1.0 - (ce + cw + cn + cs + ct + cb);

  printf("Running diffusion kernel %d times\n", count);
  fflush(stdout);
  gettimeofday(&time_begin, NULL);
  diffusion_baseline(f1, f2, nx, ny, nz, ce, cw, cn,
                     cs, ct, cb, cc, dt, count);
  gettimeofday(&time_end, NULL);
  time = count * dt;
  dump_result(f_final, nx, ny, nz,
              "diffusion_result.dat");

  init(answer, nx, ny, nz, kx, ky, kz, dx, dy, dz,
       kappa, time);
  REAL err = accuracy(f_final, answer, nx*ny*nz);
  double elapsed_time = (time_end.tv_sec -
                         time_begin.tv_sec)
      + (time_end.tv_usec - time_begin.tv_usec)*1.0e-6;
  REAL mflops = (nx*ny*nz)*13.0*count/elapsed_time
                * 1.0e-06;
  double thput = (nx * ny * nz) * sizeof(REAL) * 3.0 *
                 count / elapsed_time * 1.0e-09;

  fprintf(stderr, "Elapsed time : %.3f (s)\n",
          elapsed_time);
  fprintf(stderr, "FLOPS        : %.3f (MFlops)\n",
          mflops);
  fprintf(stderr, "Throughput   : %.3f (GB/s)\n", thput);
  fprintf(stderr, "Accuracy     : %e\n", err);

  free(f1);
  free(f2);
  return 0;
}
```

FIGURE 4.5

(Continued)

As you can see, this is a substantial set of calculations and took close to 95 minutes using just 1 core and 1 thread on the coprocessor. Our next step is to exploit the available parallelism through scaling the code across the many cores of the coprocessor.

Finding a wide boulevard: scaling the code

So, we have found a good route to get to the grocery store, but we also know we are definitely not using the fastest roads or shortest distance in combination to take advantage of the speed and maneuverability of our sports car. We want to look for a wider, easier road, like a boulevard, that has a higher speed limit and is still heading in the general direction of our grocery store. As in the other code we have worked with, we now need to apply the two key elements that makes our Intel Xeon Phi coprocessor shine, scaling and vectorizing.

First, we will look at scaling the code using OpenMP as we have done in previous chapters. Figure 4.6 shows an updated function `diffusion_openmp()` that adds OpenMP directives to distribute and scale the work across the available cores and threads. The key OpenMP clause is the `#pragma omp for collapse(2)` before the z loop. This clause tells the compiler to collapse the next two loops (z and y) into one loop and then apply the OpenMP `omp for` work division mechanism, as was used in previous chapters, to split the loop calculations among the current available threads. Conceptually, the `for` loop changes to a single loop that executes as `for(yz=0; yz<ny*nx; ++yz)` with the associated similar implied mapping for the use of y and z in the body of the loop. This will enable each thread to be assigned larger chunks of data to process more calculations, and therefore, allow more efficiency on each pass through the loop.

Now, we will compile and run the code to see what performance we get, and then we will look for opportunities to improve it further. To compile the code use the following command:

```
$ icc –openmp –mmic –std=c99 –O3 –vect-report=3 diffusion_omp.c -o diffusion_omp
```

Upload the file to the coprocessor to a working directory like /home/<*yourusername*>, set the number of threads and affinity and run the program using the following commands:

```
% export OMP_NUM_THREADS=244 (or 4x your # of cores)
% export KMP_AFFINITY=scatter
% ./diffusion_omp
```

One our test card we get the following output:

```
Running diffusion kernel 6553 times
Elapsed time : 108.311 (s)
FLOPS        : 13195.627 (MFlops)
Throughput   : 12.181 (GB/s)
Accuracy     : 1.775597e-05
```

```
void
diffusion_openmp(REAL *restrict f1, REAL *restrict f2,
 int nx, int ny, int nz, REAL ce, REAL cw, REAL cn,
 REAL cs, REAL ct,REAL cb, REAL cc, REAL dt, int count)
{
#pragma omp parallel
  {
    REAL *f1_t = f1;
    REAL *f2_t = f2;

    for (int i = 0; i < count; ++i) {
#pragma omp for collapse(2)
      for (int z = 0; z < nz; z++) {
        for (int y = 0; y < ny; y++) {
          for (int x = 0; x < nx; x++) {
            int c, w, e, n, s, b, t;
            c =  x + y * NXP + z * NXP * ny;
            w = (x == 0)     ? c : c - 1;
            e = (x == NXP-1) ? c : c + 1;
            n = (y == 0)     ? c : c - NXP;
            s = (y == ny-1)  ? c : c + NXP;
            b = (z == 0)     ? c : c - NXP * ny;
            t = (z == nz-1)  ? c : c + NXP * ny;
            f2_t[c] = cc * f1_t[c] + cw * f1_t[w]
                    + ce * f1_t[e] + cs * f1_t[s]
                    + cn * f1_t[n] + cb * f1_t[b]
                    + ct * f1_t[t];
          }
        }
      }
      REAL *t = f1_t;
      f1_t = f2_t;
      f2_t = t;
    }
  }
  return;
}
```

FIGURE 4.6

The diffusion_openmp Function.

That's an immediate benefit from scaling of about 52 times on a 61-core coprocessor. Now we can experiment with the number of threads per core to ensure that we consider balancing the access to resources to avoid conflicts and resource saturation, particularly for memory. Next we set for three threads per core and run again:

```
% export OMP_NUM_THREADS=183
% ./diffusion_omp
```

In this case our test card produces the following output:

```
Running diffusion kernel 6553 times
Elapsed time : 84.622 (s)
```

```
FLOPS          : 16889.533 (MFlops)
Throughput     : 15.590 (GB/s)
Accuracy       : 1.775597e-05
```

Now, test with two threads per core:

```
% export OMP_NUM_THREADS=122
% ./diffusion_omp
```

On our test platform the results are as follows:

```
Running diffusion kernel 6553 times
Elapsed time    : 156.857 (s)
FLOPS           : 9111.690 (MFlops)
Throughput      : 8.411 (GB/s)
Accuracy        : 1.775597e-05
```

Finally, with one thread per core:

```
% export OMP_NUM_THREADS=61
```

Results:

```
Running diffusion kernel 6553 times
Elapsed time    : 144.331 (s)
FLOPS           : 9902.489 (MFlops)
Throughput      : 9.141 (GB/s)
Accuracy        : 1.775597e-05
```

Compare the output and assess which gives the best results. In this case, three threads per core provide the best performance. The scaled code runs almost 67 times faster than the baseline. This would also be a great time to consider using a performance profiling and analysis tool like Intel® VTune™ Amplifier XE to provide insight into what the coprocessor and the application are doing and look for hot spots, cache, and memory usage while running with different numbers of threads per core. Chapter 13 describes VTune Amplifier XE in more detail.

So, we have found our "boulevard" that lets us move quite a bit faster towards our destination but we want to find even faster ways. We will look for another leap in speed to carry us to our destination in the next section.

Thunder road: ensuring vectorization

Are you a fan of or have you at least heard of Bruce Springsteen? Have you seen the movie musical *Grease* with John Travolta and Olivia Newton-John? Both "Thunder Road," in Springsteen's iconic song of the same title, and, the movie *Grease*, feature a mystical back road where you can drive fast with few impediments. Now that we have found our boulevard to speed us up a bit through scaling, our next goal is to really pick up the pace and find our town's Thunder Road for our diffusion code by vectorizing it.

Look back at the output of your vector report. Does it indicate that the innermost loop of the `diffusion_openmp()` code is vectorizing? One thing to note is that compilers, especially Intel's compilers, are in a constant state of improvement, particularly in regards to finding vectorization opportunities. So, as of the writing of this book, the compiler version we used was unable to automatically vectorize this code, but if you are using a newer compiler version, it indeed may have succeeded. Even if it did, you are bound to run into code at some point that the compiler may need a little more information to vectorize.

So, we will analyze this particular case because it shows some of the things to consider when the compiler doesn't vectorize. One of the first, maybe obvious, things to note is that simple straightforward code within a loop is more likely to vectorize. In chapter 2, our inner loops with just a few key lines generally were able to automatically vectorize without much problem. The compiler needs to ensure that it always generates correct results. If the code uses multiple pointer variables or reuses variables or array values in a way that makes one or more of the lines of code dependent, or appear to be dependent, on results from vector lanes being simultaneously calculated, the compiler will have difficulty absolutely ensuring correct results. Therefore, it will not vectorize the key lines. In the case of our innermost loop in the `diffusion_omp()` function, one complication comes with the code that deals with the boundary conditions. Another is the use of the two temporary array pointers, `f1_t` and `f2_t`. Likely the compiler vector report will indicate there is FLOW or ANTI dependence. The compiler documentation describes this message in more detail. The bottom line is that the compiler cannot interpret the ping pong, double-buffered swapping we are doing every loop iteration, and therefore cannot confirm independence between `f1_t` and `f2_t`. When the developer is sure no dependency exists, there is a directive we can use to tell the compiler to vectorize anyway. It is a `#pragma simd` directive. Figure 4.7 shows the updated code, `diffusion_openmpv()` with the added vectorization directive before the x loop.

```
void
diffusion_openmpv(REAL *restrict f1, REAL *restrict f2,
                  int nx, int ny, int nz, REAL ce,
                  REAL cw, REAL cn, REAL cs, REAL ct,
                  REAL cb, REAL cc, REAL dt, int count)
{
#pragma omp parallel
  {
    REAL *f1_t = f1;
    REAL *f2_t = f2;

    for (int i = 0; i < count; ++i) {
#pragma omp for collapse(2)
      for (int z = 0; z < nz; z++) {
        for (int y = 0; y < ny; y++) {
#pragma simd
          for (int x = 0; x < nx; x++) {
            int c, w, e, n, s, b, t;
            c =  x + y * NXP + z * NXP * ny;
            w = (x == 0)    ? c : c - 1;
            e = (x == NXP-1) ? c : c + 1;
            n = (y == 0)    ? c : c - NXP;
            s = (y == ny-1) ? c : c + NXP;
            b = (z == 0)    ? c : c - NXP * ny;
            t = (z == nz-1) ? c : c + NXP * ny;
            f2_t[c] = cc * f1_t[c] + cw * f1_t[w] +
                      ce * f1_t[e] + cs * f1_t[s] +
            cn * f1_t[n] + cb * f1_t[b] + ct * f1_t[t];
          }
        }
      }
      REAL *t = f1_t;
      f1_t = f2_t;
      f2_t = t;
    }
  }
  return;
}
```

FIGURE 4.7

The `diffusion_openmpv` Function.

The line `#pragma simd` requests the compiler to vectorize the loop regardless of potential dependencies or other potential constraints.

That was a pretty simple one line change but we created a new file for it called `diffusion_ompvect.c`. Compile it with the following:

```
$ icc –openmp –mmic –std=c99 –O3 –vect-report=3 diffusion_ompvect.c -O diffusion_ompvect
```

Note that you now should see that the vector report indicates the inner loop was indeed vectorized.

Upload the file to the coprocessor and perform four runs from the coprocessor prompt adjusting the threads per core based on the number of cores for the coprocessor on each run as below:

```
% export KMP_AFFINITY=scatter
% export OMP_NUM_THREADS=244
% ./diffusion_ompvect

Running diffusion kernel 6553 times
Elapsed time    : 18.664 (s)
FLOPS           : 76575.266 (MFlops)
Throughput      : 70.685 (GB/s)
Accuracy        : 1.558128e-05

% export OMP_NUM_THREADS=183
% ./diffusion_ompvect

Running diffusion kernel 6553 times
Elapsed time    : 19.569 (s)
FLOPS           : 73034.367 (MFlops)
Throughput      : 67.416 (GB/s)
Accuracy        : 1.558128e-05

% export OMP_NUM_THREADS=122
% ./diffusion_ompvect

Running diffusion kernel 6553 times
Elapsed time    : 25.369 (s)
FLOPS           : 56337.496 (MFlops)
Throughput      : 52.004 (GB/s)
Accuracy        : 1.558128e-05

% export OMP_NUM_THREADS=61
% ./diffusion_ompvect

Running diffusion kernel 6553 times
Elapsed time    : 30.993 (s)
FLOPS           : 46114.676 (MFlops)
Throughput      : 42.567 (GB/s)
Accuracy        : 1.558128e-05
```

Figure 4.8 shows a graph of the benefits we have seen so far. We see the significant impact of vectorization. Improving top performance by more than 4.5 times above our OpenMP changes alone and now more than 335 times our original single-threaded baseline!

So, we have found our Thunder Road enabling us to arrive sooner at our proverbial grocery store. We now have both scaled and vectorized our code, and we have seen very significant performance improvement over the baseline. Now we'll look to do a little more tuning of our "engine" to see if we can gain a bit more performance.

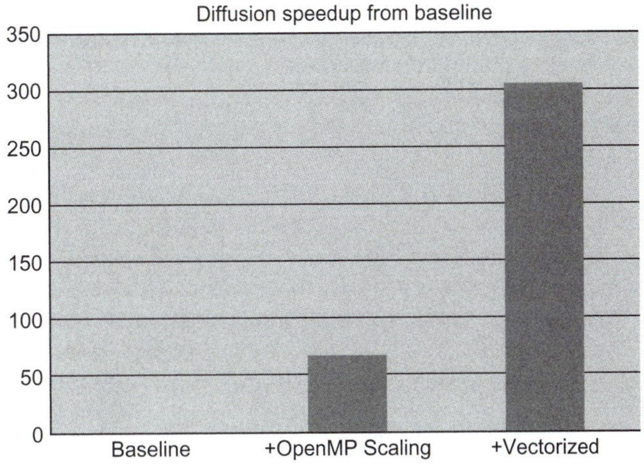

FIGURE 4.8

Accumulative Performance Benefits of Scaling and Vectorization.

Peeling out: peeling code from the inner loop

Okay, we could not help ourselves from stretching our sports car analogy to the limit and adding in a little pun for good measure. *Peeling out* or pushing hard on the gas pedal to get a car moving fast from a standstill with a little bit of tire screeching may get you to your destination a little bit faster but probably not with the large improvements we have found so far. Given the dramatic speedups we have achieved with scaling and vectorizing the code, we now are looking towards finer-grained tuning.

```
void
diffusion_peel(REAL *restrict f1, REAL *restrict f2,
               int nx, int ny, int nz, REAL ce, REAL cw,
               REAL cn, REAL cs, REAL ct,REAL cb,
               REAL cc, REAL dt, int count) {
#pragma omp parallel
  {
    REAL *f1_t = f1;
    REAL *f2_t = f2;

    for (int i = 0; i < count; ++i) {
#pragma omp for collapse(2)
      for (int z = 0; z < nz; z++) {
        for (int y = 0; y < ny; y++) {
          int x, c, n, s, b, t;
          x = 0;
          c =  x + y * NXP + z * NXP * ny;
          n = (y == 0)    ? c : c - NXP;
          s = (y == ny-1) ? c : c + NXP;
          b = (z == 0)    ? c : c - NXP * ny;
          t = (z == nz-1) ? c : c + NXP * ny;
          f2_t[c] = cc * f1_t[c] + cw * f1_t[c] + ce *
                    f1_t[c+1] + cs * f1_t[s] + cn *
                    f1_t[n] + cb * f1_t[b] + ct *
                    f1_t[t];
#pragma simd
          for (x = 1; x < nx-1; x++) {
            ++c;
            ++n;
            ++s;
            ++b;
            ++t;
            f2_t[c] = cc * f1_t[c] + cw * f1_t[c-1] +
                      ce * f1_t[c+1] + cs * f1_t[s] +
                      cn * f1_t[n] + cb * f1_t[b] +
                      ct * f1_t[t];
          }
          ++c;
          ++n;
          ++s;
          ++b;
          ++t;
          f2_t[c] = cc * f1_t[c] + cw * f1_t[c-1] +
                    ce * f1_t[c] + cs * f1_t[s] +
                    cn * f1_t[n] + cb * f1_t[b] +
                    ct * f1_t[t];
        }
      }
      REAL *t = f1_t;
      f1_t = f2_t;
      f2_t = t;
    }
  }
  return;
}
```

FIGURE 4.9

The `diffusion_peel` Function.

In this section, we will look to remove or "peel" unneeded code from the inner loop. Reviewing the code carefully, we see that the boundary check might be a candidate. Consider that for a volume of any significant size, the code will encounter a boundary that requires altering the baseline stencil usage relatively rarely. If possible, we want to look for a way to "peel out" the boundary checks from the inner loop portions because we know that the code does the bulk of its processing without encountering a boundary condition. Figure 4.9 shows one way to do it.

Since only our starting and ending x coordinates 0 and $nx-1$ will hit the boundary condition, we can create an inner loop without any boundary checks by simply ensuring we process x indices from *1* to $nx-2$. Furthermore, since the stencil always traverses in single units across the x row of sub-volumes, we can update the stencil positions by simply incrementing them. Also, we can eliminate calculating the east and west locations by referencing their positions directly in the array index ($e=c-1$ and $w=c+1$). This new inner loop now has the X-edge checks removed. The file `diffusion_peel.c` contains the code with the modifications. We can compile and run it to see if we achieved any improvement as below

```
$ icc –openmp –mmic –std=c99 –03 –vect-report=3 diffusion_peel.c -0 diffusion_peel
```

Upload the file to your working directory on the coprocessor. Set the affinity and number of threads at the coprocessor prompt iterating through the number of threads needed (based on core count) to perform one to four threads per core using the following commands:

```
% export KMP_AFFINITY=scatter
% export OMP_NUM__THREADS=244
% ./diffusion_peel

Running diffusion kernel 6553 times
Elapsed time : 15.111 (s)
FLOPS        : 94585.055 (MFlops)
Throughput   : 87.309 (GB/s)
Accuracy     : 1.580171e-05

% Export OMP_NUM_THREADS=183
% ./diffusion_peel

Running diffusion kernel 6553 times
Elapsed time : 18.980 (s)
FLOPS        : 75303.023 (MFlops)
Throughput   : 69.510 (GB/s)
Accuracy     : 1.580171e-05

% export OMP_NUM_THREADS=122
% ./diffusion_peel

Running diffusion kernel 6553 times
Elapsed time : 18.217 (s)
FLOPS        : 78457.055 (MFlops)
Throughput   : 72.422 (GB/s)
Accuracy     : 1.580171e-05
```

```
% export OMP_NUM_THREADS=61
% ./diffusion_peel

Running diffusion kernel 6553 times
Elapsed time : 23.815 (s)
FLOPS        : 60013.832 (MFlops)
Throughput   : 55.397 (GB/s)
Accuracy     : 1.580171e-05
```

As expected, we got a measureable improvement in our fastest run (244 threads) but it certainly is not as dramatic as we have seen before. However, we did improve by almost 24 percent over our prior code runs, which is a solid and beneficial improvement.

In the next sections, we will look at one more possible improvement that should be part of our standard fine-tuning repertoire.

Trying higher octane fuel: improving speed using data locality and tiling

Many high-performance cars benefit from using fuel with a higher octane rating. So far we have optimized the direction and roads we are traveling on and added some touches to get moving faster. Now we will attempt one final improvement by trying to get more power out of our fuel, the memory subsystem.

In many circumstances, improvements can be found by analyzing the data access patterns to take advantage of *data locality*. We want to create a more optimal pattern of data reuse within our innermost loops to maintain data in the L1 and L2 caches for much faster access.

Stencil operations contain data reuse patterns that make them strong candidates for exploiting data locality. *Tiling* and *blocking* are terms to describe a technique often used for improving data reuse in cache architectures. Cache architectures generally employ "least recently used" (LRU) methods to determine which data is evicted from the cache as new data is requested. Therefore, the longer data remains unused, the more likely it will be evicted from the cache and no longer available immediately when needed. Since memory accesses are significantly longer than cache accesses, a goal is to find techniques and usage patterns that can help reduce memory accesses by reusing cached data. To be most successful, reusing data in cache lines that have been used very recently or *local* to current code sequence is important.

Tiling the access pattern can exploit data that remains in the cache from recent, previous iterations. For instance, in our diffusion stencil code, each innermost loop iteration processes the x elements of a y row sequentially, and then moves on to the following y row. Ignoring the work division from scheduling multiple threads for a moment, there is a high likelihood of accessing data in the L1 or L2 cache we have used before from the current and previous y rows since our access of those y data is recent. However, the *bottom* and *top* row data on the adjacent z plane are used once and then not accessed again until the next full y plane is processed at the same row. Therefore, there is a low

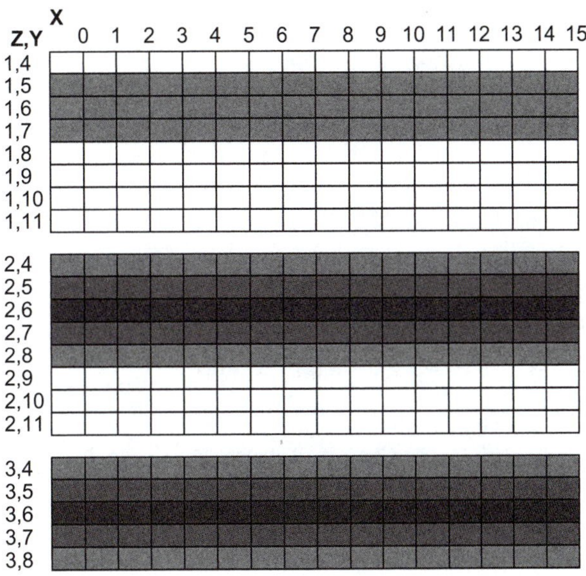

FIGURE 4.10

Cache Line Reuse in Diffusion Calculation.

likelihood that the *z* data are being reused and so they must be fetched again from memory on the next iteration of the *z* loop. If we consider processing a *rectangular tile* of *y*—actually a slab of *yx* values across a range of *z*. The top row in a given *z* iteration will still be in cache to serve as left, center, and right rows for the next *z*, and the bottom row for the *z* after that. This usage avoids additional memory requests and a performance benefit is likely possible. Figure 4.10 depicts an example of the cache access and reuse level we should be able to achieve if we tile in *y* and step across the *z* dimension within those tiles. Each block represents a 64-byte cache line, which holds sixteen contiguous *x*-dimension single-precision `float` values. The saturated highlights the reuse pattern with darker blocks representing multiple reuse of the same value across a range of *y* and *z*.

Figure 4.11 shows a code implementation of the `diffusion_tiled()` function. We select a *blocking factor* value *YBF* for the number of *y* rows we will process in each slab; the goal being to select an optimal number that will maintain the sufficient amounts of *y* and *z* data in the cache long enough to be reused during computation.

Since we will be processing a portion or *tile* of *y* rows across the full *z* dimension, we add an outer *y* loop to control stepping to the start of each tile. The inner *y* loop is then adjusted to perform the per-row processing within the current tile. The *x* processing with the peeled out boundary management is maintained so we keep that optimization intact.

So, let's compile, upload, and run the code on our coprocessor.

```
$ icc –openmp –mmic –std=c99 –O3 –vect-report=3 diffusion_tiled.c -O diffusion_tiled
```

```
void
diffusion_tiled(REAL *restrict f1, REAL *restrict f2,
                int nx, int ny, int nz,REAL ce, REAL cw,
                REAL cn, REAL cs, REAL ct, REAL cb,
                REAL cc, REAL dt, int count) {

  unsigned long tsc;
  int nthreads;
#pragma omp parallel
  {
    REAL *f1_t = f1;
    REAL *f2_t = f2;
    int mythread;

    for (int i = 0; i < count; ++i) {
#define YBF 16
#pragma omp for collapse(2)
      for (int yy = 0; yy < ny; yy += YBF) {
      for (int z = 0; z < nz; z++) {
        int ymax = yy + YBF;
        if (ymax >= ny) ymax = ny;
        for (int y = yy; y < ymax; y++) {
          int x;
          int c, n, s, b, t;
          x = 0;
          c =  x + y * NXP + z * NXP * ny;
          n = (y == 0)    ? c : c - NXP;
          s = (y == ny-1) ? c : c + NXP;
          b = (z == 0)    ? c : c - NXP * ny;
          t = (z == nz-1) ? c : c + NXP * ny;
          f2_t[c] = cc * f1_t[c] + cw * f1_t[c] + ce
              * f1_t[c+1] + cs * f1_t[s] + cn
              * f1_t[n] + cb * f1_t[b] + ct * f1_t[t];
#pragma simd
          for (x = 1; x < nx-1; x++) {
            ++c;
            ++n;
            ++s;
            ++b;
            ++t;
            f2_t[c] = cc * f1_t[c] + cw * f1_t[c-1]
                      + ce * f1_t[c+1] + cs * f1_t[s]
                      + cn * f1_t[n] + cb * f1_t[b]
                      + ct * f1_t[t];
          }
          ++c;
          ++n;
          ++s;
          ++b;
          ++t;
```

FIGURE 4.11

The `diffusion_tiled` Function.

```
f2_t[c] = cc * f1_t[c] + cw * f1_t[c-1] + ce
                     * f1_t[c] + cs * f1_t[s] + cn
                     * f1_t[n] + cb * f1_t[b] + ct
                     * f1_t[t];
        } // tile ny
      } // tile nz
      } // block ny
      REAL *t = f1_t;
      f1_t = f2_t;
      f2_t = t;
    } // count
  } // parallel
  return;
}
```

FIGURE 4.11

(Continued)

Upload the code and go to the coprocessor command prompt and run the program with each of the threads per core available:

```
% export KMP_AFFINITY = scatter
% export OMP_NUM_THREADS = 244
% ./diffusion_tiled

Running diffusion kernel 6553 times
Elapsed time    : 16.151 (s)
FLOPS           : 88490.656 (MFlops)
Throughput      : 81.684 (GB/s)
Accuracy        : 1.580171e-05
% export OMP_NUM_THREADS = 183
% ./diffusion_tiled

Running diffusion kernel 6553 times
Elapsed time    : 13.388 (s)
FLOPS           : 106752.742 (MFlops)
Throughput      : 98.541 (GB/s)
Accuracy        : 1.580171e-05

% export OMP_NUM_THREADS = 122

Running diffusion kernel 6553 times
Elapsed time    : 16.704 (s)
FLOPS           : 85561.117 (MFlops)
Throughput      : 78.979 (GB/s)
Accuracy        : 1.580171e-05
```

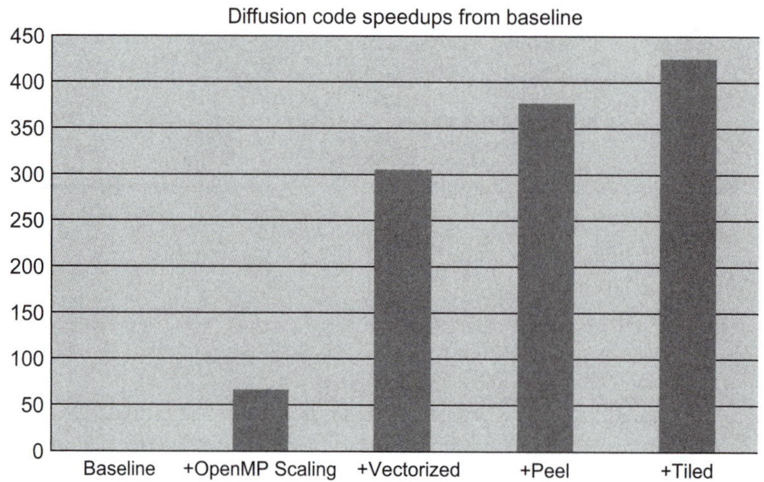

FIGURE 4.12

Accumulative Performance Improvements from Baseline to Tiling.

```
% export OMP_NUM_THREADS=61

Running diffusion kernel 6553 times
Elapsed time    : 30.993 (s)
FLOPS           : 46114.676 (MFlops)
Throughput      : 42.567 (GB/s)
Accuracy        : 1.558128e-05
```

The improved cache reuse gave us a bit more of a boost and we ended up with another 15-percent improvement over the peel improvements. That is 435 times improvement from the original single-threaded baseline. Figure 4.12 shows a graph of the performance improvements we realized while tuning the diffusion code. As with any code, there are likely some other improvements we could find with deeper analysis, particularly targeted ones with the help of analysis tools like Intel VTune Amplifier. But for our goals of this book on essentials, you have seen some of the key steps and "parallel thinking" needed to take real-world code from a serial implementation to high-speed parallel code that remains general and portable while scaling across cores and threads, and taking advantage of vectorization and cache architecture.

High speed driver certificate: summary of our high speed tour

Congratulations! You now have completed our introductory high speed "driving course" for parallel, high performance programming using the Intel Xeon Phi coprocessor. In these last three chapters, our goal was to give you an immediate hands-on, practical feel for tapping the performance potential of this new and exciting Intel product. However, it is important to understand that the parallel programming techniques, development tools, and methods we used are universally applicable to most any general purpose, parallel computing platform. For instance, the code also should see measurable performance improvements through each optimization step on past, present, and future Intel® Xeon® processors with multiple cores.

Ultimately, you can look at the Intel Xeon Phi coprocessor with its Intel Many Integrated Core architecture as taking computing architecture for parallel processing to a new level. As a software developer, to enjoy any real benefit on an Intel Xeon Phi coprocessor you must focus on parallel coding techniques or you will likely end up quite disappointed with the results on the coprocessor. We have found that, when the investment is made in optimizing code for parallel techniques such as vectorizing and scaling for multiple cores while reducing cross-task or thread dependencies, code can perform hundreds or even thousands of times faster than the original serial version.

Furthermore, your investment in parallelism pays dividends; providing improvements with many currently available processors while poised to gain further benefits as parallel computing continues to be the foreseeable norm.

We now will switch gears from practice to theory in the upcoming chapters. We will give you more insight how to exploit more parallelism in your applications and take full advantage of the Intel Xeon Phi coprocessor.

CHAPTER

Lots of Data (Vectors)

5

The Intel® Xeon Phi™ coprocessor is designed with strong support for vector level parallelism with features such as 512-bit vector math operations, hardware prefetching, software prefetch instructions, caches, and high aggregate memory bandwidth. This rich support in hardware coupled with numerous software options may seem overwhelming at first glance, but the richness available offers many solutions for diverse needs. Processors and coprocessors benefit from vectorization. Exposing opportunities to use vector instructions for vector parallel portions of algorithms is the first programming effort. Even then, the layout of data, alignment of data, and the effectiveness of prefetching into caches can affect vectorization. This chapter covers the rich set of options available for processors and Intel Xeon Phi coprocessors with little specific Intel Xeon Phi knowledge required.

The best software options are using functions in the Intel® Math Kernel Library (MKL), or programming using the vector support from any of SIMD directives, prefetching, or Intel® Cilk™ Plus. Alternatives such as intrinsics and compilers auto-vectorization can deliver excellent performance results, but the limitations in portability and future maintenance can be substantial. All together, the numerous methods to achieve vector performance on Intel Xeon Phi coprocessors are plentiful enough to help you use this important capability. In the first chapter we explained how you should aim to have at a high usage of vector instructions on Intel Xeon Phi coprocessors. These vector instructions are critical to keeping the coprocessor busy.

We break down our discussion in this chapter as follows: we start by explaining why vectorization matters, and then we give an overview of five approaches to vectorization. We introduce a six-step methodology for looking for important and easy places where a few changes might improve vectorization. The rest of the chapter then walks through the key topics for writing vectorizable code:

- Streaming through caches: data layout, alignment, prefetching, streaming stores
- Compiler tips, options, and directives
- Use of array sections in Fortran, C, and C++
- Assembly code inspection
- Numerical result variations

Why vectorize?

Performance! Full use of the vector instructions means being able to do 16 single-precision or 8 double-precision mathematical operations at once instead of one. The performance boost that offers is substantial, and is a key to the performance we should expect from an Intel Xeon Phi coprocessor. Until a couple years ago, with SSE, processors could only offer four single-precision or two double-precision operations per instruction. The advent of AVX has make that eight and four, respectively, but still half what is found in Intel Xeon Phi coprocessors.

How to vectorize

Effective vectorization comes from a combination of efficient data movement and recognition of vectorization opportunities in the program itself. Many things get in the way of vectorization: poor data layout, C/C++ language limitations, required compiler conservatism, and poor program structure. We'll start with the five approaches to vectorization that should be of most interest, then look at a six-step method that may help you, and finally we'll review the multiple obstacles and solutions such as data layout and compiler options, in order to vectorize your code! Table 5.1 summarizes techniques for achieving vectorization.

Five approaches to achieving vectorization

Vectorization occurs when code makes use of vector instructions effectively. We encourage finding a method that has the compiler generate the instructions as opposed to manually writing in

Table 5.1 Techniques to Achieve Vectorization

	Cilk Plus	Array Notations	Auto-vectorization	SIMD Directives	MKL
Languages supported	C, C++	Fortran, C, C++	Fortran, C, C++	Fortran, C, C++	Fortran, C, C++
First available	2010	2010	More than 20 years ago	2010	More than 20 years ago
Key benefit	Reliable and predictable	Intuitive syntax that reflects programmer intent.	Few code changes needed, but expect to babysit the compiler with options.	Full programmer control, reliable and predictable. Will be standard in OpenMP 4.0.	Someone else did all the hard work! Reliable and predictable, no code changes to scale forward.
Key disadvantage	New, Intel compiler only[1] (as of 2012, more expected in future)	Standard Fortran array notations are not always high performance, Cilk Plus is new for C/C++	Unreliable, too limited by language and compiler technology, not portable	SIMD directives are powerful but need to be used carefully to avoid changing program meaning	Math libraries only, not general purpose solution

[1]*There has been work on the gcc compiler in an experiment branch to support this specification too.*

assembly code or with explicit intrinsics. The compiler can do everything automatically for a very small number of examples, but usually does much better with some help from programmers to overcome limitations in the programming language or algorithm implementation. As listed in Table 5.1, five approaches to consider are:

- *Math library.* See Chapter 11. The Intel Math Kernel library has been tuned to use vectorization when possible within the library routines in Intel MKL.
- *Auto vectorization.* Count on the compiler to figure it all out. This works for only the simplest loops, and usually only with a little help overcoming programming language limitations (for instance, using the `-ansi-alias` compiler option). Figure 5.1 shows the C code for a simple add of two vectors (we illustrate later in Figure 5.6). We have inserted an alignment directive, which is important. We saw alignment directives in Chapters 2 through 4 for the same reason. There are additional tips for compiler vectorization in an upcoming section, *General Compiler Tips and Comments for Vectorization*, in this chapter.
- *Directives/pragmas to assist or require vectorization.* See Figure 5.2. The SIMD directives (expected to be standard in OpenMP 4.0 in 2013, probably with slightly different syntax) give simple and effective controls to mandate vectorization. These are much more powerful than "IVDEP" directives that did not mandate vectorization. The catch in using these directives is that the vectorization of arbitrary loops is generally unsafe or will change the meaning of the program. Use of these directives has been very popular, but requires a firm understanding of their meaning and their dangers. SIMD directives are covered in an upcoming section, *SIMD Directives*, in this chapter.
- *Array notations.* See Figure 5.3 and Figure 5.4. Array notations convey programmer intent in an intuitive notation that reflects the array operations within an algorithm. The concise semantics

```
__declspec(align(16)) float a[MAX], b[MAX], c[MAX];
for (i=0;i<MAX;i++)
   c[i]=a[i]+b[i];
```

FIGURE 5.1

Vector Addition Using Standard C, Similar Programming Can Be Done in Fortran.

```
__declspec(align(16)) float a[MAX], b[MAX], c[MAX];
#pragma simd
for (i=0;i<MAX;i++)
   c[i]=a[i]+b[i];
```

FIGURE 5.2

Vector Addition Using Standard C, Similar Programming Can Be Done in Fortran.

```
__declspec(align(16)) float a[MAX], b[MAX], c[MAX];
c[i:MAX]=a[i:MAX]+b[i:MAX];
```

FIGURE 5.3

Vector Addition Using Cilk Plus Array Notation, Similar Programming Can Be Done in Fortran.

```
__declspec(align(16)) float a[MAX], b[MAX], c[MAX];
int veclen = 16;
// Using Array syntax in C/C++
for (i=0;i<(MAX-veclen+1);i+=veclen)
   c[i:veclen]=a[i:veclen]+b[i:veclen];
// a remainder loop (process the remaining elements)
for (i=MAX-(MAX%veclen);i<MAX;i++)
   c[i]=a[i]+b[i];
```

FIGURE 5.4

Vector Addition Using Cilk Plus Array Notation, with "Short Vector" Syntax.. Similar Programming Can Be Done in Fortran.

```
__declspec(align(16)) float a[MAX], b[MAX], c[MAX];
__declspec(vector(uniform(B,C), linear(i:1)));
float foo(float *B, float *C, int i) {
  return B[i]+C[i];
}
...
for(i=0; i<MAX; i++){
  a[i] = foo(b, c, i);
}
```

FIGURE 5.5

Vector Addition Using a Cilk Plus Elemental Function, No Fortran Equivalent Exists.

of array notations match vector execution, thereby naturally avoiding unintended barriers to vectorization. Fortran has array notations in the standard, whereas array notations in C/C++ are extensions support by compilers with support for Cilk Plus.

- *Elemental functions.* See Figure 5.5. Elemental functions are very useful when a program has an existing function that does one operation at a time that could be done in parallel with vector operations. This elemental function capability of Cilk Plus allows programs to maintain their current modularity but benefit from vectorization. Another advantage is that the simple code can be inlined but more complex operations may be left as functions for efficiency.

Six step vectorization methodology

Intel has published an interesting article suggesting a six-step process for vectorizing an application. It is not specific to Intel Xeon Phi coprocessors, but rather a general methodology designed for processors that is equally appropriate for Intel Xeon Phi coprocessors. It is neatly documented in an online *Vectorization Toolkit* that includes links to additional resources for each step. The URL is given at the end of this chapter. This section is a brief overview suitable to give a taste of some interesting tools Intel has to help evaluate and guide vectorization work.

This approach is very useful in cases where incremental work can yield strong results. Scientific codes that have successfully used vector supercomputers previously, or made use of SIMD instructions such as SSE or AVX, are easily the best candidates for this approach. This six-step methodology is no panacea because it can completely miss a bigger picture of overall algorithm redesign when that might be most appropriate. Parallelism may not be easily exposed. An effective parallel program may require a more holistic approach involving restructuring (refactoring) of the algorithm and data layout to get significant gains. Whether parallelism is easily exposed, or with great difficulty, it is wise to start by looking for the easiest opportunities to expose. These six steps help explain how to look for the most accessible and easiest opportunities.

Step 1. Measure baseline release build performance

We should start with a baseline for performance so we know if changes to introduce vectorization are effective. In addition, setting a goal can be useful at this point so we can celebrate later when we achieve it. A release build should be used instead of a debug build. A release build will contain all the optimizations for our final application and may alter the hotspots or even the code that is executed. For instance a release build may optimize away a loop in a hotspot that otherwise would be a candidate for vectorization. Using a debug build would be a mistake when working to optimize. A release build is the default in the Intel Compiler. We have to specifically turn off optimizations by doing a DEBUG build on Windows (or using the `-Zi` switch) or using the `-Od` switch on Linux or OS X. If using the Intel Compiler, ensure you are using optimization levels 2 or 3 (−O2 or −O3) to enable the auto-vectorizer.

Step 2. Determine hotspots using Intel® VTune™ Amplifier XE

We can use Intel® VTune™ Amplifier XE, our performance profiler, to find the most time-consuming functions in your application. The Hotspots analysis type is recommended; although Lightweight Hotspots would work as well (it will profile the whole system as opposed to just your application).

Identifying which areas of the code are taking the most time will allow us to focus on optimization efforts in the areas where performance improvements will have the most effect. Generally we want to focus on only the top few hotspots, or functions taking at least 10 percent of the application's total time. Make note of the hotspots we want to focus on for the next step.

Step 3. Determine loop candidates using Intel Compiler vec-report

The vectorization report (or vec-report) of the Intel Compiler can tell us whether or not each loop in our code was vectorized. We should ensure that we are using Compiler optimization level 2 or 3 (−O2 or −O3) to enable the auto-vectorizer, then run the vec-report and look at the output for the hotspots we determined in Step 2. If there are loops in the hotspots that did not vectorize, we can check whether they have math, data processing, or string calculations on data in parallel (for instance in an array). If they do, they might benefit from vectorization. Continue to Step 4 if any candidates are found. To run the vec-report, use the `-vec-report2` or `/Qvec-report2` option. The vec-report option, when used with offloading, can be easier to read if the reports for the host and the coprocessor are not interspersed. The section "Vec-report Option Used with Offloads" in Chapter 7 explains how to do this.

Step 4. Get advice using the Intel Compiler GAP report and toolkit resources

Run the Intel Compiler Guided Auto-parallelization (or GAP) report to see suggestions from the compiler on how to vectorize the loop candidates from Step 3. (Note: Intel named it *guided auto-parallelization* because it helps with task and data (vector) parallelism, vectorization is really just a special type of parallel processing.) Examine the advice and refer to additional toolkit resources as needed. Run the GAP-report using the `-guide` or `/Qguide` options for the Intel Compiler.

Step 5. Implement GAP advice and other suggestions (such as using elemental functions and/or array notations)

Now that we know the GAP report suggestions for the loop, it is time to implement them if possible. The report may suggest making a code change. Make sure the change would be "safe" to do. In other words, we must make sure the change does not affect the semantics or safety of the loop. The tool can definitely suggest changes that will yield vectorization but will change the program and get the wrong answer (but it will be faster!). One way to ensure that the loop has no dependencies that may be affected is to consider if executing the loop in backwards order would change the results. Another is to think about the calculations in the loop being in a scrambled order. If the results would be changed, the loop has dependencies and vectorization would not be "safe." We may still be able to vectorize by eliminating dependencies in this case. We could modify the source to give additional information to the compiler or optimize a loop for better vectorization. At this point we may introduce some of the high-level constructs provided by Cilk Plus or Fortran to better expose the vector parallelism.

Step 6: Repeat!

Iterate through the process as needed until performance is achieved or there are no good candidates left in the identified hotspots. Please bear in mind that this six-step process does not consider opportunities that may be possible if algorithm and data restructuring are considered. This six-step approach does not attempt to identify such opportunities.

Streaming through caches: data layout, alignment, prefetching, and so on

In order for vectorization to occur efficiently, data needs to flow to and from the vector instructions without excessive overhead. Efficiency in data movement depends on data layout, alignment, prefetching and efficient store operations. Some investigation into the code produced by the compiler can be done by anyone, and is discussed in a later section in this chapter titled "Looking at What the Compiler Created."

Why data layout affects vectorization performance

Vector parallelism comes from performing the same operation on multiple pairs (or triplets with FMA) of data elements simultaneously. Figure 5.6 illustrates the concept using the same vector registers we first showed in Figure 2.1. Figure 5.6 is not particular to Intel Xeon Phi coprocessors, other than the exact width of the registers. In fact, the optimizations discussed in the chapter are essentially the same as we would do for any modern microprocessors. The Intel Xeon Phi coprocessor does offer more vector level parallelism by having wider registers and more aggregate memory bandwidth, but with the correct programming methods an application can be written to map to processors or coprocessors through use of Intel MKL or the compiler without requiring different approaches in programming.

Figure 5.6 illustrates a vector addition of two registers, each holding 16 single-precision floating-point values yielding 16 single precision sums. In general, this math is done by loading the two input registers from data in memory and then performing the addition operation. There are several issues that need to be understood and optimized to make this possible:

- *Data layout in memory, aligned and packed.* Sixteen values have to be collected into each input register. If the data is laid out in memory in the same linear order and aligned on 512-bit (64 bytes) boundary, then a simple high performance vector load will suffice. If not, the first consideration should be whether data could be laid out in order and alignment. Data that is not packed and aligned optimally will require more instructions and cache or memory accesses to collect and organize in registers in order to use the vector operations. The extra instructions and

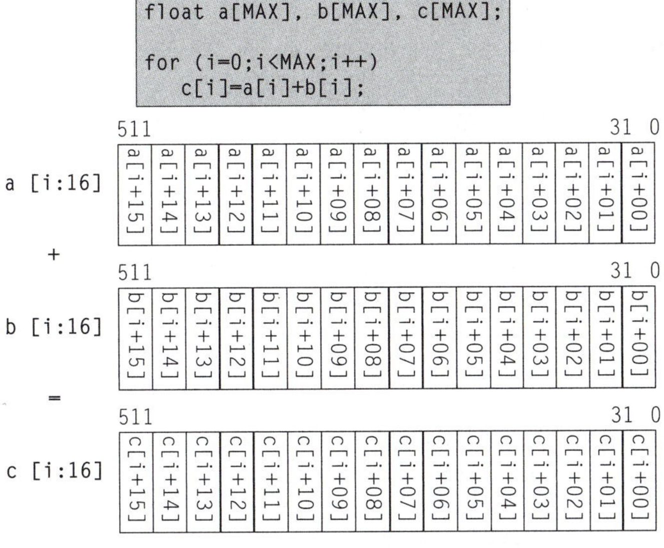

FIGURE 5.6

Vector Addition.

data accesses reduce performance. The compilers offer alignment directives and command line options, covered later in this chapter, to force or specify alignment of variables.

- *Data locality:*
  - *Fetch data from cache not memory.* Data eventually comes from memory, but at the time a vector load instruction is issued it is much faster if the data has been fetched into the closest (level 1, known as L1 cache) prior to the load instruction. On an Intel Xeon Phi coprocessor data actually travels from memory to L2 cache to L1 cache. Optimally this can be done by a prefetch of data from memory to L2, later followed by a prefetch from L2 to L1 cache, and later by the load instruction from L1 cache. The prefetches can be initiated by hardware or by software prefetches specified by the compiler automatically or manually by the programmer. L1 Prefetch instructions can ask for memory data to L1, but there are far fewer L1 prefetch operations allowed to be outstanding at the same time than the capacity for L2 prefetches to be outstanding. The compiler inserts prefetches automatically, and there are directives to help the compiler with hints and there are `mm_prefetch` intrinsics to do the prefetching manually. These are covered in a later section in this chapter.
  - *Data reuse.* If a program is fetching data into the cache that will be accessed more than once, then those accesses should occur close together. This is called temporal locality of reference. Ensuring that data is reused quickly helps reduce the chance that data will be evicted before it is needed again—resulting in a new fetch. Rearranging a program to increase temporal reuse is often a rewarding optimization. Intel MKL (Chapter 11) uses blocking in the library routines, which is a big help. For code we write explicitly, the challenge of blocking generally falls to the programmer. The good news is that cache blocking has been studied for decades for processors, and Intel Xeon Phi coprocessor relies on the same programming techniques. Before we decide to curse caches, it is worth noting that caches exist to lower power consumption and increase performance. The fact that our programming style can align with the cache designs to maximize performance is the price we pay to have more performance and power efficiency than would be possible without caches.
  - *Streaming stores.* If a program is writing data out that it will not use again, and that occupies memory linearly without gaps, then making sure streaming stores are being generated is important. Streaming stores increase cache utilization for data that matters by preventing the data being written from needlessly using up cache space.

Data alignment

If poor vectorization is detected via compiler vectorization report or assembler inspection, we may decide to improve data alignment to increase vectorization opportunities. For alignment, what is important is often the relative alignment of one array compared to another, or of one row of a matrix compared to the next. The compiler can often compensate for an overall offset in absolute alignment. Though of course, absolute alignment of everything is one way of getting relative alignment. For matrices, we may want to pad the row length (or column length, for Fortran) to be a multiple of the alignment factor. For Intel Xeon Phi coprocessors, alignment to 64-byte boundaries of all data (usually arrays) is very important in order to reach maximum performance. Aligned heap memory allocation can be achieved with calls to:

```
Void* _mm_malloc (int size, int base)
```

Alignment assertion `align(base)` can be used on statically allocated variables:

```
__attribute__((align(64))) float temp[SIZE]; /* array temp: 64byte aligned */
```

or

```
__declspec(align(64)) float temp[SIZE]; /* array temp: 64byte aligned */
```

Note: The Intel compilers accept either `__attribute__()` or `__declspec()` spellings to contain the directives for alignment. The `__attribute()` spelling is associated with gcc and Linux generally whereas `__declspec()` originated with Microsoft compilers and Windows. The Intel compiler allows source code to be used on Linux, Windows, or Mac OS X systems without changing the spelling, allowing either to be used.

The equivalent Fortran directive is

```
!DIR$ ATTRIBUTES ALIGN: base :: variable
```

Alignment assertion `__assume_aligned(pointer, base)` can be used on pointers:

```
__assume_aligned(ptr, 64); /* ptr is 64B aligned */
```

Fortran programmers would use the following to assert that the address of A(1) is 64B aligned:

```
!DIR$ ASSUME_ALIGNED A(1): 64
```

Additionally, there are compiler command line options ("align") to specify alignment of data. The Fortran compiler support variations to force alignment of arrays and `COMMON` blocks. C/C++ programs generally use only the `__attribute()` or `__declspec()` source code directives, whereas Fortran programmers often use the command line options as an alternative to the directives.

Some examples of alignment directives (shown in Fortran) include:

```
!dir$ attributes align : 32 :: A, B
```

- Directs compiler to align the start of objects A, B to 32 bytes
- Does not work for objects inside common blocks or derived types with `sequence` attribute; can be used to align start of common block itself

```
!dir$ assume_aligned A:32, B:32
```

- Tells the compiler that A and B have been aligned
- Useful if the compiler wouldn't otherwise know

```
!dir$ vector aligned
```

- Invites the compiler to vectorize a loop using aligned loads for all arrays, ignoring efficiency heuristics, provided that it is safe to do so.

```
-assume array32byte
```

- Roughly like `!dir$` attributes align:32 wherever possible

```
!dir$ attributes align
```

and

```
!dir$ assume_aligned
```

- where arrays are declared, not where they are used
- can appear together, but should not be necessary

```
!dir$ assume_aligned
```

- Most obvious use is for an incoming subroutine argument
- Cannot be used for global objects declared elsewhere or sequential objects (risk of conflicts) such as within common blocks or within modules or within structures

```
!dir$ vector aligned
```

- Applies to *all* the arrays in the following loop
- No impact on array attributes or other loops

Prefetching

The best performing applications will have well laid out data ready to be streamed to the math units to be processed. Moving the data from its tidy layout in memory to the math units is done using prefetching to avoid delays that occur as a mathematical operation has to wait for input data.

Prefetching is an important topic to consider regardless of what coding method we use to write an algorithm. To avoid having a vector load operation request data that is not in cache, we can make sure prefetch operations are happening. Any time a load requests data not in the L1 cache, a delay occurs to fetch the data from an L2 cache. If data is not in any L2 cache, an even longer delay occurs to fetch data from memory. The lengths of these delays are nontrivial, and avoiding the delays can greatly enhance the performance of an application. Optimized libraries such as Intel MKL will already utilize prefetches, so we will focus on controlling prefetches for code we are writing.

There are four sources of prefetches: automatic prefetching by the hardware to L2 caches (see Chapter 8), automatic software prefetch instructions by the compiler to L1 cache, compiler-generated prefetches (which were assisted by information from the programmer), and manual prefetch instructions by the programmer with both L2 and L1 fetch capabilities. The hardware prefetching is automatic and will automatically give way to software prefetches because they have higher priority. Figure 5.7 shows usage of prefetch directives. Figure 5.8 demonstrates the roughly equivalent using manual prefetches. It's easy to see that pragmas are far simpler to use. We recommend starting by working with the compiler, and moving to coding of manual prefetches only if required.

```
for (i=i0; i!=i1; i+=is) {
  float sum = b[i];
  int ip = srow[i];
  int c = col[ip];
  #pragma noprefetch col
  #pragma prefetch value:1:12
  #pragma noprefetch x
  for(; ip<srow[i+1]; c=col[++ip]) {
    sum -= value[ip] * x[c];
  }
  y[i] = sum;
}
```

FIGURE 5.7

Examples of Prefetching Directives.

```
Pseudo-code for compiler-generated code:
for (i=i0; i!=i1; i+=is) {
  float sum = b[i];  int ip = srow[i];
  int c = col[ip];
  /* pref for refs in outer loop with dist d2/d1 */
  /* No prefetch directive for outer loop, use
     compiler heuristics for prefetching */
  vprefetch1(&b[i+is*d2]);
  vprefetch0(&b[i+is*d1]);
  vprefetch1(&srow[i+is*d2]);
  vprefetch0(&srow[i+is*d1]);
  vprefetch1(&y[i+is*d2]);
  vprefetch0(&y[i+is*d1]);
  for(...) {
    ...
    /* vprefetch1 for value with a distance of 12, no
prefetching for others.
      If loop is   vectorized, prefetch 12 vector-iters
ahead*/
    vprefetch1(&value[ip+12*VLEN]);
  }
  y[i] = sum;
}
```

FIGURE 5.8

Roughly the “Manual Prefetches” that Are Generated from the Example in Figure 5.7 by the Compiler.

```
sum = 0.d0
do j=1,lastrow-firstrow+1
  i = rowstr(j)
  iresidue = mod( rowstr(j+1)-i, 8 )
  sum = 0.d0
  !DIR$ NOPREFETCH a,p,colidx
  do k=i,i+iresidue-1
    sum = sum +  a(k)*p(colidx(k))
  enddo
  !DIR$ NOPREFETCH p
  !DIR$ PREFETCH a:1:16
  !DIR$ PREFETCH colidx:0:8
  do k=i+iresidue, rowstr(j+1)-8, 8
    sum = sum + a(k  )*p(colidx(k  )) &
    + a(k+1)*p(colidx(k+1)) + a(k+2)*p(colidx(k+2)) &
    + a(k+3)*p(colidx(k+3)) + a(k+4)*p(colidx(k+4)) &
    + a(k+5)*p(colidx(k+5)) + a(k+6)*p(colidx(k+6)) &
    + a(k+7)*p(colidx(k+7))
  enddo
  q(j) = sum
enddo
```

FIGURE 5.9

A Prefetch Directive Example in Fortran.

```
subroutine spread(a1, b, n)
integer n
real*8 a1(:), b(:)

! Issue vprefetch0 for a1 with a distance of 4 vectorized iterations ahead
! Issue vprefetch1 for b with a distance of 40 vectorized iterations ahead
! Issue vprefetch0 for b with a distance of 8 vectorized iterations ahead
!dir$ prefetch a1:0:4
!dir$ prefetch b:1:40
!dir$ prefetch b:0:8
do i = 1,N
  a1(i) = b(i-1) + b(i+1)
enddo
return
end
```

FIGURE 5.10A

Another Prefetch Directive Example in Fortran.

Compiler prefetches

When using the Intel compiler with normal or elevated optimization levels (-O2 or greater) then prefetching is automatically set to `opt-prefetch=3`. Compiler prefetching is enabled with the `-opt-prefetch=n` option with *n* being a value 1 to 4 on Linux (Windows: `/Qopt-prefetch:n`). The higher the value, the more aggressive the compiler is with issuing prefetch instructions. If algorithm is well blocked to fit in L2 cache, prefetching is less critical but generally still useful for Intel Xeon Phi coprocessors.

In general, we recommend using the compiler to issue prefetches. If this is not perfect, there are a number of ways to give the compiler additional hints or refinements but still have the compiler generate the prefetches. We consider manual insertion of prefetch directives to be a last resort if compiler prefetching cannot be utilized for a particular need.

The first tuning to try is to use different second-level prefetch (vprefetch0) distances. We recommend trying $n = 1,2,4,8$ with `-mP2OPT_hlo_use_const_second_pref_dist=n`. In this case, $n = 2$ means use a prefetch distance of two vectorized iterations ahead (if the loop is vectorized). Instead of the compiler option, prefetch pragmas can be utilized in the source code.

Compiler prefetch controls (prefetching via pragmas/directives)

```
void foo(int *htab_p, int m1, int N)
{
  int i, j;
  for (i=0; i<N; i++) {
    #pragma prefetch htab_p:1:16
    #pragma prefetch htab_p:0:6
    // Issue vprefetch1 for htab_p with a distance
    // of 16 vectorized iterations ahead
    // Issue vprefetch0 for htab_p with a distance
    // of 6 vectorized iterations ahead
    // If pragmas are not present, compiler chooses
    // both distance values
    for (j=0; j<2*N; j++) {
      htab_p[i*m1 + j] = -1;
    }
  }
}
```

FIGURE 5.10B

A Prefetch Directive Example in C.

Instead of relying only on the compiler option, prefetch pragmas can be utilized in the source code. The compiler can be given prefetch directives to modify default behavior. The passing of addition information through directives can improve the performance of an application. The format for C/C++ and Fortran are respectively:

```
#pragma prefetch var:hint:distance
!DIR$ prefetch var:hint:distance
```

The *hint* value can be 0 (L1 cache [and L2 due to inclusion]), 1 (L2 cache, not L1). Figure 5.7 shows usage of prefetch directives and Figure 5.8 shows the roughly equivalent manual prefetches that we get from the compiler automatically with the simpler Figure 5.7 example syntax. Figures 5.9, 5.10A, 5.10B, and 5.11 give additional usage examples to examine.

Manual prefetches (using vprefetch0 and vprefetch1)

Figures 5.12 and 5.13 show examples of using manual prefetch directives. We recommend only doing this if the compiler cannot generate prefetches sufficiently even with hint covered in the prior

```
#pragma prefetch a:1:64 // Use distance of 64 vectorized iterations for a - vprefetch1
#pragma prefetch a:0:8  // Use distance of 8 vectorized iterations for a - vprefetch0
#pragma noprefetch b    // No prefetches for b
 for (i = 0; i < nn; i+=16) {
 _val = _mm512_load_ps ((void*)(&a[i]));
 _yy  = _mm512_add_ps (_val, _val);
 _mm512_extstore_ps ((void*)(&b[i]), _yy, _MM_DOWNCONV_PS_NONE, _MM_HINT_NONE);
}
```

FIGURE 5.11

C Prefetch Examples Illustrating Interoperation with Vector Intrinsics.

```
#include <stdio.h>
#include <immintrin.h>
#define N 1000
int main(int argc, char **argv) {
  int i, j, htab[N][2*N];
  for (i=0; i<N; i++) {
  #pragma noprefetch  // Turn off compiler prefetches for
this loop
    for (j=0; j<2*N; j++) {
      _mm_prefetch((const char *)&htab[i][j+20],
_MM_HINT_T1); // vprefetch1
      _mm_prefetch((const char *)&htab[i][j+2],
_MM_HINT_T0); // vprefetch0
      htab[i][j] = -1;
    }
  }
  printf("htab element is %d\n", htab[3][40]);  return 0;
}
/* constants to use with _mm_prefetch  (extracted from
*mmintrin.h) */
#define _MM_HINT_T0 1
#define _MM_HINT_T1 2
#define _MM_HINT_T2 3
#define _MM_HINT_NTA    0
#define _MM_HINT_ENTA   4
#define _MM_HINT_ET0    5
#define _MM_HINT_ET1    6
#define _MM_HINT_ET2    7
```

FIGURE 5.12

C Prefetch Intrinsics Example, Manual Prefetching.

section. These intrinsics work on processors and coprocessors both and are not specific to Intel Xeon Phi coprocessors. The intrinsics for Fortran and C/C++, respectively, are:

```
MM_PREFETCH (address [, hint])
void _mm_prefetch(char const*address, int hint)
```

The intrinsic issues a software prefetch to load one cache line of data located at *address*. The value *hint* specifies the type of prefetch operation. Values of `_MM_HINT_T0` or 0 (for L1 prefetches)

```
subroutine spread_lf (a, b)
  PARAMETER (n = 1028)
  real*8 a(n,n), b(n,n), c(n)
  do j = 1,n
    do i = 1,n
      a(i, j) = b(i-1, j) + b(i+1, j)
      call mm_prefetch (a(i+2, j), 0)
      call mm_prefetch (a(i+20, j), 1)
      call mm_prefetch (b(i+21, j), 1)
    enddo
  enddo
  print *, a(2, 567)
  stop
end
```

FIGURE 5.13

Fortran Prefetch Intrinsics Example, Manual Prefetching.

and `_MM_HINT_T1` or 1 (for L2 prefetches) are most common and are the interesting ones for use with Intel Xeon Phi coprocessors.

If we do decide to insert prefetches manually, we will want to disable automatic compiler insertion of prefetch instructions. Doing both will generally create competition for the limited prefetch capabilities of the hardware, and will result in reduced performance. If we are going through the effort to control prefetching manually, we should have already determined the compiler prefetching was not optimal. This generally happens for more complex data processing than the compiler can determine automatically.

Compiler prefetching is disabled with the `-opt-prefetch=0` or `-no-opt-prefetch` option on Linux (Windows: `/Qopt-prefetch:0` or `/Qopt-prefetch-`).

Streaming stores

Streaming stores are a special consideration in vectorization. Streaming stores are instructions especially designed for a continuous stream of output data that fills in a section of memory with no gaps between data items. They are supported by many processors, including Intel Xeon processors, as well as Intel Xeon Phi coprocessors. An interesting property of an output stream is that the result in memory does not require knowledge of the prior memory content. This means that the original data does not need to be fetched from memory. This is the problem that streaming stores solve—the ability to output a data stream but not use memory bandwidth to read data needlessly.

Having the compiler generate streaming stores can improve performance by not having the processor or coprocessor fetch caches lines from memory that will be completely overwritten. This method stores data with instructions that use a nontemporal buffer, which minimizes memory hierarchy pollution. This optimization helps with memory bandwidth utilization and is present for processors and Intel Xeon Phi coprocessors and may improve performance for both.

Use of the compiler option -opt-streaming-stores *keyword* (Linux and OS X) or /Qopt-streaming-stores:*keyword* (Windows) controls the compilers generation of streaming stores. The *keyword* can be *always*, *never* or *auto*. The default is *auto*. It is useful to know how to help the compiler understand an application enough to use streaming stores effectively.

When streaming stores will be generated for Intel® Xeon Phi™ coprocessors

The compiler is smart enough not to generate prefetches for lines for the streaming store, so as to avoid negating the value of the streaming stores. The compiler will also inject L2 cache line eviction instructions when using streaming stores. The Intel compiler generates streaming store instructions for an Intel Xeon Phi coprocessor only when:

1. It is able to vectorize the loop and generate an aligned unit-strided vector unmasked store:
   - If the store accesses in the loop are aligned properly, user can convey alignment information using pragmas/clauses
     - *Suggestion*: Use vector aligned directive before loop to convey alignment of all memory references inside loop including the stores.
   - In some cases, even when there is no directive to align the store-access, the compiler may align the store-access at runtime using a dynamic peel-loop based on its own heuristics.
   - Based on alignment analysis, compiler could prove that the store accesses are aligned (at 64 bytes)
   - Store has to be aligned and be writing to a full cache line (vstore – 64 bytes, no masks)
     - *Suggestion*: it is the responsibility of the programmer to align the data appropriately at allocation time using align clauses, `aligned_malloc`, `-align array64byte` option on Fortran, and so on.
2. Vector-stores are classified as nontemporal using one of:
   - We have specified a nontemporal pragma on the loop to mark the vector-stores as streaming
     - *Suggestion*: Use vector nontemporal directive before loop to mark aligned stores, or communicate nontemporal-property of store using a vector nontemporal *A* directive where an assignment into array *A* is the store inside the loop.
   - We have specified the compiler option `-opt-streaming-stores always` to force marking *all* aligned vector-stores as nontemporal.
     - This has the implicit effect of adding the nontemporal pragma to all loops that are vectorized by the compiler in the compilation scope
     - Using this option has few negative consequences even if used incorrectly for Intel Xeon Phi coprocessor since the data remains in the L2 cache (just not in the L1 cache)—so this option can be used if most aligned vector-stores are nontemporal. However, using this option on processors for cases where some accesses actually are temporal can cause significant performance losses since the streaming-store instructions on Intel Xeon bypass the cache altogether.

Compiler generation of clevicts

On streaming operations, the use of `clevicts` instructions allows the compiler to tell the hardware to not fetch data that will entirely be discarded (overwritten). This effectively avoids wasted prefetching efforts. Compiler has heuristics that determine whether a store is *streaming*. Usually this heuristic will kick in only when the loop has a large number of iterations specified and that is known at compile time. This is very limiting, so for applications where the calculation for the number of iterations is symbolic, there is a nontemporal pragma that allows us to mark streaming stores:

```
#pragma vector nontemporal
```

For processors, this pragma generates the nontemporal hints on stores. For Intel Xeon Phi coprocessors the compiler generates `clevicts` instead when the compiler knows the store addresses are aligned. Feature is controlled via the option:

```
-mGLOB_default_function_attrs="clevict_level=N"
```

where $N=0$, 1, 2 or 3 (default is 3)

- 0 - do not generate `clevict`
- 1 - generate L1 `clevict`
- 2 - generate L2 `clevict`

Compiler tips

There are a number of tips we can offer on how to get the most of the ability for the compiler to help with vectorization.

Avoid manual loop unrolling

The Intel® Compiler can typically generate efficient vectorized code if a loop structure is not manually unrolled. *Unrolling* means duplicating the loop body as many times as needed to operate on data using full vectors. For single precision on Intel Xeon Phi coprocessors, this commonly means unrolling 16-times. This means the loop body would do 16 iterations at once and the loop itself would need to skip ahead 16 per iteration of the new loop.

It is better to let the compiler do the unrolls, and we can control unrolling using `#pragma unroll N` (C/C++) or `!DIR$ UNROLL N` (Fortran). If *N* is specified, the optimizer unrolls the loop *N* times. If *N* is omitted, or if it is outside the allowed range, the optimizer picks the number of times to unroll the loop. Manual unrolling will generally interfere with the compiler optimizations enough to hurt performance.

To add to this, manual loop unrolling tends to tune a loop for a particular processor or architecture, making it less than optimal for some future port of the application. Generally, it is good advice to write code in the most readable, straightforward manner. This gives the compiler the best chance of optimizing a given loop structure. Here is a Fortran example where manual unrolling is done in the source:

```
m = MOD(N,4)
    if ( m /= 0 ) THEN
      do i = 1 , m
        Dy(i) = Dy(i) + Da*Dx(i)
      end do
      if ( N < 4 ) RETURN
```

```
    end if
    if (mp1 = m + 1) then
      do i = mp1 , N , 4
          Dy(i) = Dy(i) + Da*Dx(i)
          Dy(i + 1) = Dy(i + 1) + Da*Dx(i + 1)
          Dy(i + 2) = Dy(i + 2) + Da*Dx(i + 2)
          Dy(i + 3) = Dy(i + 3) + Da*Dx(i + 3)
      end do
    end if
```

It is better to express this in the simple form of:

```
  do i = 1,N
    Dy(i) = Dy(i) + Da*Dx(i)
  end do
```

This allows the compiler to generate efficient vector-code for the entire computation and also improves code readability. Here is a C/C++ example where manual unrolling is done in the source:

```
double accu1 = 0, accu2 = 0, accu3 = 0, accu4 = 0;
double accu5 = 0, accu6 = 0, accu7 = 0, accu8 = 0;
for (i = 0; i < NUM; i + = 8) {
      accu1 = src1[i + 0]*src2 + accu1;
      accu2 = src1[i + 1]*src2 + accu2;
      accu3 = src1[i + 2]*src2 + accu3;
      accu4 = src1[i + 3]*src2 + accu4;
      accu5 = src1[i + 4]*src2 + accu5;
      accu6 = src1[i + 5]*src2 + accu6;
      accu7 = src1[i + 6]*src2 + accu7;
      accu8 = src1[i + 7]*src2 + accu8;
}
accu = accu1 + accu2 + accu3 + accu4
      + accu5 + accu6 + accu7 + accu8;
```

It is better to express this in the simple form of:

```
double accu = 0;
for (i = 0; i < NUM; i++ ) {
      accu = src1[i]*src2 + accu;
}
```

Requirements for a loop to vectorize (Intel® Compiler)

Since a single iteration of a loop generally operates on one element of array, but use of vector instruction depends on operating on multiple elements of an array at once (see Figure 5.6), the "vectorization" of a loop essentially requires unrolling the loop so that it can take advantage of packed SIMD instructions to perform the same operation on multiple data elements in a single instruction.

The Intel compilers may be among the most capable and aggressive at vectorizing programs, but they still have limitations. In the most recent Intel compilers, vectorization is one of many optimizations enabled by default. Here is a list of requirements in order for a loop to potentially vectorize:

- If a loop is part of a loop nest, it must be the inner loop. Outer loops can be parallelized using OpenMP or autoparallelization (`-parallel`), but they cannot be vectorized unless the compiler is able either to fully unroll the inner loop, or to interchange the inner and outer loops. Additional high level loop transformations such as these may require `-O3`.
- The loop must contain straight-line code (a single basic block). There should be no jumps or branches, but masked assignments are allowed. A "masked assignment" simply means an assignment controlled by a conditional (such as an IF statement).
- The loop must be countable, which means that the number of iterations must be known before the loop starts to execute although it need not be known at compile time. Consequently, there must be no data-dependent exit conditions.
- There should be no backward loop-carried dependencies. For example, the loop must not require statement 2 of iteration 1 to be executed before statement 1 of iteration 2 for correct results. This allows consecutive iterations of the original loop to be executed simultaneously in a single iteration of the unrolled, vectorized loop. Figures 5.14 and 5.15 illustrate this requirement. The examples only make sense when thinking of doing multiple iterations at once due to vectorization. That is what would make Figure 5.15 illustrate a barrier to vectorization.

There should be no special operators and no function or subroutine calls, unless these are inlined, either manually or automatically by the compiler. Intrinsic math functions such as `sin()`, `log()`, and `fmax()` are allowed, since the compiler runtime library contains vectorized versions of these functions. The following math functions may be vectorized by the Intel C/C++ compiler: `sin`, `cos`, `tan`, `asin`, `acos`, `atan`, `log`, `log2`, `log10`, `exp`, `exp2`, `sinh`, `cosh`, `tanh`, `asinh`, `acosh`, `atanh`, `erf`, `erfc`, `erfinv`, `sqrt`, `cbrt`, `trunk`, `round`, `ceil`, `floor`, `fabs`, `fmin`, `fmax`, `pow`, and `atan2`. The list may not be exhaustive. Single precision versions such as `sinf` may also vectorize. The Fortran equivalents, where available, should also vectorize.

```
for (i=1; i<MAX; i++) {
  a[i] = b[i] + c[i];
  d[i] = e[i] - a[i-1]
}
```

FIGURE 5.14

Vectorizable: a[i-1] Is Always Computed Before It Is Used.

```
for (i=1; i<MAX; i++) {
  d[i] = e[i] - a[i-1];
  a[i] = b[i] + c[i]
}
```

FIGURE 5.15

Not Vectorizable: a[i-1] Might Be Needed Before It Has Been Computed (if Vectorized).

Some additional advice on how to have a loop vectorize:

- Both reductions and vector assignments to arrays are allowed.
- Try to avoid mixing vectorizable data types in the same loop (except for integer arithmetic on array subscripts). Vectorization of type conversions may be either unsupported or inefficient. Support for the vectorization of loops containing mixed data types may be extended in a future version of the Intel compiler.
- Try to access contiguous memory locations. (So loop over the first array index in Fortran, or the last array index in C). While the compiler may sometimes be able to vectorize loops with indirect or non-unit stride memory addressing, the cost of gathering data from or scattering back to memory is often too great to make vectorization worthwhile.
- The `ivdep` pragma or directive may be used to advise the compiler that there are no loop-carried dependencies that would make vectorization unsafe.
- The `vector always` pragma or directive may be used to override the compiler's heuristics that determine whether vectorization of a loop is likely to yield a performance benefit.
- To see whether a loop was or was not vectorized, and why, look at the vectorization report. This may be enabled by the command line switch `/Qvec-report3` (Windows) or `-vec-report3` (Linux or Mac OS X).
- The vec-report option, when used with offloading, can be easier to read if the reports for the host and the coprocessor are not interspersed. The section "Vec-report Option Used with Offloads" in Chapter 7 explains how to do this.

Importance of inlining, interference with simple profiling

Because vectorization happens on innermost loops consisting of straight line code (see actual rules in the prior section), inlining of functions within the loop is critical. Turning off optimizations (the default is ON) will stop automatic inlining, and that will affect the ability of loops to vectorize if they contain function calls. Instrumenting for profiling using the `–pg` option will generally do the same, and stop optimization. Better profiling can be done using the less intrusive Intel VTune Amplifier XE (see Chapter 13). Because it requires no instrumentation that will defeat inlining, we can do profiling on the release version of an application. The `-opt-report-phase-ipo_inl` option can show which functions are inlined.

Compiler options

There are many ways to share information that we know about out program that is not captured purely in the existing language. We selected a few of the most used and most effective compiler options to consider in order to boost the performance of an application:

- Use the ANSI aliasing option for C++ programs; this is not ON by default due to potential compatibility issues with older programs. This enables compiler to do type-based disambiguation (asserts that pointers and floats do not overlap). Without the flag, the compiler may assume that the count for the number of iterations is changing inside the loop if the upper bound is an object-field access. Obeying strict ANSI aliasing rules provides more room for optimization. Hence, it is highly recommended to enable for ANSI-conforming code via `-ansi-alias` (Linux and OS) or `/Qansi-alias` (Windows). This is already the default for the Intel Fortran Compiler. See an example coming up next in the section titled "Memory Disambiguation Inside Vector-Loops."

- No aliasing of arguments: on Linux and Mac OS X the option `-fargument-noalias` acts in the same way as applying the keyword `restrict` to all pointers of all function parameters throughout a compilation unit. This option is not available on Windows.

  Use optimization reports to understand what the compiler is doing:

  ```
  -opt-report-phase hlo –opt-report-phase hpo –opt-report 2
  ```

  This lets us check whether a loop of interest is properly vectorized. The "Loop Vectorized" message is the first step. We can get extra information using –vec-report 6.
- Use loop count directives to give hints to compiler; this affects prefetch distance calculation, use #pragma loop count (200), before a loop.
- The `restrict` keyword is a feature of the C99 standard that can be useful to C/C++ programmers. It can be attributed to pointers to guarantee that no other pointer overlaps the referenced memory location. Using the Intel C++ compiler does not only limit it to C99. It makes the keyword available for C89 and even for C++, simply by enabling a dedicated option: `-restrict` (Linux and Mac OS X) or `/Qrestrict` (Windows).
- In order to allow vectorization to happen, we need to avoid converting 64-bit integers to/from floating point. Use of 32-bit integers, preferable signed integers (most efficient).

Memory disambiguation inside vector-loops

Consider vectorization for a simple loop:

```
void vectorize(float *a, float *b, float *c, float *d, int n) {
    int i;
    for (i = 0; i<n; i++) {
      a[i] = c[i] * d[i];
      b[i] = a[i] + c[i] - d[i];
    }
}
```

Here, the compiler has no idea as to where those four pointers are pointing. As programmers, we may know they point to totally independent locations. The compiler thinks differently. Unless the programmer explicitly tells the compiler that they point to independent locations, the compiler has to assume the worst case aliasing is happening. For example, `c[1]` and `a[0]` may be at the same address and thus the loop cannot be vectorized at all.

When the number of unknown pointers are very small, the compiler can generate a runtime check and generate optimized and unoptimized versions of the loops (with overhead in compile time, code size, and also runtime testing). Since the overhead grows quickly, that very small number has to be really small—like two—and even then we are paying the price for not telling the compiler that "pointers are independent."

So, the better thing to do is to tell the compiler that "pointers are independent." One way to do it is to use C99 `restrict pointer` keyword. Even if we are not compiling with C99 standard, we can use `-restrict` (Linux) and `-Qrestrict` (Windows) flag to let the Intel compilers to accept `restrict` as a keyword. In the following example, we tell the compiler that `a` isn't aliased with anything else, and `b` isn't aliased with anything else:

```
void vectorize(float *restrict a, float *restrict b, float *c, float *d, int n) {
    int i;
    for (i=0; i<n; i++) {
      a[i] = c[i] * d[i];
      b[i] = a[i] + c[i] - d[i];
    }
}
```

Another way is to use IVDEP pragma. Semantics of IVDEP is different from the restrict pointer, but it allows the compiler to eliminate some of the assumed dependencies—just enough to let the compiler think vectorization is safe.

```
void vectorize(float *a, float *b,
               float *c, float *d, int n) {
    int i;
#pragma ivdep
    for (i=0; i<n; i++) {
       a[i] = c[i] * d[i];
       b[i] = a[i] + c[i] - d[i];
    }
}
```

Compiler directives

When we work to get the key part of an algorithm (usually a loop) to vectorize, we may quickly realize that there are two barriers: (1) getting the code to be vectorizable, (2) expressing the algorithm so the compiler accepts that it is vectorizable. The former is our responsibility as programmers. The nuisances of programming languages complicate the latter so that even the most brilliant compiler cannot auto-vectorize most loops written with no hints at all. In general, the presence of pointers that are too flexible in the C/C++ languages tend to make this problem most significant in C/C++ code and less for Fortran. Nevertheless, the challenge to completely specify our intent so that a compiler will vectorize is why we have directives. In a later section, we will review array notation and elemental functions as more elegant coding styles that can do much the same thing if we rewrite our code using a better notation. The directive is a bit more like a hammer—we use directives to force our current program to vectorize assuming it should. Code transformations to make the code vectorize is a prerequisite, the directive simply finishes reassuring the compiler so that it does the vectorization.

Traditionally, directives have been hints to the compiler to remove certain restrictions it may enforces. Assuming the concerns that blocked vectorization were removed, then the compiler will vectorize the code. These offer safety, but can be less portable and less predictable, even from release to release, as the heuristics in a compiler shift and change. The VECTOR and IVDEP directives are examples—they give the compiler hints but still rely on the compiler checking and approving all concerns for which the hints do not apply.

The SIMD directives are a different approach; they force the compiler to vectorize and essentially place all the burden on the programmer to ensure correctness. Gone are the days of fighting the compiler? Perhaps, but the programmer has to do the work and ensure correctness. For many, it is a dream come true: no compiler to fight. For many others, it is difficult without the compiler to help verify correctness.

SIMD directives

The SIMD directives enforce vectorization of loops. SIMD directives are an important capability to understand for vectorization work. SIMD directives come in two forms for C/C++ and Fortran, respectively:

```
#pragma simd [clause[ [,] clause]...]
!DIR$ SIMD [clause[[,] clause]...]
```

Analogously to how `cilk_for` gives permission to parallelize a loop (see Chapter 6), but does *not* require it, marking a `for` loop with `#pragma simd` similarly gives a compiler permission to execute a loop with vectorization. Usually this vectorization will be performed in small chunks whose size will depend on the vector width of the machine. For example, writing:

```
extern float a[];
#pragma  simd
for ( int  i = 0; i < 1000; ++i ) {
  a[i] =  2  *  a[i + 1];
}
```

grants the compiler permission to transform the code equivalently into:

```
extern float a[];
#pragma  simd
for ( int  i = 0; i < 1000; i + = 4 ) {
  float  tmp[4];
  tmp[0:4] =  2  *  a[i + 1:4];
  a[i:4] =  tmp[0:4];
}
```

The original loop in our example would not be legal to parallelize with `cilk_for`, because of the dependence between iterations. A `#pragma simd` is okay in the example because the chunked reads of locations still precede chunked writes of those locations. However, if the original loop body reversed the subscripts and assigned `a[i + 1] = 2 * a[i]`, then the chunked loop would not preserve the original semantics, because each iteration needs the value of the previous iteration.

In general, `#pragma simd` is legal on any loop for which `cilk_for` is legal, but not vice versa. In cases where only `#pragma simd` appears to be legal, study dependences carefully to be sure that it is really legal.

Note that `#pragma simd` is not restricted to inner loops. For example, the following code grants the compiler permission to vectorize the *outer* loop:

```
#pragma  simd
for ( int i=1;  i<1000000; ++i ) {
  while ( a[i]>1 )
  a[i] *=  0.5f;

}
```

In theory, a compiler can vectorize the outer loop by using masking to emulate the control flow of the inner `while` loop. Whether a compiler actually does so depends on the implementation. The Intel compiler detects and handles many forms of masking.

Requirements to vectorize with SIMD directives (Intel® Compiler)

The SIMD directives ask the compiler to relax some of its requirements and to make every possible effort to vectorize a loop. If an `ASSERT` clause is present, the compilation will fail if the loop is not successfully vectorized. This has led it to be sometimes called the "vectorize or die" directive.

The directive (`#pragma simd` in C/C++, or `!DIR$ SIMD` in Fortran) behaves somewhat like a combination of `#pragma vector always` and `#pragma ivdep`, but is more powerful. The compiler does not try to assess whether vectorization is likely to lead to performance gain, it does not check for aliasing or dependencies that might cause incorrect results after vectorization, and it does not protect against illegal memory references. `#pragma ivdep` overrides potential dependencies, but the compiler still performs a dependency analysis, and will not vectorize if it finds a proven dependency that would affect results. With `#pragma simd`, the compiler does no such analysis, and tries to vectorize regardless. It is the programmer's responsibility to ensure that there are no backward dependencies that might impact correctness. The semantics of `#pragma simd` are rather similar to those of the OpenMP `#pragma omp parallel for`. It accepts optional clauses such as `REDUCTION`, `PRIVATE`, `FIRSTPRIVATE`, and `LASTPRIVATE`. `SIMD`-specific clauses are `VECTORLENGTH` (implies the loop unroll factor), and `LINEAR`, which can specify different strides for different variables. Pragma SIMD allows a wider variety of loops to be vectorized, including loops containing multiple branches or function calls. It is particularly powerful in conjunction with the vector functions of Intel Cilk Plus.

Nevertheless, the technology underlying the SIMD directives is still that of the compiler vectorizer, and some restrictions remain on what types of loop can be vectorized:

- The loop must be countable. This means that the number of iterations must be known before the loop starts to execute, although it need not be known at compile time. Consequently, there must be no data-dependent exit conditions, such as `break` (C/C++) or `EXIT` (Fortran) statements. This also excludes most `while` loops. Typical diagnostic messages for incorrect application are similar to

  ```
  error: invalid simd pragma // warning #8410: Directive SIMD must be followed by
  counted DO loop.
  ```

- Certain special, nonmathematical operators are not supported, and also certain combinations of operators and of data types, with diagnostic messages such as "operation not supported," "unsupported reduction," and "unsupported data type."
- Very complex array subscripts or pointer arithmetic may not be vectorized, a typical diagnostic message is "dereference too complex."
- Loops with very low number of iterations (also referred to as a *low trip count*) may not be vectorized. Typical diagnostic: "remark: loop was not vectorized: low trip count."
- Extremely large loop bodies (very many lines and symbols) may not be vectorized. The compiler has internal limits that prevent it from vectorizing loops that would require a very large number of vector registers, with many spills and restores to and from memory.
- SIMD directives may not be applied to Fortran array assignments or to Intel Cilk Plus array notation.
- SIMD directives may not be applied to loops containing C++ exception handling code.

A number of the requirements detailed in the prior section "Requirements for a Loop to Vectorize (Intel® Compiler)" are relaxed for SIMD directives, in addition to the above-mentioned ones relating to dependencies and performance estimates. Loops that are not the innermost loop may be vectorized in certain cases; more mixing of different data types is allowed; function calls are possible and more complex control flow is supported. Nevertheless, the advice in the prior section should be followed where possible, since it is likely to improve performance.

It is worth noting that with SIMD directives, loops are vectorized under the "fast" floating-point model, corresponding to `/fp:fast` (`-fp-model=fast`). The command line option `/fp:precise` (`-fp-model precise`) is not respected by a loop vectorized with a SIMD directive; such a loop might not give identical results to a loop without the directive. For further information about the floating-point model, see "Consistency of Floating-Point Results using the Intel® Compiler" (listed in additional reading at the end of the chapter).

SIMD directive clauses

A SIMD directive can be modified by additional clauses, which control chunk size or allow for some C/C++ programmers' fondness for bumping pointers or indices inside the loop. The SIMD directives come in two forms for C/C++ and Fortran, respectively:

```
#pragma simd [clause[ [,] clause]...]
!DIR$ SIMD [clause[[,] clause]...]
```

If we specify the SIMD directive with no clause, default rules are in effect for variable attributes, vector length, and so forth. The `VECTORLENGTH` and `VECTORLENGTHFOR` clauses are mutually exclusive. We cannot use the `VECTORLENGTH` clause with the `VECTORLENGTHFOR` clause, and vice versa.

If we do not explicitly specify a `VECTORLENGTH` or `VECTORLENGTHFOR` clause, the compiler will choose a `VECTORLENGTH` using its own cost model. Misclassification of variables into `PRIVATE`, `FIRSTPRIVATE`, `LASTPRIVATE`, `LINEAR`, and `REDUCTION`, or the lack of appropriate classification of variables, may lead to unintended consequences such as runtime failures and/or incorrect results.

We can only specify a particular variable in at most one instance of a `PRIVATE`, `LINEAR`, or `REDUCTION` clause. If the compiler is unable to vectorize a loop, a warning occurs by default.

However, if ASSERT is specified, an error occurs instead. If the vectorizer has to stop vectorizing a loop for some reason, the fast floating-point model is used for the SIMD loop. A SIMD loop may contain one or more nested loops or be contained in a loop nest. Only the loop preceded by the SIMD directive is processed for SIMD vectorization.

The vectorization performed on this loop by the SIMD directive overrides any setting we may specify for options -fp-model (Linux OS and OS X) and /fp (Windows) for this loop.

VECTORLENGTH (*n1* [,*n2*]...)

n is a vector length (VL). It must be an integer that is a power of 2 (16 or less for C/C++); the value must be 2, 4, 8, or 16. If we specify more than one *n*, the vectorizor will choose the VL from the values specified. This clause causes each iteration in the vector loop to execute the computation equivalent to *n* iterations of scalar loop execution. Multiple VECTORLENGTH clauses will cause a syntax error.

VECTORLENGTHFOR (*data-type*)

data-type is one of the following intrinsic data types in Fortran or built-in integer, pointer, float, double or complex types in C/C++. This clause causes each iteration in the vector loop to execute the computation equivalent to *n* iterations of scalar loop execution where *n* is computed from size_of_vector_register/sizeof(data_type).

For example, VECTORLENGTHFOR (REAL (KIND=4)) or vectorlengthfor(float) results in $n=4$ for SSE2 to SSE4.2 targets (packed float operations available on 128-bit XMM registers) and $n=8$ for AVX target (packed float operations available on 256-bit YMM registers) and $n=16$ for Intel Xeon Phi coprocessors. The VECTORLENGTHFOR and VECTORLENGTH clauses are mutually exclusive. We cannot use the VECTORLENGTHFOR clause with the VECTORLENGTH clause, and vice versa. Multiple VECTORLENGTHFOR clauses cause a syntax error.

LINEAR (var1:step1 [, var2:step2]...)

var is a scalar variable; *step* is a compile-time positive, integer constant expression. For each iteration of a scalar loop, *var1* is incremented by *step1*, *var2* is incremented by *step2*, and so on. Therefore, every iteration of the vector loop increments the variables by VL*step1, VL*step2, ..., to VL*stepN, respectively. If more than one step is specified for a var, a compile-time error occurs. Multiple LINEAR clauses are merged as a union. A variable in a LINEAR clause cannot appear in a REDUCTION, PRIVATE, FIRSTPRIVATE, or LASTPRIVATE clause.

REDUCTION (*oper*:*var1*[,*var2*]...)

oper is a reduction operator (+, *, −, .AND., .OR., .EQV., or .NEQV.); *var* is a scalar variable. Applies the vector reduction indicated by *oper* to *var1*, *var2*, ..., *varN*. A SIMD directive can have multiple reduction clauses using the same or different operators. If more than one reduction operator is associated with a *var*, a compile-time error occurs. A variable in a REDUCTION clause cannot appear in a LINEAR, PRIVATE, FIRSTPRIVATE, or LASTPRIVATE clause.

[NO]ASSERT

Directs the compiler to assert (produce an error) or not to assert (produce a warning) when the vectorization fails. The default is NOASSERT. If this clause is specified more than once, a compile-time error occurs.

```
PRIVATE (var1 [, var2]...)
```

var is a scalar variable. Causes each variable to be private to each iteration of a loop. Its initial and last values are undefined upon entering and exiting the SIMD loop. Multiple `PRIVATE` clauses are merged as a union. A variable that is part of another variable (for example, as an array or structure element) cannot appear in a `PRIVATE` clause. A variable in a `PRIVATE` clause cannot appear in a `LINEAR`, `REDUCTION`, `FIRSTPRIVATE`, or `LASTPRIVATE` clause.

```
FIRSTPRIVATE (var1 [, var2]...)
```

var is a scalar variable. Provides a superset of the functionality provided by the `PRIVATE` clause. Variables that appear in a `FIRSTPRIVATE` list are subject to `PRIVATE` clause semantics. In addition, its initial value is broadcast to all private instances for each iteration upon entering the SIMD loop. A variable in a `FIRSTPRIVATE` clause can appear in a `LASTPRIVATE` clause. A variable in a `FIRSTPRIVATE` clause cannot appear in a `LINEAR`, `REDUCTION`, or `PRIVATE` clause.

```
LASTPRIVATE (var1 [, var2]...)
```

var is a scalar variable. Provides a superset of the functionality provided by the `PRIVATE` clause. Variables that appear in a `LASTPRIVATE` list are subject to `PRIVATE` clause semantics. In addition, when the SIMD loop is exited, each variable has the value that resulted from the sequentially last iteration of the SIMD loop (which may be undefined if the last iteration does not assign to the variable). A variable in a `LASTPRIVATE` clause can appear in a `FIRSTPRIVATE` clause. A variable in a `LASTPRIVATE` clause cannot appear in a `LINEAR`, `REDUCTION`, or `PRIVATE` clause.

```
[NO]VECREMAINDER
```

Directs the compiler to vectorize (or not to vectorize) the remainder loop when the original loop is vectorized. If `!DIR$ VECTOR ALWAYS` is specified, the following occurs: if neither the `VECREMAINDER` or `NOVECREMAINDER` clause is specified, the compiler overrides efficiency heuristics of the vectorizer and it determines whether the loop can be vectorized. If `VECREMAINDER` is specified, the compiler vectorizes remainder loops when the original main loop is vectorized. If `NOVECREMAINDER` is specified, the compiler does not vectorize the remainder loop when the original main loop is vectorized.

Use SIMD directives with care

The SIMD directives are most powerful in forcing vectorization, but come with the danger that the implications of vectorization need to be understood to avoid changing the program behavior in unexpected ways. They should be used with care. First-time users generally make mistakes and learn from them. We advise working on loops where the output values can be tested during development to provide rapid feedback. Some instructors advise "stick in SIMD directives and start debugging." We find that suggestion a little scary, but it seems to work with many developers quite well. Just be advised that it is hard to see the changes in a loop that are unexpected and problematic. On the other hand, SIMD directives free us from another evil: everything looks good, but we cannot figure out how to get the compiler to do the vectorization. Take your pick: SIMD to force the compiler to vectorize but we have to be careful, or auto-vectorization where the burden is on the compiler to keep things correct to the limits of its ability to analyze an application. The

VECTOR and IVDEP directives give us some "in between" options, which share the burden by retaining some compiler checking but giving us more control.

The VECTOR and NOVECTOR directives

Unlike SIMD directives, VECTOR and NOVECTOR are generally hints to modify compiler heuristics. The VECTOR and NOVECTOR overrides the default heuristics for vectorization of FORTRAN `DO` loops and C/C++ `for` loops. They can also affect certain optimizations. Their format is:

```
!DIR$ VECTOR [clause[[,] clause]...]
!DIR$ NOVECTOR
#pragma vector [clause[[,] clause]...]
#pragma vector nontemporal[(var1[, var2, ...])]
```

clause is an optional vectorization or optimizer clause. It can be one or more of the following:

`ALWAYS [ASSERT]`

Enables or disables vectorization of a loop. The `ALWAYS` clause overrides efficiency heuristics of the vectorizer, but it only works if the loop can actually be vectorized. If the `ASSERT` keyword is added, the compiler will generate an error-level assertion message saying that the compiler efficiency heuristics indicate that the loop cannot be vectorized. We should use the IVDEP directive to ignore assumed dependences or SIMD directive to ignore virtually everything. This makes `VECTOR ALWAYS` safer for the programmer in a way but leaves room for the compiler to be more conservative than might be strictly necessary. IVDEP and SIMD all shift more burden to the programmer to check that the vectorization is safe (preserves the programmer's intent).

`ALIGNED | UNALIGNED`

Specifies that all data is aligned or no data is aligned in a loop. These clauses override efficiency heuristics in the optimizer. The clauses `ALIGNED` and `UNALIGNED` instruct the compiler to use, respectively, aligned and unaligned data movement instructions for all array references. These clauses disable all the advanced alignment optimizations of the compiler, such as determining alignment properties from the program context or using dynamic loop peeling to make references aligned.

Be careful when using the `ALIGNED` clause. Instructing the compiler to implement all array references with aligned data movement instructions will cause a runtime exception if some of the access patterns are actually unaligned.

`TEMPORAL | NONTEMPORAL [(var1 [, var2]...)]`

var is an optional memory reference in the form of a variable name. This controls how the "stores" of register contents to storage are performed (streaming versus non-streaming). The `TEMPORAL` clause directs the compiler to use temporal (that is, non-streaming) stores. The `NONTEMPORAL` clause directs the compiler to use non-temporal (that is, streaming) stores. For Intel Xeon Phi coprocessors, the compiler generates clevict (cache-line-evict) instructions after the stores based on the non-temporal directive when the compiler knows that the store addresses are aligned.

By default, the compiler automatically determines whether a streaming store should be used for each variable. Streaming stores may enable significant performance improvements over non-streaming stores for large numbers on certain processors. However, the misuse of streaming stores can significantly degrade performance.

`VECREMAINDER | NOVECREMAINDER`

Same as the `[NO]VECREMAINDER` clause for SIMD directives (see above).

Use VECTOR directives with care

The VECTOR directive should be used with care. Overriding the efficiency heuristics of the compiler should only be done if we are absolutely sure the vectorization will improve performance.

For instance, the compiler normally does not vectorize loops that have a large number of non-unit stride references (compared to the number of unit stride references). In the following example, vectorization would be disabled by default, but the directive overrides this behavior:

```
!DIR$ VECTOR ALWAYS
  do i = 1, 100, 2
    ! two references with stride 2 follow
    a(i) = b(i)
  enddo
```

There may be cases where we want to explicitly avoid vectorization of a loop; for example, if vectorization would result in a performance regression rather than an improvement. In these cases, we can use the NOVECTOR directive to disable vectorization of the loop.

In the following example, vectorization would be performed by default, but the directive overrides this behavior:

```
!DIR$ NOVECTOR
  do i = 1, 100
    a(i) = b(i) + c(i)
  enddo
```

The IVDEP directive

Unlike SIMD directives, IVDEP gives specific hints to modify compiler heuristics about dependencies. Specifically, the compiler will assume dependencies between loops when it cannot prove they do not exist. The IVDEP directive instructs the compiler to ignore assumed vector dependencies. The format for C/C++ and Fortran, respectively, is:

`#pragma ivdep`

`!DIR$ IVDEP [: option]`

`!DIR$ IVDEP` with no *option* can also be spelled `!DIR$ INIT_DEP_FWD (INITialize DEPendences ForWarD)`

To ensure correct code, the compiler will prevents vectorization in the presence of assumed dependencies. This pragma overrides that decision. Use this pragma only when we know that the assumed loop dependencies are safe to ignore.

In Fortran, the *option* LOOP implies no loop-carried dependencies and the option BACK implies no backward dependencies. When no option is specified, the compiler begins dependence analysis by assuming all dependences occur in the same forward direction as their appearance in the normal scalar execution order. This contrasts with normal compiler behavior, which is for the dependence analysis to make no initial assumptions about the direction of dependence.

IVDEP example in fortran

In the following example, the IVDEP directive provides more information about the dependences within the loop, which may enable loop transformations to occur:

```
!DIR$ IVDEP
  DO I = 1, N
    A(INDARR(I)) = A(INDARR(I)) + B(I)
  END DO
```

In this case, the scalar execution order follows:

3. Retrieve `INDARR(I)`.
4. Use the result from step 1 to retrieve `A(INDARR(I))`.
5. Retrieve `B(I)`.
6. Add the results from steps 2 and 3.
7. Store the results from step 4 into the location indicated by `A(INDARR(I))` from step 1.

IVDEP directs the compiler to initially assume that when steps 1 and 5 access a common memory location, step 1 always accesses the location first because step 1 occurs earlier in the execution sequence. This approach lets the compiler reorder instructions, as long as it chooses an instruction schedule that maintains the relative order of the array references.

IVDEP examples in C

The loop in this example will not vectorize without the `ivdep` pragma, since the value of k is not known; vectorization would be illegal if $k < 0$:

```
void ignore_vec_dep(int *a, int k, int c, int m)
{
  #pragma ivdep
  for (int i = 0; i < m; i++)
    a[i] = a[i + k] * c;
}
```

The pragma binds only the `for` loop contained in current function. This includes a `for` loop contained in a sub-function called by the current function.

The following loop requires the parallel option in addition to the `ivdep` pragma to indicate there are no loop-carried dependencies:

```
#pragma ivdep
for (i=1; i<n; i++)
{
  e[ix[2][i]] = e[ix[2][i]]+1.0;
```

```
    e[ix[3][i]] = e[ix[3][i]] + 2.0;
}
```

The following loop requires the parallel option in addition to the `ivdep` pragma to ensure there is no loop-carried dependency for the store into `a()`:

```
#pragma ivdep
for (j = 0; j < n; j++)
{
    a[b[j]] = a[b[j]] + 1;
}
```

Random number function vectorization

```
double drand48(void);
double erand48(unsigned short xsubi[3]);
long int lrand48(void);
long int nrand48(unsigned short xsubi[3]);
long int mrand48(void);
long int jrand48(unsigned short xsubi[3]);
```

FIGURE 5.16

Supported C/C++ Functions.

```
#include <stdlib.h>
#include <stdio.h>
#define ASIZE 1024
int main(int argc, char *argv[])
{
      int i;
      double rand_number[ASIZE] = {0};
      unsigned short seed[3] = {155,0,155};
      // Initialize Seed Value For Random Number
      seed48(&seed[0]);
      for (i = 0; i < ASIZE; i++) {
          rand_number[i] = drand48();
      }
      // Print Sample Array Element
      printf("%f\n", rand_number[ASIZE-1]);
      return 0;
}
```

FIGURE 5.17

Example of drand48 Vectorization.

The Intel Compiler supports a vectorized version of the random number function. This is the `drand48` family of random number functions in C/C++ and `RANF` and `Random_Number` functions (single and double precision) in Fortran. Figure 5.16 shows the list of supported C/C++ functions and Figures 5.17 through 5.22 show examples using them.

```
#include <stdlib.h>
#include <stdio.h>
#define ASIZE 1024
int main(int argc,  char *argv[])
{
      int i;
      double rand_number [ASIZE] = {0};
      unsigned short seed[3] = {155,0,155};
      #pragma ivdep
      for (i = 0; i < ASIZE; i++) {
          rand_number[i] = erand48(&seed[0]);
      }
      // Print Sample Array Element
      printf("%f\n", rand_number[ASIZE-1]);
      return 0;
}
```

FIGURE 5.18

erand38 Vectorization; Seed Value Is Passed as an Argument.

```
#include <stdlib.h>
#include <stdio.h>
#define ASIZE 1024
int main(int argc, char *argv[]) {
      int i;
      long rand_number[ASIZE] = {0};
      unsigned short seed[3] = {155,0,155};
      // Initialize Seed Value For Random Number
      seed48(&seed[0]);
      for (i = 0; i < ASIZE; i++) {
          rand_number[i] = lrand48();
      }
      printf("%ld\n", rand_number[ASIZE-1]);
      return 0;
}
```

FIGURE 5.19

lrand38 Vectorization.

Utilizing full vectors, -opt-assume-safe-padding

Efficient vectorization involves making full use of the vector hardware. This implies that users should strive to get most code to be executed in the kernel-vector loop as opposed to peel loop and/or remainder loop.

```
#include <stdlib.h>
#include <stdio.h>
#define ASIZE 1024
int main(int argc,  char *argv[]) {
  int i;      long rand_number[ASIZE] = {0};
  unsigned short seed[3] = {155,0,155};
  #pragma ivdep
  for (i = 0; i < ASIZE; i++){
    rand_number[i] = nrand48(&seed[0]);
  }
  // Sample Array Element
  printf("%ld\n", rand_number[ASIZE-1]);
  return 0;
}
```

FIGURE 5.20

nrand48 Vectorization; Seed Value ID Passed as an Argument.

```
#include <stdlib.h>
#include <stdio.h>
#define ASIZE 1024
int main(int argc,  char *argv[]) {
  int i;
  long rand_number[ASIZE] = {0};
  unsigned short seed[3] = {155,0,155};
  // Initialize Seed Value For Random Number
  seed48(&seed[0]);
  for (i = 0; i < ASIZE; i++) {
    rand_number[i] = mrand48();
  }
  printf("%ld\n", rand_number[ASIZE-1]);
  return 0;
}
```

FIGURE 5.21

mrand48 Vectorization.

Remainder loop

A remainder loop is created to execute the remaining iterations when the number of loop iterations (trip count) for a vectorized loop is not a multiple of the vector length. While this is unavoidable in many cases, having a large amount of time spent in remainder loops will lead to performance inefficiencies. For example, if the vectorized loop trip count is 20 and the vector length is 16, it means every time the kernel loop gets executed once, the remainder 4 iterations have to be executed in the remainder-loop. Though the Intel Xeon Phi compiler may vectorize the remainder-loop (as reported by -vec-report6), it won't be as efficient as the kernel loop. For example, the remainder-loop will use masks, and may have to use gathers/scatters instead of unit-strided loads/stores (due to memory-fault-protection issues). The best way to address this is to refactor the algorithm/code in such a way that the remainder-loop is *not* executed at runtime (by making trip counts a multiple of

```
#include <stdlib.h>
#include <stdio.h>
#define ASIZE 1024
int main(int argc,  char *argv[]) {
  int i;
  long rand_number[ASIZE] = {0};
  unsigned short seed[3] = {155,0,155};
  #pragma ivdep
  for (i = 0; i < ASIZE; i++) {
    rand_number[i] = jrand48(&seed[0]);
  }
  printf("%ld\n", rand_number[ASIZE-1]);
  return 0;
}
```

FIGURE 5.22

jrand48 Vectorization; Seed Value Is Passed as an Argument.

vector length) and/or making the trip count large compared to the vector length (so that the overhead of any execution in the remainder loop is low).

The compiler optimizations also take into account any knowledge of actual trip count values. So if the trip count is 20, compiler usually makes better decisions if it knows that the trip count is 20 (trip count is a constant known statically to the compiler) as opposed to a trip count of *n* (symbolic value) that happens to have a value of 20 at runtime (maybe it is an input value read in from a file). In the latter case, we can help the compiler by using a `#pragma loop_count (20)` in C/C++, or `CDEC$ LOOP COUNT (20)` in Fortran, before the loop.

Also take into account any unrolling of the vector-loop done by the compiler (by studying output from -vec-report6 option). For example, if the compiler vectorizes a loop (of trip count *n* and vector length 16) and unrolls the loop by 2 (after vectorization), each kernel loop is designed to execute 32 iterations of the original src loop. If the dynamic trip count happens to be 20, the kernel loop gets skipped completely and all execution will happen in the remainder loop. If we encounter this issue, we can use the `#pragma nounroll` in C/C++ or `CDEC$ NOUNROLL` in Fortran to turn off the unrolling of the vector loop. (We can also use the `loop_count` pragma described earlier instead to influence the compiler heuristics).

If we want to disable vectorization of the remainder loop generated by the compiler, use `#pragma vector novecremainder` in C/C++ or `CDEC$ vector noremainder` in Fortran pragma/directive before the loop (using this also disables vectorization of any peel loop generated by the compiler for this loop). We can also use the compiler internal option `-mP2OPT_hpo_vec_remainder=F` to disable remainder loop vectorization (for all loops in the scope of the compilation). This is typically useful if we are analyzing the assembly code of the vector loop, and we want to identify clearly the vector-kernel loop from the line numbers (otherwise we have to carefully sift through multiple versions of the loop in the assembly—kernel/remainder/peel to identify which one we are looking at).

Peel loop

The compiler generates dynamic peel loops typically to align one of the memory accesses inside the loop. The peel loop peels a few iterations of the original src loop until the candidate memory access gets aligned. The peel loop is guaranteed to have a trip count that is smaller than the vector length. This optimization is done so that the kernel vector loop can utilize more aligned load/store instructions—thus increasing the performance efficiency of the kernel loop. But the peel loop itself (even though it may be vectorized by the compiler) is less efficient (study the-vec-report6 output from the compiler). The best way to address this is to refactor the algorithm/code in such a way that the accesses are aligned and the compiler knows about the alignment following the vectorizer alignment BKMs. If the compiler knows that all accesses are aligned (say if the user correctly uses `#pragma vector aligned` before the loop so that the compiler can safely assume all memory accesses inside the loop are aligned), then there will be no peel loop generated by the compiler.

We can also use the `loop_count` pragma described earlier to influence the compiler decision of whether or not to create a peel loop.

We can instruct the compiler to *not* generate a dynamic peel loop by adding `#pragma vector unaligned` in C/C++ or `CDEC$ vector unaligned` in Fortran pragma/directive before the loop in the source.

We can use the vector pragma/directive with the `novecremainder` clause (as mentioned above) to disable vectorization of the peel loop generated by the compiler. We can also use the compiler internal option `-mP2OPT_hpo_vec_peel=F` to disable peel-loop vectorization (for all loops in the scope of the compilation).

```
% cat -n t2.c
#include <stdio.h>
void foo1(float *a, float *b, float *c, int n)
{
  int i;
  #pragma ivdep
  for (i=0; i<n; i++) {
    a[i] *= b[i] + c[i];
  }
}
void foo2(float *a, float *b, float *c, int n)
{
  int i;
  #pragma ivdep
  for (i=0; i<20; i++) {
    a[i] *= b[i] - c[i];
  }
}
```

For the loop in function `foo1`, the compiler generates a kernel-vector loop (unrolled after vectorization by a factor of 2), a peel loop and remainder loop, both of which are vectorized. For the loop in function `foo2`, the compiler takes advantage of the fact that the trip count is a constant (20) and generates a kernel loop that is vectorized (and not unrolled). The remainder loop (of 4 iterations) is completely unrolled by the compiler (and not vectorized). There is no peel loop generated.

Option -opt-assume-safe-padding

We can increase the size of arrays by using the compiler option `-opt-assume-safe-padding`, which can improve performance. This option determines whether the compiler assumes that variables and dynamically allocated memory are padded past the end of the object.

When `-opt-assume-safe-padding` is specified, the compiler assumes that variables and dynamically allocated memory are padded. This means that code can access up to 64 bytes beyond what is specified in our program. The compiler does not add any padding for static and automatic objects when this option is used, but it assumes that code can access up to 64 bytes beyond the end of the object, wherever the object appears in the program. To satisfy this assumption, we must increase the size of static and automatic objects in our programs when we use this option.

One example of where this option can help is in the sequences generated by the compiler for vector-remainder and vector-peel loops. This option may improve performance of memory operations in such loops. If this option is used in the compilation above, the compiler will assume that the arrays *a*, *b*, and *c* have a padding of at least 64 bytes beyond *n*. If these arrays were allocated using `malloc`, such as:

```
ptr = (float *)malloc(sizeof(float) * n);
```

then they should be changed by the user to say:

```
ptr = (float *)malloc(sizeof(float) * n + 64);
```

After making such changes (to satisfy the legality requirements for using this option), we get a higher-performing sequence for the peel loop generated for loop at line 7.

Data alignment to assist vectorization

Data alignment is a method to force the compiler to create data objects in memory on specific byte boundaries. This is done to increase efficiency of data loads and stores to and from the processor. Without going into great detail, processors are designed to efficiently move data when that data can be moved to and from memory addresses that are on specific byte boundaries. For the Intel Xeon Phi coprocessor, memory movement is optimal when the data starting address lies on 64-byte boundaries. Thus, it is desired to force the compiler to create data objects with starting addresses that are modulo 64 bytes.

In addition to creating the data on aligned boundaries, the compiler is able to make optimizations when the data is known to be aligned by 64 bytes. By default, the compiler cannot know and cannot assume data alignment when that data is created outside of the current scope. Thus, we must also inform the compiler of this alignment via pragmas (C/C++) or directives (Fortran) so that the compiler can generate optimal code. The one exception is that Fortran module data receives alignment information at USE sites. To summarize, two steps are needed:

1. Align the data
2. Use pragmas/directives in performance critical regions where the data is used to tell the compiler that the arguments are aligned

Step 1: Aligning the data

It is important for performance to align data. It is also important for optimization to inform the compiler of the alignment information in critical regions of the code. If we align data but do not tell the compiler, we can end up getting less optimal code and/or longer compilation time.

How to define aligned STATIC arrays

Here is an example for statically declaring a 1000-element single-precision floating-point array A on a 64-byte boundary, optimal on Windows C/C++:

```
__declspec(align(64)) float A[1000];
```

on Linux or OS X C/C++:

```
float A[1000] __attribute__((aligned(64)));
```

For Fortran simple arrays, the easiest way to get array data aligned is to use compiler option `-align array64byte` to get all arrays, static or dynamic, aligned on a 64-byte boundary. This option does not align data in COMMON blocks, nor elements within derived types. We can also align arrays with a directive. Directives in our code remove the need to remember the `-align array64-byte` compiler option by explicitly calling out the alignment in our code where the variable is declared. Here is an example:

```
real :: A(1000)
!dir$ attributes align: 64:: A
```

For Fortran COMMON data, use `-align zcommons` to align all common block entities on 32-byte boundaries by adding padding bytes as needed. This is *not* the ideal data alignment for Intel Xeon Phi coprocessors, but is ideal for AVX. For the coprocessor, we have a 50/50 chance of full 64-byte alignment. Note: padding bytes may break many legacy applications that assume COMMON entities are packed and have no padding. So be sure to check results from our application to insure correctness with this compiler option.

For a Fortran derived-type data element, use `-align recnbyte`. To align data elements contained within a derived type on the 64-byte boundary optimal for the coprocessor, use the compiler option `-align rec64byte`. This option aligns components of derived types and fields within record structures on the boundary specified by (`n`). Each derived type element after the first is stored on either the size of the member type or n-byte boundaries, whichever is smaller. Fortran module data:

```
module mymod
real, allocatable :: a(:), b(:)
!dir$ attributes align:64 :: a
!dir$ attributes align:64 :: b
...
end module mymod
```

For alignment of dynamic data in C/C++ we replace `malloc()` and `free()` with alignment-specified replacements `_mm_malloc()` and `_mm_free()`. The arguments are identical. These `_mm_` replacements provided by the Intel C++ Composer XE use the same argument and return types as `malloc()` and `free()`. The returned data from `_mm_malloc()` will be 64-byte aligned.

```
_aligned_malloc()
_mm_malloc() and _mm_free()
```

For alignment of dynamic data in Fortran we use the `-align arraynbyte` and `-align recnbyte` compiler options as discussed previously.

Step 2: Inform the compiler of the alignment

Now that we have aligned our data, it is necessary to inform the compiler that this data is aligned where that data is actually used in the program. For example, when we pass data as arguments to a performance-critical function or subroutine, how does the compiler know if the arguments are aligned or unaligned? This information must be provided by us since the compiler has no information on the arguments.

Here's an example in C/C++: for a specific variable, use the `__assume_aligned` macro to inform the compiler that a particular variable or argument is aligned. For example, to inform the compiler that an array passed in as an argument or in global data is aligned we would do the following:

```
void myfunc( double p[] ) {
   __assume_aligned(p, 64);
   for (int i = 0; i < N; i++){
      p[i]++;
   }
}
void myfunc2( double *p2, double *p3, double *p4, int n) {
   for (int j = 0; j < n; j+ = 8) {
      __assume_aligned(p2, 64);
      __assume_aligned(p3, 64);
      __assume_aligned(p4, 64);
      p2[j:8] = p3[j:8] * p4[j:8];
   }
}
```

Here's an example in Fortran: use the directive `ASSUME_ALIGNED`. The general syntax is:

```
cDEC$ ASSUME_ALIGNED address1:n1 [, address2:n2]...
```

If we specify more than one `address:n` item, they must be separated by a comma. If `address` is a Cray `POINTER` or it has the `POINTER` attribute, it is the `POINTER` and not the pointee or the `TARGET` that is assumed aligned. If we specify an invalid value for *n*, an error message is displayed.

```
!DIR$ ASSUME_ALIGNED A: 64
do i = 1, N
A(I) = A(I) + 1
end do
```

```
!DIR$ ASSUME_ALIGNED A: 64
A = A + 1
```

How to tell the vectorizer all memory references are nicely aligned for the target

A more general pragma or directive can be put in front of a loop to tell the compiler that *all* data in the loop is aligned. In this way, we do not have to specify each variable using the methods above.

Example in C/C++

```
#pragma vector aligned
for (i = 0; i<n; i++){
  A[i] = B[i] * C[i] + D[i];

}
//Add pragma just before an array-notation stmt to
//specify alignment for arrays used
#pragma vector aligned
A[0:n] = B[0:n] * C[0:n] + D[0:n];
```

Examples in Fortran:

```
!DIR$ VECTOR ALIGNED
do I = 1, N
  A(I) = B(I) * C(I) + D(I)

end do
!DIR$ VECTOR ALIGNED
A = B * C + D
```

Some notes: these clauses override the efficiency heuristics in the compiler vectorizer. These clauses cause the compiler to use aligned data movement instructions for all array references. These clauses disable all the advanced alignment optimizations of the compiler, such as determining alignment properties from the program context or using dynamic loop peeling to make references aligned. Be careful when using these clauses. Instructing the compiler to implement all array references with aligned data movement instructions will cause a runtime exception if some of the access patterns are actually unaligned.

Mixing aligned and unaligned accesses: how to tell the vectorizer all RHS memory references are 64-Byte aligned

Data alignment is a method to force the compiler to create data objects in memory on specific byte boundaries. This is done to increase efficiency of data loads and stores to and from the processor. For The Intel® Many Integrated Core Architecture (Intel® MIC Architecture) products such as the Intel Xeon Phi coprocessor, memory movement is optimal when the data starting address lies on 64-byte boundaries.

In addition to creating the data on aligned boundaries, the compiler is able to make optimizations when the data is known to be aligned by 64 bytes. Thus, we must also inform the compiler of this alignment via pragmas (C/C++) or directives (Fortran) so that the compiler can generate optimal code. The one exception is that Fortran module data receives alignment information at USE sites.

This example shows alignment being asserted to help the compiler optimize as much as possible:

```
float *p, *p1;
__assume_aligned(p,64);
```

```
__assume_aligned(p1,64);
__assume(n1%16==0);
__assume(n2%16==0);
__assume(n3%16==0);
__assume(n4%16==0);
__assume(n5%16==0);
for(i=0;i<n;i++){
  q[i] = p[i]+p[i+n1]+p[i+n2]+p[i+n3]+p[i+n4]+p[i+n5];

}
for(i=0;i<n;i++){
  q1[i] =
    p1[i]+p1[i+n1]+p1[i+n2]+p1[i+n3]+p1[i+n4]+p1[i+n5];

}
```

Tradeoffs in array notations due to vector lengths

When converting code to array notation, it is useful to keep in mind what operations are directly supported by the target hardware. Consider this scalar code:

```
void scalar(T *R, T *A, T *B, int S, T k) {
  // S is size __assume_aligned(R,64);
  __assume_aligned(A,64);
  __assume_aligned(B,64);
  for (int i = 0; i < S; i++) {
    T tmp = A[i] * k - B[i];
    if (tmp > 5.0f) {
      tmp = tmp * sin(B[i]);
    }
    A[i] = tmp;
  }

}
```

If the scalar code were converted directly to array notation using the basic technique of replacing loop-index-subscripts `[i]` with array notation `[0:S]`, this code would be the result:

```
void longvector(T *R, T *A, T *B, int S, T k) {
  __assume_aligned(R,64);
  __assume_aligned(A,64);
  __assume_aligned(B,64);
  T tmp[S];
  tmp[0:S] = A[0:S] * k - B[0:S];
  if (tmp[0:S] > 5.0f) {
    tmp[0:S] = tmp[0:S] * sin(B[0:S]);
```

```
    }
    A[0:S] = tmp[0:S];
}
```

If the array size S is large (larger than L2 cache size), the above code may not perform optimally because the array sections are very large. Specifically:

1. The temporary array tmp, which was a single scalar value in the original code, is now a large array. This data is reused several times in the algorithm, but does not fit in the cache and must be reloaded from memory. It may even lead to stack allocation problems.
2. The array B has the same problem: it is reused but does not fit in the cache.
3. The size S array section operations are much larger than hardware vector length. The compiler must decide how to break them up for efficient vectorization.

The compiler may be able to "fuse" all the code together, which will improve reuse, but it may be hampered by the unknown size S and the generic declaration of the arrays as kpointers to T.

A way to write the above code that relies less on aggressive compiler analysis is:

```
void shortvector(T *R, T *A, T *B, int S, T k) {
  __assume_aligned(R,64);
  __assume_aligned(A,64);
  __assume_aligned(B,64);
  for (int i = 0; i < S; i + = VLEN) {
    T tmp[VLEN];
    tmp[:] = A[i:VLEN] * k - B[i:VLEN];
    if (tmp[:] > 5.0f) {
      tmp[:] = tmp[:] * sin(B[i:VLEN]);
    }
    A[i:VLEN] = tmp[:];
  }
}
```

This "short vector" style reintroduces the for loop and iterates through the loop in groups of VLEN elements. Within the loop, the compiler will generate operations that handle VLEN elements at a time. If VLEN is chosen to match the target hardware vector length, these operations can map directly into vector instructions and register operations.

The obvious question to ask is: isn't the short vector style more complicated to read than the original for loop? Wouldn't it be better to use a scalar for loop and rely on compiler vectorization and other optimizations? The answer is "it depends." The advantage of the short vector style is that it tells the compiler exactly what is expected and assists with dependency analysis due to the array notation semantics (array notation implies no dependencies within a statement). If the scalar for loop performs optimally, of course there is no reason to use this style. But if the compiler is not providing the desired code generation with the scalar for loop, then short vectors are a good way to tune the loop without unnatural looking constructions like strip-mining.

Another natural question is: "What is the optimal value of VLEN?" A good rule of thumb is to start with the target hardware vector size and try multiplying or dividing by 2. Increasing the size will increase the number of vector registers that are needed to compute the loop, but may increase performance by reducing trip count and exposing more optimization opportunities. Decreasing the size will increase trip count, but may be needed if the loop operations require more vector registers than are available (it is a good idea to reduce VLEN when mixing floats and doubles, for instance). For the Intel Xeon Phi coprocessor, 16 seems to be the optimal VLEN for the above routine.

On the Intel Xeon Phi coprocessor, the short vector code above ran 25 percent faster in our tests than the native scalar code. Here is the full code:

```
// Example of short vector style coding vs. scalar.
#include <stdio.h>
#include <stdlib.h>
#include <math.h>
#define S 8192*4
#define T float
#define ITERS 100
#define VLEN 16

// Reduce for AVX,SSE,etc.
__declspec(noinline) void scalar(T *R,T *A, T *B, T k) {
    __assume_aligned(R,64);
    __assume_aligned(A,64);
    __assume_aligned(B,64);
    for (int i = 0; i < S; i++) {
      T tmp = A[i] * k - B[i];
      if (tmp > 5.0f) {
        tmp = tmp * sin(B[i]);
      }
      A[i] = tmp;
    }

}
// NOT EXECUTED; CAUSES STACK OVERFLOW DUE TO LARGE stack allocation
__declspec(noinline) void longvector(T *R,T *A, T *B, T k) {
//__declspec(noinline) void longvector(T R[S],T A[S], T B[S], T k) {
    __assume_aligned(R,64);
    __assume_aligned(A,64);
    __assume_aligned(B,64);
    T tmp[S];
    tmp[0:S] = A[0:S] * k - B[0:S];
    if (tmp[0:S] > 5.0f) {
      tmp[0:S] = tmp[0:S] * sin(B[0:S]);
    } A[0:S] = tmp[0:S];

}
```

```
__declspec(noinline) void shortvector(T *R,T *A, T *B, T k) {
    __assume_aligned(R,64);
    __assume_aligned(A,64);
    __assume_aligned(B,64);
    for (int i = 0; i < S; i + = VLEN) {
      T tmp[VLEN];
      tmp[:] = A[i:VLEN] * k - B[i:VLEN];
      if (tmp[:] > 5.0f) {
        tmp[:] = tmp[:] * sin(B[i:VLEN]);
      } A[i:VLEN] = tmp[:];
    }

}
bool compare(T ref, T cean) {
    return (fabs(ref - cean) < 0.00001);

}
//__declspec(align(64)) T A[S],B[S],C[S]; int main() {
    volatile __int64 start=0, end=0, perf_ref=0, perf_short=0, max, tmpdiff;
    T *A,*B,*C;
    posix_memalign((void **)&A, 64, sizeof(T)*S);
    posix_memalign((void **)&B, 64, sizeof(T)*S);
    posix_memalign((void **)&C, 64, sizeof(T)*S);
    //__declspec(align(64)) T A[S],B[S],C[S];
    int short_vs_ref;
    T ref_result, short_result;
    float k = 0.5;
    max = 0;
    for (int i = 0; i < ITERS; i++) {
      A[0:S] = __sec_implicit_index(0);
      B[0:S] = __sec_implicit_index(0);
      C[0:S] = __sec_implicit_index(0);
      start = __rdtsc();
      scalar(A,B,C,k);
      tmpdiff = __rdtsc() - start;
      perf_ref + = tmpdiff;
      if (max < tmpdiff) max = tmpdiff;
      ref_result = __sec_reduce_add(A[0:S]);
    }
    perf_ref - = max;
    tmpdiff = (perf_ref - perf_short) * 100 / perf_ref;
    short_vs_ref = (int)tmpdiff;
    if (!compare(ref_result, short_result)) {
      printf("MISCOMPARE SHORT: FAILEDn");
      return -1;
```

```
        } else if (short_vs_ref < 15) {
          printf("SHORT VECTOR IS < 15%% FASTER THAN SCALAR : %d%%n", short_vs_ref);
          printf("FAILEDn"); return -2;
        }
        printf("SHORT VS SCALAR SPEEDUP >= 15%%: %d%%n", short_vs_ref);
        printf("PASSEDn");
        return 0;
}
```

C++ Array Notation is part of Intel Cilk Plus, which is a feature of the Intel® C++ Composer XE. Array Notation is one way to express parallelism. Array Notation helps the compiler with vectorization. However, one has to be careful in its use. Array expressions often require creation of temporary copies of the intermediate arrays used in evaluation of the expression. A side effect could be that these temporary vectors spill out of cache, eliminating reuse and causing a performance loss compared to the original loop equivalent. Rewriting the array syntax in shorter vectors can avoid this cache overflow.

Use array sections to encourage vectorization

Use of array sections in Fortran or C/C++ are better at explaining our intent as programmers. This in turn helps the compiler have the information it needs to vectorize the loop because it is has less of the implied dependencies that creep up from the use of loops.

Fortran array sections

An array section is a portion of an array that is an array itself. It is an array sub-object. A section subscript list (appended to the array or array component) determines which portion is being referred to. A reference to an array section takes the following form `array(sect-subscript-list)`, where `array` is the name of the array, *`sect-subscript-list`* is a list of one or more section subscripts (subscripts, subscript triplets, or vector subscripts) indicating a set of elements along a particular dimension. At least one of the items in the section subscript list must be a subscript triplet or vector subscript. A subscript triplet specifies array elements in increasing or decreasing order at a given stride. A vector subscript specifies elements in any order. Each subscript and subscript triplet must be a scalar integer (or other numeric) expression. Each vector subscript must be a rank-one integer expression.

If no section subscript list is specified, the rank and shape of the array section is the same as the parent array. Otherwise, the rank of the array section is the number of vector subscripts and subscript triplets that appear in the list. Its shape is a rank-one array where each element is the number of integer values in the sequence indicated by the corresponding subscript triplet or vector subscript.

If any of these sequences is empty, the array section has a size of zero. The subscript order of the elements of an array section is that of the array object that the array section represents.

Each array section inherits the type, kind type parameter, and certain attributes (`INTENT`, `PARAMETER`, and `TARGET`) of the parent array. An array section cannot inherit the `POINTER` attribute. If an array (or array component) is of type character, it can be followed by a substring range in parentheses.

Subscript triplets

A subscript triplet is a set of three values representing the lower bound of the array section, the upper bound of the array section, and the increment (stride) between them. It takes the following form `[first-bound] : [last-bound] [:stride]`, where `first-bound` is a scalar integer (or other numeric) expression representing the first value in the subscript sequence. If omitted, the declared lower bound of the dimension is used, `last-bound` is a scalar integer (or other numeric) expression representing the last value in the subscript sequence. If omitted, the declared upper bound of the dimension is used. When indicating sections of an assumed-size array, this subscript must be specified. Here `stride` is a scalar integer (or other numeric) expression representing the increment between successive subscripts in the sequence. It must have a nonzero value. If it is omitted, it is assumed to be 1.

If the stride is positive, the subscript range starts with the first subscript and is incremented by the value of the stride, until the largest value less than or equal to the second subscript is attained. If the first subscript is greater than the second subscript, the range is empty. If the stride is negative, the subscript range starts with the value of the first subscript and is decremented by the absolute value of the stride, until the smallest value greater than or equal to the second subscript is attained. If the second subscript is greater than the first subscript, the range is empty. If a range specified by the stride is empty, the array section has a size of zero.

A subscript in a subscript triplet need not be within the declared bounds for that dimension if all values used to select the array elements are within the declared bounds. For example, if an array has been declared as A(15), the array section specified as A(4:16:10) is valid. The section is a rank-one array with shape (2) and size 2. It consists of elements A(4) and A(14).

If the subscript triplet does not specify bounds or stride, but only a colon (:), the entire declared range for the dimension is used. If all subscripts are omitted, the section defaults to the entire extent in that dimension.

Vector subscripts

A vector subscript is a one-dimensional (rank one) array of integer values (within the declared bounds for the dimension) that selects a section of a whole (parent) array. The elements in the section do not have to be in order and the section can contain duplicate values. An array section with a vector subscript that has two or more elements with the same value is called a many-one array section. A many-one section must not appear on the left of the equal sign in an assignment statement, or as an input item in a `READ` statement.

Implications for array copies, efficiency issues

Unlike the array section definition for C/C++ with Cilk Plus, the Fortran language semantics sometimes require the compiler to make a temporary copy of an array or array slice. Situations where this can occur include:

- Passing a noncontiguous array to a procedure that does not declare it as assumed-shape
- Array expressions, especially those involving `RESHAPE`, `PACK`, and `MERGE`

- Assignments of arrays where the array appears on both the left- and right-hand sides of the assignment
- Assignments of POINTER arrays

By default, these temporary values are created on the stack and, if large, may result in a "stack overflow" error at runtime. The size of the stack can be increased, but with limitations dependent on the operating system. Use of the /heap-arrays (Windows) or -heap-arrays (Linux) compiler option tells the compiler to use heap allocation, rather than the stack, for such temporary copies. Heap allocation adds a small amount of overhead when creating and removing the temporary values, but this is usually inconsequential in comparison to the rest of the code.

Performance can be further improved by eliminating the need for a temporary copy entirely. For the first case above, passing a noncontiguous array to a procedure expecting a contiguous array, enabling the /check: arg_temp_created (Windows OS) or -check arg_temp_created (Linux OS) compiler option, will produce a runtime informational message when the compiler determines that the argument being passed is not contiguous. A runtime test is made and, if the argument is contiguous, no copy is made. However, this option will not issue a diagnostic for other uses of temporary copies.

One way to avoid temporary copies for array arguments is to change the called procedure to declare the array as assumed-shape, with the DIMENSION(:) attribute. Such procedures require an explicit interface to be visible to the caller. This is best provided by placing the called procedure in a module or a CONTAINS section. As an alternative, an INTERFACE block can be declared.

Use of POINTER arrays makes it difficult for the compiler to know if a temporary value can be avoided. Where possible, replace POINTER with ALLOCATABLE, especially as components of derived types. The language definition allows the compiler to assume that ALLOCATABLE arrays are contiguous and that they do not overlap other variables, unlike POINTERs.

Another situation where the temporary values can be created is for automatic arrays, where an array's bounds are dependent on a routine argument, use or host associated variable, or COMMON variable, and the array is a local variable in the procedure. As above, these automatic arrays are created on the stack by default; the /heap-arrays (Windows) or -heap-arrays (Linux) compiler option will create them on the heap. Consider making such arrays ALLOCATABLE instead; local ALLOCATABLE variables that do not have the SAVE attribute are automatically deallocated when the routine exits. For example, replace:

```
SUBROUTINE SUB (N)
INTEGER, INTENT(IN) :: N
REAL :: A(N)
```

with:

```
SUBROUTINE SUB(N)
INTEGER, INTENT(IN) :: N
REAL, ALLOCATABLE :: A(:)
ALLOCATE (A(N))
```

Cilk Plus array sections and elemental functions

Cilk Plus extends C and C++ with array notation and elemental functions, which lets the programmer specify array sections, operations on array sections, and scalar operations to be applied on vectors. These are the parts of Cilk Plus that enable vector programming and are therefore covered in this chapter. The task-oriented features of Cilk Plus are covered in Chapter 6.

Programming with array notation achieves predictable performance based on mapping parallel constructs to the underlying hardware vector parallelism, and possibly thread parallelism in the future. The notation is explicit, easy to understand, and enables compilers to exploit vector and thread parallelism with less reliance on alias and dependence analysis. For example:

```
a[0:n] =  b[10:n] *  c[20:n];
```

is an unordered equivalent of:

```
for ( int i=0; i<n; ++i )
  a[i] =  b[10+i] +  c[20+i];
```

Use array notation where our operations on arrays do not require a specific order of operations among elements of the arrays.

Specifying array sections

An array section operator is written as one of the following:

```
[first:length:stride]
[first:length]
[:]
```

where:

- `first` is the index of the first element in the section.
- `length` is the number of elements in the section.
- `stride` is the difference between successive indices. The `stride` is optional, and if omitted is implicitly 1. The stride can be positive, zero, or negative.

All three of these values must be integers, but they can be computed at runtime (they do not need to be known at compile time). The notation `expr[:]` is a shorthand for a whole array dimension if `expr` has array type before decay (conversion to pointer type) and the size of the array is known. If either first or length is specified, then both must be specified.

Operations on array sections

Most C and C++ scalar operations act element-wise on array sections and return an element-wise result. For example, `a[10:n]-b[20:n]` returns an array section of length `n` where the j element is `a[10+j]-b[20+j]`. Each operand must have the same shape, unless it is a scalar operand. Scalar operands are reshaped by replication to match the shape of the non-scalar operands. Function calls are also applied element-wise. The few operators that are not applied element-wise or have peculiar rank rules are:

- *Comma operator.* The rank of x, y is the rank of y.
- *Array section operator.* As described earlier, the rank of $a[i : n : k]$ is one more than the rank of a.
- *Subscript operator.* As described earlier, the rank of the result of `a[i]` is the sum of the ranks of a and i. The j element of `a[k[0 : n]]` is `a[k[j]]`. Trickier is the second subscript

in b[0 : m][k[0 : n]]. Both b[0 : m] and k[0 : n] have rank 1, so the result is a rank-two section where the element at subscript i, j is b[i][k[j]].

Note that pointer arithmetic follows the element-wise rule just like other arithmetic. A consequence is that a[i] is not always the same as *(a + i) when array sections are involved. For example, if both a and i have rank one, then a[i] has rank two, but *(a + i) has rank one, because it is element-wise unary * applied to the result of element-wise addition.

Historical note: In the design of array notation, an alternative was explored that preserved the identity *(a + i) ≡ a[i], but it broke the identity (a + i) + j ≡ a + (i + j) when a is a pointer type, and made the rank of $a + i$ dependent on the type (not just the rank) of a. It turns out that array notation must break one of the two identities, and breaking associativity was deemed the worse of two evils.

Reductions on array sections

There are built-in operations for efficient reductions of array sections. For example, _sec_reduce_add(a[0:n]) sums the values of array section a[0:n]. Table 5.2 is a summary of the built-in operations. The last column shows the result of reducing a zero-length section.

The "$-\infty$" and "∞" are shorthand for the minimum and maximum representable values of the type. The result of a reduction is always a scalar. For most of these reductions, the rank of a can be one or greater. The exception is that the rank of a must be one for _sec_reduce_max_ind and _sec_reduce_min_ind.

Avoid partial overlap of array sections

In C and C++, the effect of a structure assignment *p = *q is undefined if *p and *q point to structures that partially overlap in memory. The assignment is well defined if *p and *q are either completely disjoint or are aliases for exactly the same structure. Cilk Plus extends this rule to array sections. Examples:

```
extern float  a[15];
a[0:4] =   a[5:4]; // Okay, disjoint
a[0:5] =   a[4:5]; // WRONG! Partial overlap
a[0:5] =   a[0:5]+1;        // Okay, exact overlap
a[0:5:2] =   a[1:5:2];  // Okay, disjoint, no locations shared
a[0:5:2] =     a[1:5:3]; // WRONG! Partial overlap (both share a [4])
a[0:5] =   a[5:5]+a[6:5];   // Okay, reads can partially overlap
```

The last example shows how partial overlap of reads is okay. It is partial overlap of a write with another read or write that is undefined. This definition for array notation, which makes partial overlap ill defined, is different from the "well-defined but inefficient" choice made by APL and Fortran. Experience showed that doing so required a compiler to often generate temporary arrays, so it could fully evaluate the right side of a statement before doing an assignment. These temporary arrays hurt performance and caused unpredictable space consumption, both at odds with the C++ philosophy of providing abstractions with minimal performance penalty. So the specification was changed to match the rules for structure assignment in C/C++. Perhaps future compilers will offer to insert partial overlap checks into code for debugging.

Table 5.2 Built-in Operations

Operation	Result	If Empty
sec_reduce_add	$\Sigma i\ ai$	0
sec_reduce_mul	$\Pi i\ ai$	1
sec_reduce_max	max*i* *ai*	"$-\infty$"
sec_reduce_min	min*i* *ai*	"∞"
sec_reduce_max_ind	j such that $\forall i : ai \geq aj$	unspecified
sec_reduce_min_ind	j such that $\forall i : ai \leq aj$	unspecified
sec_reduce_all_zero	$\forall i : ai = 0\ ?\ 1 : 0$	1
sec_reduce_all_nonzero	$\forall i : ai\ /=\ 0\ ?\ 1 : 0$	0
sec_reduce_any_zero	$\exists i : ai = 0\ ?\ 1 : 0$	1
sec_reduce_any_nonzero	$\exists i : ai\ /=\ 0\ ?\ 1 : 0$	0

Elemental functions

An elemental function is a scalar function with markup that tells the compiler to generate extra versions of it optimized to evaluate multiple iterations in parallel. These are well-suited to converting legacy code where such functions already exist and can be converted without changing the rest of the program. It is a convenient notation that is useful to consider in writing new code as well because it holds up well over time as hardware vector lengths change.

When we call an elemental function from a parallel context, the compiler can call the parallel version instead of the serial version, even if the function is defined in a different source file than the calling context. The steps for using an elemental function are:

1. Write a function in scalar form using standard C/C++.
2. Add `__declspec(vector)`, and perhaps with optional control clauses, to the function declaration so that the compiler understands the intended parallel context(s) for calling it. Use additional clauses let you tell the compiler the expected nature of the parameters:
   - `uniform(b)` indicates that parameter b will be the same for all invocations from a parallel loop.
   - `linear(a:k)` indicates that parameter a will step by k in each successive invocation from the original serial loop. For example, `linear(p:4)` says that parameter `p` steps by 4 on each invocation. Omitting `:k` is the same as using `:1`.
3. Invoke the function from a loop marked with `#pragma simd` or with array section arguments.

The examples in Figures 5.23 and 5.24 show definition and use respectively of an elemental function. This code will likely perform better than a program where the function is not marked as elemental, particularly when the function is defined in a separate file. Writing in this manner exposes the opportunity explicitly instead of hoping that a super-optimizing compiler will discover the opportunity, which is particularly important in examples less trivial than this one.

Specifying unit-stride accesses inside elemental functions

If an elemental function accesses memory in unit-stride, these are the two ways we can write the function to achieve good performance, as shown in Figure 5.25.

```
__declspec(vector(linear(a),uniform(b)))
void bar(float  *a,  float *b,  int  c,  int  d) {
  if( *a>0 )
  *a =  b[c+d];
}
```

FIGURE 5.23

Defining an elemental function. The `declspec` tells the compiler to generate, in addition to the usual code, a specialized version for efficiently handling vectorized chunks where *a* has unit stride and *b* is invariant.

```
__declspec(vector(linear(a),uniform(b)))
void bar(float  *a,  float *b,  int c, int d);
void foo(float  *a,  float *b,  int*  c, int*  d, int  n) {
#pragma simd
  for( int  i=0; i<n; ++i )
  bar( a+i, b, c[i],  d[i] );
}
```

FIGURE 5.24

Calling an elemental function from a vectorizable loop. The `declspec` on the prototype tells the compiler that the specialized version from the prior example exists. As usual in C/C++, a separate prototype is unnecessary if the function is defined first in the same file.

```
// uniform pointer indexed by linear integer
__declspec(vector(uniform(a),linear(i:1)))
float foo(float *a, int i){
  return a[i]++;
}

// linear pointer
__declspec(vector(linear(a:1)))
float foo1(float *a){
  return (*a)++;
}
```

FIGURE 5.25

Two ways to promise unit-stride for vector (elemental) functions.

Look at what the compiler created: assembly code inspection

There are several ways to gain insight into how well applications were vectorized for the Intel® MIC architecture. The Vectorization Intensity performance metric, discussed in Chapter 13, quantifies the efficiency of an application's vectorization in terms of how many elements operations applied to. The Vectorization report (`-vec-report`) compiler option, introduced in this chapter, gives detailed information on which loops vectorized. Another handy tool for judging vectorization is assembly code inspection.

Visual inspection of assembly code can help identify performance problems that may merit further investigation. Understanding generated assembly code and its impact on application execution is a complex subject that can require years of study. We don't attempt to tackle that whole subject in this chapter. Instead we will share possible signs of trouble that anyone can look for in generated assembly for the Intel Xeon Phi coprocessor.

How to find the assembly code

There are two methods for obtaining the assembly code for your coprocessor application. The first is by using the `-S` option (Linux) for the Intel Compiler. This will produce an assembly file instead of a typical executable, and it will end in .s unless otherwise specified. If an offload application is being compiled to assembly, two files will be generated: one with a `.s` and the other ending in `MIC.s`, which will contain the specific binary to be run on the coprocessor. When using the `-S` option, we recommend removing `-g` (debug information) as it will remove a great deal of extra symbolic labeling in the assembly file and make it easier to read. Looking at an assembly listing presents several challenges though. The sheer length of most assembly listings can be intimidating. A trick for finding relevant code regions in an Intel Compiler assembly file is to search for '`#linenumber`' in the file (for example, '`#206`' for line 206). Even after doing this, however, you will often see hundreds of lines of assembly corresponding to one or two lines of source. For example, the compiler will typically try to align one or more memory references in a `for` loop dynamically. If, for example, a loop is accessing floats in an array and the first reference happens to be to a piece of data that is the eleventh element in a cacheline, the compiler will generate three loops. The first is a "peel" loop, which will perform the first five iterations of the loop (accessing the last five elements in the first cacheline). Then will be the main loop, accessing elements aligned to cachelines (16 elements per line). Then will be a remainder loop, to access any remaining elements in the final cacheline. Many other types of performance enhancements the compiler performs have the effect of making the assembly language very different from a straightline interpretation of the original source. Another source of confusion in assembly files can come from parallelism libraries like OpenMP, which create a function for the parallel region and result in loop code being found in a different location than expected.

Given the challenges outlined above, many people prefer to use the second method for viewing assembly, which is the source/assembly viewer in Intel® VTune™ Amplifier XE. VTune Amplifier XE can display the assembly for an application you are analyzing without needing any special compilation options. If symbolic information is available, the assembly code can be displayed side-by-side with the original source code. When a line of source code is selected, the corresponding assembly lines are displayed. This makes it easier to locate the assembly code of interest, but doesn't completely solve the issue of sorting out things like where the body of a loop that has been parallelized will appear in the assembly. Another way that the Intel VTune Amplifier XE can make things easier: loop analysis. Using loop analysis mode (Figure 5.26), VTune Amplifier XE will display hot information for the loops in your code instead of the functions. This makes it even easier to select a loop to focus on, and then view the source just for that loop and the corresponding lines of assembly (Figure 5.27). When looking at the assembly, you can using the line-by-line event count information to see how much time each instruction took to execute, allowing you to focus on the main loop body (higher execution times) instead of peel/remainder loops.

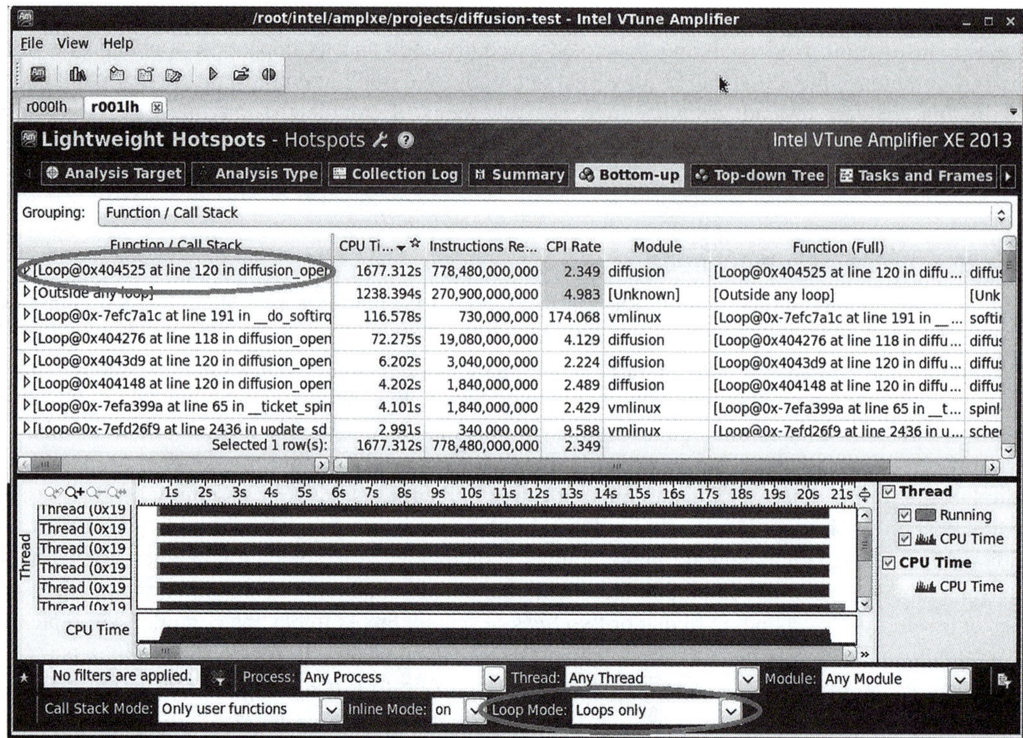

FIGURE 5.26

Loop Analysis, using VTune.

Quick inspection of assembly code

After determining which assembly code is relevant to look at for your loop or function, the next thing to understand is what it means. Understanding the instruction set for the Intel Xeon Phi coprocessor is beyond the scope of this book and is covered in the Intel Xeon Phi Coprocessor Instruction Set Architecture Reference Manual (see "For More Information" at the end of this chapter). This section focuses on spotting potential performance issues with a *quick* inspection. Since vectorization is so important to performance on the Intel Xeon Phi coprocessor, all of the assembly language issues that we cover here will pertain to vectorization.

Symptom 1: usage of unaligned loads and stores

Loading or storing unaligned data in a loop can result in the compiler using two instructions for each memory access. Generally, the compiler will try to dynamically align accesses using peel/remainder loops as discussed above, but in some situations this may not be possible. If the `vloadunpackld/hd` (low data/high data) or `vstoreunpackld/hd` instruction pairs are observed in a *main* loop body (not a peel or remainder loop), it indicates compiler was not able to enforce alignment

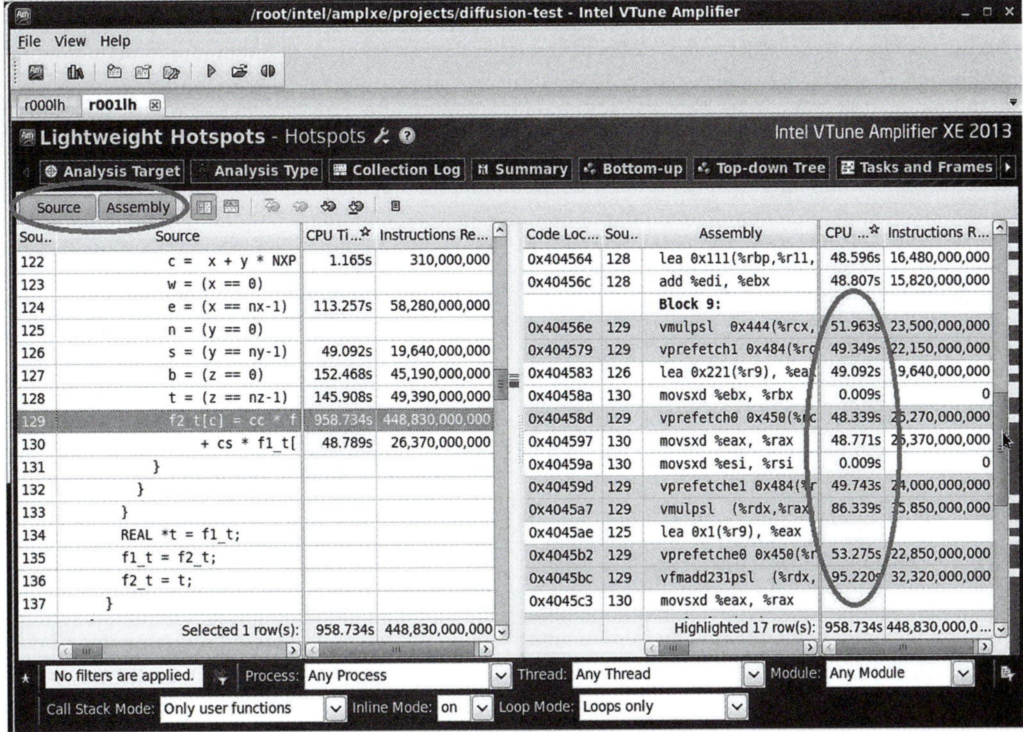

FIGURE 5.27

Assembly Code View Selected, using VTune.

dynamically and this is likely impacting performance. To address this issue, you should both align your data accesses and tell the compiler they are aligned. Both are important. Alignment is discussed in the section "Data Layout, Alignment, Prefetching, and So On" earlier in this chapter. In an illustrative example, a simple for loop (Figure 5.28) results in unaligned loads and stores (Figure 5.29). After telling the compiler that alignment is enforced using the #pragma vector aligned, the `vmovaps` instruction can be used just once for each data access (Figure 5.30) for a much more efficient loop.

Symptom 2: usage of %k1 mask

If the vector instructions for the Xeon Phi coprocessor are all masked, this may indicate inefficiencies. Masks are used for marking which elements in a vector register to which to apply the operation. Instructions that are generated by the compiler with a `%k0` mask apply to every element in a vector register – mask `%k0` is automatically all 1 s. The compiler can use a different mask with an instruction to indicate that it should apply to less than a full vector (to fewer than all elements in a 512bit vector register). For a thorough explanation of how the masks are used, see section 2.1.2 of the Intel® Xeon Phi™ Coprocessor Instruction Set Architecture Reference Manual.

```
for (int i = 0; i < n; ++i)
  a[i] = b[i] + c[i];
```

FIGURE 5.28

Source Code for the Loop.

```
vloadunpackld (%r12,%rsi), %zmm4
vloadunpackld (%r12,%rdx), %zmm5
vloadunpackhd 64(%r12,%rsi), %zmm4
vloadunpackhd 64(%r12,%rdx), %zmm5
nop
vaddps    %zmm5, %zmm4, %zmm6
nop
nop                                         #5.9 c15
vpackstoreld %zmm6, (%r12,%rdi)             #5.9 c18 stall 1
vpackstorehd %zmm6, 64(%r12,%rdi)           #5.9 c20
```

FIGURE 5.29

Unaligned Version of the Loop.

```
vmovaps    (%rax,%rdx), %zmm4               #6.16 c1
nop                                         #6.23 c3
vaddps     (%rax,%rcx), %zmm4, %zmm5        #6.23 c5
nop                                         #6.9 c7
nop                                         #6.9 c9
vmovaps    %zmm5, (%rax,%rdi)               #6.9 c12 stall 1
```

FIGURE 5.30

Aligned Version of the Loop.

If scalar code (not vectorized) is being generated, typically the compiler will still use a vector instruction with a mask of `%k1`. Earlier in the code the compiler will have set %k1 to have a value of 1 – so, the vector instruction being used will only apply to 1 element in the vector register. Seeing the `%k1` mask being used is not a definite sign of an issue – but, it is likely that less than full registers are being operated on and so vectorization is not as efficient as it could be. Again, this is something to be concerned about when looking at the assembly code for the main loop body, which should have aligned memory accesses and operate on full vector registers. Peel and remainder loops will have instructions operation on fewer elements and so may use masking effectively.

If this symptom is present, examine the compiler vectorization report for the loops in question. Using the highest level of diagnostic information (level 6) gives information on which loops were not vectorized and why. Figure 5.31 shows instructions not operating on full vectors. Instructions

```
## Usually, %k1 will be set to 1 in code:
movq      %rax, (%rsp)
pushq     $1
popq      %rax
movq      %rbx, 72(%rsp)
kmov      %rax, %k1
## Later, instructions using %k1 mask:
vmulps %zmm3, %zmm3, %k1, %zmm4
vaddpsl  0x1986960(%rax){1to16}, %zmm2, %k1, %zmm7
```

FIGURE 5.31

Instructions using %k1 Mask.

```
vmulps %zmm3, %zmm3, %k0, %zmm4
vaddpsl  0x1986960(%rax){1to16}, %zmm2, %k0, %zmm7
```

FIGURE 5.32

Full Vectors Being Operated On.

```
vmulps %zmm3, %zmm3, %zmm4
vaddpsl  %rax, %zmm2, %zmm7
```

FIGURE 5.33

Full Vectors: No Mask Being Used At All.

operating on full vectors are shown in Figure 5.32. Or, depending on the format, the `%k0` mask may be left out to indicate no mask is being given as shown in Figure 5.33.

Symptom 3: usage of scatters or gathers

Like symptoms 1 and 2, usage of scatter or gather instructions, see Figure 5.34, should cause concern only if observed in a main loop body and not a peel or remainder loop. Scatter and gather instructions are used to load or store multiple elements at a time. Gathers load elements into a vector register to be operated on, and scatters store elements back to multiple memory locations (cachelines) at once. They are useful instructions in the case where the application code is performing true indirect memory accesses, such as in a sparse data structure. However, due to their nature of loading/storing many elements they can have a long execution latency. In some cases, such as strided accesses, the application code can be restructured to have stride 1 access and avoid long latency scatter/gather operations. (When memory is accessed with a stride of 1, a single cacheline can hold a full vector register's worth of data to be operated on.)

```
vgatherdps (%r12,%zmm29,4), %zmm26{%k3}
vscatterdps %zmm30, (%r12,%zmm29,4){%k1}
```

FIGURE 5.34

Example Scatter/Gather Instructions.

```
vprefetch0 4(%rdi,%rsi,4)
movq       816(%rsp), %rax
vprefetch0 68(%rdi,%rsi,4)
movq       808(%rsp), %r14
movslq     %r8d, %r8
vprefetch0 132(%rdi,%rsi,4)
movq       800(%rsp), %r11
lea        (%rdi,%r13,4), %r9
vprefetch0 196(%rdi,%rsi,4)
vprefetch0 260(%rdi,%rsi,4)
vprefetch0 324(%rdi,%rsi,4)
lea        (%rdx,%r13,4), %rdx
lea        (%rdi,%rsi,4), %rbx
lea        (%rdi,%rax,4), %rax
lea        (%rdi,%r14,4), %r14
lea        (%rdi,%r11,4), %r12
```

FIGURE 5.35

Example: 6 Prefetches Followed by 6 Loads.

A typical case of strided accesses is an array of structures, often seen in molecular dynamics codes. These arrays holding structs (X, Y, and Z coordinates for example) are usually accessed in a strided fashion—moving through memory accessing all the X elements for example. Restructuring the code to access a structure of arrays—with all the Xs in one array, the Ys in another array, and so on, can change the access pattern to stride 1, which is far more beneficial. Section 5 of the *Guide to Vectorization with Intel C++ Compilers* (see "For More Information" at end of this chapter) discusses the structure of arrays concept with an example.

Symptom 4: lack of prefetch instructions

Software prefetch is an important strategy for improving performance on the Intel Xeon Phi coprocessor. Within loops, the compiler will usually insert prefetch instructions into code for you. One prefetch methodology used by the compiler is to prefetch data first into the local L2 cache with a `vprefetch1` instruction, and then into the L1 cache with a `vprefetch0` instruction. Typically you will see 1 or 2 prefetch instructions prior to each data load in a loop, as in Figure 5.35, and these could be a mixture of `vprefetch0` and `vprefetch1`, and sometimes `vprefetche1` or 2 (for stores). The absence of these prefetch instructions could indicate that the compiler is using an alternate prefetching methodology. If you see few or no prefetch instructions, and are seeing a poor L1 hit rate (see Chapter 13), it may be worth trying some of the compiler pragmas governing prefetch. A number of prefetch options are configurable and may yield better performance. The earlier section "Prefetching" in this chapter discusses these options.

Symptoms: quick inspections

The quick inspections we have shown give some things to look for in assembly code that may point to less than optimal code being generated for the Intel Xeon Phi coprocessor. These inspections can be useful tool in searching for top performance, and do not require great expertise in assembly language code.

Numerical result variations with vectorization

Generally vectorized reductions do not produce numerically identical results to scalar loops. Additionally, sometimes they may not be reproducible from one run to the next due to concurrency, even for identical executables running on identical data on the identical processor or coprocessor. If this is an issue, we can try the `–fp-model precise`, which, amongst other things, disables vectorization of reductions. Performance will be reduced by such an option.

Summary

The vector parallel capabilities of the Intel Xeon Phi coprocessor are utilized in the same manner as vectorization for processors. The big difference being that the level of performance possible due to the extra wide vectors makes it more important than for processors with smaller vector capabilities. Best use of the vector capability requires vectorization to create the vector instructions and good data layout and streaming to enable efficient movement of data to and from the vector instructions. This gives rise to many models to expose the vector parallelism so vectorization occurs, as well as influencing prefetching of data into levels of the data cache. This chapter gave the fundamentals, which are the same techniques we'd find in most any tutorial or reference on vectorization for processors. The Intel compiler documentation has more examples and options for advanced usage.

For more information

Here are some additional reading materials we recommend related to this chapter.

- Intel documentation including compiler reference manuals: http://software.intel.com/en-us/articles/intel-parallel-studio-xe-for-linux-documentation/
- *Vectorization Toolkit*. The toolkit also includes links to additional resources for a step-by-step vectorization methodology. http://tinyurl.com/intelveckit
- *Guide to Vectorization with Intel C++ Compilers*, http://tinyurl.com/intelautovec
- The article "Cache Blocking Techniques" provides more background on this general purpose technique that helps processor and coprocessor performance http://tinyurl.com/intelcacheblock
- The article "Memory Layout Transformations" provides more background the "array of structures" vs. "structures of array" topic. Understanding this general-purpose transformation can motivate changes to benefit processor and coprocessor performance. http://tinyurl.com/intelmemlayout

- In the article "Fortran Array Data and Arguments and Vectorization," various Fortran array data types and arguments are vectorized by the Intel compiler. This information may be helpful in generating effective vectorized programs. http://tinyurl.com/intelfortranarrays
- Article titled "Consistency of Floating-Point Results using the Intel® Compiler," http://tinyurl.com/intelfpconsist
- Reference material titled "Quick-Reference Guide to Optimization with Intel® Compilers," http://software.intel.com/en-us/intel-composer-xe/
- Intel Xeon Phi Coprocessor Instruction Set Architecture Reference Manual, http://intel.com/software/mic

CHAPTER

Lots of Tasks (not Threads)

6

The advice in this chapter is this: you need lots of task-level parallelism and you should first consider using OpenMP, Fortran 2008 `DO CONCURRENT`, Intel® Threading Building Blocks (TBB), and Intel® Cilk™ Plus. Alternatives such as direct use of pthreads or use of OpenCL can deliver excellent performance results, but the limitations in terms of being portable and difficulties in maintaining can be substantial. All together, the numerous methods to achieve scaling on Intel® Xeon Phi™ coprocessors are plentiful enough to help you have enough task-level parallelism, and the resulting code will work on processors and coprocessors alike.

It is important to understand that these tasking/threading models dispatch only within the shared memory space of a single coprocessor, or a collection of processors that share memory. Since coprocessors do not have a hardware-coherent shared memory with other coprocessors or processors, the threads and tasks created on a coprocessor thread will always stay somewhere on the coprocessor. Likewise, tasks (or threads) on the processor do not extend across to the coprocessor (s) automatically. It is possible to consider adding extensions to do such, but as of writing this book no such extensions exist. It is a topic of some discussion with TBB and Cilk Plus, so the future may offer additional options. The offload models discussed in Chapter 7 (Offload) have a number of options that blur the distinction a little, specifically `_Cilk_Shared`, but still manage distinct task/thread pools on each coprocessor and the host.

In the first chapter, we explained how you should have at least a hundred threads on Intel® Xeon Phi™ coprocessors (more likely 150 or more will be needed for maximum performance). These threads are critical to keeping the coprocessor busy and productive because they help hide latencies that are inherent in in-order microarchitecture such as that used in Intel Xeon Phi coprocessors.

Loops are the first place most developers look to create tasks because considering every iteration of a loop to be a task can often keep a large number of threads active. Loops usually get special treatment to avoid creating a thread for every iteration since the number of iterations can be much larger than the number of threads on any machine. There is no sense in creating a million threads on an Intel Xeon Phi coprocessor. In fact, it would cause a problem in terms of overhead and memory usage. Instead, we like to think of creating the *opportunity* for a million threads if the loop has a million iterations. To express the opportunity for parallelism, OpenMP has a parallel loop directive (`PARALLEL DO`), Fortran has `DO CONCURRENT`, Threading Building Blocks has a parallel for template (`parallel_for`) and Cilk Plus has a parallel for keyword (`cilk_for`). Loops are special and often the best first place to look to create parallel tasks. Explicitly creating parallel tasks without a loop to tap into requires more thinking and generally source code changes in more diverse locations. Both loop level parallelism and task parallelism are provided for by the various models, but loop level parallelism is easily the most used, easiest to learn, and easiest to understand in a program.

If you choose to have multiple MPI ranks (see Chapter 12) on each coprocessor, then the number of threads per rank will be large but need not be a hundred. Since you should not provide a hundred threads by setting up a hundred MPI ranks, you need to create lots of threads. A typical usage with MPI might be 4 to 10 ranks on a coprocessor to service about 60 cores (120 threads), so that threading in each rank needs to provide 12 to 30 threads per rank. A program with a single rank per coprocessor would need to have over a hundred threads created. The importance of using some form of threading is very evident with and without use of MPI. More discussion of MPI programming can be found in Chapter 12.

As a programmer you should program in tasks, not threads. What we means by that is this: the programmer should expose parallelism and share the opportunities for parallelism as tasks, but the work to map tasks to threads should not be encoded into an application. There are several reasons for this, including the difficulty of doing so, the inflexibility programs have at scaling on future hardware, and the fact that so many good options now exist to program in tasks. It is very unwise to mix the concept of exposing tasks with the effort to map tasks to hardware threads. Separated, tasks are the job of the application writer and mapping onto hardware is the job of a tasking package such as OpenMP, Intel Threading Building Blocks (TBB), or Intel Cilk™ Plus. Similarly, the Intel Math Kernel Library (MKL) hides pthreads by using OpenMP, which in turn is built using pthreads. Use of native threads (for example, pthreads) directly by an application is the parallel programming equivalent of writing in assembly language complete with managing the contents of the machine registers. The advice to use tasks, not threads, is strictly an argument about how to be efficient at programming but still get great results. The choice remains yours, because Intel Xeon Phi coprocessors support all these choices. After all, OpenMP, TBB, Cilk Plus and MKL are all eventually just libraries that use pthreads on Linux (or Windows threads on Windows).

OpenMP, Fortran 2008, Intel® TBB, Intel® Cilk™ Plus, Intel® MKL

OpenMP, Fortran 2008, TBB, Cilk Plus are standards to program with in terms of tasks not threads. MKL is mentioned because it uses OpenMP internally and fills the same needs whenever one of its math algorithms is utilized by an application. MKL is covered in Chapter 11. We will discuss OpenMP, Fortran 2008, TBB, and Cilk Plus in this chapter. Table 6.1 offers a brief comparison of the models.

Choosing between the models depends on your needs. OpenMP is well established, caters to Fortran and C programming, but does not cater to C++ programming and is not completely composable. Fortran 2008 is obviously Fortran only, with support appearing in most Fortran compilers, and is a full ISO standard. TBB caters to C++ programming, does not support Fortran or C, is composable, and is the only of the three that requires no compiler modifications. Cilk Plus caters well to C and C++ programming, is composable, provides strong *guarantees* on scheduler performance and stack *space*, and has features to also assist with vectorization (use of SIMD instructions).

Task creation needs to happen on the coprocessor

Whether you program natively (run directly on the coprocessor) or you run with an offload model (only the offloaded code runs on the coprocessor), you need to create enough tasks for the

Table 6.1 OpenMP vs. Fortran 2008 vs. Intel® TBB vs. Intel® Cilk™ Plus

	OpenMP	Fortran 2008	Intel® TBB	Intel® Cilk™ Plus
Website	openmp.org	fortranwiki.org	opentbb.org	cilkplus.org
first available	1997	2010	2006	2010
Languages supported	Fortran, C, and C++	Fortran	C++	C and C++
Summary	standardization of extensions via compiler directives to add parallelism to Fortran and C	extend Fortran for task parallelism via language extensions	extend C++ for rich parallelism via C++ template libraries	extend C/C++ for essential task and rich vector parallelism with language extensions
Approach	Compiler directives (pragmas), runtime library	Language keywords and syntax, runtime library	Compiler independent C++ Template Library, runtime library	Language keywords, attributes and directives (pragmas), runtime library
Specification	open specification by OpenMP	ISO/IEC 1539-1:2010 standard	open source project started by Intel	open specification by Intel
Features	parallel loops, tasking model, portable locks	Fortran language with extensions for concurrent programming.	parallel loops and algorithms, tasking model, portable locks, pipeline and flow graph models, scalable memory allocator	parallel loops, tasking model, vector loops, array notations, elemental functions, interoperate with TBB
Features that uniquely distinguish from the other two (which lack these)	largest HPC adoption, not completely composable	`DO CONCURRENT`, Coarrays[1]	largest general usage adoption, can work with any compiler (does not require compiler changes), pipeline and flow graph models, scalable memory allocator	provides strong *guarantees* on scheduler performance and stack *space*, vector loops, array notations, elemental functions

[1]*Coarrays are not yet supported on Intel Xeon Phi coprocessors at the time of this book being published. This is an exciting new feature that had only recently appeared in the Intel compiler for Xeon processors (it originated in Cray compilers and then was added to the standard). We think this is an important addition to the Fortran standard that will eventually gain adoption in compilers and by Fortran programmers.*

coprocessor within the code that runs on the coprocessor. In general, the large numbers of tasks for the coprocessor are generated on the coprocessor itself. Therefore, the OpenMP directives, the Fortran `DO CONCURRENT`, the TBB algorithms, the Cilk Plus loops or spawns, or the thread creates in pthreads, need to actually be run on the coprocessor either natively or inside an offload region of your code. The notable exceptions are calls to MKL, which can automatically create offloads from within the library if called on a processor with enough work to do (this is covered in Chapter 11).

Importance of thread pools

Applications should ultimately rest on top of thread pools so as to avoid the high overhead of creating and destroying threads repeatedly. If you are using pthreads, you should create all the threads you want only once and then reuse them through the life of the application. Fortunately, this is what OpenMP, TBB, Fortran 2008, and Cilk Plus all do for us automatically. Without having to reinvent them yourself, solutions for load balancing plus scheduling algorithms, to map work to threads, are details taken care of by well-engineered and tuned schedulers you can rely on from OpenMP, TBB, Fortran 2008 and Cilk Plus. In general, one software thread per hardware thread (four hardware threads per core) is the right upper bound for the coprocessor. This is a parameter worth experimenting with to see the performance changes in your own application. Not running threads on the core with the active OS routines running on it is important when using offload, because offload data transfers tends to keep the OS busy. The general rule of thumb is to use *N* code natively, or *N*-1 cores if using them via offload because of the one core that is busy doing data movement. Spreading the threads out evenly over the cores is done using affinity, which is important for OpenMP and TBB, and automatic with Cilk Plus. The manual controls available in OpenMP and TBB can be very important, which can theoretically put Cilk Plus at a disadvantage but in practice this seems uncommon as Cilk Plus delivers good performance in real applications too. All applications should use thread pools, either manually with pthreads or automatically with OpenMP, TBB, Cilk Plus, or MKL.

OpenMP

OpenMP is a set of directives to a compiler that can be ignored and the program should simply work in a nonparallel mode (sequential). When a compiler recognizes OpenMP directives (requires the `-openmp` switch on the Intel compilers), then the directives are interpreted to give direction on how to create parallel tasks in order to speed execution of a program through parallelism. OpenMP has also been extended with offload directives and those will be covered separately in Chapter 7. For creating tasks, OpenMP offers a large variety of directives for invoking parallelism. The most widely used are the directives that simply distribute a loop in parallel. OpenMP offers enough options to have inspired quite a number of books dedicated to the topic as well as online training and reference materials. We'll briefly cover only the essentials with an eye toward those that are most popular. Also we'll explain some of the coprocessor-oriented considerations when using OpenMP with the Intel Xeon Phi coprocessor.

Parallel processing model

A program containing OpenMP directives begins execution as a single thread known as the initial thread of execution. This initial thread executes sequentially until the first parallel construct is encountered. The `PARALLEL` (`!$OMP PARALLEL` or `#pragma omp parallel`) directive defines the extent of the parallel construct. When the initial thread encounters a parallel construct, it creates a team of threads (a thread pool), with the initial thread becoming the master of the team. All program statements enclosed by the parallel construct are executed in parallel by each thread in the team, including all routines called from within the enclosed statements.

The statements enclosed lexically within a construct define the static extent of the construct. The dynamic extent includes all statements encountered during the execution of a construct by a thread, including all called routines.

When a thread encounters the end of a structured block enclosed by a parallel construct, the thread waits until all threads in the team have arrived. When that happens the team is dissolved, and only the master thread continues execution of the code following the parallel construct. The other threads in the team enter a wait state until they are needed to form another team. You can specify any number of parallel constructs in a single program. As a result, thread teams can be created and dissolved many times during program execution. Implementations will actually maintain a thread pool after the first creation so that creating and dissolving thread teams is not an expensive operation.

Directives

OpenMP directives are disguised differently in C and C++ versus Fortran but both with the intent of being invisible to compilers that lack OpenMP support. For C and C++, an OpenMP directive will begin with `#pragma omp`. In Fortran, an OpenMP directive will begin with `!$OMP`. The most used OpenMP directives are listed in Table 6.2.

Significant controls over OpenMP

One thing that characterizes OpenMP is the rich set of controls that are offered to allow performance-oriented work many knobs to turn. Aside from the many clauses available to augment simple OpenMP directives, there are a number of OpenMP controls with wide-reaching implications for your programs. In general, OpenMP controls are available as function calls to be made within a program and via environment variables, which can be set and modified without changing the program. Function calls overrule environment variables if they are used. Use of environment variables are especially popular for describing items that may vary from machine to machine, or

Table 6.2 Most Used OpenMP Directives

Directive Name (put after `#pragma omp` or `!$OMP`)	Description
`PARALLEL` and `END PARALLEL`	Defines a parallel region where all threads are executing everything, no just the "master" thread.
`PARALLEL DO` and `END PARALLEL DO`	A shortcut for a PARALLEL region that contains a single DO directive.
`MASTER` and `END MASTER`	Defines a serial region where only the master thread is executing.
`CRITICAL` and `END CRITICAL`	Defines a serial region where only one thread can run at a time.
`THREADPRIVATE`	Makes the named COMMON blocks or variables private to a thread. The list argument consists of a comma-separated list of COMMON blocks or variables.
`TARGET`	Proposed for OpenMP 4.0, see Chapter 7.

depending on how much of a machine you are using. The compiler documentation contains a long list of these controls with details on their function. In Table 6.3, we list a few key controls that we believe are the most important to know about.

These controls also control parallelism generated by the Intel compiler, using the `-parallel` (`/Qparallel` on Windows) compile option, including parallel code generated from use of "do concurrent."

Nesting

OpenMP is unfortunately not fully composable, which can be a serious limitation when compared with the other abstract parallel programming models discussed in this chapter. Nesting of OpenMP can create explosive numbers of threads in recursive situations, which rapidly exhaust system resources, especially stack space, and require that the program be shut down. To prevent this, the maximum number of levels of parallel nesting that will activated when using OpenMP is set to one by default. While this is somewhat limiting (nested parallelism as supported by TBB and Cilk Plus is incredibly useful), it avoids a generally intolerable condition. With the continued popularity of OpenMP being so strong, we can expect additional proposals to refine OpenMP into a better ability to exploit nested parallelism opportunities when they exist. Without such solutions, programs are best to avoid relying on nesting of parallelism in order to get performance if using OpenMP.

Table 6.3 OpenMP Controls

Environment Variable Name	Description
`LD_LIBRARY_PATH` and `MIC_LD_LIBRARY_PATH`	Specifies the path for shared (.so) library files. Needs to point to where the OpenMP library is located.
`OMP_NUM_THREADS`	Sets the maximum number of threads to use for OpenMP parallel regions if no other value is specified in the application. Best values can range from 2–4 times the number of coprocessor cores you wish to use. The number of cores to use should be the number of core on the coprocessor unless you are using offload, in which case you decrease by one to allow the offload code in the OS a place to work, or if you choose to use less because you are running multiple MPI ranks on a coprocessor.
`KMP_AFFINITY`	Enables runtime library to bind threads to physical processing units. A popular setting is export `KMP_AFFINITY = SCATTER`, which scatters across cores before using multiple threads on a given core. Another is `COMPACT`, which is usually not wanted since it favors using all threads on a core before using other cores. See the "Thread Affinity Interface" section of the compiler documentation to see the numerous controls available include exact enumeration of locations.
`KMP_STACKSIZE` and `MIC_STACKSIZE`	Sets the number of bytes to allocate for each OpenMP thread to use as its private stack. Recommended size is 16 Mb on a processor but the default is far smaller. The default on a coprocessor is a more reasonable 12 Mb. This is often an important option to use.
`OFFLOAD_REPORT`	Enables printing diagnostics that show offload execution time, in seconds, and the amount of data transferred in bytes. Values should be 1 for a little and 2 for more information.

Fortran 2008

Fortran 2008 introduces two important features to support parallelism in the FORTRAN language: Coarrays and DO CONCURRENT.

We will focus on DO CONCURRENT; we will not cover Coarrays, which offer a Partitioned Global Address Space (PGAS) model of programming. We think Coarrays will eventually be very important. Coarrays remain very new and are implemented in very few compilers. Coarrays are *not* yet supported on Intel Xeon Phi coprocessors at the time of this book being published. We think this is an important addition to the Fortran standard that will eventually gain adoption in compilers and by Fortran programmers.

When choosing DO CONCURRENT, it is important to note that the Intel compiler will not produce parallel code from do concurrent unless -parallel (/Qparallel on Windows) compile options are used. This is consistent with the Intel compiler avoiding creating concurrent code unless the compile line authorizes it. This helps avoid surprises when doing a simple recompile using an old Makefile. When parallelization is enabled, the Intel compiler maps "do concurrent" onto OpenMP automatically thereby making the APIs and environment variable controls of OpenMP apply equally to use of "do concurrent."

DO CONCURRENT

The DO CONCURRENT construct specifies that there are no data dependencies between the iterations of a DO loop and it looks like this:

```
REAL :: SUM

  DO CONCURRENT (I = 1:N)
    SUM = BX(I) + CX(I)
    AX(I) = SUM + COS(SUM) + 3
  END DO
```

DO CONCURRENT and DATA RACES

A confusing part of the standard is this: the use of SUM in this example is required to be defined before it is used in each iteration. This prevents a dependence on the ordering of the execution of iterations, so that the order the iterations are actually performed does not matter. However, the use of a single SUM in every iteration does create a conflict (a data race) if iterations are executed in parallel. The Fortran standard does not mandate that a compiler do anything to prevent the data race. The use of SUM in every iteration creates a data race if this loop is used concurrently (in parallel), so this is not advisable for a parallel loop. It is technically possible for a compiler to privatize the variable, since this would seem to be the intent, but even if one compiler did that others may not. The "fix" for this would be use of the BLOCK construct to create variables local to each iteration. The code example would change to:

```
DO CONCURRENT (I = 1:N)
  BLOCK
    REAL :: SUM
```

```
            SUM = BX(I) + CX(I)
            AX(I) = SUM + COS(SUM) + 3
        END BLOCK
    END DO
```

Unfortunately, this is currently not supported in most Fortran compilers including the Intel Fortran compilers.

DO CONCURRENT definition

The formal definition of DO CONCURRENT is shown in Table 6.4.

The DO CONCURRENT range is executed for every active combination of the *index-name* values.

Each execution of the range is an iteration. The executions are free to occur in any order, so we need to be sure this is what we intend. A consequence of not knowing the order is that any variable modified in more than one iteration does not have a guaranteed outcome based on the iteration count. Branching is allowed within a given iteration but is not allowed to branch outside the DO CONCURRENT. Therefore branching cannot be used to terminate a DO CONCURRENT.

If *type* appears, the *index-name* has the specified type and type parameters. Otherwise, it has the type and type parameters that it would have if it were the name of a variable in the innermost executable construct or scoping unit.

If *type* does not appear, the *index-name* must not be the same as a local identifier, an accessible global identifier, or an identifier of an outer construct entity, except for a common block name or a scalar variable name.

The *index-name* of a contained FORALL or DO CONCURRENT construct must not be the same as an *index-name* of any of its containing FORALL or DO CONCURRENT constructs.

The following cannot appear in a DO CONCURRENT construct:

- A RETURN statement
- An image control statement
- A reference to a nonpure procedure
- A reference to module IEEE_EXCEPTIONS procedure IEEE_GET_FLAG, IEEE_SET_HALTING_MODE, or IEEE_GET_HALTING_MODE
- An EXIT statement must not appear within a DO CONCURRENT construct if it belongs to that construct or an outer construct.

Table 6.4 DO [,] CONCURRENT ([*type*::]*forall-spec*[, *mask-expr*])

Part	Definition
type	is an integer data type
forall-spec	*index-variable-name* = *forall-limit* : *forall-limit* [: *forall-step*]
forall-limit	is a scalar integer expression
forall-step	is a scalar integer expression
mask-expr	a mask expression that is scalar and of type logical

The following are additional rules for DO CONCURRENT constructs:

- A variable that is referenced in an iteration must be previously defined during that iteration, or it must not be defined or become undefined during any other iteration.
- A variable that is defined or becomes undefined by more than one iteration becomes undefined when the loop terminates.
- An allocatable object that is allocated in more than one iteration must be subsequently deallocated during the same iteration in which it was allocated.
- An object that is allocated or deallocated in only one iteration must not be referenced, allocated, deallocated, defined, or become undefined in a different iteration.
- A pointer that is referenced in an iteration must have been pointer associated previously during that iteration, or it must not have its pointer association changed during any iteration.
- A pointer that has its pointer association changed in more than one iteration has an association status of undefined when the construct terminates.
- An input/output statement must not write data to a file record or position in one iteration and read from the same record or position in a different iteration.
- Records written by output statements in the range of the loop to a sequential-access file appear in the file in an indeterminate order.

The restrictions on referencing variables defined in an iteration of a DO CONCURRENT construct also apply to any procedure invoked within the loop.

These restrictions ensure no interdependencies occur that might affect code optimizations.

Note that if compiler option -parallel (Linux and OS X) or /Qparallel (Windows) is specified, the compiler will attempt to parallelize the construct, otherwise no performance benefit will come from use of this construct instead of a simple DO loop.

DO CONCURRENT vs. FOR ALL

We've seen DO CONCURRENT referred to as "FORALL done right." The problem with FORALL was its semantics as a series of array assignments that had to be executed one after the other. Unfortunately, many people thought of FORALL as a "parallel DO," which it was not, and it proved to be difficult to parallelize effectively. DO CONCURRENT is much simpler and specifies that each instance of the DO body can be executed in any order. The Intel compiler will try to parallelize DO CONCURRENT when the compiler "parallel" option is specified.

The statements within the DO CONCURRENT are executed in order, in each iteration, but there is no dependence on other iterations. FORALL could have array assignments only, but each assignment needed to be completed by all iterations before the next one executed, effectively creating a "wait for all" after each assignment. The initial idea of FORALL was to help with parallelization, but like a lot of High-Performance Fortran, the obsolete variant from which FORALL comes, it was not well thought through and parallelization was much more difficult than it seemed it would be at the time to many.

DO CONCURRENT vs. OpenMP "Parallel"

DO CONCURRENT is roughly equivalent to OMP PARALLEL used with a DO statement. The biggest difference in practice seems to be the lack of an explicit way to create private copies of variables within the loop when using `DO CONCURRENT` unless your Fortran compiler also supports the `BLOCK` construct from the Fortran 2008 standard. Since Fortran 2008 remains a standard with very uneven support in the industry, the use of OpenMP instead is likely to be preferred. Intel's support of Fortran 2008 is fairly complete by industry standards, but lacks the `BLOCK` construct support as of this book being published. It is reasonable to expect this will be implement by Intel and others, and then `DO CONCURRENT` offers a Fortran-specific language method to declare concurrency that should be attractive. The decision, by Intel, to map "do concurrent" on top of OpenMP and thereby have a consistent method to control affinity, number of threads used, and so on, is a decision that hopefully other compilers will follow as well.

Intel® TBB

Intel Threading Building Blocks is a widely used and highly portable template library that provides a comprehensive set of solutions to program using tasks in C++. It also provides a set of supporting functionality that can be used with or without the tasking infrastructure, such as concurrency-safe STL-compatible data structures, memory allocation, and portable atomics. Although we focus on tasks in this book due to their increased machine independence, safety, and scalability over threads, TBB also implements a significant subset of the C++11 standard's thread support, including platform-independent mutexes and condition variables. Much more information is available at http://threadingbuildingblocks.org.

Like Cilk Plus and OpenMP, use of TBB as a threading model must exist only in a single memory space. Any use TBB on a given coprocessor will only influence tasks and threading on the same coprocessor, and any use on the host (processor[s] with shared memory between them) will apply only to the host processor(s). An offload directive (see Chapter 7) can invoke TBB and such actions will impact only where the offload is executed. Since offload regions can potentially be run on the host (if no coprocessor is available), this can be a little confusing or very convenient if you have the right mindset.

"Intel Threading Building Blocks" is a book that introduces TBB and provides many examples. The book predates lambdas and a number of additional advanced features of TBB. The documentation that accompanies TBB (http://threadingbuildingblocks.org) is exceptional, and a reliable source of current information on all the features of the latest TBB.

TBB is a collection of components that outfits C++ for parallel programming. Figure 6.1 illustrates these components. At the heart of TBB is a task scheduler that is most often used indirectly via the parallel algorithms in TBB, such as `tbb::parallel_for`. The rest of TBB provides thread-aware memory allocation, portable synchronization primitives, scalable containers (thread safe versions of key STL containers), and a variety of useful utilities. Each part is important for parallelism. Indeed the non-tasking features are intended for use with other parallelism frameworks like Cilk Plus and OpenMP, so that those frameworks do not have to duplicate key functionality.

TBB shares many of the key attributes of Cilk Plus but it differs from Cilk Plus on several points:

- TBB is designed to work without any compiler changes, and thus be quickly portable to new platforms. As a result, TBB has been ported to a multitude of key operating systems and processors, and code written with TBB can likewise be easily ported.

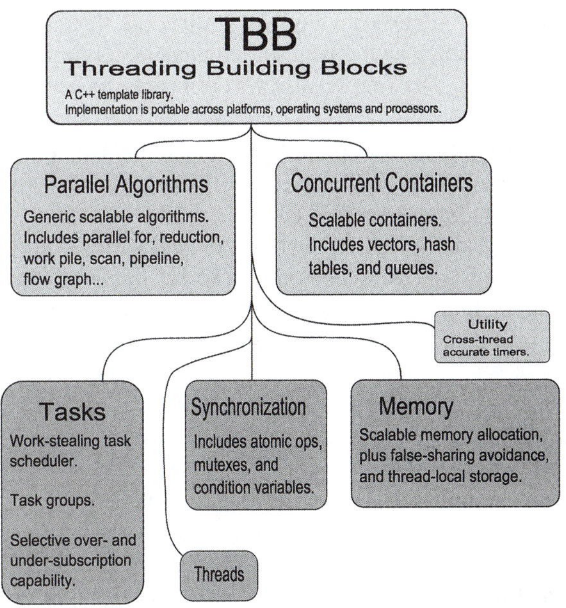

FIGURE 6.1

Overview of Threading Building Blocks.

- As a consequence of avoiding any need for compiler support, TBB does not have direct support for vector parallelism. However, TBB combined with array notation or #pragma simd from Cilk Plus or auto-vectorization can be an effective tool for exploiting both thread and vector parallelism.
- TBB is designed to provide comprehensive support for C++ developers in one package. It supports multiple paradigms of parallel programming. It goes beyond the strict fork-join model of Cilk Plus by supporting pipelines, dataflow, and unstructured task graphs. The additional power of these features bring is sometimes worth the additional complexity they bring to a program.
- TBB is intended to provide low-level services such as memory allocation and atomic operations that can be used by programs using other frameworks, including Cilk Plus.

TBB is an active open source project. It is widely adopted and often cited in articles about parallelism in C++. It continues to grow as the parallel ecosystem evolves.

History

TBB was first available as a commercial library from Intel in the summer of 2006, not long after Intel shipped its first dual-core processors. It provided a much needed comprehensive answer to the question "what must be fixed or added to C++ for parallel programming." TBB's key programming abstractions for parallelism focused on logical specification of parallelism via algorithm templates. By also including a taskstealing scheduler, a thread-aware memory allocator, portable mutexes, global timestamps and concurrent containers, TBB provided what was needed to program for parallelism in C++. The first release was primarily focused on strict fork/join or loop-type data parallelism.

The success of Intel TBB would, however, have been limited if it had remained a proprietary solution. Even during the release of v1.0, Intel was in discussions with early customers on the future direction of TBB in both features and licensing.

Watching and listening to early adopters, such as Autodesk Maya, highlighted that much of the value of TBB was not only for data parallelism but also for more general parallelism using tasks, pipelines, scalable memory allocation, and lower-level constructs like synchronization primitives. Intel also received encouragement to make TBB portable by creating and supporting it via an open source project.

This customer feedback and encouragement led, only a year later, to version 2.0, which included a GPL v2 with the runtime exception version of both the source and binaries, as well as maintaining the availability of non-GPL binaries. Customers had said that this would maximize adoption, and the results have definitely shown they were right.

Intel increased the staffing on TBB, worked proactively to build a community to support the project, and continued to innovate with new usage models and features over the next few years. We have been amazed and humbled by the response of customers like Adobe Systems, Avid, Epic Games, DreamWorks, and many others, along with that of our community members. TBB now has a very large user community, and has had contributions that have led to Intel TBB being ported to many operating systems, platforms and processors. We appreciate Intel's willingness to let us prove that an open source project initiated by Intel, yet supporting non-x86 processors, not only made sense—but would be very popular with developers. We've definitely proven that!

Through the involvement of customers and community, TBB has grown to be the most feature-rich and comprehensive solution for parallel application development available today. It has also become the most popular!

The TBB project was grown by a steady addition of ports to a wide variety of machines and operating systems, and the addition of numerous new features that have added to the applicability and power of TBB.

TBB was one of the inspirations for Microsoft's Task Parallel Library (TPL) for .NET and Microsoft's Parallel Patterns Library (PPL) for C++. Intel and Microsoft have worked jointly to specify and implement a common subset of functionality shared by TBB and Microsoft's Parallel Patterns Library (PPL). In some cases, Intel and Microsoft have exchanged implementations and tests to ensure compatibility. An appendix of *The TBB Reference Manual* summarizes the common subset.

TBB 4.0 added a powerful capability for expressing parallelism as data flowing through a graph. Support for Intel Xeon Phi coprocessors started use a couple years before the launch of the coprocessor. Use of TBB continues to grow, and the open source project enjoys serious support from Intel and others.

The Intel Cilk Plus project complements TBB by supplying C interfaces, simpler syntax, better opportunity for compiler optimization, and data parallel operations that lead to effective vectorization. None of these are possible without direct compiler support. Intel briefly considered calling Cilk Plus simply "compiled TBB." While this conveyed the desire to extend TBB for the objectives mentioned, it proved complicated to explain the name so the name Cilk Plus was introduced. The full interoperability between TBB and Cilk Plus increases the number of options for software developers without adding complications. Like TBB, Intel has open sourced Cilk Plus to help encourage adoption and contribution to the project. TBB and Cilk Plus are sister projects at Intel.

Using TBB

Include the header `<tbb/tbb.h>` to use TBB in a source file. All public identifiers are in namespace `tbb` or `tbb::flow`. In the following descriptions, the phrase "in parallel" indicates that parallelism is permitted if resources allow, but is not mandated. As with Cilk Plus, the license to ignore unnecessary parallelism enables the TBB task scheduler to use parallelism efficiently.

parallel_for

The function template `parallel_for` maps a functor across range of values. The template takes several forms. The simplest is:

```
tbb::parallel_for(first,last,f )
```

where *f* is a functor. It evaluates the expression *f* (*i*) in parallel for all *i* in the half-open interval [*first*,*last*), Both *first* and *last* must be of the same integral type. It is a parallel equivalent of:

```
for (auto i = first; i < last; ++i) f(i);
```

A slight variation specifies a stride:

```
tbb::parallel_for(first,last,stride,f )
```

It is like the previous version, except that the possible values of *i* step by *stride*, starting with *first*. This form is a parallel equivalent of:

```
for (auto i = first; i < last; i+ = stride ) f(i);
```

Another form of `parallel_for` takes two arguments:

```
tbb::parallel_for(range,f)
```

It decomposes *range* into subranges and applies *f* to each subrange, in parallel. Hence the programmer has the opportunity to optimize *f* to operate on an entire subrange instead of a single index. This version in effect exposes the tiled implementation of the map pattern used by TBB.

This form of parallel for also generalizes the parallel map pattern beyond onedimensional ranges. The argument *range* can be any *recursively splittable range* type.

blocked_range

The most commonly used recursive range is `tbb::blocked_range`. It is typically used with integral types or random-access iterator types. For example, `blocked_range<int>(0,8)` represents the index range {0, 1, 2, 3, 4, 5, 6, 7}. An optional third argument called the *grainsize* specifies the maximum size for splitting. It defaults to 1. For example, the following snippet splits a range of size 30 with grainsize 20 into two indivisible subranges of size 15:

```
// Construct half -open
interval [0,30) with grainsize of 20
blocked_range<int> r(0,30,20); assert(r.is_divisible());

// Call splitting constructor
blocked_range<int> s(r);
// Now r = [0,15) and s = [15,30) and both have a grainsize 20
// inherited from the original value of r.
assert(!r.is_divisible()); assert(!s.is_divisible());
```

There is a two-dimensional variant called `tbb::blocked_range2d`. It permits the use of a single `parallel_for` to iterate over two dimensions at once, which sometimes yields better cache behavior than nesting two one-dimensional instances of `parallel_for`.

Partitioners

The range form of `parallel_for` takes an optional *partitioner* argument, which lets the programmer specify performance-related tactics. The argument can have one of three types:

- *auto partitioner.* The runtime will try to subdivide the range sufficiently to balance load, but no further. This behavior is the same as when no partitioner is specified.
- *simple partitioner.* The runtime must subdivide the range into subranges as finely as possible; that is method `is_divisible` will be false for the final subranges.
- *affinity partitioner.* Request that the assignment of subranges to underlying threads be similar to a previous invocation of `parallel_for` or `parallel_reduce` with the same `affinity_partitioner` object.

These partitioners also work with `parallel_reduce`. An invocation of `parallel_for` with a `simple_partitioner` looks like:

```
parallel_for(r,f,simple_partitioner());
```

This partitioner is useful in two scenarios:

- The functor *f* uses a fixed amount of memory for temporary storage, and hence cannot deal with subranges of arbitrary size. For example, if *r* is a `blocked_range` the partitioner guarantees that *f* is invoked on subranges not exceeding the grainsize of *r*.
- The work for *f* (*r*) is highly unbalanced in a way that fools the `auto_partitioner` heuristic into not dividing work finely enough to balance load.

An `affinity_partitioner` can be used for cache-fusion. Unlike the other two partitioners, it carries state. The state holds information for replaying the assignment of subranges to threads. Figure 6.2 shows an example of its use in a common pattern—serially iterating a map. In the listing, variable *ap* enables cache fusion of each map to the next map. Because it is carrying information between serial iterations, it must be declared outside the serial loop. TBB uses the variable *ap* to remember on which threads ran which subranges of the previous invocation of `parallel_for`,

```
void relax(
  double* a,  // pointer to array of data
  double* b,  // pointer to temporary storage
  size_t n,      // number of data elements
  int iterations // number of serial iterations
) {
  assert(iterations%2==0);
  //  Partitioner should be declared outside the loop .
  tbb::affinity_partitioner ap;
  //  Serial loop around a parallel loop .
  for( size_t t=0; t<iterations; ++t ) {
    tbb::parallel_for(
      tbb::blocked_range<size_t>(1,n-1),
        [=]( tbb::blocked_range<size_t> r ) {
          size_t e = r.end();
 #pragma simd
          for( size_t i=r.begin(); i<e; ++i )
            b[i] = (a[i-1]+a[i]+a[i+1])*(1/3.0);
        },
        ap);
    std::swap(a,b);
  }
}
```

FIGURE 6.2

Example of `affinity_partitioner`.

and biases execution toward replaying that assignment. The `pragma simd` is for showmanship. It makes the impact of the partitioner more dramatic, by raising arithmetic speed so that memory bandwidth becomes the limiting resource.

parallel_reduce

Function template `parallel_reduce` performs a reduction over a recursive range. It has several forms. The form used in this book is:

```
T result =
tbb::parallel_reduce(range,identity,subrange reduction,combine);
```

where:

- *range* is a recursive range as for `parallel_for`, such as `blocked_range`.

- *identity* is the identity element of type *T*. The type of this argument determines the type used to accumulate the reduction value, so be careful about what type it has.
- *subrange reduction* is a functor such that *subrange reduction*(*subrange*,*init*) returns a reduction value over *init* and *subrange*. The type of *subrange* is the type of the *range* argument to parallel_reduce. The type of *init* is *T*, and the returned reduction value must be convertible to type *T*. Do not forget to include the contribution of *init* to the reduction value.
- *combine* is a functor such that *combine*(*x, y*) that takes two arguments of type *T* and returns a reduction value for them. This function must be *associative* but does not need to be *commutative*.

An alternative way to do reduction is via class `tbb::enumerable_thread_specific`. General advice on which to use:

- If type *T* takes little space and is cheap to copy, or the reduction operation is noncommutative, use `parallel_reduce`.
- If type *T* is large and expensive to copy and the reduction operation is commutative, use `enumerable_thread_specific`.

parallel_invoke

Template function `parallel_invoke` evaluates a fixed set of functors in parallel. For example:

```
tbb::parallel_invoke(f,g,h);
```

evaluates the expressions `f()`, `g()`, and `h()` in parallel and waits until they all complete. Anywhere from 2 to 10 functors are currently supported. The `task_group` class allows an arbitrary number of functors to be run in parallel.

Notes on C++11

Though TBB works fine with C++98, it is simpler to use with C++11. In particular, C++11 introduces lambda expressions and auto declarations that simplify use of TBB and other template libraries. Lambda expressions are already implemented in the latest versions of major C++ compilers. We strongly recommend using them to teach, learn, and use TBB, because once you get past the novelty, they make TBB code easier to write and easier to read.

Additionally, TBB implements most of some C++11 features related to threading, thus giving you an immediate migration path for taking advantage of these features even before they are implemented by C++ compilers. This path is further simplified by the way that TBB's injection of these features into namespace `std` is optional. These features are:

- `std::mutex` A mutex with a superset of the C++11 interface. The superset includes TBB's interface for mutexes.
- `std::lock guard` C++11 support for exception-safe scoped locking.
- `std::thread` A way to create a thread and wait for it to complete. Sometimes threads really are a better solution than tasks, particularly if the "work" must be preemptively scheduled or mostly involves waiting for something to happen. Also, note that threads provide mandatory

parallelism, which may be important when interacting with the outside world or in a user interface. Tasks provide optional parallelism, which is better for efficient computation.

- `std::condition variable` A way to wait until state protected by a mutex meets a condition.

The parts of the C++11 interface not implemented in TBB are those that involve time intervals, since those would have involved implementing the C++11 time facilities. However, TBB does have equivalents to this functionality, based on TBB's existing `tick_count` interface for time.

A condition variable solves the problem of letting a thread wait until state protected by a mutex meets a condition. It is used when threads need to wait for some other thread to update some state protected by a mutex. The waiting thread(s) acquire the mutex, check the state, and decide whether to wait. They wait on an associated condition variable. The wait member function atomically releases the mutex and starts the wait. Another thread acquires mutex associated with the condition, modifies state protected by the mutex; then it signals one or all of the waiter(s) when it is done. Once the mutex is released, the waiters reacquire the mutex and can recheck the state to see if they can proceed or need to continue waiting.

Condition variables should be the method of choice to have a thread wait until a condition changes. TBB makes this method of choice portable to more operating systems.

TBB summary

TBB is a powerful solution for C++ programmers to address tasking in general, and a number of related C++ issues like thread-aware memory allocation, thread safe versions of key STL container classes, portable locks and atomics, and timing solutions. We have scratched the surface in terms of TBB capabilities here to offer a place to begin. We recommend the book *Intel Threading Building Blocks* and the online documentation as ways to learn more. If being C++ specific is useful, then TBB certainly will be an excellent choice.

Cilk Plus

Cilk (pronounced "silk") started as a linguistic and runtime technology for algorithmic multithreaded programming developed at MIT. Its philosophical approach is that a programmer should concentrate on structuring programs to expose parallelism and exploit locality while leaving a runtime system to be responsible for scheduling computations to run efficiently on a given platform. The Cilk runtime system takes care of details like load balancing, synchronization, and communication protocols. Unique to Cilk, the runtime system guarantees efficient and predictable performance and also guarantees bounds on stack size. MIT licensed Cilk technology to Cilk Arts, Inc. of Lexington, MA, a venture-funded start-up founded by Professor Charles E. Leiserson and Matteo Frigo, which later transitioned to Intel where former Cilk Art developers added the technology to the Intel compilers. Additionally, Intel extended the task-oriented solutions of Cilk with vector solutions and released an open specification with the name Cilk Plus, shown in Figure 6.3, and their implementation in the Intel compilers known as Intel Cilk Plus. Intel has also open-sourced their Cilk Plus runtime, which will enable additional compilers to implement the specification more easily. The specification is portable across platforms, operating systems, and processors.

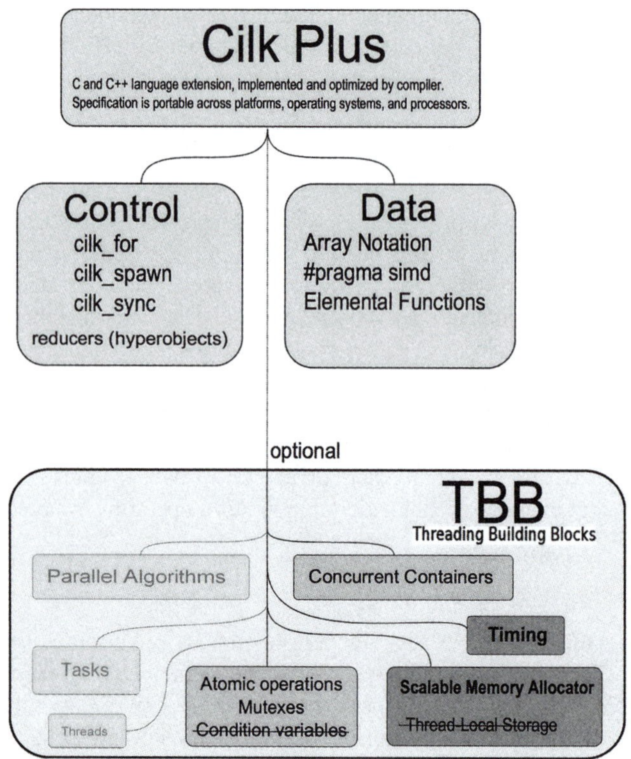

FIGURE 6.3

Cilk Plus with the optional ability to utilize features in TBB. Darker TBB boxes have proven to be the most commonly utilized by Cilk Plus users. The crossed-out portions of TBB carry risks that require understanding.

The original Cilk home at the Massachusetts Institute of Technology (MIT) continues to maintain useful samples, tutorials and papers about Cilk. Visiting it at http://supertech.csail.mit.edu is recommended to learn more about Cilk. Intel and the related open source project for Cilk Plus maintain http://cilkplus.org.

Cilk Plus is distinguished by its focus on minimal but sufficient support for parallelism in C and C++. It is easy to learn, able to support sophisticated debugging tools, and provides guarantees that bound stack usage. Cilk Plus does this while also scaling to high degrees of thread *and* vector parallelism. Cilk Plus seeks to address shortcomings of a template library approach (as used by TBB) to provide:

- Usability in C, not just C++
- Support for vector parallelism
- Serial elision; a Cilk Plus program that is run with one thread behaves as if the Cilk Plus keywords are replaced with standard C/C++
- A parallel structure to the compiler at a higher level than a template library, which enables more optimization opportunities

These items require compiler support and are therefore beyond the scope of a template library such as TBB.

History

The Cilk language has been developed since 1994 at the MIT Laboratory for Computer Science. It is based on ANSI C, with the addition of just a handful of Cilk-specific keywords.

Cilk is a faithful extension of C and the serial elision of any well-defined Cilk program is always a valid serial implementation in C that matches the semantics of the parallel Cilk program. Despite several similarities, Cilk is not directly related to AT&T Bell Labs' Concurrent C.

In the original MIT Cilk implementation, the first Cilk keyword was cilk, which identified a function as written in Cilk. This keyword was needed to distinguish Cilk code from C code, because in the original implementation, Cilk procedures could call C procedures directly, but C procedures could not directly call or spawn Cilk procedures.

A commercial version of Cilk, called Cilk++, that supported C++ and was compatible with both GCC and Microsoft C++ compilers, was developed by Cilk Arts, Inc. The cilk keyword morphed into extern "Cilk". Cilk++ introduced the notion of hyperobjects [FHLLB09], which elegantly eliminated the need for several keywords in the original Cilk pertaining to reductions.

In July 2009, Intel Corporation acquired, from Cilk Arts, the Cilk++ technology and the Cilk trademark. In 2010, Intel released a commercial implementation in its compilers combined with some data parallel constructs, under the name Intel Cilk Plus. Intel has also released specifications, libraries, code and the free ability to use the "Cilk Plus" name (trademark) with other implementations.

Intel Cilk Plus extends Cilk and Cilk++ by adding array extensions, being incorporated in a commercial compiler (from Intel), and having compatibility with existing debuggers. Intel Cilk Plus adopted a significant simplication proposed by Cilk++ team: eliminate the need to distingush Cilk linkage from C/C++ linkage. This was a major improvement in usability, particularly for highly templated libraries, where linkage specifications can become confusing or impossible. Furthermore, erasing the distinction between Cilk and C/C++ functions enabled C/C++ functions to be spawned directly.

Intel has published both a language specification and an ABI specification to enable other compilers to implement Cilk Plus in a compatible way and to optionally utilize the Intel runtime. The Cilk Plus extensions to C and C++ have also been implemented in a branch version of the GCC compiler.

Intel has stated its desire to refine Cilk Plus and to enable it to be implemented by other compilers to gain industry wide adoption.

Borrowing components from TBB

Cilk Plus does not duplicate functionality that can be borrowed from TBB. You are encouraged to use components of TBB that are orthogonal to expression of parallelism. These components of TBB include the scalable memory allocator and `tick_count` timing facility. Some portions of TBB are okay to use, but are not the Cilk Plus ideal because they break determinism or greedy scheduling theory. These include mutexes, atomic objects, and concurrent containers. For these, it is generally better to consider alternative solutions based on Cilk Plus hyperobjects to get the benefits of determinism. The parallel algorithms and tasks in TBB can interoperate with Cilk Plus, but using them instead of Cilk Plus forgoes the key value proposition of Cilk Plus. Hyperobjects are usually an excellent alternative to thread-local storage.

Loaning components to TBB

The Cilk Plus features for vector parallelism (array notations and `#pragma simd`) are an excellent way to exploit vector parallelism in a TBB programs, even if the tasking model supported by Cilk Plus is not used. Note that if you express vector parallelism using only elemental functions and the `#pragma simd`, the code will still be portable to other compilers, since ignoring these constructs still gives the expected result.

Keyword spelling

This book's spelling of the keywords requires inclusion of the header `<cilk/cilk.h>`, which has:

```
#define cilk_spawn _Cilk_spawn
#define cilk_sync _Cilk_sync
#define cilk_for _Cilk_for
```

The compiler recognizes only the keywords on the right because new keywords by a compiler are limited, by convention and standards, to names beginning with an underscore followed by an uppercase letter. Such symbols are reserved to compiler implementers and should never cause a conflict with application code. The header provides more aesthetically pleasing spellings. Including the `<cilk/cilk_stub.h>` header file converts a program to its serial elision by defining:

```
#define _Cilk_spawn
#define _Cilk_sync
#define _Cilk_for     for
```

These substitutions revert a program to a serial program that can be compiled by any C++ compiler. The resulting code will behave just like a Cilk Plus program running on a single thread.

cilk_for

A `cilk_for` (see Figure 6.4) is a direct replacement for the `for` keyword with a few critical differences in semantics and rules for usage:

- Use of `cilk_for` allows iterations to run in parallel, even if there are dependencies that would have forbidden it for the regular `for` loop.

```
// cilk_for ( initialization;  condition;  increment )
body
cilk_for (int  i=ivalue; i<limit; ++i)  {
  a[i] =  foo(b[i],c[i]) *  3.0;
}
```

FIGURE 6.4

Sample Usage of `cilk_for`.

- Control may not be explicitly transferred out of the body or into it. In particular, return and break are prohibited. A `goto` must not jump from inside the body to outside of it, or vice versa. However, control may be implicitly transferred out of the body by an exception. In that case, which other iterations execute depends on the implementation, and might not be deterministic. The exception thrown from the `cilk_for` is the same as the serial elision would have thrown, even if multiple iterations throw.
- The *initialization* shall declare or initialize a single variable only. This is called the *control variable*. In C, the *control variable* may be declared outside the `cilk_for` loop. In C++, the *initialization* must declare the control variable. The variable cannot be declared `const` or `volatile`.
- The control variable may not be modified within the loop body.
- The *increment* must have one of the following forms: `i++`, `++i`, `i--`, `-I`, `i += step` or `i -= step`, where `i` stands for the control variable, and `step` can be any loop invariant expression.
- The *condition* must consist of the control variable *i* compared with another expression, which we will call the `limit`. The comparison can be =>, >, <=, <, != or ==.
- The `step` (if any) and `limit` expressions must not be modified within the loop body. This is so that the number of iterations can be computed correctly before any iteration commences. For C programs, the value of the control variable, if declared outside the loop, has the same value after a `cilk_for` loop as it would have after a for loop.
- The Cilk Plus Language Specification at http://cilkplus.org can be consulted for some of the finer details or more precise descriptions.

cilk_spawn and cilk_sync

The `cilk_spawn` keyword specifies that the caller of a function may continue to run without waiting for called function to return (see Figure 6.5).

Execution of a statement with the `cilk_spawn` keyword is called a *spawn*. The function, try block or `cilk_for` body that contains the spawn is called the *spawning block*. Note that compound statements containing a spawn are *not* spawning blocks unless they fit one of the categories above.

Execution of a `cilk_sync` statement is called a *sync*. A sync waits only for spawns that have occurred in the same spawning block and has no effect on spawns done by other tasks, done by other threads, nor those done prior to entering the current spawning block. An implicit sync occurs when exiting the enclosing spawning block. Thus when a spawning block completes, any parallelism that it created is finished. This property simplifies reasoning about program

```
// simple functional call
cilk_spawn bar(1);
// lambdas allowed
cilk_spawn []{ bar(2); }();
// results allowed
result = cilk_spawn bar(4);
// innermost call completes before spawn
result = cilk_spawn bar( bar(9) );
// spawn not used , no need, potentially wasteful
bar(5);
// wait for all spawns
cilk_sync;
```

FIGURE 6.5

Examples of Using `cilk_spawn` and `cilk_sync`.

composition and correspondence with its serial elision. The following snippet illustrates some of these points:

```
void foo() {
  for (int i = 0; i<3; ++i) {
    cilk_spawn bar(i);
    if (i%2) cilk_sync;
  }
  // implicit cilk sync
}
```

The snippet has one spawning block: the function body. The body of the `for` loop is *not* a spawning block because it is not the body of a function, try block, or `cilk_for`. The code operates thusly:

1. Spawn bar(0) and bar(1).
2. Execute a sync that waits for the spawned calls.
3. Spawn bar(2)
4. Execute the implicit `cilk_sync`.

The scope of the explicit sync is dynamic, not lexical. It applies to all prior spawns by the current invocation of `foo()`, since that is the innermost spawning block.

Jumping into, or out of, a spawning block results in undefined behavior. This includes use of `goto`, `setjmp`, and `longjmp`. "Undefined behavior" is a term of art in language specifications that means *anything* could happen, including crashing your program or turning your computer into a frog. You have been warned.

Behavior is defined if a spawned function throws an exception and does not catch it. The exception is rethrown when execution leaves the corresponding sync. If there are multiple such exceptions for the sync, the sync rethrows the exception that the serial elision would have thrown. The extra exceptions are destroyed without being caught.

Reducers (Hyperobjects)

Hyperobjects enable multiple strands of execution to operate in parallel on the same logical object, without locking, yet get the same result as the serial elision would get. Furthermore, hyperobjects avoid contention bottlenecks, because parallel strands get separate local views of the logical object.

A *reducer* is a hyperobject intended for doing reductions. Cilk Plus reducers work for any operation that can be reassociated. Cilk Plus predefines reducers for common associative operations including min, max, addition, subtraction, bitwise AND/OR/XOR, string concatenation and reducer version of `std::ostream`. C++ and C syntax formats are supported.

Array notation and elemental functions

Cilk Plus extends C and C++ with array notation and elemental functions, which lets the programmer specify array sections, operations on array sections and scalar operations to be applied on vectors. These are part of Cilk Plus to enable vector programming, and are therefore covered in Chapter 5.

Cilk Plus summary

Cilk Plus is a language specification that provides for both thread and vector parallelism in C and C++ via keywords, syntax for array operations, elemental functions, and pragmas. Much more information is available at http://cilkplus.org.

Summary

Intel Xeon Phi coprocessors have many cores, which in turn offer a high ability for parallel execution. Feeding them is important in order to see the potential of these coprocessors. The rich environment of options available for programming processors and coprocessors alike offer the ability to program in a consistent and effective style that spans processors and coprocessors. Our recommendation is to utilize OpenMP, Fortran 2008, TBB, Cilk Plus, or MKL; but other viable options including OpenCL and pthreads exist. Even with new entries, we expect OpenMP, Fortran 2008, TBB, Cilk Plus, and MKL to remain the best options for effective scaling in terms of giving both short term benefits and holding up well over time.

If you have any doubts about the need to abandon threads in programming in favor of tasks, "The Problem with Threads" is recommended reading. We think of it as a modern version of the classic "Go To Statement Considered Harmful" which is so commonly accepted today that it is hard to recall the controversy the "Go To" paper raised for more than a decade after its publication. Programming with threads will go the way of "Go To" and these are the key papers that are explain the need for change.

With the foundations of vectorization and tasking to give work for our coprocessors, the next chapter discusses applying the techniques for vectorization and scaling (Chapters 5 and 6) in

Offload mode (Chapter 7). In Chapter 11, we discuss applying MKL. In Chapter 12, we discuss MPI that can combine with all the techniques of the prior chapters.

For more information

Here are some additional reading materials we recommend on various threading models.

- Intel online product documentation: http://tinyurl.com/inteldocs
- Intel Threading Building Blocks: http://opentbb.org
- Intel Cilk Plus: http://cilkplus.org
- M.I.T. Cilk: http://supertech.csail.mit.edu
- Fortran 2008: http://fortranwiki.org
- OpenMP: http://openmp.org
- James Reinders. *Intel Threading Building Blocks*. O'Reilly & Associates, Inc., Sebastopol, CA, USA, first edition, 2007.
- Michael McCool, Arch Robison, James Reinders, *Structured Parallel Programming: Patterns for Efficient Computation*, Morgan Kaufmann Publishers Inc., San Francisco, CA, USA, 2012.
- Michael J. Quinn. *Parallel Programming in C with MPI and OpenMP*. McGraw-Hill Education Group, 2003.
- Edward A. Lee. *The problem with threads*. Technical Report UCB/EECS-2006-1, EECS Department, University of California, Berkeley, Jan 2006. A published version of this paper is in IEEE Computer 39(5):33–42, May 2006.
- Edsger Dijkstra (March 1968). "Go To Statement Considered Harmful" (PDF). Communications of the ACM 11 (3): 147–148.

CHAPTER

Offload

7

Offload refers to writing a program from the point of view of running on processor(s) and offloading work from the host to one or more coprocessors. Execution begins on the host and, based on user-defined code, some sections are offloaded to the coprocessor, if present, or run on the host if not. A key feature of offload is that the resulting binary runs whether or not a coprocessor is present (unless you choose to use `#pragma offload target(mic:coproc-num` or `_Cilk_offload_to)` to specify that a coprocessor is required.)

Offloading could simply be thought of an inline code that may be run on a coprocessor, as shown in Figure 7.1.

When needed, the compiler produces the required activity to copy data to the memory for the coprocessor, run the code on the coprocessor, and then copy the results back to the memory for the processor.

This simplistic use will work, but performance may be limited by the lack of any concurrency between the processor and coprocessor as well as the implied movement of data before and after the offloaded code. In order to control the movement of data, many additional controls are available and are important to understand if programming using offload appeals to you. It's these "extras" that make this worthy of a full chapter.

Offload can be a good programming approach as long as the code spends a lot of time doing computation without I/O, the computationally intensive portion of the code and the data on which it works is relatively easy to encapsulate, the computation time is substantially higher than the data transfer time (that is, N^2 computation for N data), and the data fits in coprocessor memory or can be partitioned for coprocessor memory. The best fits also have the ability to structure computation and data so that multiple agents can perform computations and data transfer asynchronously especially to overlap them.

```
// code running on processor
foo(9);
x[i] = 9;
#pragma offload target(mic)
  foo(1202); // runs on the coprocessor
bar(19); // back on the processor
```

FIGURE 7.1

Running Code on a Processor and Offloading to a Coprocessor.

Two offload models

A number of offload controls and features are needed because the host and the coprocessor do not share common system memory. This leads to the need to move data back and forth between the host and the coprocessor.

The compiler supports two distinct programming models, which differ in their approach to dealing with the lack of shared system memory, the *non-shared memory model* and the *virtual-shared memory model.* You can use both models of offloading in a single program. However, the data manipulated by the two models should be distinct. Table 7.1 provides a comparison of the offload options.

In both models, specifying that something should run on the coprocessor does not guarantee that it will. The availability of an Intel® Xeon Phi™ coprocessor at the offload point determines if the offload succeeds. When an offload fails, the construct will execute on the host instead. This fallback, and the shared programming models between coprocessors and processors, makes portable programming a straightforward effort.

Table 7.1 Comparison of the Two Offload Models

	Pragma Offload	**Shared VM Model**
Programming languages	Fortran, C, C++ (C++ functions may be called, but C++ classes cannot be transferred)	C, C++

Syntax	C/C++:
	`#pragma offload in C/C++`
	Fortran:
	`!dir$ omp offload`
	More details in Tables 7.4 and 7.5.
		`_Cilk_shared _Cilk_offload`
		More details in Tables 7.7 and 7.8.

Used for	Offloads that transfer contiguous blocks of data back and forth with complete user control.	Offloads that transfer all or parts of complex data structures, or many small pieces of data, on demand (no explicit controls)
Offloaded data allowed	Scalars, arrays, bit-wise structures that can be copied. No simple way to offload non-sequence derived types.	All data types (pointer-based data, structures, classes, locks, and so on.)
When data movement occurs	User has explicit control of data movement at start of each offload directive	`_Cilk_shared` data synchronized on demand inside `_Cilk_offload` statements
When offload code is copied to coprocessor	At first offload pragma or directive	At program start-up.
Function and variables available	All functions and variables are available on host processor(s) always.	
	Only functions and variables are available on coprocessors only if marked `using an offload` pragma, attribute or directive	Only functions and variables are available on coprocessors only if marked `_Cilk_offload` or `_Cilk_shared`.
Performance	Offers the highest performance of the two offload models, because no overhead from software coherency will occur.	Offers convenience (software coherency) that imposes some overhead.

Choosing offload vs. native execution

When to choose to use an Offload model vs. a Native Execution model is likely to be a lively debate for some time. We can offer some insight into the key criteria to consider. If you are using MPI, you should read Chapter 12 for insights for choosing Offload vs. Native modes while using MPI. Offload is most appropriate when the program cannot be made highly parallel consistently throughout most of the application:

- I/O intensive codes that have hot computational sections. The host best handles I/O.
- Large complex applications with a reasonably small number of hotspots such as compute phases or computational time-intensive filters or effects modules. Note that the computation in the offload has to justify the data transfer costs.
- Programs with memory needs that are two high where offloading computational kernels can be done with more bounded memory needs.

Native is good for programs that are largely doing operations that map to parallelism either in threads or vectors, and are not doing significant amounts of I/O or serial execution.

Offload has some additional concerns. Asynchronous allocation, copies, and deallocation of data are possible with asynchronous offload execution. Another challenge of offloading is that it requires two levels of memory blocking: one to fit the input data into the coprocessor, and another within the offload code to fit within the processor caches and not oversaturate the processor memory subsystem when all cores are busy.

Non-shared memory model: using offload pragmas/directives

A non-shared memory model uses the `offload` pragma or directives, and other pragmas or directives with the prefix `offload_`. This model is appropriate for dealing with flat data structures such as scalars, arrays, and structs that are bit-wise copyable (do not contain pointers, and does not invoke constructors or destructors). Data in this model is copied back and forth between the processor and the coprocessor around regions of offloaded code. The data selected for transfer is a combination of variables implicitly transferred because they are lexically referenced within offload constructs, and variables explicitly listed in clauses in the pragma. C/C++ simple offload is done via `#pragma offload target(mic)` while Fortran simple offload is done via `!dir$ offload target(mic)`.

Shared virtual memory model: using offload with shared VM

A shared virtual memory (VM) model is integrated with the Intel® Cilk™ Plus and uses `_Cilk_shared` and `_Cilk_offload` keywords for C/C++ programming. There is no Fortran support for this shared virtual memory offload model. In this model, variables that need to be shared between processor(s) and coprocessor(s) are marked `_Cilk_shared`; such variables can then be used in both host and coprocessor code. Dynamically allocated memory you wish to share must be allocated with special functions: `_Offload_shared_malloc`, `_Offload_shared_aligned_malloc`, `_Offload_shared_free`, and `_Offload_shared_aligned_free`. The compiler and runtime automatically maintains coherence at the beginning and end of offload statements. Only modified data is transferred when using this model.

This model is appropriate for dealing with complex pointer-based data structures, such as linked lists, trees, and the like. This model uses a software implementation of virtual memory that is shared between the host processor and the coprocessor. Code looks like

```
_Cilk_shared double foo;
```

and

```
_Cilk_offload func(y);
```

Shared Virtual Memory offers convenience (software coherency) that imposes some overhead when updates are made and need to be transferred. An update on a coprocessor will need transferring before it can be used on a processor or another coprocessor. Not accessing shared data simultaneously will improve performance as data tracking is not required.

Intel® Math Kernel Library (Intel MKL) automatic offload

The Intel® Math Kernel Library (Intel MKL) has automatic offloading capabilities. These are discussed in Chapter 11 with the rest of the discussion of Intel MKL rather than here.

Language extensions for offload

Intel introduced two models for offloading with Intel Xeon Phi coprocessors: *offload pragmas* and *share virtual memory offload*. At the same time, Intel and many others have participated in discussions of adding what Intel calls *pragma offload* functionality to a future OpenMP specification. nVidia's OpenACC was introduced during this time as a subset suitable for nVidia GPUs with loss of the generality of an OpenMP based model. This included loss of key features to fully utilize Intel Xeon Phi coprocessors. Efforts to resolve these two approaches remained work for the OpenMP committee to create a convergence that will supersede nVidia's OpenACC and Intel's original offload implementation. In November 2012, OpenMP released their first public review document detailing their proposed solution. It is called "Technical Report 1 on Directives for Attached Accelerators" and was discussed in their Birds-of-a-Feather (BoF) at the Supercomputing 2012 (SC12) conference in Salt Lake City, Utah. Intel compilers added support for this draft in January 2013, and these directives are expected to be included in the next OpenMP specification in 2013 (expected to be called OpenMP 4.0). The concepts are the same, but the syntax may differ slightly for the most part and the keyword "offload" is expected to be "target." You will be able to use the original Intel syntax or the new OpenMP syntax in the Intel compilers for the foreseeable future.

The Intel compilers provide the language extensions listed in Table 7.2 to facilitate programming for Intel® MIC Architecture. Table 7.3 is a translation table for comparing the newly proposed OpenMP target model described in OpenMP TR1, with nVidia's OpenACC, with Intel's Language Extensions for Offload (LEO). The Intel compilers support OpenMP TR1 and Intel's LEO.

Table 7.2 Intel Language Extensions for Offload

Name of Feature	Description of Feature

C/C++ pragma (start with `#pragma`):
`offload`
`offload_attribute`
`offload_transfer`
`offload_wait`
	Pragmas and directives to control the data transfer between the processor and the coprocessor.

Fortran directive (start with `!dir$ omp`):
`OFFLOAD`
`OFFLOAD_ATTRIBUTE`
`OFFLOAD_TRANSFER`
`OFFLOAD_WAIT`
`OFFLOAD BEGIN`
`END OFFLOAD`	

`ATTRIBUTES OFFLOAD`
`_Cilk_offload keyword`
`_Cilk_shared keyword`
	C/C++ only. Keywords to control the data transfer between the processor and the coprocessor. The data to be exchanged between the processor and the coprocessor can be arbitrarily complex.

`__MIC__ macro` `__KNC__ macro__`	Predefined macros for Intel® MIC Architecture. See Table 7.4 for more information.
`INTEL_OFFLOAD macro` APIs in offload.h or mic_lib.f90	A set of functions for: • dealing with multiple coprocessors • calling functions on the processor to modify the coprocessor's execution environment • writing code that should not be built for processor-only execution

Compiler options and environment variables for offload

The compiler provides several compiler options and environment variables that you can use when building a binary for Intel Xeon Phi coprocessors. You can use the compiler options to:

1. Ignore language constructs for offloading (`no-offload`)
2. Build an application that runs natively on Intel MIC Architecture (`mmic`)
3. Flag every global routine and global data object in the source file with the offload attribute `target(mic)(offload-attribute-target)`
4. Specify options to be used for the specified target and tool (`offload-option`)
5. Specify the offload optimizer phase to use when optimization reports are generated (`opt-report-phase=offload`)
6. You can use environment variables for a variety of tasks, including:
   - Setting the stack size on the coprocessor (`MIC_STACKSIZE`)

Table 7.3 Offload Models: OpenMP Target (TR1), OpenACC, Intel LEO

Topic	OpenMP Target (Intel Compiler Supports it, New in 2013)	OpenACC	Intel LEO (Documented and Used in this Chapter)
Data placement			
Memory Model	host and target region data env on device memory	Host and device memory	host and offload region data env on device memory
data clauses	`map-{to,from}`, `scratch`	`present_or_copy,-{in,out}`, `nocopy`	`inout`, `in`, `out`, `nocopy`, `alloc_if`, `free_if`
data construct (structured block data placement)	target data	acc data	paired `offload_transfer`
update construct (Data motion initiated by the host)	target update	acc update	`offload_transfer`
resident / mirror / `declspec` directive (unstructured data placement)	declare target mirror	acc mirror	`__declspec(target(mic))` `__attribute__(target(mic))`
link	declare target linkable	acc linkable	`__declspec(target(mic))` `__attribute__*target(mic))`
free/alloc API routines	Yes	yes	yes
Code placement			
Execution model	host-centric, device executes the region		
Offloading	#pragma omp target	#pragma acc parallel	#pragma offload
parallel for / sections	#pragma omp parallel for / #pragma omp parallel sections	acc loop	support full OpenMP inside)
resident/declspec function declare construct	declare target function	declare acc function	`__declspec(target(mic))` / `__attribute_-((target(mic)))`
Multiple device support of same type			
device clause	device clause, ICV	device clause, ICV	`target(mic)`
API routines	get/set dev num	get/set dev num	get/set dev num
Asynchonronous / Synchronous control	thread waits on device @task scheduling point (use tasking model)	async clause and API funcs	async/signal clause / `offload_wait`
array shape/size	array sections	array sections	array sections

- Controlling environment variables passed to the coprocessor (`MIC_ENV_PREFIX`)
- Controlling MIC I/O proxy (`MIC_PROXY_FS_ROOT` and `MIC_PROXY_IO`)
- Diagnostic information printed during execution (`OFFLOAD_REPORT`). Set to a value of 1 for a condensed report or 2 for a more verbose report.

7. Offload-specific arguments to the Intel Compilers:
   - `-offload-build`: Generate host + coprocessor code (by default only host code is generated). This activates `–openmp`.
   - `-opt-report-phase:offload`: Produce a report of offload data transfers at compile time (not runtime):
   - `-offload-copts:"switches"`: Add Intel MIC Architecture compiler switches
   - `-offload-aropts:"switches"`: Add Intel MIC Architecture archiver switches
   - `-offload-ldopts:"switches"`: Add Intel MIC Architecture linker switches
8. Caveats:
   - Standalone programs and their data need to be copied manually by the user using ftp, or scp.
   - Shared libraries, such as libiomp5.so (which has no static counterpart) may need to be copied manually, even if you link your program statically.

Sharing environment variables for offload

By default, all environment variables set on the host are passed to the coprocessor and affect execution on the coprocessor during offload execution. This can be modified by using `MIC_ENV_PREFIX` to control environment variables passed to the coprocessor. The common usage is to set `MIC_ENV_PREFIX=MIC` so that the system only passes environment variables that have a prefix of `MIC`. Note this does not change the variable names that are transferred at all, so the `MIC_LD_LIBRARY_PATH` variable is not stripped and passed to the coprocessor. This means that you cannot use `MIC_ENV_PREFIX=MIC` to change the `LD_LIBRARY_PATH` on the coprocessor.

Offloading to multiple coprocessors

A system may have multiple Intel Xeon Phi coprocessors. Using offload to each coprocessor can be programmed by having a parallel loop which distributes work to each coprocessor explicitly, as shown in Figure 7.2. Using a parallel loop like that is one way of doing it. An alternative is to do it without threads (remove the OpenMP directive) on the host to use a serial loop, and to use a signal clause `signal(&var)` (instead of just `offload`). Using `signal` makes them into asynchronous offloads that launch work on the coprocessor and gives control back to the host right after having launched the work, not after the work completes, so you can use a simple loop to launch for multiple cards. Another pragma, or looped on pragmas, can use a `wait(&var)` clause with the offload construct.

Using pragma/directive offload

The first of the two offload models we'll examine might be called the *non-shared memory* model because shared memory is not available across all the cores and nothing in this model tried to provide for a common address space. However, there is shared memory amongst the processors cores, and a separate shared memory space on each coprocessor that is shared by all cores on a single Intel Xeon Phi coprocessor.

```
int num_coprocessors = _Offload_number_of_devices();
// add code here to handle what to do if there are
// no coprocessors in the system; the following code
// assumes there are one or more coprocessors...
#pragma omp parallel for num_threads(num_coprocessors) \
      schedule(static,1)
for ( int k = 0; k < num_coprocessors; k++ )
{
      #pragma offload target(mic : k)
      {
            // code to run on a coprocessor
      }
}
```

FIGURE 7.2

Sample Code to Offload to Multiple Coprocessors.

The advantage of the pragma/directive offload model is the ability to control data movement very precisely but with some loss in generality because the data to transfer has to be specified. If you want to exchange more complex or dynamic data structures, you should consider the *offload with shared virtual memory* model that we will explore later in this chapter.

This pragma/directive offload model is suitable when the data exchanged between the processor and the coprocessor consists of scalars, arrays, and structs that could be copied from one variable to another using a simple `memcpy`. This model puts you in control of the data transfer between the processor and the coprocessor, with help from the compiler. You can select the data to be transferred at the point of offload, without needing to declare or allocate it in any special way.

This focus on flat, or noncomplex. data structures allows us to precisely specify what blocks of data need to be transferred to and from the coprocessor. Of course, data that is not exchanged has no restrictions and can be arbitrarily complex, including multidimensional arrays, C++ classes of any types, and any composition of data structures using pointers, arrays, and structs.

We can place an offload pragma before any statement, including a compound statement as shown in Figure 7.3. The statement prefixed with the offload pragma can also be an OpenMP parallel pragma. We can place the Fortran `OFFLOAD` directive before a subroutine call statement, a function call statement of the form `x = func()` or an OpenMP parallel directive as shown in Figure 7.4.

The code in Figure 7.3 and Figure 7.4 finds the first ten even numbers and then puts those numbers into an array. At the start of the code excerpt is the offload pragma. The compiler builds the code block to run on both the processor and coprocessor. Table 7.4 shows the support available in C, C++ and Fortran for offload.

Code using OpenMP and offload together may look like Figure 7.5.

The host processor and coprocessors do not share the same system memory. An implication of this is that the variables used by the code block must be duplicated so that distinct copies exist on both the host processor and coprocessor. The pragmas use specifiers to define the variables to copy between the host processor and coprocessor:

- The `in` specifier defines a variable as strictly an input to the coprocessor. The value is not copied back to the host processor.

```
#pragma offload target(mic : target_id) \
                    in(all_Vals : length(MAXSZ)) \
                    inout(numEEs) \
                    out(EE_vals : length(MAXSZ/2) )
  for (k=0; k < MAXSZ; k++) {
      if ( all_Vals[k] % 2 == 0 ) {
         EE_vals[numEEs] = all_Vals[k];
         numEEs++;
      }
  }
```

FIGURE 7.3

An Offload Pragma Can Be Placed Before Any Statement.

```
!DIR$ OFFLOAD BEGIN target(mic : target_id) &
                   inout(numEs) in(all_Vals)
out(E_vals)
    do k = 1, MAXSZ
       if ( MODULO(all_Vals(k),2) == 0 ) then
           numEs = numEs + 1
           E_vals(numEs) = all_Vals(k)
       endif
    enddo
!DIR$ END OFFLOAD
```

FIGURE 7.4

An Offload Directive Can Be Placed in a Subroutine Call Statement, a Function Call Statement of the Form `x = func()` or an OpenMP Parallel Directive.

Table 7.4 Offload Support

	C/C++	Semantics
Offload pragma	`#pragma offload <clauses> <statement>`	Next statement can execute on coprocessor if available, else processor.
Function and variable declarations	`__attribute__((target(mic)))`	Compile function for, or allocate variable on, both coprocessors and processors
Whole Blocks of code	`#pragma offload_attribute(push,\ target(mic)) // code #pragma offload_attribute(pop)`	Mark entire files of large blocks of code for being available both for coprocessor and processor
	Fortran	Semantics
Offload directive	`!dir$ omp offload <clause> <statement>`	The next OpenMP parallel construct can execute on coprocessor if available, else processor.
	`!dir$ offload <clauses> <statement>`	The next statement can execute on coprocessor if available, else processor.
Function and variable declarations	`!dir$ attributes offload:<mic> :: <ret-name> OR <var1,var2,...>`	Compile function for, or allocate variable on, both coprocessors and processors

```
// C/C++ OpenMP
#pragma offload target(mic)
#pragma omp parallel for
for (i=0; i<count; i++)
{
    a[i] = b[i] * c + d;
}
!  Fortran OpenMP
!dir$ omp offload target(mic)
!$omp parallel do
    do i=1, count
      A(i) = B(i) * c + d
    end do
!$omp end parallel do
```

FIGURE 7.5

Example of OpenMP and Offload Used Together.

- The `out` specifier defines a variable as strictly an output of the coprocessor. The host processor does not copy the variable to the coprocessor.
- The `inout` specifier defines a variable that is both copied from the host processor to the coprocessor and back from the coprocessor to the host processor.

Allocation and deallocation are by default associated with the `in/out/inout` specifiers, but they can be separated to enable persistence via `alloc-if` and `free_if`, which are discussed later. The pragma also has the `target (mic:`*target_number*`)` specifier to direct the code to a specific coprocessor in a system with multiple coprocessors. Since data is not shared coprocessor(s), this is an important concept when using multiple cards. Data is only copied between coprocessors and the host using offload directives; there is no method for coprocessor to coprocessor using the offload directives.

By default the compiler builds an application that runs on both the host processor and coprocessor. You can override this and compile to run on just the processor using the `-no-offload` compiler option.

Placing variables and functions on the coprocessor

All functions in a program are always compiled for the processor and are available to be called on the processor. However, only functions marked with the special `target(mic)` attributes are available to be called by offloaded code, and only these functions can be called on the coprocessor.

Global variables are treated in a similar fashion. All global variables are always present in the processor code. But only global variables with the target attribute are compiled into the binary offloaded to the coprocessor.

Compiling only functions and data explicitly marked with the target attribute into the coprocessor binary ensures that the code on the coprocessor is as small as possible.

```
__declspec(target(mic)) int global = 55;
__declspec(target(mic)) int foo()
{
        return ++global;
}
main() {
      int i;
      #pragma offload target(mic) in(global) out(i, global)
      {
          i = foo();
      }
      printf("global = %d, i = %d (should be the same)\n",
              global, i);
}
```

FIGURE 7.6

C/++ Shared Data Needs to Be Declared.

The compiler issues warnings for functions and data referenced within offloaded code that do not have the target attribute.

Use of `target(mic)` attributes ensure that variables and functions are available on the coprocessor.

The statement following an offload pragma or directive is converted into a function that runs on the coprocessor. This code is permitted to call other functions. To ensure that these called functions are also available on the coprocessor, you must specify one of the following special function attributes:

In C/C++:

```
__declspec( target (mic)) function-declaration
__declspec( target (mic)) variable-declaration
__attribute__ (( target (mic))) function-declaration
__attribute__ (( target (mic))) variable-declaration
```

in Fortran:

```
!DIR$ ATTRIBUTES OFFLOAD:target-name :: routine-name
!DIR$ ATTRIBUTES OFFLOAD:target-name :: variable-name
```

Multiple names can be listed on the directive with commas in between, as shown in Figure 7.6 and Figure 7.7.

Note that the presence of a function call within an offloaded construct with a target attribute does not automatically declare that function as available on that target. The function definition must include the appropriate target attribute to ensure that the function is available on the target.

Also, the definition and all declarations of a variable or function with a target attribute must be consistent with each other across all compilation units.

```
module offload_test
public

!DIR$ ATTRIBUTES OFFLOAD:mic :: global_value
integer :: global_value

contains
    !DIR$ ATTRIBUTES OFFLOAD:mic :: incr_global
    integer function incr_global
    global_value = global_value + 1
    incr_global = global_value
    return
    end function incr_global
end module offload_test

program main
 use offload_test
  integer i
  i = incr_global()
  print *, "global = ", global_value, "i = ", i,
        " (should be the same)"
```

FIGURE 7.7

Fortran Shared Data Needs to Be Declared.

Managing memory allocation for pointer variables

Conceptually an offload consists of five activities, four of which are memory management activities:

1. Coprocessor data space allocation
2. Input data copies to the coprocessor memory
3. Offloaded execution on the coprocessor
4. Coping of results back to the host processor memory
5. Deallocation of data space allocated on the coprocessor

All five of these can be done in a single offload pragma. Doing multiple offload pragmas sequentially will definitely feel the effects of Amdahl's law because all of these activities, other than the offloaded execution, are sequential operations.

The compiler provides for controlling each of these activities individually. This allows overlapped communication and computation as well as the opportunity to allow persistent data on the coprocessor between offload directives instead of having the data copied back and forth. Table 7.5 shows the clauses and modifiers for use on pragmas or directives to control data movement and allocation. Variables and pointers used in these copy clauses are restricted to scalars, structs that are bitwise copyable, and arrays of scalars or bitwise copyable structs. These restrictions apply only to data that is copied between coprocessors and processors; it does not reduce the data types that can be used on processors or coprocessors. If the copy restrictions of this model prove problematic, you should consider the shared virtual memory model for offload,

Table 7.5 Offload Explicit Copy Modifiers

Clauses / modifiers	Syntax	Semantics
Target specification	`target( name[: coprocessor_number] )`	Where to run
Conditional offload	`if (condition)`	Boolean determines if offload is allowed (FALSE means it must run on processor)
Inputs	`in(var-list` *`modifiersopt`*`)`	Copy from the processor memory to a coprocessor memory
Outputs	`out(var-list` *`modifiersopt`*`)`	Copy from a coprocessor memory to the processor memory
Inputs and outputs	`inout(var-list` *`modifiersopt`*`)`	Copy to coprocessor memory before offload and back afterwards
Non-copied data	`nocopy(var-list` *`modifiersopt`*`)`	Data is local to target (use this with globals or static only if you need them to persist on coprocessor between offloads)
`modifiersopt`:		
Specify pointer length	`length(N)`	Copy *N* elements of the pointer's type *`(specifies to copy N*sizeof(element) bytes)`*
Control pointer memory allocation	`alloc_if ( condition )`	Allocate memory to hold data referenced by pointer if condition is true
Control freeing of pointer memory	`free_if ( condition )`	Free memory used by pointer if condition is true
Control target data alignment	`align ( expression )`	Specify minimum memory alignment on target

Naturally, memory management on the processor for pointer variables used in offloaded programs is the same as non-offload programs. That is, the offload pragmas do not affect memory allocation and freeing on the processor. As usual, you, the programmer, must do this.

Memory management on the coprocessor for pointer variables named in `in` and `out` clauses of the offload pragma or directive is done automatically by the compiler and runtime system. Memory management is unique to the coprocessor designated in the target clause of the offload pragma or directive. Use of a specific target clause is recommended in order to work in systems with more than one coprocessor. A program that uses persistent memory without a target clause will almost certainly not work on a system with more than one coprocessor, because the offload runtime may select a different coprocessor for each consecutive offload!

Length Parameter in Fortran

You cannot use length parameter to offload part of an array. Instead, you can create a Fortran pointer and use that. For instance:

```
!DIR$ OFFLOAD IN(FPTR:length(n):free_if(.false.))
```

Coprocessor memory management for input pointer variables

For in variables of a `#pragma offload` or `!DIR$ OFFLOAD` the default behavior is to do a fresh memory allocation for each pointer variable. On return from the construct the memory is deallocated.

In order to retain data between offloads, you can use the alloc_if and free_if qualifiers to modify the memory allocation defaults on the coprocessor.

The alloc_if qualifier specifies a Boolean condition that controls whether the pointer variables in the in clause are allocated a fresh block of memory on the target when the construct is executed on the target. If the expression evaluates to TRUE, a fresh memory allocation is performed for each variable listed in the clause. If the condition evaluates to FALSE, the existing pointer values on the target are reused. The programmer must ensure that a block of memory of sufficient size has been previously allocated for the variables on the target, either through an explicit memory allocation by user-written code or by use of a free_if(FALSE) or free_if(.false.) clause on an earlier offload.

The free_if qualifier specifies a Boolean condition that controls whether to free the memory allocated for the pointer variables in an in clause. If the expression evaluates to true, the memory pointed to by each variable listed in the clause is freed. If the condition evaluates to false, no action is taken on the memory pointed to by the variables in the list. A subsequent clause will be able to reuse the allocated memory.

The alloc_if and free_if Boolean expressions are evaluated on the processor at the point the construct is offloaded to the target.

Target memory management for output pointer variables

By default an out variable is allocated fresh memory on the target at the start of an offload and the memory is freed at the end of the offload. The alloc_if and free_if modifiers change the defaults. The expressions are evaluated on the host and used to control coprocessor memory allocation.

When the output value is received on the host, no memory allocation is done. The variables listed in out clauses must point to allocated memory of sufficient size to receive the results on the host.

Transferring data into pre-allocated memory on the target

As described in the previous section, a pointer variable in an in, out, inout, or nocopy clause can retain the target memory allocation when you set the free_if modifier to false. You can reuse that memory in subsequent offloads by using in, out, inout, or nocopy and specifying alloc_if(0). When target memory is allocated it is associated with the value of the processor pointer variable used as the destination in the in, out, inout, or nocopy clause. When target memory is to be reused, it is located using the value of the processor pointer variable that is the destination of that transfer. The offload runtime library automatically maintains the associations between the processor address and the target memory addresses as needed and thereby keeping the directive syntax very simple. The associations are created or dropped along with target memory allocation or deallocation; in other words it creates an association at allocation time when you use alloc_if(1) free_if(0) [Fortran: alloc_if(.true.) free_if(.false.)] and it deletes the association at deallocation time when you use free_if(1) [Fortran: free-if(.true.)].

Pointers to static data on the processor are special-cased. The alloc_if and free_if modifiers are ignored when the following are both true:

- The processor address used during creation of a target memory association points to statically allocated data.
- The variable is also available in the target binary because it has __declspec(target(mic)) or ATTRIBUTES OFFLOAD:mic.

The statically allocated memory on the coprocessor is used as the destination of the transfer. This target memory is not dynamically allocated and never freed.

There is only one block of target memory associated with a processor address. It is an error to call `alloc_if(1)` [Fortran: `alloc-if(.true.)`] to create a second association for a processor address before freeing the existing one. The new association overwrites the earlier one, which has the potential for causing memory leaks on the target.

It is an error to call `free_if(1)` [Fortran: `free-if(.true.)`] for a transferred pointer if a matching association is not found. The attempted removal of an association is silently ignored. An association can be made with a processor address, and a certain length, and another association made with a different processor address within that range. Since origin addresses are different; you can use `alloc_if` and `free_if` to create distinct target allocations.

Alignment of pointer variables

When memory is allocated for a pointer variable on the target, it is aligned at the natural boundary for the type of the data pointed to by the pointer. Sometimes it may be necessary to request that the data be aligned on larger boundaries, such as, for example, when the program expects to use assembly code or intrinsic functions or array notation that operate on data with more stringent alignment requirements. In these cases, the align modifier may be used to specify an alignment. The operand of the align modifier must be an integral expression that evaluates to a power of two. The expression is evaluated on the host and the region of memory allocated for the pointer on the target is aligned at a boundary that is greater than or equal to the value of the expression. When the output value is received on the host, no memory allocation is done. The variables listed in out clauses must point to allocated memory of sufficient size to receive the results.

It is important to note that for optimal data transfer performance, by default, the target memory address for a transfer through a pointer is made to match the offset within 64 bytes of the processor data. That is, if the processor source address is 16 bytes past a 64-byte boundary, the target data address will also be 16 bytes past a 64-byte boundary.

The align modifier overrides this default and aligns the target memory at the requested alignment. To get the benefits of fast data transfer and the necessary alignment on the target, ensure that the processor data is aligned on the same boundary as the alignment specified in the align modifier. Doing so meets the requirements for fast data transfer and the requirements for target data alignment.

C/C++ offload pragma examples

Let's start by defining a few macros to make the modifiers in the offload clauses more understandable:

```
#define ALLOC alloc_if(1)
#define FREE free_if(1)
#define RETAIN free_if(0)
#define REUSE alloc_if(0)
```

The first example illustrates the default behavior, which is no data persistence on the coprocessor. The compiler allocates and frees data around the offload. No `alloc` or `free` modifiers are necessary.

```
#pragma offload target(mic) in( p:length(l) )
```

The next example illustrates keeping data on the coprocessor between offloads. This code allocates memory for p as part of this offload, and keeps the memory allocated for p after the offload. Notice that ALLOC is the default, and you do not need to explicitly specify it.

```
#pragma offload target(mic) in(p:length(l) ALLOC RETAIN)
```

The next example reuses the memory allocated for p previously. It only transfers fresh data into that memory, and after the offload completes, it continues to retain the memory.

```
#pragma offload target(mic) in(p:length(l) REUSE RETAIN)
```

The next example reuses the memory allocated for p previously. However, it frees the memory for p after this offload. Notice that FREE is the default, and you do not need to explicitly specify it.

```
#pragma offload target(mic) in(p:length(l) REUSE FREE)
```

The next example, shown in Figure 7.8, uses a pointer to create a memory allocation on the target. Then the pointer value is passed to another function. Through the pointer value, the target memory can be reused.

The code in Figure 7.9 transfers static data to the target. The target static data allocation for the matching processor variable is automatically used.

The code in Figure 7.10 shows mixing of pointers to statics and pointers to dynamically allocated memory on the processor.

Fortran offload pragma examples

The following example illustrates the default behavior, which is no data persistence on the coprocessor. The compiler allocates and frees data around the offload. No alloc or free modifiers are necessary.

```
// Transfer through a function parameter
int *p = (int *) malloc(…);
int count;
void bar()
{
        …
// Allocate memory on the coprocessor,
        // and transfer data
        #pragma offload_transfer … in( p[0:count] : ALLOC )
        foo(p, 1);
}
void foo(int *arg_p, int count)
{
        // Transfer will succeed
        #pragma offload … in( arg_p[0:count] : REUSE )
        …
}
```

FIGURE 7.8

C Example of Allocated Persistent Storage on Coprocessor.

```
// When bar is called with
//   array_processor_only, dynamic memory is
//   used on target
// When bar is called with array_both,
//   the target array_both is used
__declspec(target(mic)) int array_both[1000];
int array_processor_only[1000];
void foo()
{
      bar(&array_processor_only[0]);
      bar(&array_both[0]);
}
void bar(int *p, int count)
{
      #pragma offload … in(p[0:count] : REUSE)
      …
}
```

FIGURE 7.9

C Example showing Static vs. Dynamic Memory Declarations.

```
// Associations created by offloading named variables and
// pointers to dynamically allocated variables are treated
// the same way
__declspec(target(mic)) int array[1000];
main()
{
      // copies array to mic
      #pragma offload target(mic) in(array)
     {   ...  }
      // bar1 will use dynamically
      // allocated memory on the target
      printf("%e\n", bar2());
      // bar1 will use statically allocated "array"
      printf("%e\n", bar1(&array[0], 100));
}
float bar2()
{
    float *my_p = (float *) malloc(100 * sizeof(float));
    #pragma offload target(mic) in(my_p[0:100] : RETAIN )
    {  ...  }
    return bar1(my_p, 100);
}
float bar1(float *p, int n)
{
    float sum;
    #pragma offload target(mic) nocopy(p[0:n] : REUSE RETAIN)
    {  sum = … <sum of elements in p>  }
      return sum;
}
```

FIGURE 7.10

C Example of Using Pointers for Various Allocation Types.

```
real, dimension(:), pointer :: p
!DIR$ ATTRIBUTES OFFLOAD:mic :: p
real, dimension(10), target :: targ
!DIR$ ATTRIBUTES OFFLOAD:mic :: targ

p->targ
!DIR$ OFFLOAD TARGET (mic) in (p)
```

The following examples illustrate keeping data on the coprocessor between offloads. The following code allocates memory for p as part of this offload, and keeps the memory allocated for p after the offload. Notice that ALLOC is the default, and you do not need to explicitly specify it.

```
!DIR$ OFFLOAD TARGET (mic) in (p : alloc_if(.true.) free_if(.false.))
```

The following code reuses the memory allocated for p previously. It only transfers fresh data into that memory, and after the offload completes, it continues to retain the memory.

```
!DIR$ OFFLOAD TARGET (mic) in (p : alloc_if(.false.) free_if(.false.))
```

The following code reuses the memory allocated for p previously. However, it frees the memory for p after this offload. Notice that FREE is the default, and you do not need to explicitly specify it.

```
!DIR$ OFFLOAD TARGET (mic) in (p : alloc_if(.false.) free_if(.true.))
```

The code in Figure 7.11 uses a pointer to create a memory allocation on the target. Then the pointer value is passed to another function. Through the pointer value, the target memory can be reused.

The code in Figure 7.12 transfers static data to the target. The target static data allocation for the matching processor variable is automatically used.

The code in Figure 7.13 shows mixing of pointers to statics and pointers to dynamically allocated memory on the processor.

Optimization for time: another reason to persist allocations

The allocation of space is an expensive operation on the coprocessor when using offload largely because the request is dispatched by the host to be done on the coprocessor operating system. It is worth persisting data even if the data is not needed, if allocations and deallocations can be avoided. This has proven to be a highly valuable optimization when doing offload code. You must make sure the next offload occurs to the same card using `target(mic:card_number)` to make use of the persistent data any time there may be more than one coprocessor.

Target-specific code using a pragma in C/C++

You can write functions that you intend to run on a target, and sections of offloaded code, to take advantage of target-specific intrinsic functions.

When the compiler generates code for the coprocessor, it defines the macro `__MIC__`. You can write target-specific code within an `#ifdef __MIC__` section, as shown in Figure 7.14.

You should not use the `__MIC__` macro inside the statement following a `#pragma offload` statement. You can, however, use this macro in a subprogram called from the pragma.

```
! Transfer through a routine argument
Module m
integer, pointer :: p(:)
!dir$ attributes offload:mic :: p
   contains
         subroutine foo (arg_p, count)
        !dir$ attributes offload:mic :: foo
         integer arg_p(:)
        integer count
           …
        end subroutine foo
end module m

program test
use m

allocate(p(100000))
!dir$ offload_transfer target (mic:0) in(p : alloc_if(.true.))
call foo (p, 100000)
end
```

FIGURE 7.11

Fortran Example of Allocated Persistent Storage on Coprocessor.

```
! When bar is called with array_cpu_only, dynamic memory
! is used on target
! when bar is called with array_both, the target array_both is used

module m
   integer array_both(1000)
!dir$ attributes offload : mic :: array_both
  integer array_cpu_only(1000)
end module m

subroutine foo()
use m
          call bar(array_cpu_only, 1000)
           call bar(array_both, 1000)
end subroutine foo

subroutine bar(iarray, count)
      integer iarray(count)
      !dec$ offload begin target (mic:0) in(iarray : alloc_if(.false.))
      iarray=4
      !dec$ END OFFLOAD
end subroutine bar
```

FIGURE 7.12

Fortran Example Showing Static vs. Dynamic Memory Declarations.

```
module mod
integer, target, allocatable :: arr(:)
integer, pointer, dimension(:) :: ptr
!dec$ attributes offload:mic :: ptr, arr
end module mod

program main
    use mic_lib
    use mod
    integer sum

    allocate(arr(1000))
    ptr => arr(1:500)
    !dec$ offload begin target(mic:1) in (arr)
      !! do something
    !dec$ END OFFLOAD

    ! bar2 will use dynamically allocated memory on the target
    print *, bar2()

    ! bar1 will use statically allocated "arr" from above
    print *, bar1(ptr, 500)

end program main

integer function bar2()
     integer, allocatable :: my_p(:)
     integer sum

     allocate (my_p(500))
     !dec$ offload begin target(mic:1) &
           in (my_p:length(500) free_if(.false.))
           !! do something
     !dec$ END OFFLOAD
     bar2 =  bar1(my_p, 500)
end function bar2

integer function bar1(iarray, len)
     integer iarray(len)
     integer sum
     !dec$ offload begin target(mic:1) &
           nocopy(iarray:length(len) &
           alloc_if(.false.) free_if(.false.))
        do i = 1, len
          sum = sum + iarray(i)
        end do
     !dec$ END OFFLOAD
     bar1 = sum
 end function bar1
```

FIGURE 7.13

Fortran Example of Using Pointers for Various Allocation Types.

```
// The class F32vec will be used in offloaded code
// It needs the target(mic) attribute
#pragma offload_attribute(push,target(mic))
// Use customized versions for the processor
//          and the coprocessor
#ifdef __MIC__
      // The Intel(R) MIC Architecture version
      //   of the class is in micvec.h
      #include <micvec.h>
#else
      // The processor version is written inline
      class F32vec16
      {
            public:
            ...
            friend F32vec16 sqrt(const F32vec16& a);
      };
#endif

#pragma offload_attribute(pop)
int main()
{
      #pragma offload target(mic)
      {
            #ifdef __MIC__
            F32vec16 w = ...;
            F32vec16 s;
            s = sqrt(w);
            #endif
      }
      ...
}
```

FIGURE 7.14

C Example of Target Specific Code.

The implementation of the class F32vec is specialized for the processor and the coprocessor. The offloaded code can use the specialized version if it runs on the coprocessor. If the offload fails and the construct runs on the processor, it uses the processor version.

Target-specific code using a directive in fortran

You can write functions that you intend to run on a target, and sections of offloaded code, to take advantage of target-specific intrinsic functions.

When the compiler generates code for the coprocessor, it defines the macro __MIC__. You can write target-specific code within a !DIR$ if defined __MIC__ section, as shown in Figure 7.15.

Code that should not be built for processor-only execution

You can write code that should not be built when the target is a processor-only executable. By default, the compiler defines the macro __INTEL_OFFLOAD. You can write code within an #ifdef

```
!DIR$ ATTRIBUTES OFFLOAD : mic :: foo
integer function foo()
        implicit none
!DIR$ if defined  (__MIC__)
        foo = 1 ! Code is running on coprocessor
!DIR$ else
        foo = 0 ! Code is running on host
!DIR$ endif
end function foo

program main
        implicit none

        ! Local variables
        integer :: result
        integer :: foo

        !DIR$ ATTRIBUTES OFFLOAD : mic :: foo

        ! Call foo on host
        result = foo()

        ! Print results
        if ( result ) then
                write (*,*) "Code ran on coprocessor"
        else
                write (*,*) "Code ran on host"
        end if

        ! Call foo on MIC
        !DIR$ OFFLOAD TARGET(mic)
        result = foo()

        ! Print results
        if ( result ) then
                write (*,*) "Code ran on coprocessor"
        else
                write (*,*) "Code ran on host"
        end if
end program main
```

FIGURE 7.15

Fortran Example of Target Specific Code.

`__INTEL_OFFLOAD` section when the source code is customized for running on the coprocessor, either heterogeneously or natively.

For example, you can use this macro to protect code on the host that should only be executed for an offload build, such as C/C++ calls to the `omp_set_num_threads_target` family of APIs in `offload.h` or Fortran calls to the `omp_set_num_threads_target` family of APIs in mic_lib.f90.

The section for the host compiler works only when you compile with the `-no-offload` compiler option.

C/C++:

```
#ifdef __INTEL_OFFLOAD
  #ifdef __MIC__
    printf("Using offload: Hello from coprocessor\n");
  #else /* __MIC__ */
    printf("Using offload: Hello from processor\n");
  #endif /* __MIC__ */
#else
  printf("Using host only: Hello from the processor\n");
#endif
```

Fortran:

```
#ifdef __INTEL_OFFLOAD
   #ifdef __MIC__
      PRINT *,"Using offload compiler : Hello from the coprocessor"
   #else /* __MIC__ */
      PRINT *,"Using offload compiler : Hello from the processor"
   #endif /* __MIC__ */
   #else
    #ifdef __MIC__
        PRINT *,"Using native compiler : Hello from the coprocessor"
    #else
        PRINT *,"Using host compiler : Hello from the processor"
    #endif
#endif
```

Predefined macros for Intel® MIC architecture

Fortran arrays

A Fortran array variable can be one of four major types: explicit-shape, assumed-shape, deferred-shape, and assumed-size. The runtime descriptor for the first three types makes that array variable's size known at compile time or at runtime. The last dimension of an assumed-size array is the length of its variable.

By default, the compiler copies explicit-shape, assumed-shape, and deferred-shape arrays in their entirety. They do not need an element-count expression. However, you can use an optional element-count expression to specify the total number of elements to copy, which limits the number of elements copied back and forth in the last dimension of the array.

You must specify an assumed-size array with an element-count expression specification, because the compiler does not know the total size of the array. The value of the element-count expression is the total number of elements of the array to be copied.

Table 7.6 Predefined Macros for Intel® MIC Architecture

Name of Macro	When it is Defined as TRUE
`__MIC__`	Predefined only while building code to run on the coprocessor. You can use this macro to protect code that should only be compiled for and executed on the coprocessor, such as intrinsic functions that only run on Intel® MIC Architecture, or the corresponding header files, such as `zmmintrins.h`. Do not use the `__MIC__` macro inside the statement following an offload pragma or directive. You can, however, use this macro in a subprogram called from the offloaded code.
`__KNC__`	A deprecated name for `__MIC__`. Same definition.
`__INTEL_OFFLOAD`	Predefined only when offload compilation is enabled.You can use this macro in conjunction with the `no-offload` compiler option to protect code on the host that should only be executed for an offload build, such as calls to the `omp_set_num_threads_target` family of APIs in `offload.h`.

Allocating memory for parts of C/C++ arrays

The `alloc` modifier can be used with the offload set of pragmas. The `alloc` modifier contains an array section reference. When you specify it, then the allocation on the coprocessor is limited to that shape of array. Only unit stride is allowed in the section. When a section has a rank greater than one, the second and subsequent index expressions must specify all elements at that dimension. The array section must be contiguous.

Data is transferred into that portion of the array specified by the in or out expression. Thus memory allocation and the data transfer can use separate array slice references.

When the lower bound of the first dimension of a section used in the `alloc` modifier is nonzero, then the memory allocation begins with that element. The memory preceding the lower bound is unallocated and should not be referenced by your program. By not referencing it, you enable a smaller section of the array to be transferred to the coprocessor without requiring that the entire array be allocated. In the following example:

- The `alloc(p[5:1000])` modifier allocates 1000 elements on the coprocessor.
- The first usable element has index 5 and the last has index 1004. Thus only elements 5 through 1004 are accessible on the coprocessor.
- Data transfer is specified by the `in(p[10:100])` clause. 100 elements are transferred into the allocated memory in the range `p[10]` through `p[109]`.

```
int *p;
// 1000 elements allocated. Data transferred into p[10:100]
#pragma offload ... in ( p[10:100] : alloc(p[5:1000]) )
{ ... }

typedef int ARRAY[4][4];
```

```
ARRAY *p;
p = (ARRAY*)malloc(...);

// On the coprocessor, 16 elements are allocated
// for an array of shape 5x4.
// The first row is unallocated.
// Data is transferred into row 2 only
#pragma offload ... in ( (*p)[2][:] : alloc(p[1:4][:]) )
{ ... }
```

Allocating memory for parts of fortran arrays

This topic discusses using the ALLOC modifier with the OFFLOAD set of directives.

The ALLOC modifier contains an array section reference. When you specify it, then the allocation on the coprocessor is limited to that shape of array. Only unit stride is allowed in the section. When a section has a rank greater than one, the second and subsequent index expressions must specify all elements at that dimension. The array section must be contiguous.

Data is transferred into that portion of the array specified by the IN or OUT expression. Thus memory allocation and the data transfer can use separate array slice references.

When the lower bound of the first dimension of a section used in the ALLOC modifier is nonzero, then the memory allocation begins with that element. The memory preceding the lower bound is unallocated and should not be referenced by your program. By not referencing it, you enable a smaller section of the array to be transferred to the coprocessor without requiring that the entire array be allocated. In the following example:

- The array A has 15 elements on the processor, A(1:15).
- The ALLOC modifier allocates 8 elements A(3:10).
- On the coprocessor, the elements A(1:2) are uninitialized.
- The IN clause transfers elements A(4:8) from the processor to the coprocessor.
- B is allowed 5 rows, 4 columns on the processor.
- On the coprocessor, the ALLOC modifier allocates rows 2 through 5, all columns.
- On the coprocessor, row 1, is not allocated.
- The IN clause transfers the third row (3: :) to the coprocessor.

```
INTEGER :: A (15)
!       8 elements allocated
!       5 data elements transferred starting at element 4
!DIR$ OFFLOAD ... IN ( A(4:8) : ALLOC ( (3:10) ) ...
...

INTEGER, ALLOCATABLE :: B (:,:)
ALLOCATE (B (5,4))

! On the coprocessor: 16 elements allocated (rows 2 through 5)
!     Shape of array is 5x4, first row is unallocated
```

```
!      Data is transferred into row 3 only
!DIR$ OFFLOAD ... IN ( B (3, :) : ALLOC ( 2:5, : ) ...
```

Moving data from one variable to another

The `into` modifier enables you to transfer data from a variable on the processor to another on the coprocessor, and the reverse, from a variable on the coprocessor to another on the processor. Only one item is allowed in the *variable-ref* list when using the `into` modifier. Thus a one to one correspondence is established between a single source and destination.

Note that this effectively breaks the notion that you can comment out the pragmas and still use the code, since the variable names inside the offload region are going to have a different name because of the `into` clause. This is not likely to be a problem, but it is worth noting.

When you use into with the `in` clause, data is copied from the processor object to the coprocessor object. The `alloc_if`, `free_if`, and `alloc` modifiers apply to the `into` expression.

When you use `into` with the `out` clause, data is copied from the coprocessor object to the processor object. The `alloc_if`, `free_if`, and `alloc` modifiers apply to the out expression.

The `into` modifier is not allowed with `inout` and `nocopy` clauses.

When you use the `into` modifier, the source expression generates a stream of elements to be copied into the memory ranges specified by the `into` expression. Overlap between the source and destination memory ranges leads to undefined behavior. No ordering can be assumed between transfers from different `in` and `out` clauses. Here are some examples in C/C++:

```
int p[1000], p1[2000];
int rank1[1000], rank2[10][100];
// Partial copy
#pragma offload ... in( p[0:500] : into (p1[500:500]) )
// Overlapping copy; result undefined
#pragma offload ...  in( p[0:600]   : into (p1[0:600]) )   \
                     in( p[601:400] : into (p1[100:400]) )
// Shape change is not allowed
// Error!
#pragma offload ...  out( rank1 : into(rank2) )
```

In the following Fortran example:

- The "Partial copy" case copies the first 500 elements of P to the last 500 elements of P1.
- The "Overlapping copy" case copies the first 600 elements of P into P1 but then tries to copy the last 400 elements of P into P1(100) and beyond, but P1 (100) was initialized by the previous IN clause
- The "rank change" is an error because rank 2 data on the coprocessor is being copied back to rank 1 data on the processor, even though the sizes are the same.

```
INTEGER :: P (1000), P1 (2000)
INTEGER :: RANK1 (1000), RANK2 (10, 100)
!       Partial copy
!DIR$ OFLOAD... IN ( P (1:500) : INTO ( P1 (501:1000) ) )...
!       Overlapping copy; result undefined
!DUR$ OFFLOAD... IN ( P (1:600) : INTO ( P1 (1:600) ) )... &
&       IN ( P (601:1000) : INTO ( P1 (100:499) ) )...
!       Rank change is not allowed – error
!DIR $ OFFLOAD... OUT ( RANK1, OUT (RANK2) )...
```

Restrictions on offloaded code using a pragma

Offloaded code has the following restrictions:

- Exception handling may be done as usual within code running on the processor and within code running on the coprocessor. So exceptions can be raised, caught, and handled on the processor, or raised, caught, and handled on the coprocessor. However it is not possible to propagate an exception from the coprocessor to the processor.
- Multiple host processor threads can execute concurrently while one host processor thread offloads a section of code. In this case synchronization mechanisms such as locks, atomics, mutexes, OpenMP atomic operations, OpenMP critical, OpenMP taskwait, and OpenMP barriers do not work between host processor code and code offloaded to the target. However, if parallelism on the host processor is enabled using OpenMP, then OpenMP synchronization at the end of a parallel region is guaranteed to work even if some part of the OpenMP parallel region has been offloaded to the target.
- Global variables referenced by functions called from within offloaded code must be declared with matching target attributes to ensure that the variable is available on the target. The offloaded code cannot access the host processor global variables. This is enforced by the compiler. By default, pointer variables are assumed to point to a single element of the corresponding type. The offloaded code may dereference the pointer and access a single element. The data element pointed to is automatically copied into target memory and the pointer value adjusted accordingly. The *element-count-expr* expression available with `in` / `out` / `inout` parameters enable variable-length data to be copied back and forth.
- Only pointers to non-pointer types are supported. In Fortran, these non-pointer types must have the `TARGET` attribute. Pointers to pointer variables are not supported. The compiler enforces this restriction.
- Arrays are supported provided the array element type is a scalar or bitwise copyable derived type in Fortran or in C/C++ a bitwise copyable `struct` or `class`. So, arrays of pointers are not supported.
- Because pointers are not copied across the host-target interface, but instead the data they point to is copied, do not assume that the relative distance between pointers that point to distinct variables

remains the same between the host and target. Pointers within the same data structure still have the same distance between them after offload. Thus, some pointer comparisons and arithmetic that were meaningful on the host processor can no longer be used reliably on the target.

- Similarly, although the data pointed to is available after offload, the program cannot assume that the same user variable is pointed to after variable. For example, consider the following line of code: {int a = 55; int *p = &a; #pragma offload { q = p; ... } Although `q` on the target will point to the value `55`, the value of `q` will not be `&a` on the target.
- Unions containing a combination of pointer and non-pointer members are treated as holding the non-pointer value type. Thus, no special treatment is given to the pointer, and the data pointed to is not copied to the target.
- Unions consisting entirely of pointer members are not allowed to be copied between the host and the target.
- If an offloaded statement calls a function defined in a separate file and that function references global variables, then those global variables cannot be copied in or out because the references are not visible to the compiler. Those variables are copied in or out if they are also referenced in the offloaded statement. Global variables such as these must be explicitly named in `in` and `out` clauses in the offload specification. When these global variables are file-scope static variables, then they cannot be named in the `in` or `out` clauses. You need to access their values using one of the following methods:
  - Make them external and add them to the `in` or `out` clauses in the offload specification.
  - Fetch the variable values into local variables using functions designed specifically for that purpose, and then add the local variables to the in or out clauses.
- You cannot use objects that are not bitwise copyable, such as the `ostream` object `std::cout`, inside a `#pragma offload` or `!DIR$ OFFLOAD` region. The compiler enforces this restriction and issues an error such as: `error: variable "std::cout"` is not bitwise copyable.
- There are three Intel Cilk Plus constructs: `_Cilk_spawn`, `_Cilk_sync`, and `_Cilk_for`. You can use all of these in functions called from a #pragma offload construct, but you can only use `_Cilk_for` directly within the offloaded construct. You cannot use `_Cilk_spawn` and `_Cilk_sync` within a `#pragma offload` construct, because it is illegal to offload only a portion of an Intel Cilk Plus spawning routine. The whole spawning routine must be offloaded. For example, the first pragma in the following code is illegal while the second pragma is legal code:

```
#pragma offload target(mic) // this example is illegal
{
    _Cilk_spawn f();          // _Cilk_spawn used within
}                             // offloaded construct
#pragma offload target(mic) // this example is legal
{
                g();
}
...
void g()
{
    _Cilk_spawn f();         // _Cilk_spawn used within
}                            // offloaded function
```

Table 7.7 _Cilk_shared for Data and Functions

Clauses / Modifiers	Syntax	Semantics
Function	`int _Cilk_shared f(int x) { return x+1; }`	Versions generated for both processor(s) and coprocessor(s); may be called from either side
Global	`_Cilk_shared int x = 0;`	Visible on both sides
File/Function static	`static _Cilk_shared int x;`	Visible on both sides, only to code within the file/function
Class	`class _Cilk_shared x {...};`	Class methods, members, and `and` operators are available on both sides
Pointer to shared data	`int _Cilk_shared *p;`	`p` is local (not shared), can point to shared data
A shared pointer	`int *_Cilk_shared p;`	`p` is shared; should only point at shared data

Entire blocks of code	`#pragma offload_attribute( push, _Cilk_shared)`
	`// code/data to mark __Cilk_shared`
	`#pragma offload_attribute(pop)`
		Mark entire files or large blocks of code `_Cilk_shared` using this pragma

Using offload with shared virtual memory

The other offload model is the *shared virtual memory (VM)* model, which uses `_Cilk_shared` and `_Cilk_offload` keywords. An overview of each can be seen in Tables 7.7 and 7.8. This model is appropriate for dealing with complex pointer-based data structures, such as linked lists, trees, and the like. This model uses a software implementation of virtual memory that is shared between the host processor and the coprocessor. You either declare data to be exchanged during offloads as shared, or if the data is dynamic it is allocated using special `alloc` and `free` calls.

This programming model is suitable when the data exchanged between the processor and the coprocessor is more complex than scalars, arrays, and structs that can be copied from one variable to another using a simple `memcpy`. The data to be exchanged between the processor and the coprocessor can be arbitrarily complex. It can use pointers, and any composition of structs and pointers.

Data exchanged in this model is unrestricted in data structural complexity. However, at the point of offload, the data must already be in the shared memory region, either as a result of its being declared `_Cilk_shared`, or because it was allocated using `_Offload_shared_malloc()` or `_Offload_shared_aligned_malloc()`.

Using shared memory and shared variables

The offload runtime system maintains a section of memory at the same virtual address on the processor and the coprocessor. The keyword `_Cilk_shared` enables you to use this shared memory as follows:

- It places variables in this shared memory address range.
- It specifies that a function is defined on both the processor and the coprocessor.

Table 7.8 _Cilk_offload

Feature	Examples	Description
Offloading a function call	`x = _Cilk_offload func(y);`	*func* executes on coprocessor if possible
Offloading asynchronously	`x = _Cilk_offload_to (coproc_num) func(y);`	*func* must execute on specified coprocessor
	`x = _Cilk_spawn _Cilk_offload func(y);`	Nonblocking offload
Offload a parallel for-loop	`_Cilk_offload _Cilk_for(i=0; i<N; i++) { a[i] = b[i] + c[i]; }`	Loop executes in parallel on target. The loop is implicitly outlined as a function call.

The compiler allocates shared variables such that:

- their virtual addresses are the same on the processor and the coprocessor
- their values are synchronized between the processor and the coprocessor at a predefined point

Pointers to shared variables have the same value on processor and coprocessors, because shared variables have the same addresses, so offloaded code can easily operate on linked data structures. Memory is synchronized between the processors and the coprocessors only at offload call sites.

You cannot conditionally control shared variables when you compile them to run on a coprocessor. When a variable is marked `_Cilk_shared`, the memory allocation for the variable is dynamic instead of static, and only the host allocates the memory, within the memory space that the host and the coprocessor share. When the program is compiled, the host generates code to create the shared memory dynamically, so if the host does not see the shared variable, it doesn't allocate any memory for the variable. Since the memory is not allocated in the shared space, when the coprocessor tries to access this memory an illegal access occurs.

Because the host allocates memory for the shared variable, the variable must be visible on the host even if the host does not use the variable.

For example, the following code is incorrect because the variable is only conditionally compiled for the coprocessor. Therefore, no code is generated on the host to allocate memory for the variable.

```
#ifdef __MIC__
_Cilk_shared int res;
#endif
```

If you compile the variable conditionally for the coprocessor, the `_Cilk_shared` keyword is not necessary because the host does not access the variable. Use `_Cilk_shared` only when sharing data between the host and the coprocessor.

About shared functions

When you do not use the no-offload option, the compiler builds two binary files:

- A processor version: Includes all functions in the source code, whether marked `_Cilk_shared` or not.
- A coprocessor version: Includes only functions marked `_Cilk_shared` in the source code.

Shared memory management functions

The functions described below are available for allocating and freeing shared memory to work with the `_Cilk_shared` and `_Cilk_offload` keywords. These functions revert to the standard `malloc` or `free` versions if Intel MIC Architecture-based hardware is not installed in the system, or if the Intel MIC Architecture driver is not loaded.

```
void *_Offload_shared_malloc(size_t size);
void *_Offload_shared_aligned_malloc(size_t size,
                                     size_t alignment);
_Offload_shared_free(void *p);
_Offload_shared_aligned_free(void *p);
```

Synchronous and asynchronous function execution: _cilk_offload

The `_Cilk_offload` keyword controls synchronous and asynchronous execution of functions on the processor and coprocessor. Examples of the syntax are as follows:

```
lvalue = _Cilk_offload func_name ( rvalue )
lvalue = _Cilk_offload_to ( target-number )
                           func_name ( rvalue )
lvalue = _Cilk_spawn _Cilk_offload func_name ( rvalue )
lvalue = _Cilk_spawn _Cilk_offload_to ( target-number )
                            func_name ( rvalue )
_Cilk_offload _Cilk_for ( init-expr; test-expr; incr-expr)
_Cilk_offload_to ( target-number )
              _Cilk_for ( init-expr; test-expr; incr-expr)
```

Arguments above are defined as:

- *lvalue*: An expression that designates an object.
- *rvalue*: An expression that represents a value. Note: all examples show only a single parameter, but multiple parameters are definitely permitted!
- *func_name*: A function name.
- *target-number*: An expression whose value is interpreted as follows:

  `-1`: This value specifies execution on the coprocessor. The runtime system chooses the specific coprocessor. Execution on the processor is not allowed. If the correct target hardware needed to run the offloaded program is not available on the system, the program fails with an error message.

> = 0 : A value greater than or equal to zero specifies execution on a specific coprocessor. The specific coprocessor is determined as follows:
coprocessor = target – number % number_of_coprocs
If the correct target hardware needed to run the offloaded program is not available on the system, the program fails with an error message.
< -1 : This value is reserved.
For example, in a system with 4 coprocessors:
specifying 2 or 6 tells the runtime systems to execute the code on coprocessor 2, because both 2 % 4 and 6 % 4 equal 2.

- Specifying 1000 tells the runtime systems to execute the code on coprocessor 0, because 1000 % 4 = 0.
- *init-expr* : An initialization expression for a `_Cilk_for` loop.
- *test-expr* : A test expression for a `_Cilk_for` loop.
- *incr-expr* : An increment expression for a `_Cilk_for` loop.

`_Cilk_offload` before a function call indicates that the runtime system chooses whether to execute the function being called on the coprocessor synchronously, or the processor, and if multiple coprocessors are available, on which coprocessor.

Placing the keyword `_Cilk_offload` between a `_Cilk_spawn` keyword and a call results in asynchronous execution on the processor using the normal Intel Cilk Plus rules, and a synchronous offload of the function by an Intel Cilk Plus task, effectively doing an asynchronous offload. Just as in normal Intel Cilk Plus usage, you need a `_Cilk_sync` keyword before the processor can use the results of the offloaded function.

`_Cilk_offload` before a `_Cilk_for` loop specifies that the entire loop be executed on the coprocessor.
`_Cilk_offload_to` (*target-number*) specifies mandatory offload to a coprocessor. *target-number* determines the specific coprocessor. Note that the convenience of `_Cilk_offload_` may come with a cost, as it is usually somewhat lower performing than `#pragma offload`. Here are some examples of offload function calls:

```
z = _Cilk_offload func(a);
z = _Cilk_spawn _Cilk_offload func(a);

Offload _Cilk_for loop:
_Cilk_offload _Cilk_for ( init-expr; test-expr; incr-expr ) {
...
}
```

Sharing variables and functions: _cilk_shared

The `_Cilk_shared` keyword shares a variable or function. When applied to functions, it is identical in functionality to `__declspec( target (mic))`. It is recommended that `declspec` is used on functions instead of `_Cilk_shared` as a convention. The syntax is illustrated here:

```
_Cilk_shared type variable(s)
```

```
_Cilk_shared type func_def
__declspec(target (mic)) type func_def // preferred
```

Arguments above are defined as:

- *type :* The type of the variable or variables being declared.
- *variable(s) :* One or more variables.
- *func_def* : A function definition or declaration.

Using `_Cilk_shared` with a variable allocates the variable to shared memory. Using `_Cilk_shared` with a function definition or declaration makes the function available to the processor and the coprocessor. Some examples are shown in Figure 7.16.

```
// Examples: Variables
// A shared declaration:
_Cilk_shared int x, y, z;

// A shared typedef:
typedef _Cilk_shared str_type shr_str_type;
 shr_str_type a;

// Examples: Pointers
// p is a pointer to a shared int,
// but the pointer itself is not shared:
int _Cilk_shared *p;

// p is itself in shared memory:
int * _Cilk_shared p;

// Examples: Functions
// A shared function definition:
__declspec(target (mic)) void func() {
  x = y + z;
}
// A shared function declaration:
__declspec(target (mic)) int bar();
// Examples: Functions
// Using pragma offload-attribute to apply
// this attribute to multiple declarations:
#pragma offload_attribute(push, _Cilk_shared)
#include <math.h>
void function_1();
void function_2();
#pragma offload_attribute(pop)
void function_3();
int main(){
   _Cilk_offload function_1();
   function_3();
   _Cilk_offload function_2();
}
_Cilk_shared int bar();
```

FIGURE 7.16

C Example of Shared Variables and Functions Using Cilk Plus.

Rules for using _cilk_shared and _cilk_offload

Follow these rules for using `_Cilk_shared` and `_Cilk_offload` for correct execution. In most cases the compiler issues diagnostics for incorrect usage.

Correct and Permitted Usage:

- When applied to a C++ class, all member functions are shared and all objects of that class type are shared.
- On static fields of a class.
- Assigning pointer-to-shared to pointer-to-non-shared.
- Assigning the address of a shared variable to a shared pointer.
- The named function called by `_Cilk_offload` *func* must be marked `_Cilk_shared` and must have external linkage.
- The function pointer in `_Cilk_offload`*indirect-call* must be of the type pointer-to-shared.
- Shared functions whose address is taken must have external linkage.
- Pointer arguments passed to an offloaded function call must be pointer-to-shared.
- Global variables referenced within `_Cilk_offload _Cilk_for` must have the attribute `_Cilk_shared`.
- Functions called from `_Cilk_offload _Cilk_for` must be shared.
- Pointers referenced within `_Cilk_offload _Cilk_for` must be pointers to shared variables.
- Global variables referenced inside functions marked `_Cilk_shared` must have the attribute `_Cilk_shared`.

Incorrect and Non-permitted Usage:

- `_Cilk_shared` on a field of a structure is not allowed.
- `_Cilk_shared` on static variables is not allowed.
- `_Cilk_shared` on variables local to a function is not allowed.
- Assigning pointer-to-non-shared to pointer-to-shared is not allowed.

The example in Figure 7.17 demonstrates incorrect usage of `_Cilk_shared`. The code attempts to declare a `_Cilk_shared` object named mark as a local variable to a `function`.

In the example of correct usage shown in Figure 7.18, the object mark has been allocated statically, and its usage modified slightly:

Synchronization between the processor and the target

Memory synchronization between the processor and the target occurs at the following predefined points:

- When an offloaded function is called by the processor, and upon entering the offloaded function on the target
- When an offloaded function on the target returns, and upon the return of the function to the processor

Currently no other synchronization points exist, so any simultaneous access to the shared memory location between the predefined points is treated as a race condition, and the behavior is undefined.

```
#pragma offload_attribute(push, _Cilk_shared)
#include <vector>
#include "tbb/concurrent_vector.h"
#pragma offload_attribute(pop, _Cilk_shared)
class _Cilk_shared Thing
{
public:
  Thing(void) { m_size = 100; }
  void work();
  int m_size;
};

void Thing::work() {
  std::vector<bool> mark(m_size);     // Error
  tbb::concurrent_vector< std::pair<unsigned int, unsigned int> > m_hits(m_size);
}
```

FIGURE 7.17

Incorrect Usage of _Cilk_shared.

```
#include <vector>
#include "tbb/concurrent_vector.h"

_Cilk_shared std::vector<bool> mark;
_Cilk_shared tbb::concurrent_vector< std::pair<unsigned int, unsigned int> > m_hits;

class _Cilk_shared Thing
{
public:
  Thing(void) { m_size = 100; }
  void work();
  int m_size;
};
void Thing::work() {
  mark.resize(m_size);
  m_hits.resize(m_size);
}
```

FIGURE 7.18

Correct Usage of _Cilk_shared.

Writing target-specific code with _cilk_offload

You can write offloaded sections of code to take advantage of target-specific intrinsic functions. When the compiler generates code for the coprocessor, it defines the macro `__MIC__`. You can write target-specific code within an `#ifdef __MIC__ section`.

The example in Figure 7.19 shows how target-specific code may be written within an `#ifdef __MIC__` section. The implementation of the class `F32vec` is specialized for the processor and the coprocessor. The offloaded code can use the specialized version if it runs on the coprocessor.

```
// The class F32vec will be used in offloaded code
// It needs the target(mic) attribute
#pragma offload_attribute(push,_Cilk_shared)

// Use customized versions for processor and coprocessor
#ifdef __MIC__
      // The Intel(R) MIC Architecture version
      // of the class is in micvec.h
      #include <micvec.h>
#else
      // The processor version is written inline
      class F32vec16
      {
            public:
            ...
            friend F32vec16 sqrt(const F32vec16& a);
      };
#endif

#pragma offload_attribute(pop)
_Cilk_shared void function_3()
{
      F32vec16 w = ...;
      F32vec16 s;
      s = sqrt(w);
      ...
}
```

FIGURE 7.19

Target Specific Code Using _Cilk_offload.

If `function_1` is executed on the processor, it uses the processor version of the class `F32vec`. If it runs on the coprocessor, it uses the definition from `micvec.h`.

Restrictions on offloaded code using shared virtual memory

Offloaded code using virtual shared memory has the following restrictions:

- Multiple host processor threads can execute concurrently while one host processor thread offloads a section of code. In this case, synchronization mechanisms such as locks, atomics, mutexes, OpenMP atomic operations, OpenMP critical, OpenMP taskwait, OpenMP and barriers do not work between the host processor code and code that is offloaded to the coprocessor. However, if parallelism on the host processor is enabled using OpenMP, then OpenMP synchronization at the end of a parallel region is guaranteed to work even if some part of the OpenMP parallel region has been offloaded to the coprocessor.
- Exception handling may be done as usual within code running on the processor and within code running on the coprocessor. So exceptions can be raised, caught, and handled on the processor, or raised, caught, and handled on the coprocessor. However it is not possible to propagate an exception from the coprocessor to the processor.

- Virtual shared memory classes that allocate and free memory must use either using the `_Offload_shared_malloc()` and `_Offload_shared_free()` or `_Offload_shared_aligned_malloc()` and `_Offload_shared_aligned_free()` APIs instead of standard allocate and free APIs. For an example, see `installdir/Samples/en_US/C++/mic_samples/LEO_tutorial/tbo_sort.c`(`/opt/intel/composer_xe_2013` is the default *installdir* directory at the time we are writing this). Standard Template libraries which provide classes that allocate and free their own memory are not usable currently with `_Cilk_shared` unless they are modified to use the `_Offload_shared_*` specific APIs mentioned above.
- Runtime Type Information (RTTI) is not supported under the Shared Virtual memory programming method. Specifically, use of `dynamic_cast<>` and `typeid()` is not supported.

Persistent data when using shared virtual memory

There may be times you want data to persist between segments of offloaded code, but you do not need the data to ever be available on the host. Consider the following desired variables and behaviors:

1. `float* mic_only_data;` - this array must exist only on the MIC. During the offload, it gets modified on the coprocessor, and it should persist between offloads. This data is never needed by the host, and hence should not be copied to the host.
2. `float* shared_data;` - this array exists both on the coprocessor and the host. During the offload, the coprocessor modifies it and it is sent back to the host.

With the non-shared memory model (`#pragma offload`), orchestrating this is easy: declare both with the `offload attribute target(mic)` and prepend the offloaded code with:

```
#pragma offload nocopy(mic_only_data) out(shared_data : length(N) alloc_if(first_call)
free_if(last_call))
```

The solution is this: if the data pointed to by coprocessor-only data is not meant to be shared, just use `malloc` to allocate it locally. Hold on to the pointer (valid only on the coprocessor) using a `_Cilk_shared` variable. For instance, consider the follow C code:

```
#define N 100
typedef float *fp;
_Cilk_shared fp p;
_Cilk_shared void foo()
{
    int i;
    p = (fp)malloc(N*sizeof(float));
    for (i=0; i<N; i++)
    {
        p[i] = i;
    }
```

```
}
_Cilk_shared void bar()
{
    int i;
    for (i = 0; i < N; i++)
    {
#ifdef __MIC__
      printf("p[%d] = %f\n", i, p[i]);
#endif
    }
    fflush(0);
}
int main()
{
    _Cilk_offload foo();
    _Cilk_offload bar();
    return 0;
}
```

Note that:

```
float _Cilk_shared p;
```

is equivalent to

```
typedef float fp; _Cilk_shared fp p;
```

An example in C++, showing `new` used with shared data and then with coprocessor-only data (in routine foo) is:

```
#include <stdio.h>
#include <stdlib.h>
#include <new>
class _Cilk_shared myclass {
    char label;
  public:
    myclass(char l){
    label = l;
    }
    void print(){
#ifdef __MIC__
```

```
    printf("MIC: ");
#else
    printf("CPU: ");
#endif
    printf("%c\n", label);
    }
};
myclass* _Cilk_shared mic_only;
myclass* _Cilk_shared shared_data;
_Cilk_shared void foo() {
    mic_only = new _Cilk_shared myclass('M'); // 'M' for "MIC-only"
}
int main()
{
    //Shared data is initialized as 'S'
    shared_data = new((_Cilk_sharedmyclass*)
      _Offload_shared_malloc(sizeof(myclass))) myclass('S');
    // The MIC should print the value 'S'
    _Cilk_offload(*shared_data).print();
    (*shared_data).print(); // The CPU should print the value 'S'
    _Cilk_offload foo(); // MIC-only data is initialized as 'M'
    _Cilk_offload (*mic_only).print(); // The MIC should print the value 'M'
    // Should result in an error:
    // MIC-only class is not available on the CPU
      (*mic_only).print();
            return 0;
}
```

C++ declarations of persistent data with shared virtual memory

A pointer object can be shared or not shared but can point to shared objects or not. Examples of using `_Cilk_shared` to declare these cases are shown here:

1.
```
// Shared pointer, points to shared object
   _Cilk_shared myclass * _Cilk_shared mic_only;
```
2.
```
// shared pointer, points to non shared object
   myclass *_Cilk_shared mic_only;
```
3.
```
// non shared pointer, points to shared object.
   _Cilk_shared myclass *mic_only;
```

Note, you can use the push/pop syntax to do any of these also. For instance, to do the same as #2 we can write:

```
#pragma offload_attribute(push, _Cilk_shared)
myclass* mic_only;
#pragma offload_attribute(pop)
```

This may be easier to read.

About asynchronous computation

By default, the offload pragma or directive causes the processor thread that encounters the offload pragma or directive to wait for completion of the offload before continuing to the next statement. You can execute an asynchronous offload computation, which enables the processor to initiate the offload and immediately continue to the next statement.

To specify an asynchronous offloaded computation, specify a `signal` clause in the offload pragma or directive to initiate the computation, and subsequently use the `offload_wait` pragma or `OFFLOAD_WAIT` directive to wait for completion of the offloaded computation.

The following example enables the processor to issue offloaded computations and continue concurrent activity without using any additional processor threads:

C/C++:

```
char signal_var;
do {

    #pragma offload target(mic) signal(&signal_var)
    {
          long_running_mic_compute();
    }
    concurrent_cpu_activity();
    #pragma offload_wait (&signal_var)

} while (1);
```

Fortran:

```
integer signal_var
integer counter
counter = 10000
!DIR$ ATTRIBUTES OFFLOAD:MIC :: long_running_mic_compute
do while (counter .gt. 0)

    !DIR$ OFFLOAD TARGET(MIC:0) SIGNAL(signal_var)
        call long_running_mic_compute()
    call concurrent_cpu_activity()
    !DIR$ OFFLOAD_WAIT TARGET(MIC:0) WAIT (signal_var)
```

```
    counter = counter - 1
end do
end
```

About asynchronous data transfer

To transfer data between the processor and the coprocessor, use the `offload_transfer` pragma or directive with either all in clauses or all out clauses. This pragma does no offload work, only data management! This is the same as a regular offload pragma with an empty statement following it, but is easier to read and avoids mistakes in future editing of the program.

Without a signal clause the data transfer is synchronous: The next statement is executed only after the data transfer is complete.

Using `offload_transfer` with a `signal` makes the data transfer asynchronous. The tag specified in the `signal` clause is an address expression associated with that data set. The data transfer is initiated and the processor can continue past the offload pragma or directive.

A later pragma or directive written with a `wait` clause causes the activity specified in the pragma or directive to begin only after all the data associated with the tag has been received. The data is placed into the variables specified when the data transfer was initiated. These variables must still be accessible.

Asynchronous data transfer from the processor to the coprocessor

To transfer data asynchronously from the processor to the coprocessor, use a signal clause in an `offload_transfer` with `in` clauses. The variables listed in the `in` clauses form a data set. The pragma or directive initiates the data transfer of those variables from the processor to the coprocessor. A subsequent offload pragma or directive with a `wait` clause that uses the same value for *tag* as that used in the `signal` clause causes the statement controlled by the pragma or directive to begin execution on the coprocessor only after the data transfer is complete.

If, during an asynchronous offload, a signal is created in one thread, Thread A, and waited for in a different thread, Thread B, you are responsible for ensuring that Thread B does not query the signal before Thread A has initiated the asynchronous offload to set up the signal. Thread B querying the signal before Thread A has initiated the asynchronous offload to set up the signal results in undefined behavior and a runtime abort of the application.

C/C++ Asynchronous data transfer from the processor to the coprocessor

In the following C/C++ example, the data transfer of the floating-point arrays f1 and f2 is initiated at line 11. The offload does not initiate a computation. Its only purpose is to start transferring f1 and f2 to the coprocessor. At line 22 the processor initiates the computation of the function foo on the coprocessor. The function uses the data f1 and f2, whose transfer was initiated earlier. The execution of the offloaded region on the coprocessor begins only after the transfer of f1 and f2 completes. The variable result returns the results of the computation.

```
01  const int N = 4086;
02  float *f1, *f2;
```

```
float result;
f1 = (float *)memalign(64, N*sizeof(float));
f2 = (float *)memalign(64, N*sizeof(float));
...
// The processor issues send and continues
#pragma offload_transfer in( f1, f2 : length(N) ) signal(f1)

...
// The processor issues request to do computation
// The coprocessor receives offload request and waits for pre-sent data
#pragma offload wait(f1) out( result )
{
        result = foo(N, f1, f2);
}
```

Multiple independent asynchronous data transfers can occur at any time. The example below uses offload_transfer to send f1 and f2 to the coprocessor at different times, first f1 in line 11, and then f2 in line 21.

```
01  const int N = 4086;
02  float *f1, *f2;
03  float result;
04  f1 = (float *)memalign(64, N*sizeof(float));
05  f2 = (float *)memalign(64, N*sizeof(float));
...
10  // The processor issues send and continues
11  #pragma offload_transfer in( f1 : length(N) ) signal(f1)
12
...
20  // The processor issues send and continues
21  #pragma offload_transfer in( f2 : length(N) ) signal(f2)
22
...
30  // The processor issues request to do computation using f1 and f2
31  // The coprocessor begins execution only after pre-sent data is received
32  #pragma offload wait(f1, f2) out( result )
33  {
34          result = foo(N, f1, f2);
35  }
```

C/C++ asynchronous data transfer from the coprocessor to the processor

To transfer data asynchronously from the coprocessor to the processor, use the signal and wait clauses in two different pragmas/directives. The first offload performs the computation, but only initiates the data transfer. The second pragma causes a wait for the data transfer to complete.

In the following example, the data transfer of the floating-point arrays f1 and f2 is initiated at line 11. The offload does not initiate a computation. Its only purpose is to start transferring f1 and f2 to the coprocessor. At line 22 the processor initiates the computation of the function foo on the coprocessor. The function uses the data f1 and f2, whose transfer was initiated earlier. The execution of the offloaded region on the coprocessor begins only after the transfer of f1 and f2 completes. The variable result returns the results of the computation.

```
01  const int N = 4086;
02  float *f1, *f2;
03  f1 = (float *)memalign(64, N*sizeof(float));
04  f2 = (float *)memalign(64, N*sizeof(float));
...
10  // processor sends f1 as input synchronously
11  // The output is in f2, but is not needed immediately
12  #pragma offload in( f1 : length(N) ) \
13          nocopy( f2 : length(N) ) signal(f2)
14  {
15     foo(N, f1, f2);
16  }
..
20  #pragma offload_transfer wait(f2) out( f2 : length(N)
21
22  // processor can now use the result in f2
23  ...
```

The following example double buffers inputs to an offload.

```
#pragma offload_attribute(push, target(mic))
int count = 25000000;
int iter = 10;
float *in1, *out1;
float *in2, *out2;
#pragma offload_attribute(pop)
void do_async_in()
{

     int i;
     #pragma offload_transfer target(mic:0) \
          in(in1:length(count) alloc_if(0) free_if(0)) \
          signal(in1)
     for (i = 0; i < iter; i++)
     {
                    if (i%2 = = 0) {
                          #pragma offload_transfertarget(mic:0) \
                               if (i!5iter-1) \
```

```
                        in(in2:length(count) alloc_if(0) free_if(0)) \
                        signal(in2)
                    #pragma offloadtarget(mic:0) \
                        nocopy(in1) wait(in1) \
                        out(out1:length(count)) \
                        alloc_if(0)free_if(0))
                compute(in1, out1);
            } else {
                    #pragma offload_transfer target(mic:0) \
                        if(i!5iter-1) in(in1:length(count) \
                        alloc_if(0) free_if(0)) signal(in1)
                    #pragma offloadtarget(mic:0) \
                        nocopy(in2) wait(in2) \
                        out(out2:length(count) \
                          alloc_if(0) free_if(0))
                  compute(in2, out2);
        }
      }
}
```

Fortran asynchronous data transfer from the processor to the coprocessor

In the following Fortran example, the data transfer of the floating-point array f1 is initiated at line 10, and f2 is initiated at line 12. The offloads do not initiate a computation. Their only purpose is to start transferring f1 and f2 to the coprocessor. At line 14 the processor initiates the computation of the function `foo` on the coprocessor. The function uses the data f1 and f2, whose transfer was initiated earlier. The execution of the offloaded region on the coprocessor begins only after the transfer of f1 and f2 completes. The variable result returns the results of the computation.

```
01  integer, parameter:: n = 4086
02  real, allocatable :: f1(:), f2(:), result
03  !dir$ attributes offload:mic :: f1, f2, foo
04  integer :: signal_1, signal_2

05  !dir$ attributes align : 64 :: f1
06  !dir$ attributes align : 64 :: f2
07  allocate(f1(n))
08  allocate(f2(n))
09  = 1.0
10  !dir$ offload_transfer target (mic:0) in(f1) signal(signal_1)
11  f2 = 3.14
12  !dir$ offload_transfer target (mic:0) in(f2) signal(signal_2)
13  !dir$ offload begin target(mic:0) wait (signal_1, signal_2)
14  result = foo(n, f1, f2)
```

```
!dir$ END OFFLOAD
```

Multiple independent asynchronous data transfers can occur at any time. The example below uses `offload_transfer` to send f1 and f2 to the coprocessor at different times, first f1 in line 10, and then f2 in line 13.

```
01 program main
02 integer, parameter:: n=4086
03 real, allocatable :: f1(:), f2(:), result
04 !dir$ attributes offload:mic :: f1, f2, foo
05 integer :: signal_1, signal_2
06 !dir$ attributes align : 64 :: f1
07 !dir$ attributes align : 64 :: f2
08 allocate(f1(n))
09 allocate(f2(n))
10 !dir$ offload begin target(mic:0) in (f1 ) nocopy (f2) signal(signal_1)
11 call foo(N, f1, f2)
12 !dir$ END OFFLOAD
13 !dir$ offload_transfer target(mic:0) wait(signal_1) out (f2)
14 end program main
```

Fortran asynchronous data transfer from the coprocessor to the processor

To transfer data asynchronously from the coprocessor to the processor, use the `signal` and `wait` clauses in two different pragmas/directives. The first offload performs the computation, but only initiates the data transfer. The second directive causes a wait for the data transfer to complete.

In the following example, the data transfer of the floating-point arrays `in1` and `in2` is initiated at line 15. The offload does not initiate a computation. Its only purpose is to start transferring `in1` to the coprocessor. Within the `do` loop, either `in1` or `in2` is transferred to the coprocessor, and computation starts on whichever set has already been transferred. At line 20 the processor initiates the computation of the function compute on the coprocessor, and tells it to work on `in1`. At line 24, the processor initiates the computation of the function compute on the coprocessor, but tells it to work on `in2`, which was transferred at line 23.

The following example double buffers inputs to an offload.

```
01 module M
02 integer, parameter :: NNN = 100
03 integer, parameter :: count = 25000000

04 integer :: arr(NNN)
05 real   :: dd
06 !dec$ attributes offload:mic::arr, dd
07 end module M

08 subroutine do_async_in()
09 !dir$ attributes offload:mic :: compute
10 use m
```

```
integer i, signal_1, signal_2, iter
real, allocatable :: in1(:), in2(:)
real, allocatable :: out1(:), out2(:)
iter = 10
!dir$ offload_transfer target(mic:0)&
in(in1 : length(count) alloc_if(.false.) free_if(.false.) ) signal(signal_1)
do i = 1, iter
if (mod(i,2) = = 0) then
!dir$ offload_transfer target(mic:0) if(i .ne. iter-1)&
in(in2 : length(count) alloc_if(.false.) free_if(.false.) ) &
signal(signal_2)
!dir$ offload target(mic:0) nocopy(in1) wait(signal_1)&
out(out1 : length(count) alloc_if(.false.) free_if(.false.) )
call compute(in1, out1)
else
!dir$ offload_transfer target(mic:0) if(i .ne. iter-1) &
in(in1 : length(count) alloc_if(.false.) free_if(.false.) ) &
signal(signal_1)
!dir$ offload target(mic:0) nocopy(in2) wait(signal_2) &
out(out2 : length(count) alloc_if(.false.) free_if(.false.) )
call compute(in2, out2)
endif
end do
end subroutine do_async_in
```

Applying the target attribute to multiple declarations

When you have several data and function declarations, rather than specifying each declaration with its own target attribute, you can enclose a group of data and function declarations between the push and pop variants of the `offload_attribute` pragma or directive.

When offloaded code makes use of declarations from C standard headers, Intel® Threading Building Blocks (Intel® TBB), Intel Cilk Plus, or user-written `#include` declarations, you must enclose those declarations within the `offload_attribute` pragma or directive, with a specified target-name corresponding to the offload model under which the declarations are used.

The code represented by the external routine in the header files must exist on the coprocessor either as a system library or as a user library that can run on Intel MIC Architecture.

Enclose the calls to the include files when offloading using a pragma as follows:

```
#pragma offload_attribute(push, target(mic))
...
#pragma offload_attribute(pop)
```

Enclose the calls to the include files when offloading using shared virtual memory as follows:

```
#pragma offload_attribute(push, _Cilk_shared)
...
#pragma offload_attribute(pop)
```

You can only use functions and data under a single offload model within your program, so any include file you call can only be marked for use under a single offload model. Consequently, you cannot use the keyword `_Cilk_offload` with any include file enclosed between `#pragma offload_attribute(push, target(mic))` and `#pragma offload_attribute(pop)`.

Conversely, you cannot use the #pragma offload statement with any include file enclosed between #pragma offload_attribute(push, _Cilk_shared) and #pragma offload_attribute(pop).

There is one important exception for the virtual shared memory model: do not enclose C standard headers within `#pragma offload_attribute(push, _Cilk_shared)` and `#pragma offload_attribute (pop)`. Such decoration is unnecessary and may lead to undefined symbols at runtime.

In the following example, the functions `function_1` and `function_2` each need the target attribute, as do all the declarations within some include files. It is convenient to put the `offload_attribute` pragma around all those declarations.

```
#pragma offload_attribute(push,target(mic))
#include <stdio.h>
#include <math.h>

void function_1();
void function_2();
#pragma offload_attribute(pop)

int main()
{

    #pragma offload target(mic)
    {
      function_1();
      printf("...");
    }
    ...
    #pragma offload target(mic)
    function_2();
    ...

}
```

Vec-report option used with offloads

By default, when we compile a program with offloading and use a `vec-report` compiler option, we get one report from the host compiler and another from the offload cross-compiler for the coprocessor. The messages are labeled to indicate whether they are for coprocessor (MIC) or not, but that can be confusing because they are interspersed. It is especially confusing if a loop is vectorized by one compiler but not by the other. It can make sense to limit the vectorization reports to be only for the coprocessor compilation. To get messages from the coprocessor compiler only, we can compile with:

```
-vec-report0 –offload-option,mic,compiler,"-vec-report3"
```

Similarly, for the host only compilation messages we can use:

```
-vec-report3 –offload-option,mic,compiler,"-vec-report0"
```

Measuring timing and data in offload regions

You can measure both the amount of time it takes to execute an offload region of code, as well as the amount of data transferred during the execution of the offload region.

Use one of the following mechanisms:

- Set the `OFFLOAD_REPORT` environment variable.
- Use the __Offload_report API.

__Offload_report

Controls printing offload execution time and the amount of data transferred.

```
Syntax: __Offload_report(integer)
```

The argument is either 1 or 2. If 1, it prints the offload computation time, in seconds. If 2, it prints the offload computation time, in seconds, and the amount of data transferred, in bytes.

This API enables you to time offload regions and measure the amount of data transferred during their execution. Using this API is equivalent to setting the environment variable OFFLOAD_REPORT. Setting `__Offload_report(1)` prints the offload computation time. For example:

```
[FILE]    filename.c
[LINE]    line_no
[processor-TIME]    0.278886
[MIC-TIME]    0.000177
```

Setting `__Offload_report(2)` prints the offload computation time and the amount of data transferred. For example:

```
[FILE]    filename.c
[LINE]    line_no
[processor-TIME]    0.52
[processor->MIC DATA]  0
[MIC-TIME]    0.000151
[MIC->processor DATA]  4
```

Using libraries in offloaded code

The heterogeneous compilation environment consists of a host processor compilation environment and a coprocessor compilation environment. Each environment consists of the compiler, linker, and standard libraries. Code for the host processor is compiled within the host environment and offloaded code within the coprocessor environment. The coprocessor environment may supply its own sets of standard libraries and these would be available to be called from offloaded code with no need to use special syntax or runtime features.

Some common libraries, such as the Intel® Math Kernel Library (Intel® MKL) and Intel® Performance Primitives (Intel® IPP) will be available in processor versions as well as coprocessor versions.

When the coprocessor is available, the coprocessor executable is loaded when the processor version of the executable is loaded, or when the first offload is attempted. At this time the libraries linked with the coprocessor code are initialized. The loaded coprocessor executable remains in the coprocessor memory until the host program terminates. Thus, any global state maintained by the library is maintained across offload instances.

It is worth noting that separate copies of libraries are linked or loaded with the host program and the offloaded coprocessor code. So there are two sets of global state: one on the host processor and one on the coprocessor. The host processor code only sees the host processor state and the offloaded code only sees the state of the library on the coprocessor.

About creating offload libraries with xiar and xild

Using `xiar` or the equivalent `xild -lib` to create a static archive library containing routines with offload code requires the following actions:

- Specify the `-qoffload-build` option, which causes xiar to create both a library that for the processor, *lib*.a, and a corresponding library for the coprocessor, *lib*MIC.a.
- When supplying the name of the library and the list of its member files to `xiar` or `xild`, include only the file names associated with the processor library and processor object files, such as `lib.a` and `file.o`. `xiar` and `xild` automatically manipulate the corresponding coprocessor library and member files, `libMIC.a` and `fileMIC.o`, respectively.
- Use the same options available to `ar`, including `d` (Delete), r (Replace), m (Move) and x (Extract). For more information, see the man page for ar. The syntax to use these options is as follows: `xiar –qoffload-build`*ar options archive* [*member*...] `xild -lib –qoffload-build`*ar options archive* [*member*...]
- When linking a static archive that contains offload code, use the linker options -L*path* and -l*libname*. The compiler driver automatically incorporates the corresponding coprocessor library, *lib*MIC.a, into the linking phase. The following `xiar` command creates or modifies the processor library libsample.a and coprocessor library libsampleMIC.a:

  ```
  xiar -qoffload-build rcs libsample.a obj1.o obj2.o
  ```
  `libsample.a` contains the processor object files `obj1.o` and `obj2.o`. `libsampleMIC.a` contains the coprocessor object files obj1MIC.o and `obj2MIC.o`.

Either of the following commands compiles and links myprogram.c with the static library:

```
icc myprogram.c libsample.a
icc myprogram.c -lsample
```

Performing file I/O on the coprocessor

Code running on the coprocessor can read and write files, as code can on the host. To enable reading or writing on the coprocessor, from the offloaded code you must write to the special directory ./proxyfs/, which is on the coprocessor. Files written to or read from this directory are proxied to the host under the parent directory structure defined by the host environmental variable `MIC_PROXY_FS_ROOT`. For example, when `MIC_PROXY_FS_ROOT = /home/user/app`, the proxied host directory is `/home/user/app/proxyfs/`.

The offloaded code can read or write to what appears to it to be a local file, and that file I/O is automatically proxied over to the host system. This file only exists on the host. No cached copy is maintained on the coprocessor. So there is an expected communication penalty.

It is worth noting that the coprocessor proxy directory's name, `./proxyfs/`, is predefined. You cannot modify it.

If you don't include the dot (.) before the forward slash (/) the offloaded code's file I/O is not proxied to the host, and the I/O attempts to write to the coprocessor's local directory `/proxyfs/` instead.

Files and directories that offloaded code creates outside of the directory `./proxyfs/` are not proxied to the host. They exist only locally on the coprocessor file system. For example, writing to `/tmp/testFile.dat` writes to the local coprocessor file system only.

A file written on the host in the proxied directory can also be read from the coprocessor, and the converse is true as well: A file written on the coprocessor in `./proxyfs/` can also be read from the host. The file needs to be closed for writing before it can be opened for reading.

To create a local file, that is, a file not proxied to the host, from an offloaded section of code, write a file to any directory other than ./proxyfs/.

Please note the environment variable MIC_PROXY_IO controls proxying to `stdout` and `stderr`. By default it is set to 1, which implies that `stdout` and `stderr` are proxied to the host. To disable stdout and stderr proxying to host set `MIC_PROXY_IO` to 0.

You can disable file proxying by setting `MIC_PROXY_FS_ROOT` to an empty value, or unsetting it altogether.

The default directory on the coprocessor to which files are written is `/tmp/coi_procs/`*`coprocessr_num/PID`* if you don't specify a directory for the file I/O. So if an offload is done to coprocessor #1, and the offload is handled by process PID#2929, then the default directory on the coprocessor is `/tmp/coi_procs/1/2929`.

Please note that the numbering of the coprocessors on the system starts at 1. For example, the first coprocessor, located at 192.168.1.100, is coprocessor #1. This is different than in the offload pragma target specification `target(mic:0)`.

It is also worth noting that output to `stdout` may not be immediately visible on the processor. To ensure output is visible you must execute a `fflush(0);` operation after each `printf` operation.

```
#pragma offload_attribute(push,target(mic))
#include <stdio.h>
#include <stdlib.h>
#include <string.h>
#pragma offload_attribute(pop)
int main()
{
    FILE *fp;
    char buffer[7];
    #pragma offload target(mic) nocopy(fp)
    {
      fp = fopen("./proxyfs/myfile.txt", "wb");
      if (fp == NULL)
      {
                    fprintf(stderr,
        "Failed to open myfile.txt for write\n");
                    exit(1);
    }
      fwrite("Hello\n", 1, 7, fp);
      fclose(fp);
    }
      #pragma offload target(mic) nocopy(fp) out(buffer)
    {
      fp = fopen("./proxyfs/myfile.txt", "rb");
      if (fp == NULL)
        {
        fprintf(stderr,
        "Failed to open myfile.txt for read\n");
        exit(1);
      }
      fread(buffer, 1, 7, fp);
        fclose(fp);
        if (strcmp(buffer, "Hello\n") != 0)
        {
                      fprintf(stderr,
        "File incorrectly read back on coproc\n");
                      exit(1);
      }
```

```
    }
    printf("%s", buffer);
    return 0;
}
```

Logging stdout and stderr from offloaded code

Capturing C/C++ program output to `stdout` and `stderr` from writes performed inside offloaded code may require calling `fflush()`. This function is under the control of the coprocessor offload interface (COI) layer, not the compiler or compiler run-time libraries.

Writes performed in offloaded code may be buffered when they are directed to a file, while writes to the console happen immediately. If the application exits prior to the buffer threshold being reached then the output data may be lost. Therefore, I/O to a file requires an additional explicit `fflush()` on the coprocessor to capture this output data, as shown in the sample.c example:

```
#pragma offload_attribute(push,target(mic))
#include <stdio.h>
void sub()
{
  printf("hello from MIC\n");
  fflush(0);
}
#pragma offload_attribute(pop)
int main(int argc, char* argv[])
{
  printf("hello from main\n");
  #pragma offload target(mic)
  sub();
}
```

Compile and execute the above example as follows:

```
$ icc -offload-build –o sample sample.c
$ ./sample > log.txt
$ cat log.txt hello from MIC hello from main
```

When calling fflush(), you can control directing stdout and stderr to the same or separate output files. For example, to send the stdout (1) and stderr (2) to log.txt, enter:

```
$ ./sample > log.txt 2>&1
```

To redirect stdout to one file and stderr to another, use:

```
$ ./sample > log.txt 2> log_err.txt
```

Summary

Offload models are one way to utilize Intel Xeon Phi coprocessors. There are two distinct models—one that requires all data to be shared to be managed explicitly, and one which allows certain variables to be shared automatically.

Applications are suitable for using offload when the code spends significant time doing computation without I/O, the computationally intensive portion of the code and the data on which it works is relatively easy to encapsulate, the computation time is substantially higher than the data transfer time, and the data fits or can be blocked into coprocessor memory. Additional performance comes from the ability to structure computation and data so that computations and data transfers can be asynchronous and overlap.

The alternative to offload models is simply called native programming since every thread just runs and communicates with other threads explicitly including explicit programming to exchange data with methods like MPI. The choice of which to use should be made based on what fits the structure of existing programs best, and what you feel is best for your code going forward. Neither model has an intrinsic advantage over the other in terms of theoretical maximum performance. Which is easier to utilize will depend on your code.

For more information

Here are some additional reading materials we recommend on various threading models:

- OpenMP: http://openmp.org (specifications, including the Technical Report 1 on Directives for Attached Accelerators can be found on this website)
- Updated information (eventually) for this book, especially regarding changes in Offload support by OpenMP: http://lotsofcores.com

CHAPTER

Coprocessor Architecture

8

Symmetric multiprocessor (SMP) on-a-chip is a good description for the Intel® Many Integrated Core (Intel® MIC) architecture and the very first product to use Intel MIC architecture, the Intel® Xeon Phi™ coprocessor. We know the future of computing is parallel; history seems likely to record this as an inevitable step in the miniaturization of computers and expansion of parallel computing. It is nevertheless a giant leap into the future.

Utilizing almost five billion transistors, offering up to sixty-one cores and significant reliability features while offering a familiar programming environment for a highly parallel device, is a notable accomplishment. When launched in November 2012, Intel Xeon Phi coprocessors were already in seven of the world's faster supercomputers (per the "Top 500" list, top500.org) and the power-efficient compute engine used to build the world's most power-efficient supercomputer (per "Green 500" list, green500.org). The Intel Xeon Phi coprocessor is a true engineering marvel in many ways.

This chapter dives into describing the hardware in more detail than most programmers will ever need and probably less information than some will want. We will create a firm foundation of understanding, which in turn will make Intel's detailed documentation more approachable if needed.

The ambitious goal for the coprocessor was to simultaneously enable evolutionary *and* revolutionary paths forward for scientific discovery through efficient, high performance, technical computing. Evolutionary in creating a generally programmable solution that matches the training, application investments, standards, and computing environments of an existing, vibrant High Performance Computing (HPC) development community. Revolutionary in enabling powerful new parallel focused computing elements that give a new target for long term sustainable parallel programming optimization. In this chapter, we examine the key elements behind the design of this new Intel computing product line.

The coprocessor is available in several models, each one attaches to an Intel® Xeon™ processor–based host platform via a PCI Express bus interface. The heart of the coprocessor card is the Intel Xeon Phi coprocessor silicon chip. The coprocessor comprises up to sixty-one Intel® Architecture cores that execute Intel Architecture instructions, connected by a high performance on-die bidirectional interconnect. Each core includes a 512-bit wide vector processing unit (VPU) with an extended math unit (EMU) for key transcendental functions. In addition to the cores, the coprocessor has up to eight memory controllers supporting two GDDR5 (high speed) memory channels each, plus other device interfaces including the PCI Express system interface. As we progress through the chapter, we will delve into the important capabilities of the coprocessor hardware, especially its primary functional component, the coprocessor silicon chip, with an emphasis on the software development and system management aspects.

The Intel® Xeon Phi™ coprocessor family

The different Intel Xeon Phi coprocessor models vary on such factors as performance, memory size and speed, thermal (cooling) solutions and form factor (type of card). All the coprocessor products interface to the Intel Xeon processor host platform through a PCI Express bus connection and consist of a coprocessor silicon chip on the coprocessor card with other components such as memory. The coprocessor card is what is commonly just called the coprocessor.

Figure 8.1 depicts the two types of double-wide PCI Express cards that are offered (passive and active cooling solutions). Not pictured are two "no thermal solution" versions.

FIGURE 8.1

Intel® Xeon Phi™ Coprocessor Card Forms (Top: Passive Cooling, Bottom: Active Cooling).

Passive heat sink cards will be used primarily in supercomputing cluster data centers where densely packed compute blade and "pizza box" style rack mount compute units (nodes) will have high throughput cooling fans drawing air through the entire unit. Active fan sink cards will typically be used in desk-side workstation units. The configurations without thermal solutions allow for custom cooling and platform solutions such as liquid cooling at the discretion of the system manufacturer.

There are three primary series of models, the 3100, 5100, and SE series, differing in core count, memory, features and performance. The 3100 series is ideal for compute-bound workloads (MonteCarlo, Black-Scholes, HPL, Life Sciences, and so on) with both active and passive cooling solutions to offer a wide range of applicability. These are generally the lowest priced and offer high performance value per dollar with solid floating-point performance but with less memory capacity and less memory speed then the 5100 series. The 5100 series is ideal for memory bandwidth–bound workloads (STREAM, Energy, and so on) offered in the lowest power, passively cooled, solutions. These offer the best balance of performance and energy efficiency with strong floating-point performance, high core count, larger memory capacity, plus very good memory transfer speeds. The SE series satisfies the most demanding usage models, all passively cooled with the option of "no thermal solution" to allow custom, usually large, deployments. These offer maximal performance with the highest number of cores, best floating-point performance and fastest memory access speeds. The SE (Special Edition) series coprocessors were designed in conjunction with some of the earliest customers and deployments of Intel Xeon Phi coprocessors. For example, Texas Advanced Computing Center's (TACC's) Stampede supercomputer uses the SE10 models of coprocessors. The SE series, at publication time, was a custom order part with this non-numeric name. It is expected that the SE series will eventually transform into a standard product in the future. We'll post a note on our Web site if and when this happens (lotsofcores.com).

Coprocessor card design

The coprocessor card can be thought of as a motherboard for a computer with up to 61 cores, complete with the silicon chip (containing the cores, caches and memory controllers), GDDR5 memory chips, flash memory, system management controller, miscellaneous electronics and connectors to attach into a computer system. A schematic view of the key components of the coprocessor card is shown in Figure 8.2. The major computational functionality is provided by the Intel Xeon Phi coprocessor silicon chip. The silicon chip is, as you'd find with many Intel Xeon processors, contained in Ball Grid Array (BGA) packaging. This BGA package is then the key component on a coprocessor card much like a processor is the key component on a computer motherboard.

Up to sixteen channels of GDDR5 memory can be utilized and using a method known as *clamshell,* up to thirty-two memory devices can be attached using wire connections routed on both sides of the card, doubling the typical memory capacity. GDDR5 is a special kind of DRAM that has higher bandwidth than that used with most general-purpose processors including PCs.

The Intel Xeon Phi coprocessor card complies with the Gen2 x16 PCI Express (PCIe) specification and supports 64, 128, and 256 byte packet transmission.

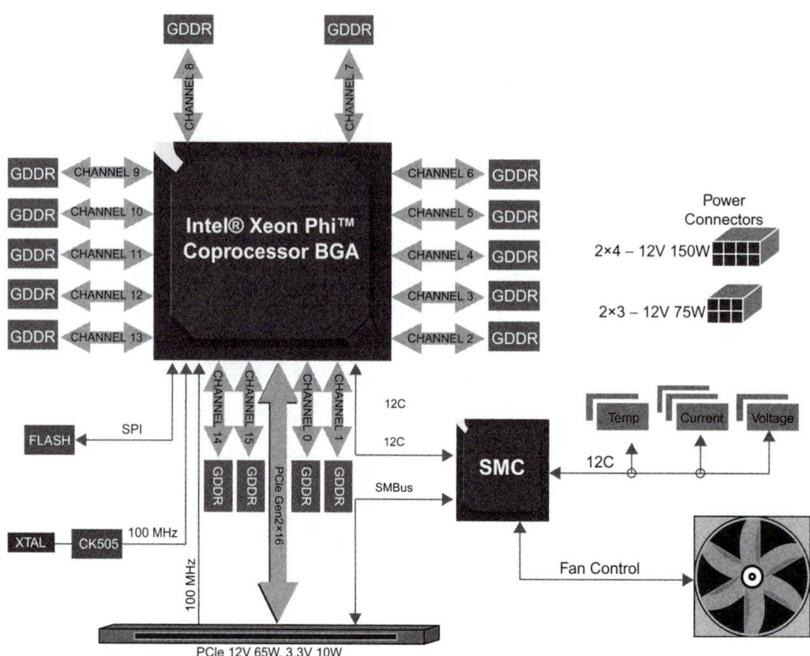

FIGURE 8.2

Intel® Xeon Phi™ Coprocessor Card Schematic. Note: On-board Fan Is Only Available on the 3100 Series Active Product.

Flash memory on the card is used to contain the coprocessor silicon's startup or bootstrap code, similar to the BIOS in an Intel Xeon processor platform.

The System Management Controller (SMC) handles monitoring and control chores such as: tracking card-level information from temperature, voltage, and current sensors, as well as adjusting the fan (if installed) accordingly to increase or decrease cooling capacity. The SMC provides the host's baseboard management controller (BMC) vital function status and control via the industry standard Intelligent Platform Management Interface (IPMI) over the System Management Bus (SMBus). The operating system software on the coprocessor chip communicates with the SMC via a standard I^2C bus implementation.

Intel® Xeon Phi™ coprocessor silicon overview

The Intel Xeon Phi coprocessor silicon implements computational and I/O capabilities. As shown in Figure 8.3, the many x86-based cores, the memory controllers, and PCI Express system I/O logic are interconnected with a high speed ring-based bidirectional on-die interconnect (ODI). Communication over the ODI is transparent to the running code with transactions managed solely by the hardware.

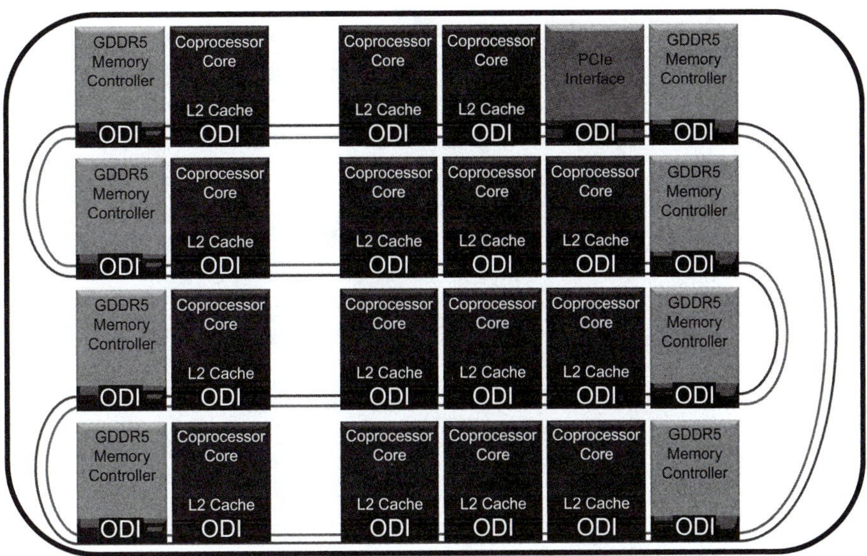

FIGURE 8.3

Overview of the Intel® Xeon Phi™ Coprocessor Silicon and the On-Die Interconnect (ODI).

Each core has an associated 512-KB Level 2 (L2) cache to provide high speed, reusable data access. Furthermore, fast access to data in another core's cache over the ODI is provided to improve performance when the data already resides "on chip." Using a distributed Tag Directory (TD) mechanism, the cache accesses are kept "coherent" such that any cached data referenced remains consistent across all cores without software intervention.

From a software development and optimization perspective, a simplified way to view the coprocessor is as a symmetric multiprocessor (SMP) with a shared Uniform Memory Access (UMA) system; each core effectively having the same memory access characteristics and priority regardless of the physical location of the referenced memory. Core-to-core transfers are not *always* significantly better than memory latency times. Optimization for better core-to-core transfers has been considered, but because of ring hashing methods and the resulting distribution of addresses around the ring, no software optimization has been found that improves on the excellent built-in hardware optimization. No doubt people will keep looking! The architects for the coprocessor, at Intel, maintain searching for such optimizations through alternate memory mappings will not matter in large part because the performance of the on-die interconnect is so high.

Individual coprocessor core architecture

A high level diagram of each processing core on the coprocessor silicon is shown in Figure 8.4. The structure of the core implies the key design goals of creating a device optimized for high level of power-efficient parallelism while retaining the familiar, Intel architecture–based general

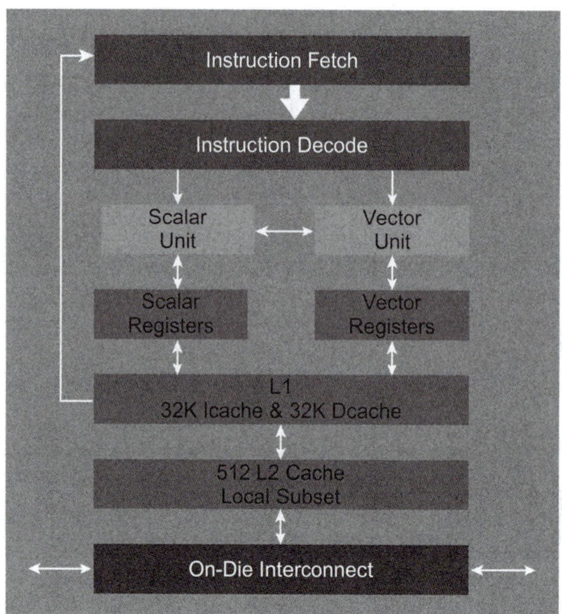

FIGURE 8.4

Intel® Xeon Phi™ Coprocessor Individual Core Structure.

programmability. A 64-bit execution environment-based on Intel64® Architecture is provided. Also, an in-order code execution model with multithreading is employed to reduce size, complexity, and power consumption of the silicon versus the deeply out-of-order, highly speculative execution support used primarily to improve serial-oriented code performance on Intel Xeon processors. This difference in instruction processing flow also reflects how a programmer might consider partitioning and targeting code and applications for platforms that include Intel Xeon Phi coprocessors. As mentioned in Chapter 1, the multithreading of the coprocessor plays a critical role in fully utilizing the in-order code execution model. Coprocessor multithreading should not be confused with hyper-threading (HT) on Intel Xeon processors. The wide range of programming model choices provided by a platform and software environment that includes coprocessors will be discussed in more detail in Chapters 9 and 10 on the software architecture and system environment.

The core includes 32-KB each of L1 instruction (code) cache and L1 data cache, as well as the private (local) 512-KB L2 cache. Code is fetched from memory into the instruction cache and then goes through the instruction decoder for dispatch and execution. There are two primary instruction processing units. The scalar unit executes code using existing traditional x86 and x87 instructions and registers. The vector processing unit (VPU) executes the newly introduced Intel Initial Many Core Instructions (IMCI) utilizing a 512-bit wide vector length enabling very high computational throughput for both single precision and double precision calculations. Note that there is no support for MMX™ instructions, Intel Advanced Vector Extensions (Intel® AVX), or any of the

Intel® Streaming SIMD Extensions (Intel® SSE). These instruction families were omitted to save space and power and to favor 512-bit SIMD capabilities unique to the Vector Processing Unit (VPU) of the Intel Xeon Phi coprocessor. Chapters 2 through 4 provided some experience with extracting the exceptional performance capabilities of the core, especially the VPU and its focus on supporting HPC workloads.

Instruction and multithread processing

Each core's instruction pipeline has an in-order superscalar architecture derived from the Intel® Pentium® P54c processor design with significant enhancements including 64-bit instruction support, vector capabilities, four-threads-per-core, power management and much more. It can execute two instructions per clock cycle, one on the U-pipe and one on the V-pipe. The V-pipe cannot execute all instruction types, and simultaneous execution is governed by instruction pairing rules. Vector instructions are mainly executed only on the U-pipe. Four independent thread contexts are available on each core. The thread management and instruction flow is pictured in Figure 8.5.

Each computational unit has an associated register file (RF) to draw operands from, in addition to potential memory operands, maintained in the L1 data cache. The instruction decoder is designed as a two-cycle fully pipelined unit, which greatly simplifies the core design allowing for higher cycle rate than otherwise could be implemented. The result is that any given hardware thread that is scheduled back-to-back will stall in decode for one cycle. Therefore, single-threaded code will only achieve a maximum of 50-percent utilization of the core's computational potential. However, if additional hardware thread contexts are utilized, a different thread's instruction may be scheduled

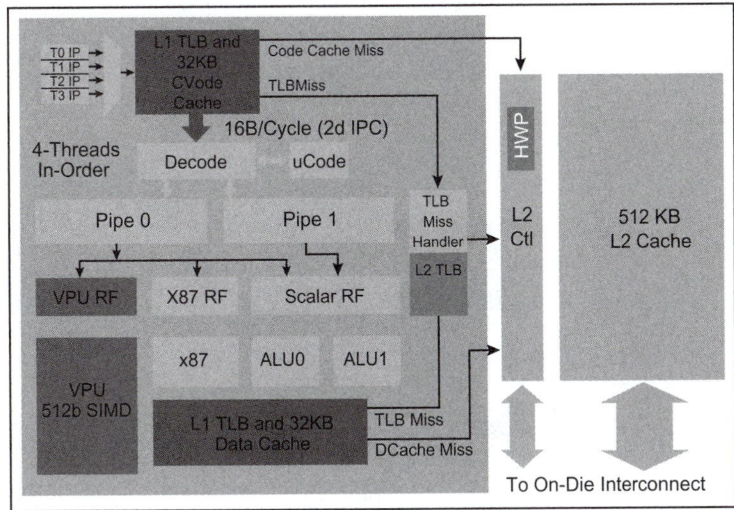

FIGURE 8.5

Intel® Xeon Phi™ Coprocessor Silicon Core Thread and Instruction Pipeline.

each cycle and full core computational throughput of the coprocessor can be realized. Therefore, to maximize the coprocessor silicon's utilization for compute-intensive application sequences, at least two hardware thread contexts should be run. As a computational engine designed for highly threaded parallel application code, the tradeoff to maximize overall clock speed for multithreaded application throughput is a reasonable one. As mentioned in Chapter 1, this differs significantly from hyper-threading (HT) on Intel Xeon processors that may not always be helpful for HPC workloads; Intel Xeon Phi coprocessor multithreading is always useful for HPC workloads although the optimal number of threads may range from 2 to 4.

A more detailed look at the hardware thread processing is depicted in Figure 8.6. The complete architectural state is replicated four times, including the general purpose registers, ST0-7, segment registers, CR, DR, EFLAGS, and EIP. Certain microarchitectural states are also replicated four times, including the prefetch buffers (described later in the chapter), the instruction pointers, the segment descriptors, and the exception logic. Thread-specific changes include adding thread ID bits to shared management structures, converting memory stall to thread-specific flush, and the introduction of thread wakeup/sleep mechanisms. Event-monitoring registers, discussed in detail in Chapter 13, allow for performance measurements on individual threads or cores. Finally, the Intel Xeon Phi coprocessor implements a "smart" round-robin multithreading.

Each of four hardware threads has a "ready to run" buffer consisting of two instruction bundles. Since each core is capable of issuing two instructions per clock cycle, each bundle represents two instructions. If the executing thread has a control transfer to a target that is not contained in this buffer, it will trigger a miss to the instruction cache, which flushes the context buffer and loads the appropriate target instructions. If the instruction cache does not have the control transfer point, a core stall will be initiated, which may result in performance penalties.

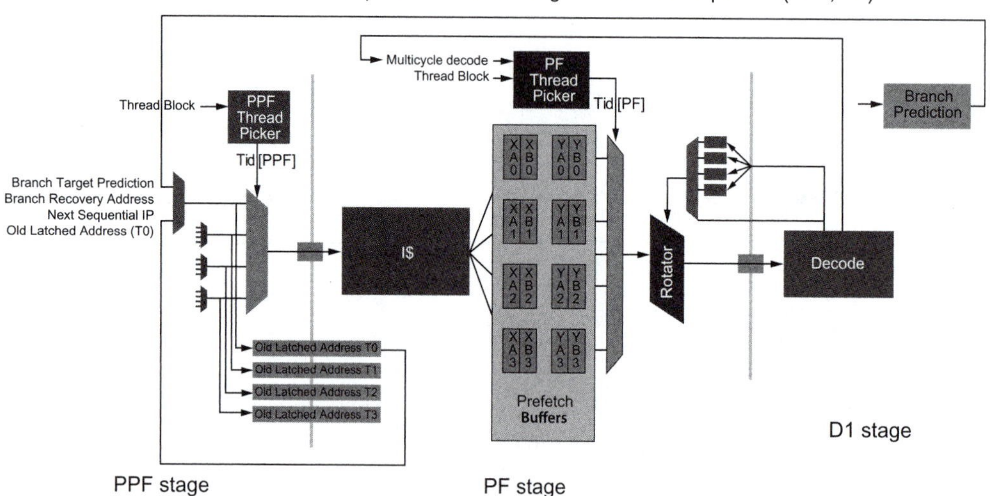

FIGURE 8.6

Intel® Xeon Phi™ Coprocessor Silicon Core Multithreading Architecture.

In general, whichever hardware context issues instructions in a given clock cycle has priority for fetching the next instruction(s) from the instruction cache. Another significant function is the picker function (PF) that chooses the next hardware context to execute. The PF behaves in a round-robin manner, issuing instructions during any one-clock cycle from a single hardware context. In cycle N, if the PF issues instruction(s) from Context 3, then in cycle $N+1$ the PF will try to issue instructions from Context 0, Context 1, or Context 2—in that order. As previously noted, it is not possible to issue instructions from the same context (Context 3 in this example) in back-to-back cycles.

Scalar unit instructions execute with 1-clock latency, while most vector instructions have a 4-clock latency with 1-clock throughput. More details on specific instruction pairing guidelines, latencies, and throughput can be found in the *Intel® Xeon Phi™ Coprocessor Instruction Set Architecture Reference Manual* referenced at the end of this chapter.

Cache organization and memory access considerations

The L2 cache organization per core is inclusive of the L1 data and instruction caches. Each core has a private (local) 512-KB L2. The L2 caches are fully coherent and can supply data to each other on-die. The private 512-KB L2 caches in aggregate comprise a total of (512-KB × # of cores) of cache on die. Common data used by multiple cores will result in copies in each local L2 for cores using the data. If no cores were to share any data or code (this is highly unlikely), then the effective total L2 size of the chip is 30.5 MB in a 61-core coprocessor, whereas, if every core shares exactly the same code and data in perfect synchronization, then the effective total L2 size of the chip is only 512 KB. Therefore, the actual size of the application-perceived L2 storage is a function of the degree of code and data sharing among cores and threads.

The key coprocessor cache structure parameters are listed in Table 8.1.

The coprocessor silicon supports virtual memory management with 4 KB (standard), 64 KB (not standard), and 2 MB (huge and standard) page sizes available and includes Translation Lookaside Buffer (TLB) page table entry cache management to speed physical to virtual address lookup as in other Intel architecture microprocessors. On a TLB miss, the hardware performs a four-level page table walk as usual stalling the current requesting thread for many more cycles than on a hit. There is an instruction TLB (ITLB) and a two-level DTLB (L1 and L2 DTLB). The

Table 8.1 Intel® Xeon Phi™ Coprocessor Silicon Key Cache Parameters

Parameter	L1	L2
Size	32 KB + 32 KB	512 KB
Associativity	8-way	8-way
Line Size	64 bytes	64 bytes
Banks	8	8
Access Time	1 cycle	11 cycles
Policy	pseudo LRU	pseudo LRU

Table 8.2 Intel® Xeon Phi™ Coprocessor Silicon TLB Parameters

	Page Size	Entries	Associativity	Maps
L1 Data TLB	4 KB	64	4-way	256 KB
	2 MB	8	4-way	16 MB
L1 Instruction TLB	4 KB	32	4-way	128 KB
L2 TLB	4 KB, 64 KB, 2 MB	64	4-way	128 MB

two DTLB levels have no connection with the concepts of L1 or L2 caches; it is simply a two level DTLB. The coprocessor's TLB characteristics are shown in Table 8.2.

In the L2 TLB, there are no restrictions on mixing page size entries. Of course, the use of smaller page size entries will result in less overall memory mapped and available for fastest access. Four-kilobyte pages have been the long-time primary standard supported by Linux operating systems. As of this writing, 64-KB page support is not prevalent in existing microprocessors and generally will not be available without specific support additions to the Linux kernel and therefore currently goes unused. Two-megabyte huge page support is available, but the application and/or environment may need modification to specifically request it. Using huge pages for large data sets and arrays can provide a significant performance boost by reducing TLB misses versus using the default of 4-KB pages depending on the application memory access patterns. However, to ensure your application uses huge pages, it may be necessary to use means other than standard library calls (malloc) to allocate memory. In C/C++, the mmap() call provides a means to request huge pages. There is also the `hugetlbfs` Linux library package that can be added to the environment that enables huge page support for standard allocation calls. Future Linux kernels supported on Intel Xeon Phi coprocessors may include transparent huge page support.

Prefetching

The Intel Xeon Phi coprocessor includes memory prefetching support to maximize the availability of data to the computation units of the cores. As the name implies, prefetching is a request to the coprocessor's cache and memory access subsystem to look ahead and begin the comparatively slow process of bringing data we expect to use in the near future into the much faster to access L1 and/or L2 caches. As an analogy, have you ever played "fetch" with very eager dogs? As soon as you lift your arm to throw, they are already running to where they anticipate the ball or stick will land to retrieve it faster. That's prefetching!

The coprocessor provides two kinds of prefetch support, software and hardware prefetching. Software prefetching is provided in the coprocessor VPU instruction set and discussed in detail in Chapter 5. The processing impact of the prefetch requests can be reduced or eliminated because the prefetch instructions can be paired on the V-pipe in the same cycle with a vector computation instruction. Compilers typically insert L1 or L2 cache prefetch instructions by default, as needed, based on the perceived access pattern of the code, so no action is necessary on the part of the application programmer. However, compiler options exist to provide further control so the programmer can to tune the prefetch insertion beyond the compiler's defaults. See Chapter 5 for the compiler control options. Prefetching is also available on Intel Xeon processors.

Also, an L2 cache hardware prefetcher (HWP) implementation is provided in the coprocessor silicon. Figure 8.5 shows its logical location in the core's L2 cache control logic section. Sixteen forward or backward sequential access data streams can be detected and managed by the HWP in each core. Once the stream direction is detected then multiple and as needed prefetch requests are made to maintain the data flow.

When effectively utilized with both software and hardware capability, prefetching can significant improve performance by reducing the possibility that all threads of the coprocessor will be stalled waiting for a memory operand to be accessible in the cache.

Vector processing unit architecture

Each core of the Intel Xeon Phi coprocessor silicon has a new SIMD 512-bit wide Vector Processing Unit (VPU) with a corresponding vector instruction set. The performance that the VPU brings for applications is almost always at least as important as using the many cores (up to 244 threads) on the coprocessor. The VPU can be used to process 16 single-precision or 8 double-precision elements per clock cycle. As depicted in Figure 8.7, there are 32 vector registers plus 8 mask registers that support per SIMD lane predicated execution. Prime (hint) instructions for scatter/gather memory access are also available. There is an Extended Math Unit (EMU) that supports single precision transcendental instructions supported in hardware for exponent, logarithm, reciprocal, and reciprocal square root operations. The VPUs are IEEE 754 2008 floating-point compliant and includes SP and DP-denormalized number support, and SAE (Suppress All Errors) support for improved performance on fdiv/sqrt. Support for streaming stores helps workloads that have large output arrays that are written to or initialized before being read.

The eight vector mask registers are denoted with a *k* prefix when used in an instruction. Each mask register is sixteen bits wide and is used by the compiler in a variety of ways, including write-masking,

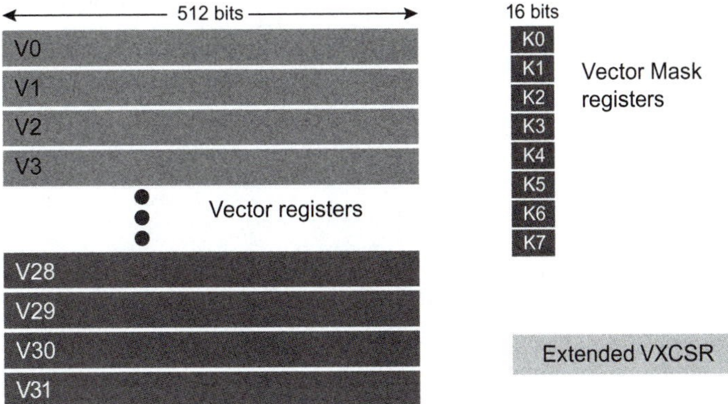

FIGURE 8.7

Intel® Xeon Phi™ Coprocessor Vector Processing Unit Registers Set.

carry/borrow flags, comparison results, and more. For instance, mask registers can allow the compiler to perform conditional (if, else) statements in vector loops maintaining high throughput even in some data dependent circumstances. A status register, VXCSR, similar in operation to an SSE status register is provided. The registers are replicated four times in the core for each of the hardware thread contexts supported.

Data type conversion to and from 32-bit or 64-bit representation occurs automatically within the same instruction cycle before and after execution respectively.

The VPU instructions support the following native data types:

- Packed 32-bit integers (or dword)
- Packed 32-bit SP FP values
- Packed 64-bit integers (or qword)
- Packed 64-bit DP FP values

For arithmetic calculations, the VPU represents values internally using 32-bit or 64-bit two's complement plus a sign bit (duplicate of the MSB) for signed integers, and 32-bit or 64-bit plus a sign bit tied to zero for unsigned integers. The VPU represents floating-point values internally using signed-magnitude with exponent bias of 128 or 1024 to adhere to the IEEE basic single-precision or double-precision format.

The Extended Math Unit (EMU) provides 1-cycle or 2-cycle throughput single precision transcendental functions. Specifically, the hardware will provide elementary functions: reciprocal (1/X, recip), reciprocal square root ($1/\sqrt{X}$, rsqrt), base 2 exponential (2^X, exp2), and logarithm base 2 (log2). Other transcendental functions can be derived from elementary functions: division (div) using recip and multiplication (mult), square root (sqrt) using rsqrt and mult, exponential base 10 (exp) using exp2 and mult, logarithm base B (logB) using log2 and mult, and power (pow) using log2, mult and exp2.

Vector instructions

Historically, SIMD implementations have a common set of semantic operations such as add, subtract, multiply, and so forth. Where most SIMD implementations differ lies in the specific number of operands to an operator, the nature of less common operations such as data permutations, and the treatment of individual elements contained inside a vector register.

Like Intel's AVX instructions, the Intel Xeon Phi coprocessor silicon uses a three-operand form for its vector SIMD instruction set. For any generic instruction operator, denoted by `vop`, the corresponding Intel® Xeon Phi™ coprocessor instruction would commonly be:

```
vop:::zmm1,:zmm2,:zmm3
```

Where `zmm1`, `zmm2`, `zmm3` are vector registers, and `vop` is the operation (add, subtract, and so on) to perform on them. The resulting expression[1] would be:

```
zmm1 = zmm2:::vop:::zmm3
```

[1]This is true for two-operand operators, such as arithmetic + or ×. For those operators that require additional operands, such as carry-propagate instructions or fused multiply-add, a different form is used.

Given that the Intel architecture is a CISC design, the Intel Xeon Phi coprocessor allows the second source operand to be a memory reference, thereby creating an *implicit memory load* operation in addition to the vector operation. The generic representation of using such a memory source is shown as:

```
vop:::zmm1,:zmm2,;[ptr]
zmm1 = zmm2:::vop:::MEM[ptr]
```

Any memory reference in the Intel Xeon Phi coprocessor instruction set conforms to standard Intel architecture conventions, so it can be a direct pointer reference (`[rax]`) or an indirect (`[rbp] + [rcx]`), and can include an immediate offset, scale, or both[2] in either direct or indirect addressing form.

While these basics are relatively straightforward and universal, the Intel Xeon Phi coprocessor introduces new operations to the vector instruction set in the form of *modifiers*. The mask registers can be understood as one type of modifier, where most vector operations take a mask register to use as a write-mask of the result:

```
vop:::zmm1:{k1},:zmm2,:zmm3 or:[ptr]
```

In the above expression, the specifier `k1` indicates that vector mask register number one is an additional source to this operation. The mask register is specified inside curly brackets {}, which indicates that the mask register is used as a write-mask register. If the vector register has `COUNT` elements inside it, then the interpretation of the write-mask behavior could be considered as:

```
for (i = 0; i < COUNT; i++)
{
if (k1[i] == 1)
  zmm1[i] = zmm2[i]vopzmm3[i]
}
```

The key observation here is that the write-mask is a nondestructive modification to the destination register; that is, where the write-mask has the value 0 no modification of the vector register's corresponding element occurs in that position. Where the mask has the value 1, the corresponding element of the destination vector register is replaced with the result of the operation indicated by `vop`.

Another modifier argument that may be specified on most SIMD vector operations is a *swizzle*, although the specific swizzle behavior is determined by whether the arguments are from registers or memory. The first type of swizzle is only permitted when all operands to the vector operation are registers:

```
vop:::zmm1:[:{k1}:],:zmm2,:zmm3:[:{swizzle}:]
```

Here, square brackets [:] denote that the write-mask and the swizzle are optional modifiers of the instruction. A swizzle is also denoted with curly brackets {:} (just as write-masks are denoted). Conceptually, an optional swizzle modifier causes the second source argument to be modified via a data pattern shuffle *for the duration of this one instruction*. It does not modify the contents of

[2]For instance, an address could be of the form [*rbp*] + ([*rax*]*2) + 0*xA*43*C*0000.

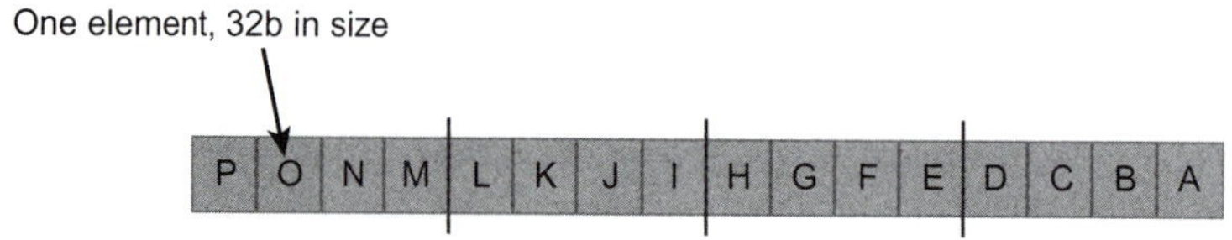

FIGURE 8.8

Per Element Vector Organization When Operating on 16 Elements of 32-bit Data.

the second source register, it only makes a temporary copy and modifies the temporary copy. The temporary copy is discarded at the end of the instruction.

The swizzle modifier that the Intel Xeon Phi coprocessor supports has an alternate form when used with the implicit load form. In this form, the swizzle acts as a broadcast modifier of the value loaded from memory. This means that a subset of memory may be read and then replicated for the entire width of the vector architecture. This can be useful for vector expansion of a scalar, for repeating values, or for common mathematical operations.

One subtle aspect of the Intel Xeon Phi coprocessor design is that each vector register is treated as though it entirely contains either 32-bit or 64-bit elements. Figure 8.8 depicts the organization of the vector register when working with 32-bit data.

When executing an Intel Xeon Phi coprocessor vector instruction, all arithmetic operations are carried out at either 32-bit or 64-bit granularity. This means that, when manipulating data of a different native size such as a two-byte float called float16, a different mathematical result might be obtained than if the operation were carried out with native float16 hardware. This can cause bit-differences between an expected result and the actual result, triggering violations of commutativity or associativity rules.

Intel Xeon Phi coprocessor includes IEEE 754-2008 [(Institute of Electrical and Electronics Engineers Standard for Floating Point Arithmetic, 2008)]-compliant, fused multiply-add (FMA) and fused multiply-subtract (FMS) instructions as well. These instructions produce results that are accurate to 0.5 ulp[3] (one-rounding) as compared to separate multiply and add instructions back-to-back, as well as, the "fused" multiply-add instructions of other architectures that produce results of 1.0 ulp (two-rounding). In the case of Intel Xeon Phi coprocessor's fused instructions, the basic three-operand instruction form is interpreted slightly differently:

```
zmm1 = zmm1:::vop1:::zmm2:::vop2:::zmm3
```

FMA operations, for example, may have `vop1` set to × and `vop2` set to +. The reality is richer than this. As mentioned previously, the ability to perform implicit memory loads for the second source argument `zmm3`, or to apply swizzles, conversions, or broadcasts to the second source argument, allows a wider range of instruction possibilities. In the presence of FMA and FMS, however, this restriction may lead to cumbersome workarounds to place the desired source field as the second source in the instruction.

Therefore, the Intel Xeon Phi coprocessor instruction set provides a series of FMA and FMS operations, each one numbered in a sequence of three digits to the order field interpretation. This allows the

[3]Unit in the Last Place (ulp), a measure of the accuracy of the least significant bit in a result.

use of the modifiers without knowing the particulars of the features. For example, the FMA operation for 32-bit floating-point data comes with these variants: `vmadd132ps`, `vmadd213ps`, and `vmadd231ps`. The logical interpretation is seen from the numeric string embedded in each mnemonic:

```
vfmadd132ps:::zmm1,zmm2,zmm3 : zmm1 = zmm1 × zmm3 + zmm2
vfmadd213ps:::zmm1,zmm2,zmm3 : zmm1 = zmm2 × zmm1 + zmm3
vfmadd231ps:::zmm1,zmm2,zmm3 : zmm1 = zmm2 × zmm3 + zmm1
```

Memory loads, modifiers such as swizzle, conversion, or broadcast, are only applicable to the `zmm3` term. By selecting a mnemonic, you can apply the modifiers to different locations in the functional expression.

The Intel Xeon Phi coprocessor also introduces a special fused multiply-add operation that acts as a scale and bias transformation in one instruction: `vfmadd233ps`. The interpretation of this instruction can be summarized in a series of equations. The `vfmadd233ps` of the form `vfmadd233ps:` $\vec{z}, \vec{u}, \vec{v}$ generates the following:

$$\vec{z}_{3..0} = \vec{u}_{3..0} \times \vec{v}_1 + \vec{v}_0$$
$$\vec{z}_{7..4} = \vec{u}_{7..4} \times \vec{v}_5 + \vec{v}_4$$
$$\vec{z}_{11..8} = \vec{u}_{11..8} \times \vec{v}_9 + \vec{v}_8$$
$$\vec{z}_{15..12} = \vec{u}_{15..12} \times \vec{v}_{13} + \vec{v}_{12}$$

The Intel Xeon Phi coprocessor also introduces vector versions of the carry-propagate instructions (CPI). As with scalar Intel architecture carry-propagate instructions, these can be combined together to support wider integer arithmetic than the hardware default. These are also building blocks for other forms of wide-arithmetic emulations. The challenge incurred in the vector version of these instructions (discussed in detail later on) is that a carry-out flag must be generated for each element in the vector. Similarly, on the propagation side, a carry-in flag must be added for each element in the vector. The Intel Xeon Phi coprocessor uses the vector mask register for both of these: as a carry-out bit vector and as a carry-in bit vector.

There are many other additions to the Intel Xeon Phi coprocessor instruction set, for use in both scalar and vector operations. A deeper, more detailed description may be found in the *Intel Xeon Phi Coprocessor Instruction Set Reference Manual* referenced in the "For More Information" section at the end of this chapter.

Coprocessor PCIe system interface and DMA

The Intel Xeon Phi coprocessor card complies with the Gen2 x16 PCI Express specification. PCI Express peer-to-peer writes and reads are also supported allowing direct communication with other PCI Express devices on the platform without host memory staging required. All data exchanges onto and off of the coprocessor traverses the PCI Express bus. Two primary means are provided to exchange data, memory-mapped virtual addressing, and DMA. Low latency memory-mapped address spaces on both the card and the host platform allow standard instructions on the processor or coprocessor to read or write data to the others address space. This is typically best for shorter data transfers and messages. Larger transfers generally benefit from asynchronous hardware managed transfers provided by the DMA logic.

DMA capabilities

Direct Memory Access (DMA) is a common hardware function within a computer system that is used to relieve the processor or coprocessor from the burden of copying large blocks of data. To move a block of data, the program constructs and fills a buffer, if one doesn't already exist, and then writes a descriptor into the DMA Channel's Descriptor Ring. A descriptor describes details such as the source and target memory addresses and the length of data in cache lines. The following data transfers are supported:

- Intel Xeon Phi coprocessor to Intel Xeon Phi coprocessor GDDR5 space (aperture)
- Intel Xeon Phi coprocessor GDDR5 to host System Memory
- Host System Memory to Intel Xeon Phi coprocessor GDDR5 (aperture or non-aperture)
- Intra-GDDR5 Block Transfers within Intel Xeon Phi coprocessor

A DMA Descriptor Ring is programmed by either the coprocessor operating system or the Host Driver. Up to eight Descriptor Rings can be opened by software; each being referred to as a DMA Channel. The coprocessor operating system or Host Driver can open a DMA Channel in either system or GDDR5 memory respectively; that is, all descriptor rings owned by the host driver must exist in system memory while rings owned by the coprocessor operating system must exist in GDDR5 memory. A programmable arbitration scheme resolves access conflicts when multiple DMA Channels vie for system or Intel Xeon Phi coprocessor resources.

The coprocessor supports host-initiated or device-initiated PCI Express Gen2/Gen1 memory, I/O, and configuration transactions. The coprocessor device-initiated memory transactions can be generated either from execution cores directly or by using the DMA engine in the SBOX.

In summary, the DMA controller has the following capabilities:

- Eight DMA channels operating simultaneously, each with its own independent hardware ring buffer that can live in either local coprocessor or system memory
- Supports transfers in either direction (host/coprocessor devices)
- Supports transfers initiated by either side
- Always transfers using physical addresses
- Interrupt generation upon completion
- 64-byte granularity for alignment and size
- Writing completion tags to either local coprocessor memory or host system

The DMA block operates at the coprocessor core clock frequency. There are eight independent channels that can move data:

- From GDDR5 Memory to System Memory
- From System Memory to GDDR5 Memory
- From GDDR5 Memory to GDDR5 Memory

The coprocessor not only supports 64-bytes (1 cache line) per PCI Express transaction, but up to a maximum of 256 bytes for each DMA-initiated transaction. This requires that the Root-Complex support 256-byte transactions. Programming the `MAX_PAYLOAD_SIZE` in the `PCI_COMMAND_STATUS` register sets the actual size of each transaction.

DMA channel arbitration

There is no notion of priority between descriptors within a DMA Channel; descriptors are fetched, and operated on, in a sequential order. Priority between descriptors is resolved by opening multiple DMA channels and performing arbitration between DMA channels in a round-robin fashion.

Descriptor ring overview

A Descriptor Ring is a circular buffer as shown in Figure 8.9. The length of a Descriptor Ring can be up to 128-KB entries, and must align to the nearest cache line boundary. Software manages the ring by advancing a Head Pointer as it fills the ring with descriptors. When the descriptors have been copied, it writes this updated Header Pointer into the DMA Head Pointer Register (`DHPR0–DHPR7`) for the appropriate DMA Channel. Each DMA Channel contains a Tail Pointer that advances as descriptors are fetched into a channel's Local Descriptor Queue. The Descriptor Queue is 64 entries, and can be thought of as a sliding window over the Descriptor Ring. The Tail Pointer is periodically written back to memory so that software can track its progress. Upon initialization,

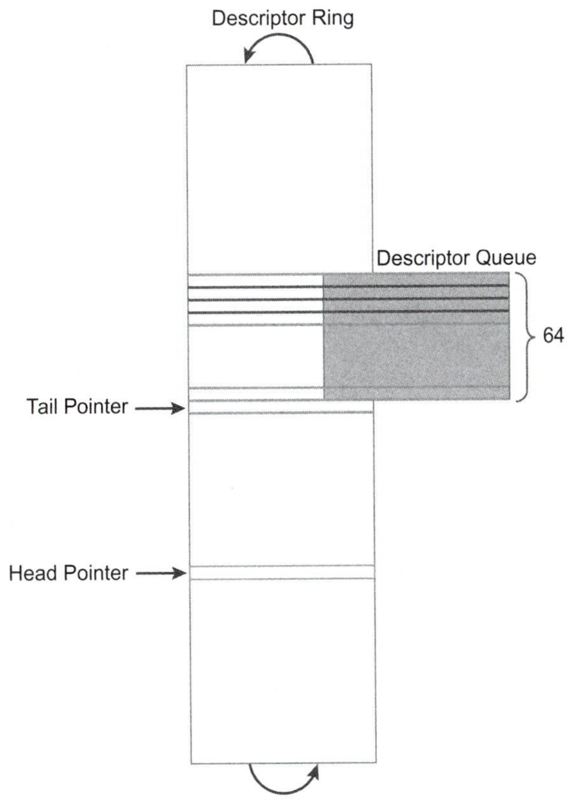

FIGURE 8.9

DMA Channel Descriptor Ring Plus Local Descriptor Queue.

software sets both the Head Pointer and Tail Pointer to point to the base of the Descriptor Ring. From the DMA Channel perspective, an empty state is approached when the Tail Pointer approaches the Head Pointer. From a software perspective, a full condition is approached when the Head Pointer approaches the Tail Pointer.

The Head and Tail Pointers are addresses. If the high-order bit is a 1, the descriptors reside in system memory; otherwise they reside in the Intel Xeon Phi coprocessor memory. Descriptors come in five different formats and are 16 bytes in length. There are no alignment restrictions when writing descriptors into the ring. However, performance is optimized when descriptors start and end on cache line boundaries because memory accesses are performed on cache line granularities, four descriptors at a time.

Coprocessor power management capabilities

Intel Xeon Phi coprocessor power management supports several Intel architecture standard power management states. Unlike the multicore family of Intel Xeon processors, there is no hardware-level power control unit (PCU); power management is controlled by the coprocessor operating system described in Chapter 10. The *Intel Xeon Phi System Software Developers Guide* referenced in the "For More Information" section at the end of this chapter has a detailed description of the power management features.

Figures 8.10 through 8.15 provide a visual description of the power management states supported on the coprocessor.

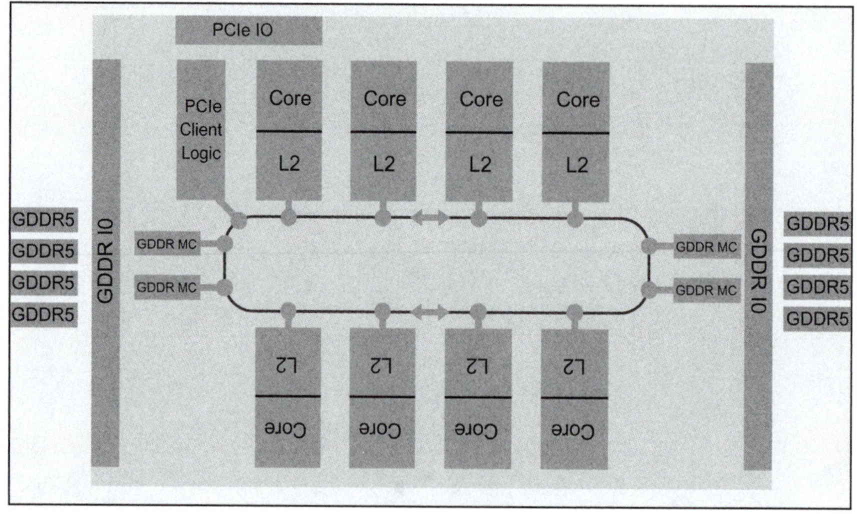

FIGURE 8.10

C0: All Coprocessor Silicon Cores and Components Running.

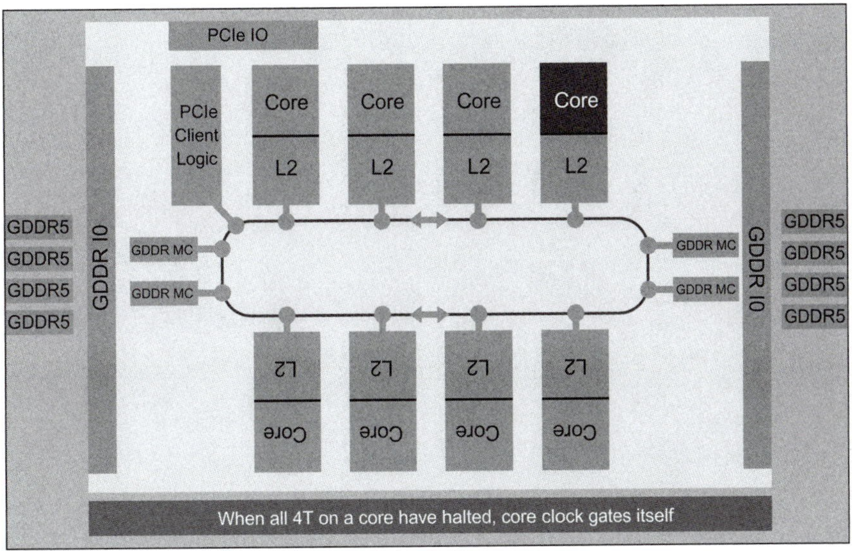

FIGURE 8.11

Single Core C1 State: Clock Gate Core.

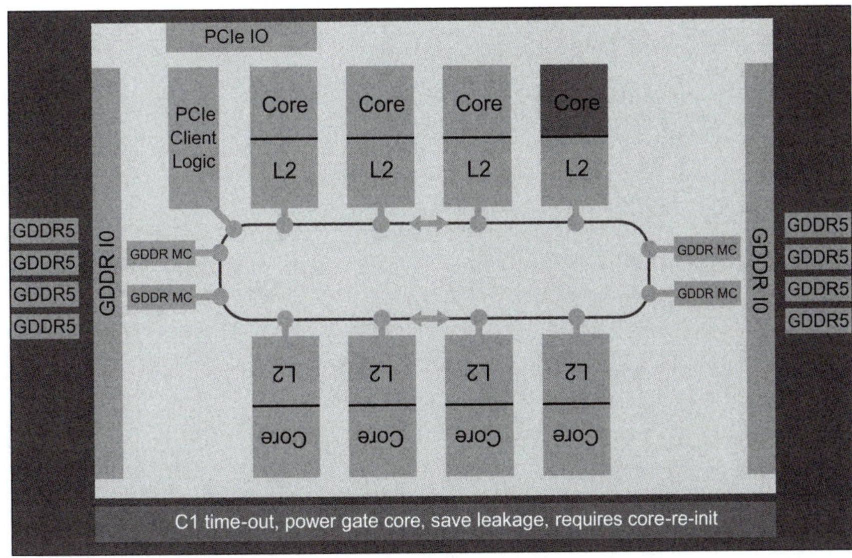

FIGURE 8.12

Single Core C6 State: Power Gate Core.

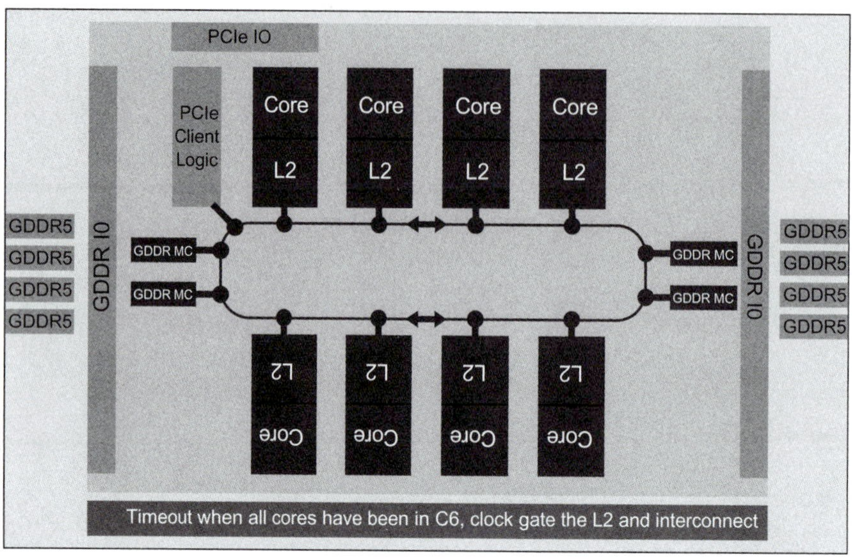

FIGURE 8.13

Whole Package Auto C3: Clock Gate L2 Cache and On-Die Interconnect.

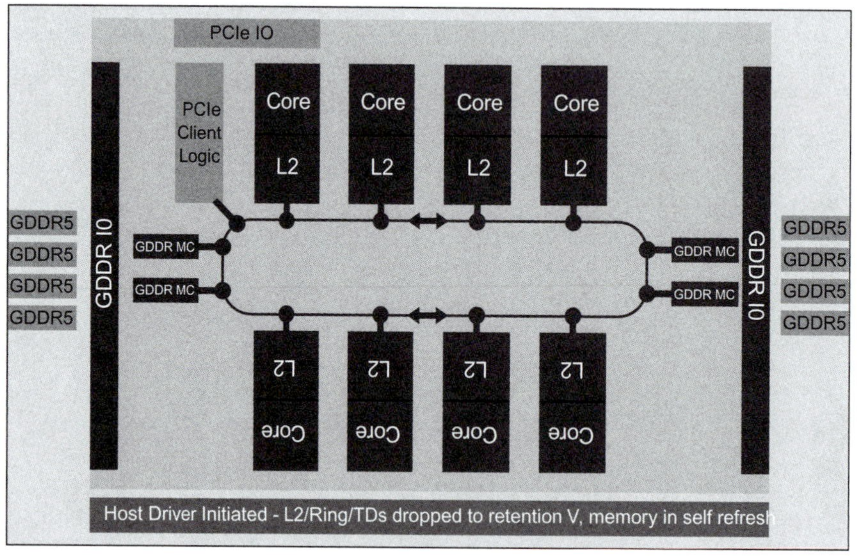

FIGURE 8.14

Whole Package Deep C3.

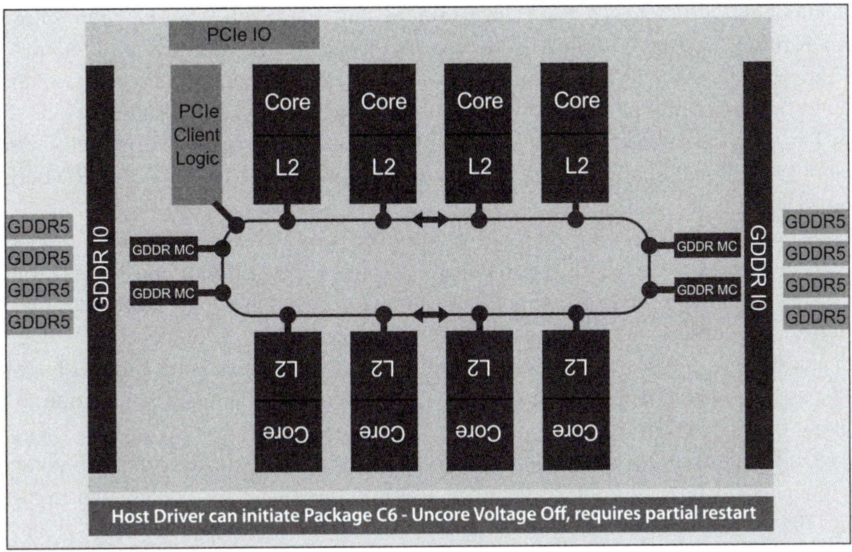

FIGURE 8.15

Whole Package C6: Lowest Power State.

Reliability, availability, and serviceability (RAS)

RAS stands for reliability, availability, and serviceability. Specifically, reliability is defined as the ability of the system to perform its actions correctly. Availability is the ability of the system to perform useful work. Serviceability is the ability of the system to be repaired when failures occur. Given that high performance long-running computing tasks may require large amounts of resources both in processing power (count of processing entities or nodes) and in processing time, node reliability becomes a limiting factor if not addressed by RAS strategies and policies. This section covers RAS strategies available in hardware and software on Intel Xeon Phi coprocessor and its host-side server.

In compute clusters, reliability and availability are traditionally handled in a two-pronged approach: by deploying hardware with advanced RAS features to reduce error rates (as exemplified in the Intel Xeon processors) and by adopting fault tolerance in high-end system software or hardware. Common software-based methods of fault tolerance are to deploy redundant cluster nodes or to implement snapshot and restore (checkpointing) mechanisms that allow a cluster manager to reduce data loss when a compute node fails by setting it to the state of last successful snapshot. Fault tolerance, in this context, is about resuming from a failure with as much of the machine state intact as possible. It does not imply that a cluster or individual compute nodes can absorb or handle failures without interrupting the task at hand.

The Intel Xeon Phi coprocessor addresses reliability and availability the same two ways. Hardware features have been added that improve reliability; for example, standard Error Correcting Codes (ECC) on both GDDR5 memory and internal memory arrays that reduce error rates. There are also additional parity checks built into critical circuits. Fault tolerance on Intel Xeon Phi coprocessor hardware improves failure detection (extended machine check architecture, or MCA). Managed properly, the result is a controlled and limited degradation allowing a node to stay in service after certain anticipated hardware failure modes manifest themselves. Fault tolerance in Intel Xeon Phi coprocessor software is assisted by the Linux coprocessor operating system, which supports application-level snapshot and restore features that are based on BLCR (Berkeley Labs Checkpoint Restart).

The Intel Xeon Phi coprocessor approach to serviceability is through software redundancy (that is, node management removes failing compute nodes from the cluster), and has no true hardware redundancy. Instead software and firmware features allow a compute node to reenter operation after failures at reduced capacity until the card can be replaced. The rationale behind this "graceful" degradation strategy is the assumption that an Intel Xeon Phi coprocessor unit with, say, one less core, will be able to resume application snapshots and therefore is a better proposition to the cluster than removing the node entirely.

A hardware failure requires the failing card to be temporarily removed from the compute cluster it is participating in. After a reboot, the card may rejoin the cluster if cluster management policies allow for it. The rebooted card may have the previously mentioned "graceful" degradation if persistent errors require turning off nonfunctional cores or parts of L2 cache, and so on.

Machine check architecture (MCA)

Machine Check Architecture is a hardware feature enabling an Intel Xeon Phi coprocessor card to report failures to software by means of interrupts or exceptions. Failures in this context are conditions where logic circuits have detected something out of order, which may have corrupted processor context or memory content. Failures are categorized by severity as either DUEs or CEs:

- DUEs (Detected Unrecoverable Errors) are errors captured by the MC logic but the corruption cannot be repaired and the system as a whole is compromised; for example, errors in L1 cache.
- CEs (Corrected Errors) are errors that have occurred and been corrected by the hardware, such as single bit errors in L2 ECC memory.

Standard Intel architecture systems implement MCA by providing two mechanisms to report MC events to software: MC exceptions (#18) for events detected in the core and NMI (#2) interrupts for events detected outside of the core (uncore).

Specifics on occurred MC exceptions are presented in MSR banks, each representing up to 32 events. The processor capability MSRs specify how many banks are supported by a given processor. The interpretation of data in MSR banks is semi-standardized; acquiring detailed raw data on an event is standardized but the interpretation of acquired raw data is not. The Intel Xeon Phi coprocessor provides three MC MSR banks.

MC events signaled through the NMI interrupt on standard Intel architecture systems come from the chipsets and represent failures in memory or I/O paths. Newer processors with built-in memory controllers also provide a separate interrupt for CEs (CMCIs) that have built-in counter dividers to throttle interrupt rates. This capability is not provided on the Intel Xeon Phi coprocessor. Instead, the coprocessor delivers both uncorrected and corrected errors that are detected in the core domain via the standard MCA interrupt (#18). Machine check events that occur in the uncore domain are delivered via the System Interface, which can be programmed to generate an NMI interrupt targeted at one or all threads. The Uncore Interrupt includes MC events related to the PCI-Express interface, Memory Controller (ECC and link training errors), or other uncore units. There is no CE error rate throttle in the coprocessor. If high error frequencies interfere with operations unnecessarily it is possible to disable the interrupt at the source of the initiating unit (L2/L1 Cache, Tag Directory, or Memory Controller).

The NMI interrupt handler software must handle a diverse range of error types on Intel Xeon Phi coprocessor. Registers to control and report uncore MC events on the coprocessor differ significantly from registers on standard Intel architecture chipsets, which means that stock operating systems have no support for uncore MC events on a coprocessor.

The Intel Xeon Phi coprocessor implements extended machine check architecture (MCA) features that allow software to detect and act on detected hardware failures in a manner allowing a "graceful" degradation of service when certain components fail. Coprocessor hardware reads bits from programmable flash memory at boot time, which may disable processor cores, cache lines, and tag directories that the MCA has reported as failing. More details on the key RAS architecture elements is available in the *Intel Xeon Phi System Software Developers Guide* referenced in the "For More Information" section at the end of this chapter.

Coprocessor system management controller (SMC)

As essentially a full computing platform packaged in a PCI Express card, features for users, administrators, and baseboard management controller software (BMC) are provided to monitor and manage the Intel Xeon Phi coprocessor. One key component enabling that manageability is an intelligent, firmware driven System Management Controller (SMC) on the card as shown in Figure 8.2.

The SMC is a microcontroller-based thermal management and communications sub-system that provides card-level control and monitoring of the coprocessor. Thermal management is achieved through monitoring the coprocessor silicon and various temperature sensors located on the coprocessor card. Card-level power management monitors the card input power draw and communicates current power conditions to the coprocessor silicon and its operating software.

The SMC communicates information via two communication channels. Communication with the onboard coprocessor silicon is done via a standard I^2C interface. Out of band communication with the host platform is done via the PCI Express supported System Management Bus (SMBus) using the industry standard Intelligent Platform Management Interface (IPMI) protocol.

Sensors

Thermal sensors located on the Intel Xeon Phi coprocessor provide information about the coprocessor silicon temperature as well as the temperature from three locations on the Intel Xeon Phi coprocessor card. Currently, one sensor is located between memory chips near the PCI Express slot while the other two are located on the east and west sides of the card. These east and west sensors are generally referred to as the "inlet" and "outlet" air temperature sensors but they do not actually indicate airflow temperatures but rather the temperature of each side of the card. These sensors can be correlated to air temperature for purposes of system thermal management.

Power sensors are attached to the power inputs from the PCI Express slot, and the two (2×3 and 2×4) auxiliary power connectors on the coprocessor card. Input power can be estimated by summing the currents over these three power connections.

Thermal design power monitoring and control

To support maintaining the coprocessor's target Thermal Design Power (TDP) level, there as several mechanisms in the SMC to signal the host and/or coprocessor silicon when thermal or power consumption limits are reached. Two programmable power consumption limits are provided and managed by the SMC. One limit defaults to 105 percent of the TDP power consumption. If this first level limit is exceeded, the SMC notifies the Intel Xeon Phi coprocessor operating system through an interrupt to reduce power by lowering the coprocessor silicon's clock speed by 100 MHz. The second power limit occurs at 125 percent generating a "throttling event," which drops to the lowest supported clock speed on the coprocessor silicon, (600–800 MHz depending on the model) in an attempt to reduce power at or below the TDP. When the SMC detects and communicates a reduction below the primary limit the core clock is restored to its nominal rate.

The SMC also monitors the thermal sensors for a maximum card temperature threshold limit. If that limit is reached then a thermal throttling condition occurs causing the coprocessor silicon to drop to its lowest supported clock speed. Again, when the temperature state is restored to operational levels the clock returns to its nominal speed.

Alternatively, on Intel Xeon Phi coprocessor models with passive thermal solutions, the host platform's baseboard management solution can utilize the PCI Express card's `B12` pin to assert a coprocessor card signal known as `PROCHOT` that is monitored by the SMC. This allows platform level thermal monitoring to request the card perform thermal throttling in support of overall platform thermal reduction.

Fan speed control

For an actively cooled card, the SMC will automatically increase and decrease the fan speed to maintain card temperature within specified limits. If the card exceeds the maximum thermal threshold the actively cooled fan will be placed at maximum speed in addition to the throttling mechanism dropping the coprocessor silicon clock to its minimum supported speed.

Potential application impact

The key impact for applications of thermal and power events is unexpected performance loss or lack of consistent, repeatable performance over multiple test runs since the primary mitigation for thermal and power issues is to lower the coprocessor clock below its nominal rate. In normal circumstances, the majority of applications should not be the cause of thermal or power events. However, should you experience unexplainable performance degradation or variability on repeated runs on the same node or across identical nodes then checking for power or thermal events by contacting your system administrator or using the available coprocessor monitoring tools described further in Chapter 9 would be something to consider.

Benchmarks

Since Intel Xeon Phi coprocessors come in so many models, and new versions are likely to continue to emerge, we choose to not dedicate pages of this book to benchmarking. Intel and some users have published a number of benchmarks already, and we will see more in the future. The Internet is an excellent resource for finding the latest claims and publications.

It is useful to note that Intel took a decidedly refreshing approach to benchmarking, which at first glance makes their benchmark numbers seem small. Intel choose to only compare the Intel Xeon Phi coprocessors when running optimized workloads to a pair of recent Intel Xeon processors also running optimized workloads. That breaks with a common practice in accelerator benchmarking of comparing an unoptimized (often single-threaded) workloads running on a (often older) processor against a highly optimized accelerator workload. In such situations, gains of "100X" could be claimed regardless of the relevance of such a comparison. Intel's approach results in some claims "only" in the "2X" realm, but along with claims of beating accelerators in terms of performance and power efficiency despite the seeming contradiction of "100X" claims by the accelerators.

Intel's choice to compare against two processors, instead of one, is an interesting one to understand as well. It turns out that two processors are closer in power consumption to a single coprocessor (or accelerator) than one processor is. This choice to level the playing field based on power consumption makes sense technically, it will remain to be seen if the market appreciates the approach. Given the intense interest in power efficiency, it seems likely Intel is onto something important here.

Summary

The Intel Xeon Phi coprocessor is optimized for highly parallel workloads while retaining the support for familiar programming languages, models and tools you would expect from a symmetric multiprocessing (SMP) system built around Intel processors. This chapter helps explain in detail the particulars of *this* SMP design, including the wider vector units that contribute an important parallel capability in addition to the large number of processing cores. The use of simpler core designs allow for more cores to fit on a single die, but important very modern features including power management are in the coprocessor also. The Intel Xeon Phi coprocessor takes advantage of having all the cores and their caches on a single die to offer performance characteristics that a discrete SMP system could not. Future products that use the Intel MIC architecture may differ from this first Intel Xeon Phi coprocessor design, but the vision for the architecture of highly parallel, highly power efficient and highly programmable shines through in this very first product to use the Intel MIC architecture from Intel.

For more information

Here are some additional reading materials we recommend related to this chapter:

- Intel® MIC Quick Start Developers Guide, http://intel.com/software/mic
- Datasheet for the Intel® Xeon Phi™ Coprocessor, http://tinyurl.com/xeonphidatasheet

- Intel® Many Integrated Core Platform Software Stack, http://intel.com/software/mic
- Intel® Xeon Phi™ Coprocessor Instruction Set Architecture Reference Manual, http://intel.com/software/mic
- An Overview of Programming for Intel® Xeon® processors and Intel® Xeon Phi™ coprocessors, http://intel.com/software/mic
- Debugging Intel® Xeon Phi™ Coprocessor: Command-Line Debugging, http://intel.com/software/mic
- Building Native Applications for Intel® Xeon Phi™ Coprocessor, http://intel.com/software/mic
- Programming and Compiling for Intel® Many Integrated Core Architecture, http://intel.com/software/mic
- Intel® Xeon Phi™ coprocessor Micro-architecture Software Stack, http://intel.com/software/mic
- Intel® Xeon Phi™ coprocessor Micro-architecture Overview, http://intel.com/software/mic
- Intel® MPI Library, http://www.intel.com/go/mpi
- Intel® MIC SCIF API Reference Manual for Kernel Mode Linux, http://intel.com/software/mic
- Intel® MIC SCIF API Reference Manual for User Mode Linux, http://intel.com/software/mic
- Intelligent Platform Management Interface Specifications, http://tinyurl.com/intelipmi
- Hotchips presentation about Intel Xeon Phi coprocessor by the lead architect for the Intel Xeon Phi coprocessor. Transcript at http://tinyurl.com/georgehotchips and presentation at http://tinyurl.com/georgehotchipspdf.

CHAPTER

Coprocessor System Software

9

The unique thing to many first introduced to the Intel® Xeon Phi™ coprocessor operational software environment and architecture is its intentional goal to *not* be unique. Because it is designed as an attached device, one could mistakenly assume the coprocessor must solely operate as a peripheral device in a master-slave relationship with its host platform processor like a network card, or an FPGA, or GPU-based computational accelerator. However, as a member of the Intel Architecture family, as discussed in Chapter 8, the coprocessor inherits many of the foundational elements and capabilities of widely used Intel Architecture processing platforms. These traits enable the coprocessor to be integrated as a peer processing platform into the well understood standard software infrastructure familiar to systems level developers, application developers and system administrators for both single workstation and large cluster supercomputers.

The most obvious indicator of broad capabilities is that the Intel Xeon Phi coprocessor bootstraps and runs a Linux operating system (OS) including Linux's substantial networking capability. The ability to run a Linux OS and communicate as a network peer is one of the primary reasons it is termed a *coprocessor* and not just an accelerator (which would require software applications to be managed by the host platform).

In this chapter, we look at the software architecture and components that enable the coprocessor to operate seamlessly in a standard environment. The architecture was designed to support a broad range of applications and programming models. Therefore, we will also discuss the variety of programming models available to take full advantage of the coprocessor capabilities. We will focus on the runtime operational environment that is in place once both the processor and the coprocessor have booted their operating systems and are ready to run applications. Chapter 10 covers the coprocessor Linux operating system management in more detail, including the boot process and the basics of configuring and managing it, given that no persistent mass storage is available directly on the coprocessor. This chapter provides important foundational information for both software developers and system administrators; the next chapter will expand and dive deeper primarily for those building and maintaining systems.

Coprocessor software architecture overview

There are two major components that comprise the software structure used to build and run applications and system services that utilize the coprocessor.

- *Development Tools and Runtimes.* The development tools and associated runtime services and libraries provided by tool packages such as Intel Parallel Studio XE 2013 and Intel Cluster

Studio XE 2013. The Intel C/C++ compiler, Intel Fortran compiler, and Intel MPI library are some of the sub-components of these development tools packages.

- *Intel® Manycore Platform Software Stack (Intel® MPSS).* The operational software specific to the coprocessor including middleware interfaces used by the development tools, device drivers for communication and control, coprocessor management utilities (such as the Control Panel), and the coprocessor's local Linux operating system. Collectively this set of software is known as the Intel Manycore Platform Software Stack.

When installing coprocessors for use in an Intel® Xeon® processor platform, an early step that normally needs to be done is to download, install, and launch the latest version of Intel MPSS (available at the http://intel.com/software/mic Web site). You will then either access an existing toolset or install the available Intel or third party development tools including compilers.

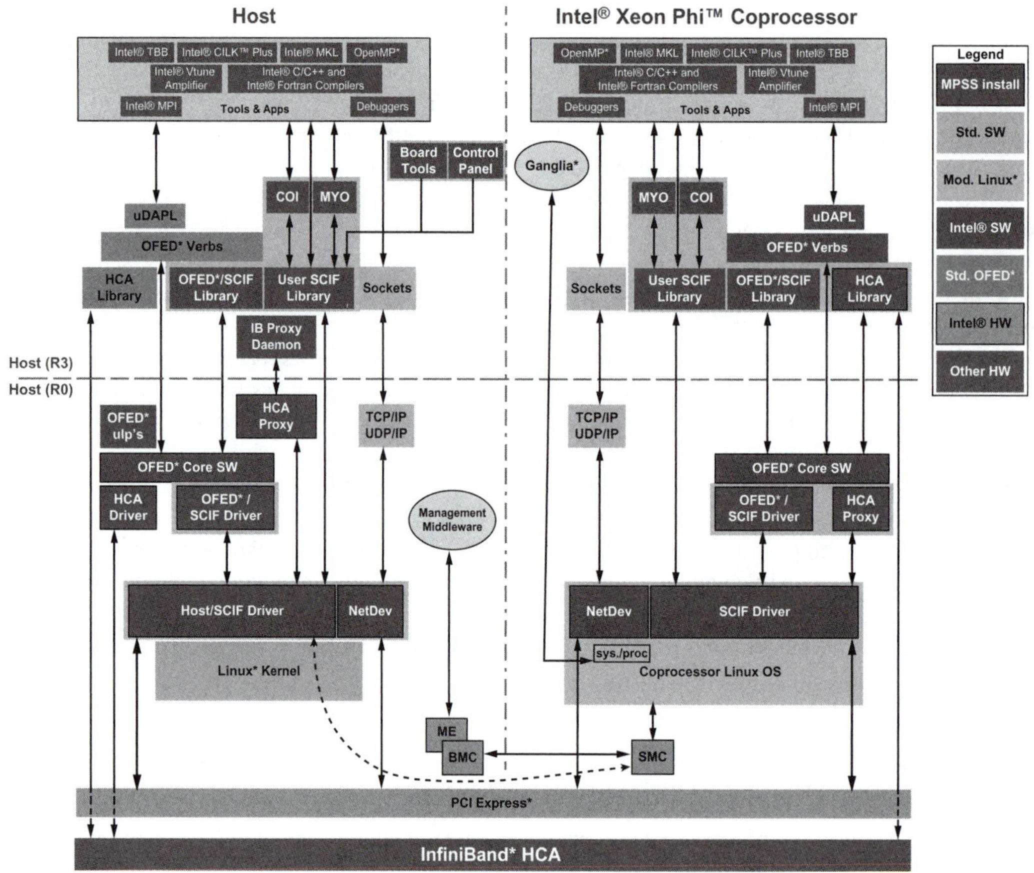

FIGURE 9.1

The Intel® Xeon Phi™ Software Architecture.

Figure 9.1 shows a block diagram of the key components that comprise the coprocessor software architecture.

Figure 9.1 is broken into left and right sides as well as top and bottom halves, represented by the dashed lines. The left side corresponds to components on the host processor platform and the right side depicts software components on the coprocessor. In the next few sections, we will touch upon the key architectural concepts this diagram implies.

Symmetry

Looking at the left and right sides of Figure 9.1 it should strike you that, with very few exceptions, the "boxes" on both sides of the diagram are the same. This belies a key underlying concept at the foundation of the software architecture for a platform with one or more coprocessors: that concept is symmetry. Making the coprocessor software components and interfaces symmetric with the host processor platform, in other words functionally identical, enables the coprocessor to be engaged by software developers in the same manner as they engage the processor.

This is a simple yet very powerful concept. This symmetry provides the fundamental basis supporting common development tools and common programming models on both the processor and coprocessor. Developers at all levels including those implementing tools, system software, and applications benefit by the familiar and common interfaces dramatically minimizing the learning curve and porting time for coprocessor targeted solutions of all kinds.

Ring levels: user and kernel

The top and bottom halves of the diagram in Figure 9.1 represent the standard operating system notion of protection domain rings with user-level application code and system interface execution at ring 3 and more trusted, system level operating system kernel and driver code running at ring 0.

It is beyond our scope to more deeply discuss these operating system design areas other than to indicate access to devices and operating system kernel services occurs virtually always through counterpart ring 3 user mode library interfaces and kernel mode ring 0 modules. The user mode library interfaces manage the ring transitions between the companion kernel-level modules, maintaining the security and integrity of the system. The concept can be seen in Figure 9.1 with like-named ring 3 user mode libraries calling upon their corresponding kernel module.

Before we more thoroughly explain the purpose of each component in Figure 9.1, we will discuss the programming models that are enabled and that influenced the creation of the coprocessor software architecture. Then the purpose of the provided system modules will have better context and be more easily described.

Coprocessor programming models and options

The overall architecture of a platform that includes Intel Xeon Phi coprocessors enables a broad array of usages. This flexibility allows a dynamic range of solutions to address many target computing needs—from mostly serial processing to highly parallel processing to a mix of both. Intel and industry partners are delivering and creating tools and standards for processor/coprocessor platforms that can be used to develop applications that are optimal for the problem at hand.

Figure 9.2 illustrates the compute spectrum enabled when coupling processors and coprocessors. Depending on the application's compute needs, execution can be initiated on either a host processor or on one or more coprocessors. Depending on the application needs and system environment, any mix of computation between the processor and coprocessor can be chosen for optimal performance.

Included in Figure 9.2 is a conceptual view of how code might be launched and executed in the key enabled programming uses. From left to right those models are:

- *Processor Hosted.* The application is launched and executed on processors only.
- *Offload.* The application is launched and primarily managed on processors and selected portions of code (usually highly parallel) are run on coprocessors using either the Intel Math Kernel Library automatic offload (See Chapter 11), Intel Language Extensions for Offload or OpenMP "target" extensions (see Chapter 7).
- *Symmetric.* The application is launched on both coprocessors and processors with cooperative communication (typically via MPI).
- *Coprocessor Hosted.* The application is launched and executed on coprocessors only.

Each of these different computation choices are discussed with running examples throughout the book, particularly in Chapters 2 (native, offload), 3 (native, host), 4 (native), and 12 (all models using MPI).

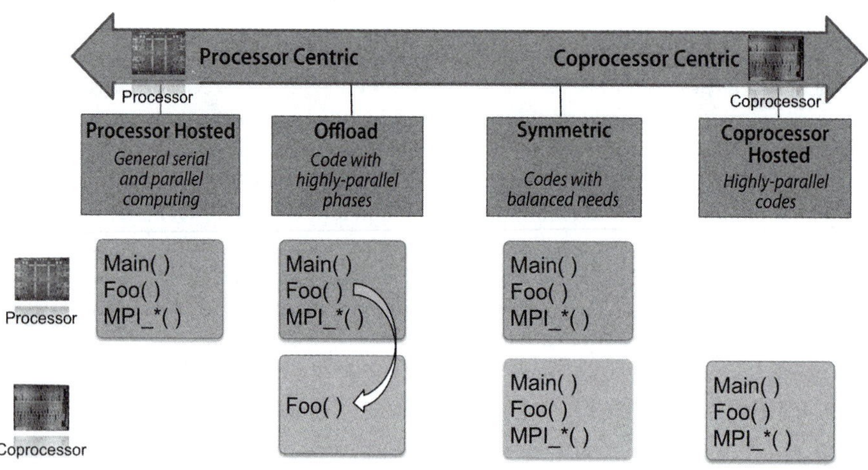

FIGURE 9.2

The Wide Spectrum of Joint Programming Models for an Intel® Xeon® Platform with a Coprocessor Including Primary Application Usages.

> **NOTE**
>
> The coprocessor-hosted model is often referred to in this book and Intel documentation as *coprocessor native* or just *native* execution. It refers to code compiled using the `-mmic` compiler option that targets code generation for launch and execution on Intel® MIC Architecture based products such as an Intel Xeon Phi coprocessor. Also, the term *host* when used alone typically refers to the processor or processor platform.

Breadth and depth

The software architecture not only enables the breadth of models shown in Figure 9.2 but also provides well known, deeper level fine controls similar to those available on other Intel Architecture processing platforms. Developers who want or need to focus on absolute maximum performance, are implementing targeted libraries and tools, or are developing specialty capabilities not otherwise fully enabled by existing tools are likely users of these programming alternatives. Figure 9.3 illustrates some of the layers and options available for developing applications with increasing levels of control, and, generally, more complexity.

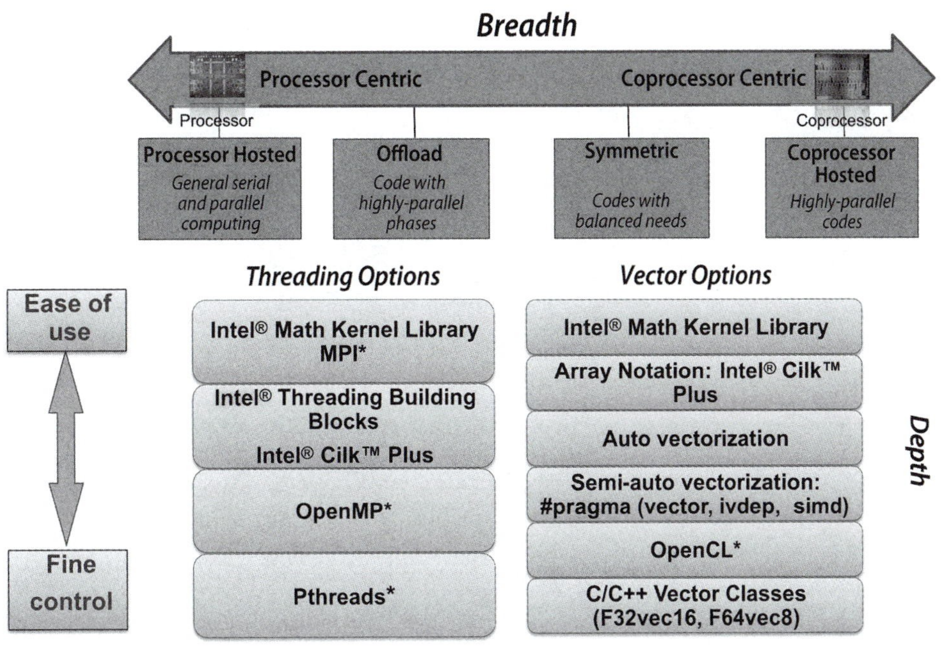

FIGURE 9.3

Coprocessor Programming Options Providing Different Methods of Control for Developers at All Levels.

Coprocessor MPI programming models

As previously mentioned, the coprocessor architecture has been designed to readily support the industry standard Message Passing Interface. In particular, the Intel® MPI library supports all the programming execution models described in Figure 9.2. MPI is the de facto library-based communication environment used to enable parallel applications to run, communicate, and scale across multiple processing cores, either between the multiple cores in a single Intel Xeon processor platform or across a connected network of nodes (individual platforms) in a cluster. Furthermore, key MPI supporting sub-component standard layers such as the Open Fabrics Alliance defined Open Fabrics Enterprise Distribution (OFED) interfaces are also supported on both the processor and the coprocessor. Chapter 12 provides programming examples and key information for getting started with MPI applications that include coprocessors. Here we will provide an overview of the available programming models.

Offload model

The offload model is characterized by the MPI communications taking place only between the host processors. The coprocessors are used exclusively through the offload capabilities as described in Chapter 7. This mode of operation is fairly straightforward, simply enabling offloading as part of existing or newly developed MPI-based applications. Making MPI library calls inside offloaded code is not supported. Figure 9.4 illustrates the MPI with offload model.

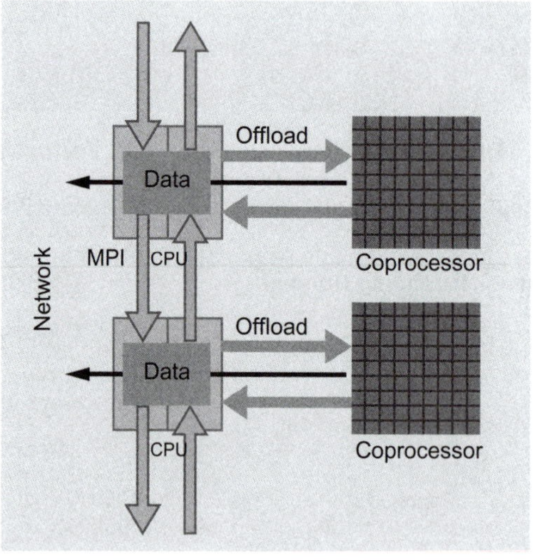

FIGURE 9.4

MPI on the Host Processor Platform Using Offload to Coprocessors.

Coprocessor-only model

The MPI coprocessor-only or *native* model has the MPI processes launched and residing solely on the coprocessor. MPI libraries, the application, and other needed libraries are uploaded to the coprocessors. Then an application can be launched from the host or from the coprocessor. Once the application is running, MPI network communications between other coprocessors (either on the local node or to other network fabric connected nodes) are managed by the Intel® Coprocessor Communications Link (Intel® CCL) services. Intel CCL provides underlying services to the MPI library to select the optimal transport for MPI messages. One such Intel CCL transport mechanism is the peer-to-peer PCI Express DMA support described in Chapter 8 to directly transfer message data between the coprocessor's memory and a peer InfiniBand (IB) adapter without host memory staging. Figure 9.5 illustrates the MPI Coprocessor-Only model. More details on the structure and components of Intel CCL are described later in this chapter.

Symmetric model

The MPI Symmetric programming model launches and executes the MPI application on both the host processor and the coprocessors. Figure 9.6 illustrates the symmetric MPI model. This is the most flexible model supporting "any to any" messaging. Message passing may occur within the coprocessor, within the host processor, between the coprocessor and the processor within the same node, and between coprocessors and processors across a cluster through several fabric mechanisms. Chapter 12 and the Intel MPI documentation describe the options available in more detail. As with the coprocessor only model, Intel® CCL optimally manages communication transport to or from processors and coprocessors across the network.

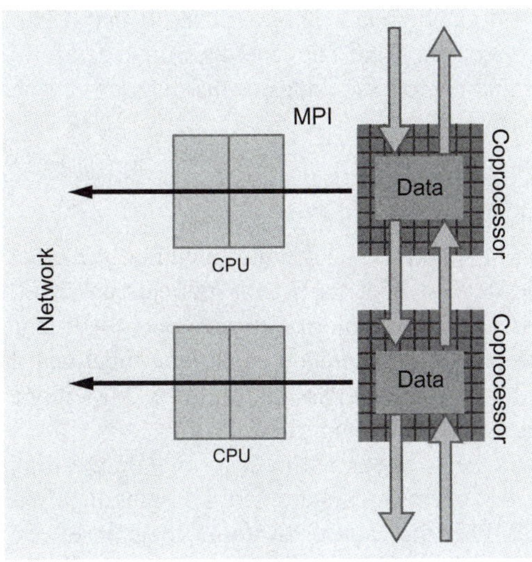

FIGURE 9.5

MPI Running on Coprocessors Only.

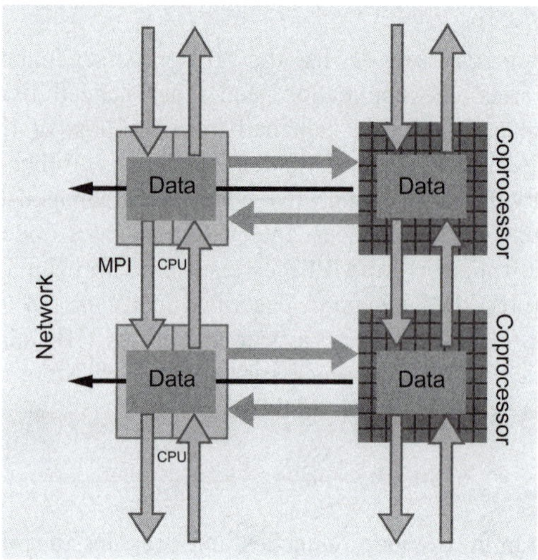

FIGURE 9.6

MPI Symmetric Communications with MPI Running on Both Processors and Coprocessors.

Coprocessor software architecture components

Now that we have an understanding for the programming models and primary usage scenarios that informed the definition of the architecture, we will describe the key purpose for each of the architecture components illustrated in Figure 9.1. You will recall that a key element of the architecture is functional symmetry between the host and coprocessor. Therefore where a component is the same on both the processor and coprocessor sides of the diagram, we need only describe it once.

Development tools and application layer

Figure 9.7 depicts a portion of software architecture including the blocks marked "Tools & Apps," which represents where the development tools and applications sit in the architecture of the full software stack. This layer is where the majority of developers will engage with both the processor and coprocessor. The development tools include compilers, functional libraries (such as the Intel® Math Kernel Library (MKL) and Message Passing Interface (MPI) libraries from Intel and the open source community), debuggers, profilers, and more.

Processor and coprocessor applications are built to include the runtime components and libraries, which in turn call upon the operating system and the immediately underlying middleware components provided in Intel MPSS that allow the tools to expose key programming models and functionality. Most programmers will be successful concentrating their development using the tools layer alone. However, as you advance in your knowledge of programming for the coprocessor, you may encounter messages or other indicators from the Intel MPSS middleware components.

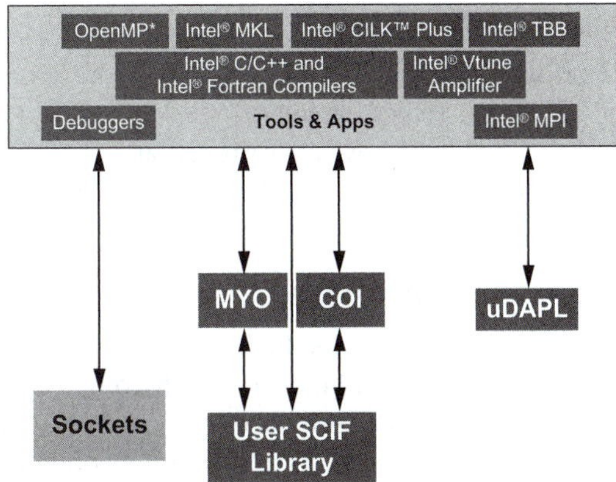

FIGURE 9.7

Development Tools and Application Components and Interface Components.

As is shown in Figure 9.7, the tools call upon service components marked Sockets, uDAPL, MYO, COI, and SCIF. Sockets and uDAPL (Direct Access Programming Library) are industry standard interfaces for communication that have readily available information resources so they will not be further described. MYO, COI, and SCIF represent Intel MPSS middleware services specific to the coprocessor environment. They will be described in the next section.

Intel® manycore platform software stack

In Figure 9.1 the legend indicates the components that make up the Intel MPSS installed components that provide the operating software for the coprocessor and the interfaces and services for the development tools and libraries. The purpose of these components is described in this section.

MYO: mine yours ours

MYO stands for Mine Yours Ours memory owners and provides a virtual shared memory capability where virtual addresses effectively point to the same data contents on the processor and coprocessor (Ours). In other words, code running on either the processor or coprocessor can literally use the same address (pointer) value to access the same memory contents. In reality there are physically distinct memory locations allocated on the processor and the coprocessor.

The concept of MYO was created by Intel Labs and has been described in several published papers. The MYO module implements a software coherence mechanism to ensure any data is properly updated when modified by either the processor or coprocessor. The primary usage is for the "virtual shared memory" offload model and semantics implemented by the Intel compiler, which is described in Chapter 7.

COI: coprocessor offload infrastructure

The Intel Coprocessor Offload Infrastructure (Intel COI) component provides much of the run-time and interface support for the "non-shared memory" offload model described thoroughly in Chapter 7. COI provides services for launching code (functions) on the coprocessor from the processor, and managing the associated parameters and data for the offloaded code.

SCIF: symmetric communications interface

SCIF is the communication backbone between the host processor and the Intel Xeon Phi coprocessor. It provides communication capabilities within a single platform. SCIF enables communications between host processors and coprocessor cards, and between coprocessor cards within the platform. It provides a uniform, symmetric API on processors and coprocessors for communicating across the platform's PCI Express system busses while delivering the full capabilities of the PCI Express transport hardware. SCIF directly exposes the DMA capabilities of the coprocessor (see Chapter 8) for high bandwidth transfer of large data segments, as well as, the ability to map memory of the host processor or map coprocessor memory into the address space of a process running on the host or on any coprocessor.

SCIF is structured as a driver with Ring 3 (User SCIF Library) and Ring 0 (SCIF Driver) components. MYO and Intel COI utilize SCIF for their data transport needs. Performance libraries such as MKL also use the SCIF, if needed, to optimize data transfer and control.

The SCIF messaging layers take advantage of the inherent reliability of PCI Express, and operates as a simple data-only network without the need for any intermediate packet inspection. Due to the data-only nature of the interface, it is not a direct replacement for higher level communication APIs, but rather provides a level of abstraction from the system hardware for these other APIs. Data transfer using SCIF is very efficient and, therefore, it is strongly recommended as the lowest level means of data transfer for coprocessor applications. The SCIF API is described further at intel.com/software/mic and the API documentation and sample programs are provided in the Intel MPSS package.

Virtual networking (NetDev), TCP/IP, and sockets

Figure 9.8 shows the portion of Figure 9.1 that depicts the standard network interfaces, sockets, Internet Protocol (IP) layer with TCP and UDP support enabling the coprocessor to operate as a standard network node. Sockets and the IP stacks are the same as any Linux OS. The key is the Intel MPSS provided *NetDev* driver implementation that maps the PCI Express bus to appear as an Ethernet device to the networking stack. The NetDev drivers emulate an Ethernet device to the next higher layer (IP layer) of the networking stack. The host can be configured to bridge the TCP/IP network (created by the NetDev drivers) to other networks that the host is connected to.

The availability of such a TCP/IP capability enables a significant number of standard networking and remote access uses including:

- Remote access to Intel Xeon Phi coprocessor devices via Telnet or SSH
- Access to MPI on TCP/IP (as an alternative to MPI on OFED)
- Network File System (NFS) access to the host or remote file systems (see Chapter 10).

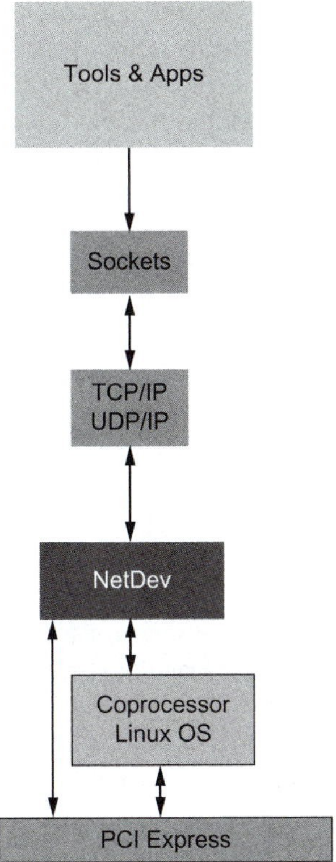

FIGURE 9.8

Standard Networking Stack with NetDev Ethernet Emulation over PCI Express.

Coprocessor system management

As an independent network computational node, the coprocessor hardware and software has been structured to provide runtime information about its operation status and to respond to platform or administrative control. Chapter 8 discussed some of these aspects from a hardware perspective; here we will focus on the software elements of managing the coprocessor.

Sysfs

Sysfs is a standard Linux 2.6 virtual file system. It exports information about devices and drivers from the kernel device model to user space *nodes*. Intel MPSS utilizes the standard sysfs to enable access to some coprocessor device characteristics. Some characteristics such as core/*cpu* utilization, process/*thread* details and system memory usage are better presented from Linux standard */proc* interfaces. The purpose of these *sysfs* nodes is to present information not otherwise available. The organization of the filesystem directory hierarchy is strict and is based on the internal organization of kernel data structures.

Sysfs is a mechanism for representing kernel objects, their attributes, and their relationships with each other. It provides two components: a kernel programming interface for exporting these items via *sysfs*, and a user interface to view and manipulate these items that maps back to the kernel objects they represent. Table 9.1 shows the mapping between internal (kernel) constructs and their external (user space) Sysfs mappings:

The current coprocessor enabled sysfs nodes are listed in Table 9.2.

Figure 9.9 illustrates the system management information flow using Sysfs and two available management agents; the Card System Management Agent and a Ganglia management agent. Intel MPSS provides a coprocessor-specific interface set in the MIC Management Software Developers Kit (SDK) to monitor and manage the card with customized tools. Several supplied tools created with the SDK are provided with the Intel MPSS installation. Also a reference implementation of the popular Ganglia open source monitoring system is provided with Intel MPSS to support remote and cluster-wide management of coprocessors for those cluster operators that are familiar with it. Other Sysfs/Proc Linux agents should interface seamlessly to the coprocessor management infrastructure.

Ganglia

Ganglia is a scalable, distributed monitoring system for high-performance computing systems such as clusters and grids. The implementation of Ganglia is robust, has been ported to an extensive set of operating systems and processor architectures, and is currently in use on thousands of clusters around the world. Ganglia uses */proc* and the *sysfs* interfaces to fetch system status information. A reference implementation of Ganglia is provided for the Intel Xeon Phi coprocessor.

Board tools, control panel, MIC Management SDK

Several utilities to manage and retrieve information from the coprocessor card are provided with Intel MPSS. These utilities are referred to in Figure 9.1 as the "board tools." These utilities are:

- *micflash.* A command utility normally used to update the coprocessor's on-board flash and system management controller (SMC).
- *micinfo.* Displays the physical settings and parameters of the card including the driver versions.
- *miccheck.* A utility that performs a set of basic checks to confirm that Intel MPSS is correctly installed and all communications links between the host and coprocessor(s), and between coprocessors are functional.

The coprocessor control panel application, *micsmc,* graphically displays information about all the coprocessors on a platform such as thermal, electrical, and usage parameters. Example parameters include coprocessor temperature, utilization on the cores, memory usage, and more. Several

Table 9.1 Sysfs Kernel to User Space Mappings

Internal	External
Kernel Objects	Directories
Object Attributes	Regular Files
Object Relationships	Symbolic Links

Table 9.2 Intel® Xeon Phi™ Sysfs Nodes

Node	Description
clst	Number of known cores
fan	Fan state
freq	Core frequencies
gddr	GDDR device info
gfreq	GDDR frequency
gvolt	GDDR voltage
hwinf	hardware info (revision, stepping, ...)
Temp	Temperature sensor readings
Vers	Version string
Volt	Core voltage

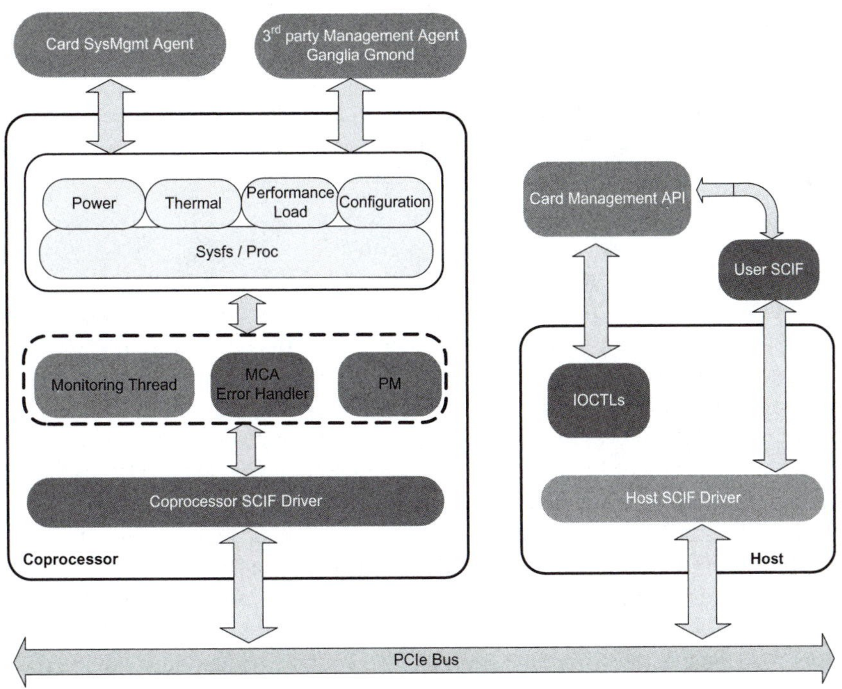

FIGURE 9.9

Intel MPSS Sysfs and Ganglia Support.

control and settings changes are also available including enabling or disabling memory error correcting codes (ECC).

These utility applications rely on the MIC Management SDK to access the coprocessor card parameters. The MIC Management SDK exposes a set of APIs enabling applications to access the coprocessor status and information. The Ring 3 system management agent running on the card handles the queries from the host and returns results to the host using SCIF for data communication.

Coprocessor components for MPI applications

The architecture of the coprocessor software stack components enable uDAPL and Infiniband verbs support for MPI. Given the significant role of MPI in high-performance computing, the Intel Xeon Phi coprocessor software stack provides support for OFED (Open Fabrics Enterprise Edition), which is widely used in high performance computing for applications that require high efficiency, wire-speed messaging, and microsecond latencies. OFED is also the preferred communications stack for the Intel MPI Library, allowing the coprocessor to take advantage of remote direct memory access (RDMA) capable transport that it exposes. Figure 9.10 shows the MPI software stack components from Figure 9.1 for the host and the coprocessor.

The Intel® MPI Library for the coprocessor utilizing OFED can use SCIF or the physical InfiniBand Host Channel Adapter (HCA) for communications between coprocessors and between coprocessors and processors. Coprocessors are treated as standalone nodes in the MPI network.

There are two implementations that cover internode and intranode communications through the InfiniBand interfaces:

- *Coprocessor Communication Link (CCL).* A set of modules that allows access to a hardware InfiniBand HCA from the coprocessor through proxy mechanisms.
- *OFED/SCIF.* A software-based InfiniBand-like device that allows verbs level communication within a single platform.

Coprocessor communication link (Intel CCL)

To efficiently communicate with remote systems, applications running on coprocessors require access to RDMA devices in the host platform. Intel CCL provides the infrastructure that enables internode communication for MPI processes running on the coprocessor.

In a heterogeneous computing environment, it is desirable to have efficient communication mechanisms from all MPI processes, whether they run on processor cores or coprocessor cores. Providing a common, standards-based programming and communication model, especially for clustered system applications, is an important goal of the coprocessor software architecture. A consistent model not only simplifies development and maintenance of applications, but allows greater flexibility for using a system to take full advantage of its performance.

RDMA architectures such as InfiniBand have been highly successful in improving performance of HPC cluster applications by reducing latency and increasing the bandwidth of message passing operations. RDMA architectures improve performance by moving the network interface closer to the application, allowing kernel bypass, direct data placement, and greater control of I/O operations to match application requirements. RDMA architectures allow process isolation, protection, and address translation to be implemented in hardware. These features are well-suited to the Intel Xeon

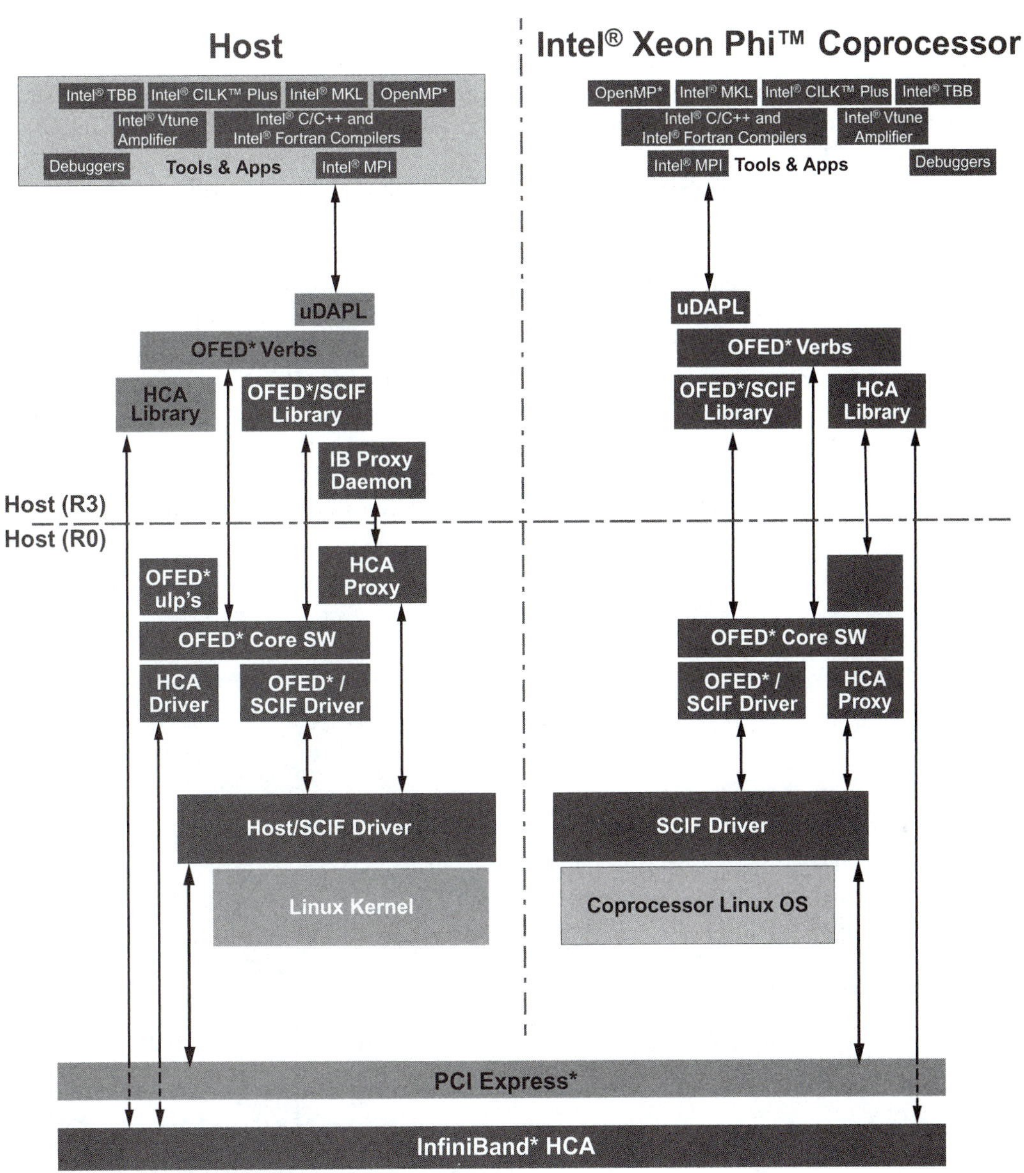

FIGURE 9.10

Coprocessor MPI Software Stack Components.

Phi coprocessor environment where host and coprocessor applications execute in separate address domains.

Intel CCL brings the benefits of RDMA architecture to the coprocessor. Figure 9.11 illustrates the operation of a direct peer to peer RDMA transfer with an RDMA Device (such as InfiniBand HCA) using Intel CCL.

Intel CCL allows RDMA device hardware to be shared between Linux-based host processor and coprocessor applications.

Figure 9.12 highlights the primary software modules (bolded rounded components) responsible for Intel CCL. The host system contains a PCI Express interface with one or more RDMA devices and one or more coprocessors. Software modules on the host processor and coprocessor communicate with each other and access RDMA devices across the PCI Express bus. The software uses a split-driver model to proxy operations across PCI Express to manage RDMA device resources allocated by the Vendor HCA Driver on the host. These modules include the IB Proxy Daemon, the IB Proxy Server, the IB Proxy Client, the Vendor HCA Proxy Drivers, and SCIF.

RDMA operations are performed by a programming interface known as *verbs*. Verbs are categorized into privileged and non-privileged classes. Privileged verbs are used to allocate and manage

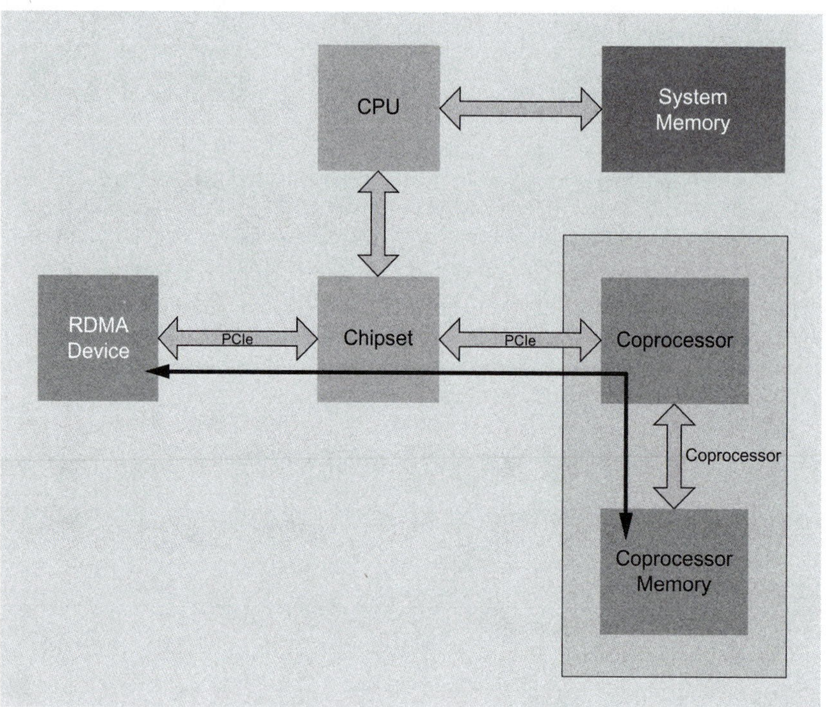

FIGURE 9.11

RDMA Peer-to-Peer Transfer with Intel® CCL.

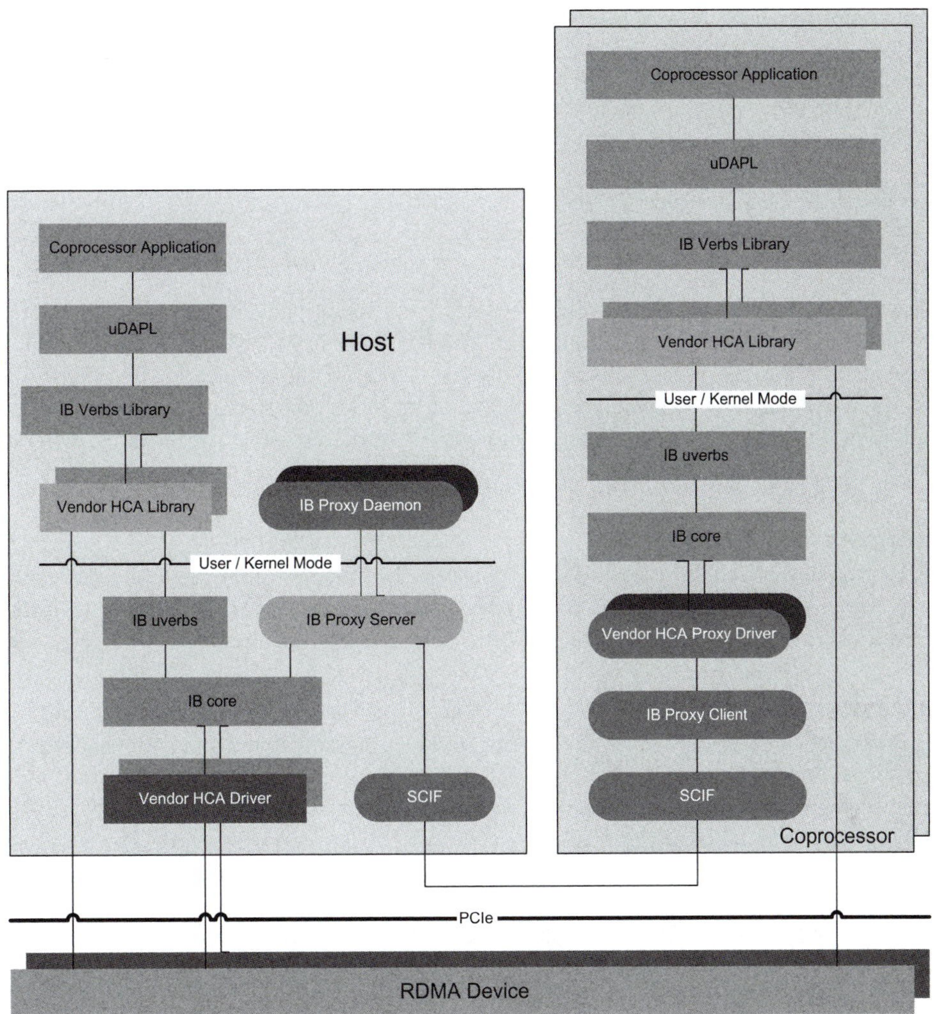

FIGURE 9.12

MPI Application using Intel® Coprocessor Communications Link.

RDMA resources. Once these resources have been initialized, non-privileged verbs are used to perform I/O operations. I/O operations can be executed directly to and from user-mode applications on the coprocessor concurrently with host I/O operations, with kernel-mode bypass, and with direct data placement. The RDMA device provides process isolation and performs address translation needed for I/O operations. Intel CCL proxies privileged verb operations between host and coprocessors with each coprocessor appearing as if it were another "user-mode" process above the host IB core stack.

IB core coprocessor modifications

The IB core module defines the kernel-mode verbs interface layer and various support functions. Support functions that allow vendor HCA drivers to access user-mode data are:

- `ib_copy_to_udata()`
- `ib_copy_from_udata()`
- `ib_umem_get()`
- `ib_umem_page_count()`
- `ib_umem_release()`

These functions may be used by vendor HCA drivers for privileged verb operations. Since the implementation of these functions assumes that data is always in host system user-space, modifications provided on the coprocessor module allow redirection of these functions for Intel CCL. The IB Proxy Server overrides the default implementation of these functions to transfer data to or from the coprocessor as needed. To be effective, vendor HCA drivers must use these IB core support functions.

IB proxy daemon

The IB Proxy Daemon is a host user-mode application. It provides a user-mode process context for IB Proxy Server calls (through the IB core) to the underlying vendor HCA drivers. An instance of the IB Proxy Daemon is started for each coprocessor by the IB Proxy Server.

IB proxy server

The IB Proxy Server is a host kernel module. It provides communication and command services for coprocessor IB Proxy Clients. The IB Proxy Server listens for client connections and relays RDMA device add, remove, and event notification messages to the IB core. The IB Proxy Server initiates kernel-mode IB verbs calls to the host IB core on behalf of coprocessor IB Proxy Clients and returns their results. The IB Proxy client on the coprocessor and the IB Proxy server communicate via SCIF.

The IB Proxy Server performs verbs on behalf of IB Proxy Clients. Received messages are dispatched to an appropriate verb handler where they are processed to generate a verb response message. Privileged verbs provide access to user-mode data to Vendor HCA Drivers through IB core support functions. The IB Proxy Server overrides the default implementation of these functions to transfer data to or from the coprocessors as needed.

IB proxy client

The IB Proxy Client is a coprocessor kernel module. The IB Proxy Client provides a programming interface to vendor HCA proxy drivers to perform IB verbs calls on the host. The interface abstracts the details of formatting commands and performing the communication. The IB Proxy Client invokes callbacks for device add, remove, and event notifications to registered Intel Xeon Phi coprocessor Vendor HCA Proxy Drivers.

The IB Proxy Client provides a verbs command interface for use by Vendor HCA Proxy Drivers. This interface is modeled after the IB Verbs Library command interface provided for user-mode Vendor HCA Libraries. A Vendor HCA Proxy Driver uses this interface to perform IB verbs calls to the Vendor HCA Driver on the host. The interface abstracts the details of formatting commands and performs the communication with the IB Proxy Server through SCIF.

Vendor HCA proxy driver

A vendor HCA proxy driver is a coprocessor kernel module. Different vendor HCA proxy drivers may be installed to support specific RDMA devices. Upon initialization, each Vendor HCA Proxy Driver registers with the IB Proxy Client for RDMA device add and remove notifications for the HCA's that it supports. The Vendor HCA Proxy Driver uses the programming interface provided by the IB Proxy Client to perform kernel-mode IB verbs calls. The Vendor Proxy Driver handles the transfer and interpretation of any private data shared between the vendor HCA library on coprocessor and vendor HCA driver on the host.

OFED/SCIF

OFED/SCIF implements a software-emulated InfiniBand HCA to allow OFED-based applications, such as the Intel MPI Library to successfully run on the coprocessor without the presence of a physical HCA. Essentially, OFED/SCIF maps OFED HCA interface calls to SCIF data transport, supporting intranode communication between one or more local coprocessors and the host processors. Intel CCL described above is used for internode communication using the physical InfiniBand HCA. By layering OFED on top of SCIF, many OFED-based HPC applications become readily available on a coprocessor based platform.

Linux support for Intel® Xeon Phi™ coprocessors

Intel Xeon Phi coprocessors have enough new features that Linux needed modifications to manage it. These modifications are available with source code on intel.com/software/mic. In time, the new drivers and the modifications to open source are likely to become standard so that Linux distributions will be fully ready for manycore coprocessors.

The reasons that standard distributions cannot currently run unmodified on the coprocessor are easy to appreciate. The very concept of a coprocessor SMP-on-a-chip that needs to communicate with a host required new drivers and capabilities. The open source software stack Intel provides consists of Linux, a minimally modified gcc, gdb, plus driver software. Separately there are also modifications available for MPI libraries and a variety of other open source projects. Changes are primarily for three reasons:

- Numerous little changes to support the unique combination of an Intel® Pentium® processor core that also supports 64-bits, four-threads-per-core, and new 512-bit SIMD vector instructions (but not MMX, SSE nor AVX).
- Power management, which is a feature not associated with the original Pentium processors. Power management is much more important when you have up to 61 cores on a single die!
- The machine check architecture, a feature not present in the original Pentium processor designs.

The use of Linux allows for experimentation with those interested in the capabilities of Intel Xeon Phi coprocessors and new paradigms in areas such as communication and power management. Running a full and open source operating system offers seemingly limitless possibilities.

Tuning memory allocation performance

For user-allocated data on the coprocessor, using large (2 MB) page allocations may improve application performance by reducing the likelihood of Translation Lookaside Buffer (TLB) misses that cause the coprocessor to perform page table lookups (page walks).

For the initial coprocessor Linux kernel version 2.6.34, the default page size is 4 KB for `malloc` and `_mm_malloc`, and there is no transparent support for Huge Pages, those pages 2 MB in size. Transparent huge page support allowing `malloc` and `_mm_malloc` to allocate 2 MB pages will come in coprocessor kernel versions 2.6.38 or greater. However, even with transparent huge page support, there is no guarantee that 2 MB will be allocated for an application. Therefore, to ensure the application uses huge pages, you must manually reserve 2 MB pages before allocating memory and allocate the memory using `mmap()`.

Not all applications benefit from using a larger page size. In general, the performance impact from a larger page size depends greatly on the data access pattern. If the application accesses multiple data structures that are allocated in different pages, having only 8 TLB entries for 2 MB pages on the coprocessor can cause performance degradation. More details on the TLB structure of the coprocessor is in Chapter 8.

Controlling the number of 2 MB pages

To control the number of 2 MB pages available to use on the coprocessor, write the desired value to the following file on the coprocessor: `/proc/sys/nr_hugepages`. For example, issuing the following command on the coprocessor configures the Linux uOS for five huge pages, each 2 MB in size.

```
echo 5 > /proc/sys/vm/nr_hugepages
```

It is recommended that the value written accommodate the total number of pages needed for all `mallocs` in the application. If the application contains two `mallocs`, where each needs P1 and P2 number of pages, the value written must reflect the total of P1 + P2. You can also parse the file to obtain the current value, add any current need, and then write the new value to the file. Requesting the total number of pages up front for all allocations improves the chance of avoiding memory fragmenting, and therefore a better chance of getting what you request.

There is no atomic interface for making this modification. This reduces the available physical memory in the free pool. When the value in this file is reduced, the coprocessor Linux OS waits until the memory is actually freed before making it available.

The compiler does not provide any user control over the requested page size. A sample method for a programmatic approach to allocating 2 MB pages is provided below.

Monitoring the number of 2 MB pages on the coprocessor

Calling `mmap()` using the `HUGE_TLB` flag guarantees 2 MB pages. If the request cannot be satisfied, the call returns `MAP_FAILED`. You can monitor the number of 2 MB pages in use on the coprocessor using`/proc/meminfo`. Use the following command on the coprocessor:

```
cat /proc/meminfo
```

The output includes the following values:

```
...
HugePages_Total:       0
HugePages_Free:        0
HugePages_Rsvd:        0
HugePages_Surp:        0
Hugepagesize:       2048 kB
...
```

A sample method for allocating 2 MB pages

The function `allocate_huge_pages()` below encapsulates a method for allocating 2 MB pages under the Linux uOS:

```
/* allocate memory using huge page support */
#define MALLOC_2M(size) \

  mmap(NULL, size, PROT_READ | PROT_WRITE, MAP_ANONYMOUS | \
      MAP_PRIVATE | MAP_HUGETLB, -1, 0);

size_t _get_huge_pages()
{

    FILE * f;
    size_t sz = 0;
    char rvalue[128] = {0};
    f = popen("cat /proc/sys/vm/nr_hugepages","r");
    if(f = = NULL)
      return -1;
    sz = fread(rvalue, 1, sizeof(rvalue)-1, f);
    if(sz = = 0) {
      pclose(f);
      return -1;
    }
    pclose(f);
    if (rvalue[0])
      return atoi(rvalue);
    else {
      errno = ENODATA;
      return -1;
    }

}
int _set_huge_pages(size_t pages)
{
```

```
    int rval = 0;
    char cmd[256];
    sprintf(cmd,
          "echo %d > /proc/sys/vm/nr_hugepages",
          int)pages);
    rval = system(cmd);
    return rval;

}
void* allocate_huge_pages(size_t size)
{

    size_t current_pages = 0;
    size_t request_pages = 0;
    current_pages = _get_huge_pages();
    if( current_pages = = -1)
      return MAP_FAILED;
    request_pages = size/1024/1024/2 + 1;
    request_pages + = current_pages;
    int err = _set_huge_pages(request_pages);
  if( err = = -1)
      return MAP_FAILED;
    return MALLOC_2M(size);

}
```

Summary

The Intel Xeon Phi coprocessor provides the software architecture and an operating environment to enable familiar usage for developers and system administrators. This chapter explained the components of the software environment and how the software architecture, based on the coprocessor's Intel Architecture heritage, allows a broad variety of programming models and application choices. By implementing a complete Linux operating system including the supporting elements to allow IP networking and InfiniBand communications, the coprocessor operates and is viewed as an independent computer in a traditional network configuration. Furthermore, by incorporating symmetry, via mirror interfaces and structure as those on the host processing environment as a foundation, the development tools and development process does not materially change for programmers at all levels and skillsets. In particular, the extensive support for MPI applications allows this prevalent model of cluster-wide application development to occur without specific new application programming knowledge to access the parallel processing capabilities inherent in the coprocessor. While the end result of this architecture is to enable application development without significant change or extensive new learning, the benefits of understanding the structure should allow developers of all types to target applications and supporting software toward the strengths of the target devices whether an Intel Xeon Processor or Intel Xeon Phi coprocessor.

This chapter had information useful for both software developers and system administrators. The next chapter will continue but primarily for the benefit of those building and maintaining systems; if your interest is purely in application development then the next chapter is not critical reading.

For more information

Here are some additional reading materials we recommend related to this chapter:

- Intel Manycore Platform Software (MPSS) documentation and downloads, http://intel.com/software/mic
- MYO, Mine Your Ours virtual shared memory, http://dl.acm.org/citation.cfm?id=1945035
- DAPL, http://www.datcollaborative.org
- Open Fabrics Alliance, OFED, https://www.openfabrics.org
- Knights Corner: Open source software stack, announcement of the first release of the open source modifications that in turn create Intel MPSS, http://tinyurl.com/announcempss

CHAPTER

Linux on the Coprocessor

10

It's *just* Linux. The very first users of the Intel® Xeon Phi™ coprocessor would always ask us general or even very specific "how to" questions about understanding how to manage, or port, or run code on the coprocessor assuming it differed from what they'd consider "normal." We were happy to surprise them. Most often, our answer would simply be "It's just Linux!" Much of why we could answer like that for application developers was explained in Chapters 8 and 9 on the hardware and software architecture of the coprocessor. We continue that in this chapter while looking at the installation and management aspects for a system.

In this chapter, we focus more on knowledge useful to the administration of a system that contains Intel Xeon Phi coprocessors. The information in this chapter is generally uninteresting if your focus is purely developing applications for the coprocessors. We will delve a little deeper into the Linux implementation on the coprocessor, how to configure it, use of the `micctrl` utility, and Intel® Cluster Checker. In particular, while it is indeed running a true Linux operating system, the nature of the design as an attached coprocessor means there are some key elements to consider and understand if you need to adapt the coprocessor Linux operating environment to specific requirements of your network, applications, and storage system. We will describe the key considerations and tools for working with and adapting the coprocessor Linux environment to your needs. We will include information on how coprocessors may be included as part of a cluster from a software perspective, and give an overview of some of resources from Intel to assist in this.

There is additional information available, including coprocessor installation documentation, "quick start" documentation, and the complete coprocessor Linux package. Further information resources are also listed at the end of this chapter.

Coprocessor Linux baseline

As explained in Chapter 9, the coprocessor does not use or boot "off the shelf" Linux distributions like, Fedora, Ubuntu, Red Hat, or SUSE. The starting point for the coprocessor Linux is the same core baseline those distributions utilize from http://kernel.org. The Linux kernel for the coprocessor uses version 2.6.34 or greater. As a growing, improving open source project, we expect the coprocessor will evolve to be adapted to newer Linux versions over time like any distribution. A goal of the adaptation to the coprocessor was to make the minimal changes required to both maintain operational compatibility with the familiar, standard Linux environment and to more easily allow future upgrades. The coprocessor Linux implementation provides typical capabilities such as process/task creation, scheduling, and memory management. It also provides configuration, power management, and server system management.

Intel® Xeon Phi™ Coprocessor High-Performance Programming.

Table 10.1 Linux Standard Base (LSB) Core Libraries on the Coprocessor

Component	Description
glibc	the GNU C standard library
libc	the C standard library
libm	the math library
libdl	programmatic interface to the dynamic linking loader
librt	POSIX real-time library (POSIX shared memory, clock and time functions, timers)
libcrypt	password and data encryption library
libutil	library of utility functions
libstdc++	the GNU C++ standard library
libgcc_s	a low-level runtime library
libz	a lossless data compression library
libcurses	a terminal-independent method of updating character screens
libpam	the Pluggable Authentication Module (PAM) interfaces allow applications to request authentication via a system administrator-defined mechanism

Given the coprocessor has a comparatively small memory footprint versus a typical Intel® Xeon® platform and no directly attached storage; a minimal, embedded Linux environment was chosen as the baseline to be ported to the coprocessor. For primary coverage of prevalent applications, the Linux Standard Base (LSB) Core libraries are also included along with a Busybox minimal shell environment. Table 10.1 lists the LSB components.

Of course, the coprocessor Linux kernel can be extended with loadable kernel modules (LKMs); LKMs may be added or removed with modprobe as with any standard distribution. An Intel Xeon Phi targeted gcc compiler for such kernel module ports is provided as part of the coprocessor Linux installation packages within the Intel® Manycore Platform Software Stack (Intel® MPSS). Finally, standard "user" level libraries from http://linux.org, open source or third parties can be ported using Intel® Parallel Studio XE or other coprocessor compatible compilers. For example, simple recompile ports of MPI libraries such as MPICH1 and MPICH2 have been done as needed by several customers. We expect optimized libraries of these and many other useful libraries to be completed over time by their primary open source contributors. Remember, "It's just Linux!"

Introduction to coprocessor Linux bootstrap and configuration

The Intel Xeon Phi coprocessors run autonomous Linux operating systems and are controlled through the host processor platform via the PCI Express bus they are plugged into. The host platform hardware and/or software provide the data communications paths to the coprocessor. To support this requirement the host must:

- Provide the Linux boot image to the coprocessor
- Instruct the coprocessor to boot, shut down, reset, and so on
- Provide the root file system for running a Linux operating system

- Provide a virtual console
- Provide a networking connection
- Provide power management control information for the coprocessor
- Provide high speed data transfer to and from the coprocessor

Software for the coprocessor is installed and configured on the host platform. This somewhat complex process is usually hidden from the system administrator by Linux OS installation scripts.

The "MPSS Boot" portion of Intel MPSS provides the software to perform the entire configuration and booting of the Linux operating system on the coprocessor. It provides the PCI Express access driver, a daemon for initialization and monitoring of the coprocessors and a utility to simplify the configuration process.

The host coprocessor driver (`mic.ko`) provides the PCI Express bus access. It contains code to inject the Linux kernel and its command line into the coprocessor's memory and signal it to begin executing (booting). It includes a virtual console driver and a virtual network driver. The host driver also coordinates the power management on the coprocessor. Finally, it implements the high speed PCI Express transfer protocol via the Symmetric Communications Interface (SCIF) that was described in Chapter 9. SCIF is utilized to provide the control and data transfer functionality required to launch and communicate with the coprocessor Linux OS.

The `mpssd` daemon controls the initialization and booting of the coprocessor based on a set of configuration files. The `mpssd` daemon is started and stopped as a Linux service (such as with the command `service mpss start`) and instructs the coprocessors on a platform to boot or shutdown. The daemon supplies the final file system image to the coprocessors when requested. It monitors the coprocessor state and logs it as it changes. It will also log error information from the coprocessor.

The `micctrl` configuration utility is the workhorse of the configuration process and has numerous options to control the configuration and the resulting Linux OS environment on the coprocessor. It also gives the system administrator the ability to individually boot and shut down coprocessors in the system. We will explain the `micctrl` utility and key uses throughout this chapter.

NOTE

We expect the `micctrl` utility will continue to grow significantly in capabilities beyond the original publishing date of this book. Our goal is to provide you the key knowledge to understand the coprocessor Linux configuration process. Please refer to latest Intel MPSS documentation for the most up-to-date information on the `micctrl` utility.

Default coprocessor Linux configuration

After the installation of Intel MPSS (consult the readme.txt file at http://intel.com/software/mic under the Intel MPSS section for installation instructions), the system administrator must complete the coprocessor configuration before starting the Intel MPSS service.

Step 1: Ensure root access

User access to each coprocessor Linux OS node is provided through the secure shell utilities, such as SSH. By default, the `mpssd` daemon enables users with existing SSH access on the host platform, although specific exclusions or inclusions of users can be controlled with configuration changes. In particular, it is important that the root user, who is typically a trusted system administrator, has access. The general method to ensure a user will have access is to generate the proper secure key file(s) configured in the standard user home directory structure. To ensure the root user has keys created, the root user must be logged in. Look in the */root/.ssh* directory for either the `id_rsa.pub` or `id_dsa.pub` key files. If no SSH keys exist, use the `ssh-keygen` command to generate a set:

```
root_prompt# ssh-keygen
```

Step 2: Generate the default configuration

Each coprocessor has a unique configuration file in the */etc/sysconfig/mic* directory. Initialize the default configuration for the all coprocessors installed on the host platform:

```
user_prompt$ sudo micctrl --initdefaults
```

The `micctrl --initdefaults` command creates and populates the default configuration files corresponding to each coprocessor installed in the system. These configuration files are *default.conf* and *micN.conf* located at */etc/sysconfig/mic/*.

NOTE

In the configuration file *micN.conf*, *N* is an integer number (0, 1, 2, 3, and so on) that identifies each coprocessor installed in the system.

Step 3: Change configuration

Examine the files in the */etc/sysconfig/mic* directory. If the default configuration meets the requirements of the system, continue to Step 4. Otherwise, edit the configuration files in */etc/sysconfig/mic* (refer to section "Changing Coprocessor Configuration").

Step 4: Start the Intel® MPSS service

By default the Intel MPSS service boots all coprocessors on the platform when it is started. Other options are available to boot specific coprocessors or delay booting any coprocessors until later. To start the Intel MPSS service, execute the Linux service command:

```
user_prompt$ sudo service mpss start
```

The call to service will complete when it determines the coprocessors have either successfully booted or failed to boot and the status of the coprocessors will be displayed.

Changing coprocessor configuration

This section focuses on configuring coprocessors, including configuration files, kernel command line parameters, and authentication.

Configurable components

On a typical Linux system, installation and configuration are performed by a graphical utility that prompts the system administrator for input. Since the Intel Xeon Phi coprocessors do not have a file system of their own, this process is replaced by:

- Installing Intel MPSS (containing the required software) on the host platform
- Configuration by a combination of the following:
  - Editing the configuration file(s)
  - Using the `micctrl` utility

The configuration parameters have three categories:

1. Parameters for the host to load the Linux kernel on the target coprocessor and initiate the boot process.
2. Parameters to define the root file system to be used for the coprocessor.
3. Parameters to configure the host processor platform's virtual Ethernet connection described in Chapter 9.

The current configuration parameters can be displayed with the `micctrl --config` command. For example, the default configuration on most systems looks like the following:

```
mic0:
==========================================
=====================
Linux Kernel:  /lib/firmware/mic/uos.img
BootOnStart:        Enabled
Shutdowntimeout: 300 seconds
ExtraCommandLine: highres=off pm_qos_cpu_dma_lat=75

UserAuthentication: Local
Root Device:     Dynamic Ram /opt/intel/mic/filesystem/mic0.image
BaseDir:     /opt/intel/mic/filesystem/base.filelist
CommonDir: /opt/intel/mic/filesystem/common.filelist
MicDir:     /opt/intel/mic/filesystem/mic0.filelist
Overlay:     /opt/intel/mic/filesystem/allinea-dev.filelist
Overlay:     /opt/intel/mic/coi/config/coi.filelist

Network: Static Pair
Hostname:  sys1-mic0tinynet.com
Host IP:   172.31.1.254
```

```
MIC IP:     172.31.1.1
Host MAC:   4a:70:e7:0c:2c:57
MIC MAC:     22:88:36:2b:0f:97
Net Bits: 24
NetMask:     255.255.255.0

Console: hvc0
VerboseLogging: Enabled
```

Configuration files

This section briefly discusses configuration file format and using the `Include` parameter, which enables one configuration file to include additional configuration files.

File location and format

Configuration is controlled by per coprocessor configuration files located in the */etc/sysconfig/mic* directory. Each coprocessor uses a file identified by its ID (that is, micN.conf, where *N* is an integer number (0, 1, 2, 3, and so forth) that identifies each coprocessor installed in the system).

Each of the configuration files contains a list of configuration parameters and their arguments. Each parameter must be on a single line. Comments begin with the "#" character and terminate at the end of the same line.

Including other configuration files

Parameter syntax:

```
Include <config_file_name>
```

Each of these configuration files has the ability to include other configuration files. The `Include` parameter lists the configuration file(s) to be included. The configuration file(s) to be included must be located in the base directory of *etc/sysconfig/mic*. The configuration parser processes each parameter sequentially. When the `Include` parameter is encountered, the included configuration file(s) are immediately processed. If the same parameter is set multiple times, the last instance of the parameter setting will be applied.

By default, the */etc/sysconfig/mic/default.conf* file is included at the start of each coprocessor specific file (e.g. mic0.conf, mic1.conf, etc.). This allows the coprocessor specific files to override any parameter set in default.conf.

The last entry in the *default.conf* file is typically the line:

```
Include conf.d/*.conf
```

This is a special rule, specifying that all the files in the */etc/sysconfig/mic/conf.d* directory will be included.

Configuring boot parameters

The host system boots the coprocessor by *injecting* the Linux kernel image and kernel command line into its memory and then instructing the coprocessor to start. To perform this operation, the host system must read the coprocessor specific configuration file and load all the parameters into the kernel command line.

What to boot

Parameter syntax:

```
OSimage <linux_kernel_image>
```

The default value for the coprocessor Linux OS image is */lib/firmware/mic/uos.img*. Optionally, the system owner can substitute a new kernel image. To do so, it is necessary to set the parameter in the correct coprocessor specific configuration file and change the image name. The change takes effect upon executing either `service mpss start` or `micctrl -b`.

When to boot

Parameter syntax:

```
BootOnStart <Enabled | Disabled>
```

This parameter controls whether the coprocessor is booted when the Intel MPSS service starts. The `BootOnStart` parameter should be defined in the coprocessor specific configuration file. If set to Enabled, the `mpssd` daemon will attempt to boot the coprocessor when `service mpss start` is called.

VerboseLogging kernel command line parameter

Parameter syntax:

```
VerboseLogging <Enabled | Disabled>
```

The `VerboseLogging` parameter specifies whether the `quiet` kernel command line parameter is passed to the coprocessor on boot. The `quiet` kernel parameter suppresses most kernel messages during kernel boot. `VerboseLogging` is enabled by default. Disabling `VerboseLogging` will reduce boot times.

Changes to `VerboseLogging` take effect upon executing `service mpss start`.

Console kernel command line parameter

Parameter syntax:

```
Console "<console device>"
```

Intel MPSS includes a PCI Express bus virtual console driver. Its device node (`hvc0`) is the default value assigned to the `Console` parameter. Other possible values are intended for internal use.

Changes to `Console` take effect upon executing `service mpss start`.

PowerManagement kernel command line parameter

Parameter syntax:

```
PowerManagement "<string>"
```

The `PowerManagement` parameter is a string of four attributes passed directly to the kernel command line for the coprocessor's power management driver. The `mpssd` daemon and micctrl utility do not validate any of the parameters in this string or its format. For more information consult the Intel MPSS power management documentation for correct values at http://intel.com/software/mic. Changes to PowerManagement take effect upon executing service mpss start.

RootDevice kernel command line parameter

Parameter syntax:

```
RootDevice RamFS <location> RootDevice StaticRamFS <location> RootDevice NFS
<location>
RootDevice SplitNFS <location> </usr location>
RootDevice InitRD
```

The RootDevice parameter defines the type of root device to mount. The type argument is a string specifying the device type. The location argument is the location information of the file system for the coprocessor. Some supported types as of this writing are RamFS, StaticRamFS, NFS, SPLITNFS, and InitRD.

The InitRD type boots to the initial RAM disk image included in the downloaded kernel. This option exists for debug purposes only.

The RamFS and StaticRamFS types have a second argument specifying the file name of the compressed cpio image to be used for the coprocessor file system. The RamFS type builds its image when the coprocessor requests download of the image file.

The StaticRamFS boot will fail if the image file is not already present.

The NFS root device type has a second argument of the directory path on the host to mount as the root directory. This directory must be correctly exported by the host as a NFS share.

The SplitNFS root device type is the same as the NFS type with a third argument specifying the location of a NFS export to mount under /usr on the embedded Linux OS. Typically the /usr NFS mount will be shared between coprocessors.

Changes to RootDev take effect upon executing service mpss start. More information on the cpio file system image will be described in the section titled "The Coprocessor File System Creation Process."

Coprocessor root file system

Every Linux operating system needs a root file system with a minimal set of files. Other nonessential files may be on the root or they may be on secondary mounts. Most modern Linux OS releases assume the root file system will be large enough to install the complete required release files. The Intel Xeon Phi coprocessor embedded file system follows the same rule. Files on the root file system fall into three categories:

1. The binaries installed with the system.
2. The files in the */etc* directory, which define an individual system.
3. The set of files for the users of the system.

The Intel MPSS configuration provides syntax for setting up the root file system.

File location parameters

Parameter syntax:

```
BaseDir <location> <descriptor file> CommonDir <location> <descriptor file>
MicDir <location> <descriptor file> OverLay <location> <descriptor file>
```

Each parameter has two required arguments. The first is the top-level directory name where the files are located. The second is a file describing where each file gets placed on the coprocessor's file system and the permissions for that file. The format of descriptor file will be explained in the section, "Adding Files to the Coprocessor Root File System."

The `BaseDir` parameter is the location of the coprocessor binaries installed by the Intel MPSS installation process. The files in this directory should never be changed since the next install will overwrite any changes.

The `CommonDir` parameter defines a set of files the system administrator wishes to have on all the coprocessor file systems installed in the host platform. The Intel MPSS installation process does not install files in this directory and any added files will be maintained across updates to the Intel MPSS installation.

The `MicDir` parameter defines the per coprocessor information for each unique coprocessor in the host platform. The Intel MPSS installation process installs no files in this directory and most of its content is created by the configuration process. Specifically, user access and network configuration each has its own set of configuration parameters.

The `Overlay` parameter is the only one of the set that is likely to be used many times in a configuration. Each entry specifies a new set of files to add to the file system. This parameter is used to add additional software to be automatically included. For an example of its syntax see */etc/sysconfig/mic/conf.d/coi.conf* in a host platform with Intel MPSS installed.

The `RamFS` root device type will use these configuration parameters to automatically build and download the file system image to the booting coprocessor. For the `StaticRamFS` type, the `micctrl --updateramfs` command can be used to update the image. The section "Coprocessor File System Creation Process" explains this further.

User access

Parameter syntax:

```
UserAuthentication None
UserAuthentication Local <low uid> < high uid>
```

User authentication for the coprocessor Linux operating system is controlled through the standard Unix */etc/passwd*, */etc/shadow* and */etc/group* files. Although the mechanisms for populating these files also copy the password defined for the use on the host system, it is recommended to control access through the secure shell.

> **NOTE**
>
> The passwords do not work with a SUSE Linux host because it uses a different encryption algorithm than the coprocessor.

The `UserAuthentication` configuration parameter specifies two default sets of users. If `None` is specified, the */etc/passwd* file on the coprocessor will default to one containing the `root`, `sshd` and `micuser` accounts. If `Local` is specified, all the users on the host between the low user ID (uid) and high user ID will also generate entries on the coprocessor files.

Changing `UserAuthentication` can be done in two ways. The first method is to edit the entry in the coprocessor specific configuration file and then run `micctrl --resetconfig`. The second, and easier, method is to use the `micctrl --userconfig` command.

NOTE

Every user to be populated to the coprocessor file system should set their secure shell configuration files with the `ssh-keygen` utility, as in the example for root authentication earlier in the chapter, before running either the `micctrl --resetconfig` or `micctrl --userconfig` commands.

The `micctrl` utility will attempt to find all users in the */etc/passwd* file and */home* directories and populate them to the coprocessor file system. After the initial user authentication configuration is completed, additional users may be added to coprocessor file system with the `micctrl --useradd` command. Further information will provided in the section "The `micctrl` Utility."

For coprocessors where it is required to strictly control user access, it is recommended to set `UserAuthentication` to `None` and add each user specifically as required.

Network access

Parameter syntax:

```
Hostname <name> HostMacAddress <address> MicMacAddress <address> BridgeName
<name>
Subnet <subnet> HostIPaddress <address> MicIPaddress <address> NetBits <bits>
MTUsize <bits>
```

On the host operating system, files are added to the network configuration based on the host OS type (RedHat or SUSE). On the coprocessor file systems, the files added are:

```
/etc/sysconfig/network/ifcfg-mic0
/etc/sysconfig/hostname
/etc/ssh/ssh_host_key
/etc/ssh/ssh_host_key.pub
/etc/ssh/ssh_host_rsa_key
/etc/ssh/ssh_host_rsa_key.pub
/etc/ssh/ssh_host_dsa_key
/etc/ssh/ssh_host_dsa_key.pub
/etc/resolv.conf
/etc/nsswitch.conf
/etc/hosts
```

All network configuration parameters take effect upon executing `service mpss start`.

Host Name Assignment. The `Hostname` parameter defines the value assigned to the host name on a coprocessor. The initial value from the `micctrl --initdefaults` command is set to the host name with a dash and the coprocessor name appended to it. The host name string may be edited in the coprocessor specific configuration.

MAC Address Assignment. Configuring the virtual network interface is a nontrivial process and differs based on the required topology. However, as a prerequisite, both ends of the virtual network need to have MAC addresses assigned.

MAC addresses for both ends of the virtual network are randomly created by the `micctrl --initdefaults` command. It is possible to generate a duplicate address when there are a large number of coprocessors in a cluster. The values in the coprocessor-specific configuration file may be edited to specific values by the system administrator.

NOTE

When editing to specific values, it is important to set bit two of the high byte to indicate the value is locally generated.

Many cluster managers use the MAC address to identify systems on the network. For this reason the MAC address assignment is a value retained as highly persistent. As such it is noted and saved by both the `micctrl --resetconfig` and `micctrl --resetdefaults` commands.

Static Pair Topology (Default). In the static pair topology, every coprocessor gets a separate subnet under the host. In the default configuration it is controlled by the `Subnet` parameter. The `BridgeName` parameter must be commented out. In the default configuration `Subnet` is set to 172.31.

Using `Subnet` to control the static pair configuration automatically assigns the `subnet` argument as the first two quads of the IP address. It is an error for the `subnet` to have more than the first two quads specified. The `micctrl --initdefault` or `micctrl --resetconfig` commands add the board number as the third quad for each coprocessor. The coprocessor side of the virtual connection is assigned 1 for the last quad and the host end is assigned 254. For example, the host end of the mic0 coprocessor will have the IP address 172.31.0.254 and the coprocessor end will be assigned the IP address 172.31.0.1.

> `Subnet` may be overridden on the coprocessor-specific configuration file by specifying the `HostIPaddress` and `MicIPaddress` parameters. They must both be provided and the IP addresses are set to the corresponding `address` values. It is an error to not specify complete, valid IP addresses using standard dot-decimal notation.

It is up to the system administrator to correctly route the virtual Ethernet nodes to the external network or each other.

Internal Bridge Topology. Linux operating systems provide a mechanism for bridging network devices to a common network. The terminology "internal bridge" in the context of Intel Xeon Phi coprocessor configuration refers to the process of bridging more than one coprocessor virtual network interface, on the same host, together.

Internal bridge configuration is specified by uncommenting the `BridgeName` parameter and setting the value to a bridge name starting with the string *mic*. The `Subnet` parameter may be left at the first two quads of the requested subnet and the third quad will become zero. Or the subnet can be further specified by providing the first three quads of the requested subnet. In either case the host is assigned the fourth quad value of 254 and each coprocessor is assigned the coprocessor number plus one.

For example, in a configuration of two Intel® Xeon Phi™ coprocessors, and where `Subnet` is 172.31.1, then the host will be assigned the IP address 172.31.1.254. The coprocessors mic0 and mic1 will be assigned IP addresses 172.31.1.1 and 172.31.1.2 respectively.

The network information will be updated when `micctrl --resetconfig` is executed. The `resetconfig` operation will create the correct network configuration files for the bridge on the host, the host side of the virtual network attachments to the bridge and the network configuration for the coprocessor.

External Bridge Topology. The Linux bridging mechanism can also bridge the coprocessor virtual connections to a physical Ethernet device. In this topology, the virtual network interfaces become configurable on the wider subnet.

To specify an external bridge topology, uncomment the `BridgeName` parameter and point it to an existing bridge connected to a physical network device. The bridge must already exist for the coprocessor configuration to become effective. As an example, the configuration files on a RedHat system may be:

```
/etc/sysconfig/network-scripts/ifcfg-br0: DEVICE = br0
TYPE = Bridge
ONBOOT = yes NM_CONTROLLED = no BOOTPROTO = dhcp STP = on
/etc/sysconfig/network-scripts/ifcfg-eth0: DEVICE = eth0
NM_CONTROLLED = yes
ONBOOT = yes
BRIDGE = br0
NAME = "System eth0"
```

NOTE

This is not a complete file listing. Please edit the appropriate files provided in the installation as needed for the particular system network topology required.

The host network configuration file for the virtual network connection will be attached to the bridge (much as the eth0 device is) and does not need an IP address.

The `Subnet` parameter needs to be set to the full IP address of the first coprocessor. It must also specify an address on a subnet the host platform exists on. Each additional coprocessor will get an IP address with the coprocessor number added to the fourth byte in the IP quad. For example: with two coprocessors in the system, if `Subnet` is set to 10.10.10.15, the first coprocessor will be assigned 10.10.10.15 and the second will be assigned 10.10.10.16.

The `Subnet` parameter may also be set to the string *dhcp*. The coprocessor network interface will attempt to retrieve its IP address using the DHCP protocol. This is the recommended value for most clusters.

Assigning the Netmask. Each network interface is assigned a netmask. The netmask for coprocessors is controlled by the `NetBits` parameter and its argument is the number of bits to assign to the mask. The default value is 24, translates into the mask FFFFFF00, and will allow a subnet with 253 devices. If bigger subnets are required, the system administrator may change this value. For instance, setting it to 22 will generate the netmask FFFFFC00 with a maximum number of devices of 1022.

Assigning the MTU size. The coprocessor virtual network defaults to packet sizes of 64 KB instead of the standard 1500 bytes. It is much more efficient, but will not route correctly over external bridge in most networks. The `MTUsize` configuration parameter will change the value of the MTU size. Its argument is the number of bytes to set it to.

Not all network hardware supports the maximum IPV4 MTU size of 64 KB. Typically clusters have the MTU size set to 9000 and `MTUsize` should be set to match.

Host Platform SSH Keys. The secure shell utilities recognize a Linux operating system on the network by their *host key files*. These files are found in the */etc/ssh* directory. The `micctrl --initdefaults` command uses the `ssh-keygen` utility to generate key values if they are not found for the coprocessor. These values, the MAC addresses, are considered to be highly persistent, and the `micctrl` command will retain their values if they exist.

In some clusters, detecting and protecting against "man in the middle" and other such attacks might not be required. In this case, the system administrator may use the `micctrl --hostkeys` command to set the host SSH keys to be the same, cluster wide.

Name Resolution Configuration. Name resolution on the coprocessor is set by creating the */etc/nsswitch* file and copying the */etc/resolve.conf* file from the host to the coprocessor file system.

The micctrl utility

The `micctrl` utility is a multipurpose toolbox for the system administrator. It provides the following categories of functionality.

- Coprocessor state control—boot, shutdown and reset control while the `mpssd` daemon is running.
- Configuration files initialization and propagation of values.
- Helper functions for modifying configuration parameters.
- Helper functions for modifying the root file system directory or associated download image.

The `micctrl` utility requires a first argument specifying the action to perform, followed by option-specific arguments. The arguments may be followed by a list of coprocessor names, which is shown in the syntax statements as [MIC coprocessor list]. If no coprocessors are specified, the host driver (`mic.ko`) must be loaded and the existing coprocessor list is probed. Otherwise, the coprocessor will be a list of the coprocessor names. For example, the list may be "mic1 mic3" if these are the coprocessors to control.

Coprocessor state control

Starting the mpssd daemon typically initiates booting of all the system's coprocessors, and stopping the daemon shuts them down. However, this global behavior is not desired if only one coprocessor needs to be restarted. The micctrl utility provides mechanisms for individual coprocessor control.

State is controlled for each coprocessor by the sysfs entry */sys/class/mic/<micname>/state*. The *micname* value is literally the name of the coprocessor and will be in the format mic0 or mic1, and so on. Reading from the state will show the current run state of the selected coprocessor. Writing to it is limited to the root user and may cause the coprocessor to change states.

Booting coprocessors

Command syntax:

```
micctrl -b [-w] [mic coprocessor list]
micctrl --boot [-w] [mic coprocessor list]
```

The coprocessor must be in the Ready state. The command writes the string *boot:linux:<image>* (where image is the OSimage configuration parameter) to the */sys/class/mic/<micname>/state* sysfs file. The host driver will inject the indicated Linux image into the coprocessors memory and start it booting.

The optional -w parameter may be specified to instruct the micctrl command to wait until the specified coprocessors have either entered the Online or Failed states. The wait option will timeout after 300 seconds.

Shutting down coprocessors

Command syntax:

```
micctrl -S [-w] [mic coprocessor list]
micctrl --shutdown [-w] [mic coprocessor list]
```

The coprocessor must be in the Online state. This command writes the string *shutdown* to the */sys/class/mic/<micname>/state* sysfs file. The driver instructs the coprocessor to perform an orderly shutdown and wait for completion. It will then reset the coprocessor to place it again in the Boot Ready state.

The optional -w parameter may be specified to instruct the micctrl command to wait until the specified coprocessors have entered the Ready state. The wait option will timeout after 300 seconds.

Rebooting the coprocessors

Command syntax:

```
micctrl -R [-w] [mic coprocessor list]
micctrl --reboot [-w] [mic coprocessor list]
```

The coprocessor must be in the Online state. This command sequentially performs the shutdown and boot functions from the sections "Shutting Down Coprocessors" and "Booting Coprocessors."

The optional `-w` parameter may be specified to instruct the `micctrl` command to wait until the specified coprocessors have entered the Ready state. The `wait` option will timeout after 300 seconds.

Resetting coprocessors

Command syntax:

```
micctrl -r [-w] [mic coprocessor list]
micctrl --reset [-w] [mic coprocessor list]
```

The coprocessor can be in any state. This command writes the string *reset* to the */sys/class/mic/ <micname>/state* sysfs file. The driver will perform a soft reset on the coprocessor.

> **NOTE**
> It is recommended to do a shutdown where possible instead of a reset.

The optional `-w` parameter may be specified to instruct the `micctrl` command to wait until the specified coprocessors have entered the Ready state. The `wait` option will timeout after 300 seconds.

Waiting for a coprocessor state change

Command syntax:

```
micctrl -w [mic coprocessor list]
micctrl --wait [mic coprocessor list]
```

The `wait` option waits for the status of the coprocessor to be either Online or Ready. It also allows for a brief pause to the Ready state during `mpssd` startup. It is intended for users to verify the `mpssd` startup procedure is complete. It has a built-in timeout value of 300 seconds.

Coprocessor status

Command syntax:

```
micctrl -s [mic coprocessor list]
micctrl --status [mic coprocessor list]
```

The `status` option displays the status of the coprocessors in the system. If the status is "online" or "booting" it also displays the name of the associated boot image.

Coprocessor configuration initialization and propagation

This section discusses the `micctrl` command options for initializing configuration files, and propagating, resetting, and cleaning configuration parameters.

Initializing the configuration files

Command syntax:

```
micctrl --initdefaults [mic coprocessor list]
```

The Intel MPSS installation does not provide the configuration files. They are created by the `micctrl --initdefaults` command. `micctrl --initdefaults` can be run anytime but will not change files if they have valid information.

The `--initdefaults` option first checks to see if the */etc/sysconfig/mic/default.conf* file is present. If not, it creates the default version of it. Then, for each supplied coprocessor, it checks for the existence of the coprocessor-specific configuration file */etc/sysconfig/mic/<micname>.conf*. If it is not present, it creates a default version with an Include parameter including the `default.conf` file.

The `--initdefaults` option then proceeds to parse the per coprocessor configuration files. For each parameter that is not set, it will add a default value to the per coprocessor configuration file. Each parameter that gets created also has its operation performed at configuration time. For example, the `UserAuthentication` parameter being set to its default of `Local` will cause the coprocessors */etc/passwd*, */etc/shadow* and */etc/group* files to be created along with any corresponding user directories and SSH key files.

Propagating changed configuration parameters

Command syntax:

```
micctrl --resetconfig [mic coprocessor list]
```

Changes to the configuration files are propagated with the `micctrl --resetconfig` command. The `--resetconfig` option first removes the files in *MicDir* created by the configuration process with the exception of the highly persistent SSH host key files. It then regenerates those files according to the parameters in the */etc/sysconfig/mic/<micname>.conf* and */etc/sysconfig/mic/default.conf* files. This process will not add default parameters, but only causes the changed parameters to be propagated.

Resetting configuration parameters

Command syntax:

```
micctrl --resetdefaults [mic coprocessor list]
```

In the event of a failed or problematic configuration process, the best remedy may be to start again. The `micctrl --resetdefaults` command deletes the configuration files and executes the same process as the `--initdefaults` option.

Since `--initdefaults` only affects the files known to the configuration, it does not delete any files the system administrator has added to a coprocessor's file system.

Cleaning configuration parameters

Command syntax:

```
micctrl --cleanconfig [mic coprocessor list]
```

Since Intel MPSS configuration commands will update the configuration when parameters change, it may not be possible to return to a previous version of the Intel MPSS software. Indeed, removing the whole coprocessor configuration may be required.

The `--cleanconfig` option not only removes a coprocessor's configuration files, but also removes all files in the *MicDir* parameter directory along with the other values specified by `RootDevice`.

Helper functions for configuration parameters

This section discusses command options for adding and removing users and groups.

Change the UserAuthentication configuration parameter

Command syntax:

```
micctrl --configuser=none [-ids] [mic coprocessor list]
micctrl --configuser=local [--low=<low uid>] \ [--high=<high uid] [-ids] [mic
coprocessor list]
```

The `--configuser` option provides an easy method for changing the `UserAuthentication` configuration parameter. It performs the same process as `--resetconfig` for this single parameter.

When specifying the `local mode`, low and high user ID values may optionally be supplied. The default values are 500 and 65000, for low and high user ID, respectively. Although any 32-bit user ID may be entered, it is not recommended to use less than 500 for the low value. This is the range where most Linux releases start user ID allocation and migrating the user IDs for system level accounts is not recommended.

The optional `-i`, `-d`, and `-s` parameters are mutually exclusive; trying to use more than one will result in an error.

The `-d` option indicates to remove all the current users in the coprocessor's file system before resetting the user authentication mode. This is the default for the `None` value.

The `-s` option indicates to save, or not delete, all the current users before changing the user authentication mode. This is the default for the `Local` value.

The `-i` option prompts the user to delete or save each current user before resetting the user authentication mode.

It is legal to specify changing the `UserAuthentication` parameter to the old value. Tying the same value to the `-i` option gives the system administrator the chance to clean up the current user list.

NOTE

Every user to be populated on the coprocessor file system should set their secure shell configuration files before running this command.

Adding users to the coprocessor file system

Command syntax:

```
micctrl --useradd=<name> -uid=<uid> -gid=<gid> \
[-home=<dir>] [-comment=<string>] [-app=<exec>] \ [-sshkeys=<keydir>] [mic
coprocessor list]
```

The `--useradd` option adds the specified user name to the */etc/passwd* and */etc/shadow* files on the coprocessor file system. The system administrator must specify the correct user and group IDs for the user.

Default values are supplied for the `-home`, `-comment`, `-app`, and `-sshkeys` arguments, and can be overridden. If a home directory for the user is not specified, one will be created in */home/<name>*. If a comment string is not specified, the user name will be placed in the comment field. The default application to execute is */bin/sh*. If a directory for the user's secure shell key files is not provided, the `--useradd` option will attempt to find them in */home/<name>/.ssh*. In addition, a default `.profile` file will be added for the user.

Removing users from the coprocessor file system

Command syntax:

```
micctrl --userdel=<name> [mic coprocessor list]
```

The `--userdel` option removes the specified user from the coprocessors */etc/passwd* and */etc/shadow* files. It also removes the directory stored in the `home` field of the */etc/passwd* file.

Adding groups to the coprocessor file system

Command syntax:

```
micctrl --groupadd=<name> -gid=<gid> [mic coprocessor list]
```

The `--groupadd` option adds the specified group name and ID to the coprocessor's */etc/group* file.

Removing groups from the coprocessor file system

Command syntax:

```
micctrl --groupdel=<name> [mic coprocessor list]
```

The `--groupdel` option removes the specified group name entry from the coprocessors */etc/group* file.

Setting the root device

Command syntax:

```
micctrl --rootdev=RamFS -target=<location> \ [mic coprocessor list]
micctrl --rootdev=StaticRamFS -target=<location> \ [mic coprocessor list]
micctrl --rootdev=NFS -target=<NFS Share> [-c] [-d] \ [mic coprocessor list]
micctrl --rootdev=NFS -target=<NFS Share> \
-usr=</usr NFS share> [-c] [-d] [mic coprocessor list]
micctrl --rootdev=InitRD [mic coprocessor list]
```

The `--rootdev` option changes the configured `RootDevice` parameter. The `target` argument is the name of the compressed cpio image to be used for the coprocessor file system. Setting `rootdev` to `NFS` optionally uses the `target` parameter to specify a valid NFS share on the host containing the root file system. If target is not specified the default name of */opt/intel/mic/filesystem/<micN>.export* will be used. If the `-c` parameter is also specified, the `micctrl` utility will create the root directory using the same information required for building the compressed cpio download image. The created directory must be in the NFS exports list on the host.

Setting `rootdev` to `SplitNFS` is the same as the `NFS` option except the `/usr` files are mounted as a separate NFS share. On a multicard system the coprocessors will typically share the same /usr NFS export. If the `usr` parameter is not specified then the default value of */opt/intel/mic/filesystem/usr.export* will be used.

Adding a NFS mount

Command syntax:

```
micctrl --addnfs=<NFS export> -dir=<mount dir> \
[-server=<server>] [mic coprocessor list]
```

The `--addnfs` option adds a NFS mount entry to the coprocessor's */etc/fstab* file. It specifies the NFS export and the mount directory. If the optional server argument is not specified, it places the IP address of the host in the server field.

Removing a NFS mount

Command syntax:

```
micctrl --remnfs=<mount dir> [mic coprocessor list]
```

The `--remnfs` option searches the */etc/fstab* for the coprocessor for the specified mount point and removes it from the file.

Specifying the host secure shell keys

Command syntax:

```
micctrl --hostkeys=<keydir> [mic coprocessor list]
```

The `--hostkeys` option removes the host keys randomly generated by the `--initdefaults` command and replaces it with the files from the specified directory. These files are considered to be highly persistent and should stay resident unless the `--resetdefaults` or `--cleanconfig` option is performed.

Other file system helper functions

Updating the compressed CPIO image

Command syntax:

```
micctrl --updateramfs [mic coprocessor list]
```

The StaticRamFS root file system image is only changed when the system administrator requests it. In many cluster systems this image will be built externally and put in place. The --updateramfs option updates the image from the same parameters used by the RamFS specification. The new image will be used the next time the coprocessor boots.

Adding software

No installation is static. Additional software eventually needs to be added. The system administrator must therefore add files to the downloaded root file system to meet user needs.

The File System Creation Process

The root file system for the coprocessor is built from the configuration parameters BaseDir, CommonDir, MicDir and Overlay. It is accomplished by using the filelist argument to each of the parameters as a list of the files to be placed into the file system image. Each filelist is processed in the order of configuration parameters stated. Here are the filelist directives:

```
dir <name> <perms> <uid> <gid>
file <name> <source> <perms> <uid> <gid>
slink <name> <to> <perms> <uid> <gid>
nod <name> <perms> <uid> <gid> <type> <major> <minor>
pipe <name> <perms> <uid> <gid>
sock <name> <perms> <uid> <gid>
```

Each filelist entry defines one of six types of files available on a Linux file system.

The dir filelist directive

The dir directive specifies a directory that must be present on the file system. It requires the information to set the permissions, user ID, and group ID of the directory. A typical entry is:

```
dir /tmp 0777 0 0
```

The example defines the directory */tmp* to be owned by user *root* and group *root* with global permissions for everybody.

The file filelist directive

The file directive specifies to create the file with name in the file system image for the file source on the host. It must also be created with the specified permission, user ID and group ID. The source file is copied from the specified string prepended with the associated directory from the original configuration parameter. For example the configuration parameter MicDir may be:

```
MicDir /opt/intel/mic/filesystem/mic0 \
/opt/intel/mic/filesystem/mic0.filelist
```

The entry to copy the */etc/passwd* file to the coprocessor's file system image is:

```
file /etc/passwd etc/passwd 644 0 0
```

This specifies using the file */opt/intel/mic/filesystem/mic0/etc/passwd* for the coprocessor's */etc/passwd* file. It will be owned by user and group root with global read permissions and root modification permission.

The slink filelist directive

The `slink` directive specifies creation of a symbolic link on the file system. It will have `name` and will link to `source`. The link will be created with the specified user and group IDs and permissions. A typical use of symbolic links is found in the Linux OS startup scripts. In the filelist associated with the `MicDir` parameter you will find:

```
slink /etc/rc3.d/S80sshd ../init.d/sshd 0755 0 0
```

This directs the creation of a symbolic link on the coprocessor's file system accessing the */etc/init.d/sshd* file when */etc/rc.d/S80sshd* is accessed.

The nod filelist directive

The `nod` directive creates a device node on the coprocessor's file system. It will be located at `name` and will be of `type`. Type must be either the character *b* for block device or *c* for character device. The arguments `major` and `minor` must be integer values defining the correct values of the node. The node will be created with the specified user and group IDs and permissions.

Most devices on Linux today are created dynamically by the device driver. However, some legacy devices still require a hard-coded entry. For example the `filelist` for `BaseDir` includes the following entry, which specifies the creation of a device node for the console:

```
nod /dev/console 0600 0 0 c 5 1
```

The pipe filelist directive

The `pipe` directive creates a device file of type `pipe` under the specified `name`. It is created with the specified user and group IDs and associated permissions.

The sock filelist directive

The `sock` directive creates a device file of type `socket` under the specified `name`. It is created with the specified user and group IDs and associated permissions.

Creating the download image file

The download image file for the `RamFS` root device type is created by processing the configuration directives `BaseDir`, `CommonDir`, `MicDir` and any `Overlays` in that order. As the configuration directives are processed, a tree of file names and their information is created.

When the tree is completely processed, `mpssd` or `micctrl --updateramfs` will create a cpio entry for the file and append it to the file name specified by the `RootDevice` directive. When processing is complete it then compresses the file.

Adding files to the root file system

Adding a file to the root file system can be done in two ways. The system administrator can add an entry to some existing `filelist`, indicating the location of the file. Alternatively, the system administrator can add new `Overlay` configuration parameter with `location` and descriptor file arguments that describe the files to be added.

Adding files by copying

When adding a file to an existing `filelist`, the first decision is whether the file should be accessible by all the cards or only a particular one. If it is required for all cards to have access, then copy the file to a location under the directory specified by the `location` argument to the `CommonDir` configuration parameter, and amend its `filelist`. Otherwise, copy the file to a location under the directory specified by the `location` argument to the `MicDir` directory, and amend its `filelist`.

If a directory had to be created for the added file, do not forget to insert the appropriate `dir` entry prior to the new `file` entry.

Adding an overlay

The process for adding an `Overlay` set is similar to the description the previous section. The file must be placed in the correct location specified under `Overlay` and added to the `filelist` file specified. The power of the `Overlay` is it may be called from a new configuration file in */etc/sysconfig/mic/conf.d*.

Example: Adding a new global file set

The Intel® Coprocessor Offload Infrastructure (Intel ®COI) as part of Intel MPSS (see Chapter 9) is configured as add-in software and is a good example of how to add a new set of software to the coprocessor file systems. The Intel COI configuration file is installed at */etc/sysconfig/mic/conf.d/coi.conf*. It contains the following:

```
# COI download files
Overlay /opt/intel/mic/coi
/opt/intel/mic/coi/config/coi.filelist
```

From this file, it is clear the files for the coprocessor file system were installed into the */opt/intel/mic/coi* directory. It has also installed a `coi.filelist` file describing the files to include in the coprocessor file systems and looks like the following:

```
dir /bin 755 0 0
file /bin/coi_daemon device-linux-release/bin/coi_daemon 755 0 0 dir /etc 755 0 0
dir /etc/init.d 755 0 0
file /etc/init.d/coi config/coi 775 0 0 dir /etc/rc3.d 755 0 0
slink /etc/rc3.d/S95coi ../init.d/coi 777 0 0
dir /lib64 755 0 0
file /lib64/libcoi_device.so device-linux-release/lib/libcoi_device.so 755 0 0 slink
/lib64/libcoi_device.so.0 libcoi_device.so 777 0 0
```

From this we can see:

- COI requires that the */bin* directory exists
- The COI daemon is at */bin/coi_daemon*
  - It is found on the host file system at */opt/intel/mic/coi/device-linux- release/bin/coi_daemon*
  - It requires read/write/execute permissions for root

  - It requires read/execute permissions for other
  - It runs under the root (0) user and group IDs
- COI requires the */etc* and */etc/init.d* directories
- The COI startup script should be put at */etc/init.d/coi*
  - It can be found on the host at */opt/intel/mic/coi/config/coi*
  - Set permissions, user ID and group ID as described.
  - For the coprocessor to start COI, it needs a reference in */etc/rc3.d*, so make sure it exists.
- The startup will find the script at */etc/rc3.d/S95coi*, so create a symbolic link to the actual startup script.
- COI requires */lib64* directory to exist.
- Install `libcoi_device.so` library.
- Create the required symbolic link to it.

Since Intel COI installs a new daemon on the file system, it needs a startup script for it. The COI startup script appears in the following code example.

```
#!/bin/sh
coiexec=/bin/coi_daemon
case "$1" in
start)
if [ ! -f $coiexec ];then exit 1;
fi

   $coiexec &
   ;;

esac
```

Coprocessor Linux boot process

As previously mentioned, the host driver and `mpssd` daemon manage the process of booting the Linux kernel on the coprocessor. Figure 10.1 shows the sequence of steps that are performed during the boot process.

Booting the coprocessor

The key steps in the process flow in Figure 10.1 performed during the Intel MPSS boot process on the coprocessor are described in this section.

Set the kernel command line

On most Intel Architecture based systems, loading and executing the Linux kernel image is controlled by the `grub` boot loader. In the `grub` configuration file, each possible kernel definition contains a number of parameters to be passed to Linux through its kernel command line. In the Intel MPSS boot system, this is done by the `mpssd` daemon parsing its configuration files. The kernel command line is created based on values in the configuration files and placed in */sys/class/mic/mic<id>/cmdline* for the driver to retrieve it.

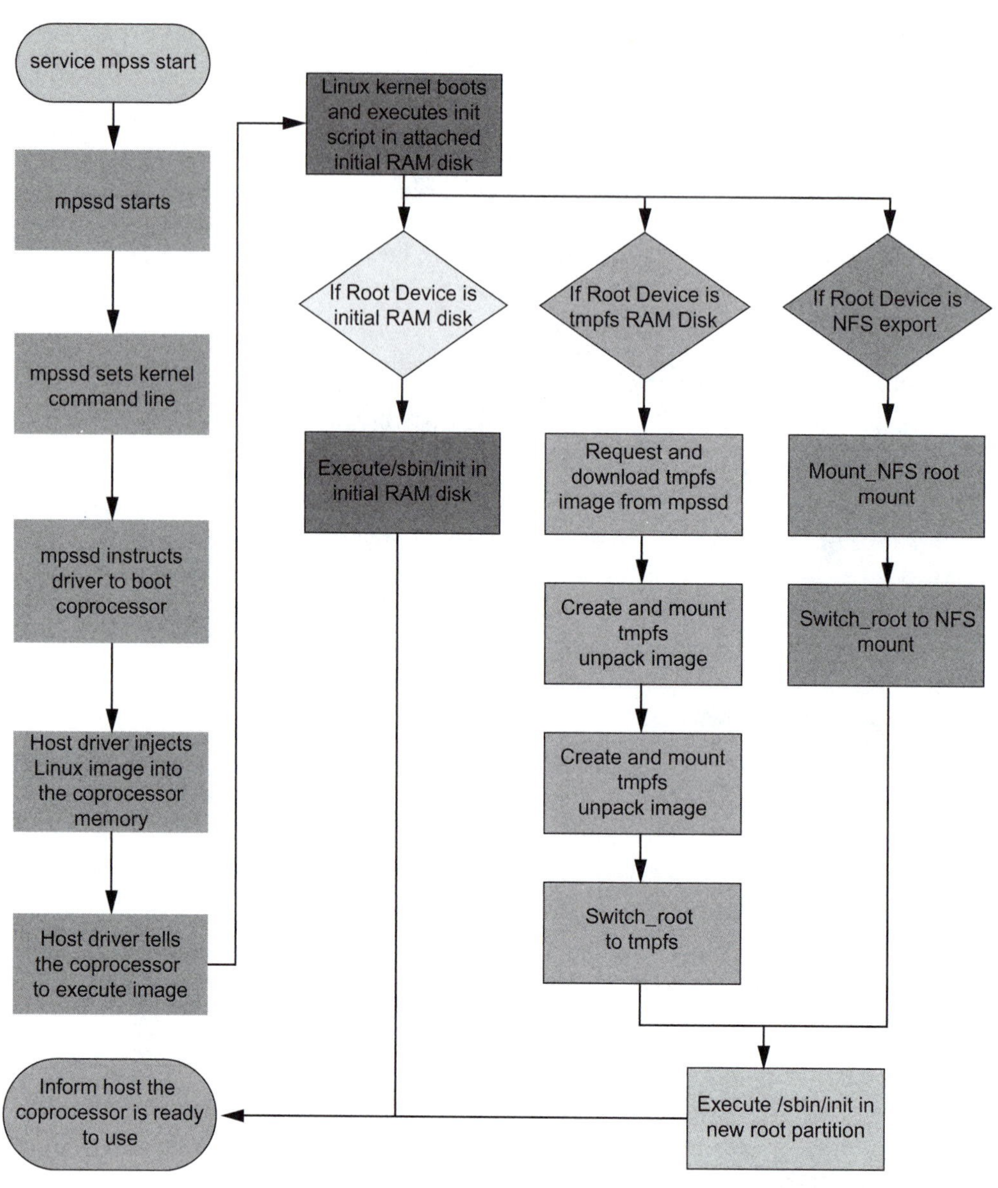

FIGURE 10.1

Boot Process for the Intel® Manycore Platform Software Stack (Intel® MPSS).

Instruct the driver to boot the coprocessor

The mpssd daemon requests the coprocessor to start executing the Linux image by writing a boot string to the */sys/class/mic/mic<id>/state* file. This file is a link into the coprocessor driver through a Linux sysfs (see Chapter 9) entry. The format of the request must be:

```
boot:linux:<Linux image file name>
```

The options reset and shutdown may also be written to state entry and will be discussed further later. The second part of the boot argument indicates to boot a Linux image. It may also be set to elf to indicate booting a standard ELF format file. This option is beyond our scope, please see standard Linux documentation for more information.

When the driver receives the boot request, it first checks to see the coprocessor is in the Ready state. If the coprocessor is not ready to boot it will return an error through the write call to the sysfs entry and not attempt to boot the coprocessor. Otherwise it sets the state of the coprocessor to Booting.

The driver then saves the image file name for later retrieval through the */sys/class/mic/mic<id>/image* sysfs entry. It also sets the mode to indicate it is booting a Linux image.

The driver will copy the kernel command line setting request by the mpssd daemon, along with a number of addresses in host memory required by various drivers in the Linux image. It then copies the requested Linux image file into the coprocessor's memory.

The last step is to write to the coprocessor register instructing it to start executing the injected image.

Execute the Linux kernel image

Executing the Linux kernel code functions as it does on any Intel Architecture based machine. It initializes hardware, starts kernel services, and sets all the CPU cores to the Online state. When the kernel is ready, it initializes its attached initial RAM disk image and starts executing the init script in the image.

The initial RAM disk contains the loadable modules required for the real root file system. Many of the arguments passed in the kernel command line are addresses required for the modules to access host memory. The init script parses the kernel command line for needed information and loads the driver modules.

The last step is for the init script to check the root parameter in the kernel command line for the type of device containing the root file system, and take the appropriate actions.

Root is the initial RAM disk

Setting the root to be the initial RAM disk is for debug purposes only. The initial RAM disk contains only a minimal set of tools and utilities.

Root is a RAM disk image

If the root is set to be a RAM file system, the init script must first download the file system information from the host. It makes a request to the mpssd daemon through a SCIF (see Chapter 9) connection and receives a compressed cpio format file.

After the file has been downloaded, the `init` script creates a `tmpfs` (Linux RAM disk file system type) in coprocessor memory and extracts the file system information into it. This image must contain everything needed to start a fully functional Linux system.

The RAM disk image is activated as the root device by calling the Linux `switch_root` utility. This special utility instructs the Linux kernel to remount the root device on the *tmpfs* mount directory, release all file system memory references to the old initial RAM disk, and start executing the new */sbin/init* function.

The */sbin/init* function performs the normal Linux user level initialization. All the information required must have already been in the compressed cpio file.

Root is a NFS export

If a NFS mount is indicated to supply the root device, the `init` script will initialize the `mic0` virtual network interface to the IP address supplied on the kernel command line and mount the NFS export from the host.

As in the RAM disk image, the NFS mount is activated as the root device by calling the Linux `switch_root` utility. This special utility instructs the Linux kernel to remount the root device on the NFS mount directory, release all file system memory references to the old initial RAM disk, and start executing the new */sbin/init* function.

The */sbin/init* function performs the normal Linux user level initialization. All the information required must have already been in the NFS export.

Notify the host that the coprocessor system is ready

The last step of any of the three initializations is to notify the host that the coprocessor is ready for access. It does this by writing to its */sys/clas/micnotify/notify/host_notified* entry. This causes an interrupt into the host driver, which updates the coprocessor's state to Booted.

Coprocessors in a Linux cluster

So far in this chapter, and much of this book, we have focused on explaining how a coprocessor is programmed and operates in a single host processor platform, In other words, a single *node* in a cluster. This focus has been intentional as we believe it is essential for success on a cluster of coprocessor-enabled platforms to first understand how to parallelize and optimize code at the node level in order to maximize use across a cluster.

Using Intel Xeon Phi coprocessors in a cluster environment is, of course, one of the primary usages. The foundation to enable it is provided by the coprocessor's Linux operating system environment and it's configurability that we have described thus far in this chapter. However, configuring, optimizing, and running code in clusters in general and further in clusters with Intel Xeon Phi coprocessors is a significant topic on its own and to cover it properly would warrant multiple chapters or even its own book. From an application development point of view, MPI is the prevalent cluster-wide scaling tool, and the software architecture for MPI and its uses on the coprocessor in Chapters 9 and 12 should be a solid basis to start cluster-wide application development.

Here, we will touch upon some key information and resources to consider when using Intel Xeon Phi coprocessors in a standard cluster configuration Intel calls Intel® Cluster Ready.

Intel® Cluster Ready

This section is particular to systems that are certified Intel Cluster Ready and therefore have access to the tools to verify and maintain that compliance. Compliance of machines and software to a common specification greatly enhances portability of software between clusters.

Intel created the Intel Cluster Ready program in collaboration with High Performance Computing (HPC) industry hardware and software vendors to make it easier to set up, to operate, and to maintain HPC clusters including those with Intel Xeon Phi coprocessors. At the heart of the program is a standard and tools to check for adherence to the standard. The compliance checks are a great checklist in setting up a system that can be used to find many issues that would otherwise take time to discover or debug.

The Intel® Cluster Checker, a key element of the Intel Cluster Ready validation process, is a software tool that helps to verify that cluster components are working well when the cluster is being deployed and help check compliance status throughout the life of the machine.

How Intel® Cluster Ready works

Intel Cluster Ready works in the following manner:

1. *Initial machine setup.* Platform providers and system integrators use the Intel Cluster Ready architecture and specification to develop interoperable clusters that are easy to deploy and manage. They ensure that all cluster components work together, so an end user can buy an Intel Cluster Ready cluster with the confidence that it will work right from the start. Intel Cluster Ready clusters must pass a certification process in order to verify they are interoperable with registered Intel Cluster Ready software.
2. *Software compliance for portability.* Software developers test their applications running representative workloads on certified Intel Cluster Ready systems to ensure that they run as expected. Once proper execution is verified, the application is registered as capable of running on any system compliant with the Intel Cluster Ready specification. An end user can choose the right cluster to run the software that has been registered with Intel Cluster Ready and experience great application performance, right from the start.
3. *Ongoing machine/environment compliance.* Intel Cluster Checker, which is provided with all Intel Cluster Ready systems, eases the headaches of traditional cluster maintenance and gives the end user the power of HPC clusters with less need for specialized experience. Intel Cluster Checker enhances system reliability, reduces total cost of ownership over the cluster's lifetime, and ensures continuing performance.

How Intel® Cluster Checker works

Before a certified Intel Cluster Ready system arrives, the platform provider has used Intel Cluster Checker to verify that the cluster fully complies with the Intel Cluster Ready specification. Application software developers have defined representative workloads and used Intel Cluster Checker to confirm that their applications run successfully on an Intel Cluster Ready system.

Intel Cluster Checker can be run as part of regular cluster maintenance, helping to keep components working together over the cluster's lifetime or spotting potential issues before they can affect productivity. If problems arise, Intel Cluster Checker can be used to identify the problems quickly and obtain detailed diagnostic information. The time required to find a solution can be reduced from days to hours or even minutes.

Intel Cluster Checker is a tool that acts a proxy for application binaries. With more than 100 checks aggregated in parallel test modules, Intel Cluster Checker can perform a wide array of cluster evaluations. This rich feature set is also extensible. Additional checks can be integrated and existing checks can be customized in order to fully exploit the potential of Intel Cluster Checker. The cluster is examined at both the node and cluster level, making sure that all components work together and deliver optimal performance. Intel Cluster Checker assesses firmware, kernel, storage, and network settings, and conducts high-level tests of node and network performance using the Intel® MPI Benchmarks, STREAM, the HPC Challenge benchmark (HPCC), and other benchmarks.

Intel® Cluster Checker support for coprocessors

One of the key benefits of Intel Cluster Checker is that it acts as a real-life user executing commands. The end user does not have to be an expert in using HPC clusters in order to be able to fully exploit the capabilities of Intel Cluster Checker. Intel Cluster Checker supports Intel Xeon Phi coprocessors and incorporates a variety of checks in order to ensure the proper functioning of the coprocessor.

For example, to ensure that the coprocessor is up and running, there are three recommended steps: two involving the execution of Intel MPSS supporting tools `micinfo` and `miccheck` described in Chapter 9 plus the execution of a benchmark on the host system that uses offload to speed up computation as described in Chapter 7.

The built-in test module `micinfo` checks whether the coprocessor information is correct and uniform across nodes. Any error, undefined value, or abnormal difference among coprocessors is reported. For example, the test module ensures that voltage, memory size, and temperature are non-zero and only differences smaller than 100,000 μV, 128 MB or 20°C are allowed. This default behavior can be altered with custom configuration if desired.

The test module `miccheck` checks the sanity of the coprocessors by running the `miccheck` diagnostic tool on every node in the cluster in parallel. Only the failing checks are reported. Since the Intel Math Kernel Library has very good support for direct offload to an Intel Xeon Phi coprocessor for certain routines, like the GEMM routines, the test module `dgemm` of Intel Cluster Checker can directly be used to also test the offload functionality and performance.

To run a benchmark that offloads work to a coprocessor, two related environment variables need to be specified (both to force offload and to enable reporting). Since the offloading of GEMM routines works best with symmetric values, the parameters to the test `dgemm` in the configuration file (default *config.xml*) should be adjusted as well.

```
<cluster>
    <include_module>micinfo</include_module>
    <include_module>miccheck</include_module>
    <test>
      <dgemm>
```

```
            <k>6000</k>
            <m>6000</m>
            <n>6000</n>
          </dgemm>
        </test>

</cluster>
```

Then run the following command to explicitly test the Intel Xeon Phi coprocessor:

```
$ source '/opt/intel/clck/<version>/bin/clckvars.sh
$ OFFLOAD_REPORT=2 MKL_MIC_ENABLE=1 clck –I micinfo –I miccheck –I dgemm
```

Here is an example of some lines of corresponding diagnostic and verbose output when running Intel Cluster Checker with the option `–certification`, which executes a larger set of test modules, including `micinfo` and `miccheck`:

```
Intel(R) Cluster Checker, Version 2.0
Commandline: '/opt/intel/clck/2.0.013/bin/clck -certification'
User: 'cmsupport'
Date: 'Thu Nov 15 20:21:45 2012'
Configuration File: '/etc/intel/clck/config.xml'
...
Nodefile: '/etc/intel/clck/nodelist'
Checking 5 nodes:

        jerry, computej-[1-4]

Modules to be executed:
...

        'micinfo'

...

        'miccheck'
        'mpi_internode'
        'hpl'
Test                              Result
_____________________________________________________________________

...

Check Intel Xeon Phi wellness and uniformity, (micinfo)........
..............................Succeeded

      subtest 'micinfo uniformity' passed
        node: computej-[1-4]: 82 fields matched
      subtest 'micinfo valid output' passed
        node: computej-[1-4]: passed
```

```
Mounted filesystems check, ...
Intel          Xeon         Phi         diagnostic         test,         (miccheck)
.........................................................................
Succeeded

      subtest 'MIC 0 Test 1 Find the MIC' passed
        node: computej-[1-4]: OK
      ...
        subtest 'Test 2 Ensure host driver is loaded' passed
          node: computej-[1-4]: OK
        subtest 'Test 3 Ensure driver matches manifest' passed
          node: computej-[1-4]: OK
        subtest 'Test 4 Detect all MICs' passed
          node: computej-[1-4]: OK

...
20 Modules passed:

      clock dgemm disk_bandwidth ethernet hardware hpl libraries miccheck micinfo mount
mpi_internode mpi_local packages ping process remote_login shells storage stream tools

0 Modules failed
Check has SUCCEEDED
Log saved in: /var/log/intel/clck/clck-20121115-202144.log
Total elapsed time: 0:03:12
```

Clusters are a challenge to build or manage but an Intel Cluster Ready certified platform with Intel Cluster Checker validation tools helps make the process more predictable and reliable.

Summary

A key goal in making the Intel Xeon Phi coprocessor a readily usable platform for high performance parallel programs is to allow developers and operational personnel the ability to focus on the delivering applications and solutions, not on learning new and different ways to interact with a new product. Adapting a standard Linux operating system to the coprocessor is at the heart of making this goal a reality.

In this chapter we provided insight into how this goal was achieved and also the tools and mechanisms allowing the coprocessor Linux operating system to be configured and booted to successfully operate as a standalone Linux computer in almost any network configuration, including the desired file system topology and the software required for target applications.

We also discussed some of the tools and considerations in using the coprocessor in cluster environments, including the Intel Cluster Ready certification program and the Intel Cluster Checker tool that allows confirming a cluster is operating properly.

In this chapter along with Chapters 8 and 9, we explained various architectural and operational aspects of the Intel Xeon Phi coprocessor to give you important foundational elements that enable high performance applications to run on the coprocessor. In the upcoming three chapters, we will now switch focus to some of the libraries and development tools that can enable you to more easily develop high performance parallel applications.

For more information

Here are some additional reading materials we recommend related to this chapter.

- Intel Manycore Platform Software (Intel MPSS) documentation and downloads, http://intel.com/software/mic
- Linux information, http://linux.org
- Linux kernel source distributions, http://kernel.org
- Information on Intel Clusters, the Intel Cluster Ready Program, and related tools: http://www.intel.com/go/cluster

CHAPTER

Math Library

11

Math libraries offer a very attractive option for using the power of Intel® Xeon Phi™ coprocessors quickly and effectively, often as easy as swapping out a processor optimized library for compatible library that uses the combined capabilities of the processor and Intel Xeon Phi coprocessors. Intel has done a great job giving several powerful options for programs that utilize the Intel® Math Kernel Library (Intel® MKL) already, or use industry standard interfaces like BLAS, CBLAS, LAPACK, LAPACKE, FFTW, and ScaLAPACK, to have access to the power of Intel processors and the Intel Xeon Phi coprocessor.

Table 11.1 lists the three programming models for using Intel MKL with Intel Xeon Phi coprocessors. These programming models are simply different interfaces to the same underlying performance capabilities of the processors and coprocessors. Multiple models can easily be utilized in the same program to meet your needs. The library does not operate in different modes; these models are just different interfaces to the same underlying performance capabilities in processors and coprocessors. The key choice is native versus offload, based on the same logic covered in Chapter 7: use native for highly parallel workloads and use offload when it is beneficial for parts of your program run specifically on a processor or coprocessor at the right time.

Table 11.1 Intel® MKL: Programming Models for Intel® Xeon Phi™ Coprocessors

Model	Description
Native	Intel MKL functions called from within an application executing natively on an Intel Xeon Phi coprocessor run on the coprocessor. Calling Intel MKL from C/C++ and Fortran is supported.
Offload, Automatic	Select Intel MKL functions are automatically distributed to run across the processor(s) and Intel Xeon Phi coprocessor(s) when present including the automatic control of data movement to/from the coprocessor(s). This mode is enabled and more finely controlled where desirable with simple service functions (or environment variables) and supports calling from both C/C++ and Fortran.
Offload, Compiler Assisted	Intel MKL functions called from within compiler offload regions (see Chapter 7) run on the Xeon Phi coprocessor(s) when present (or on the processor(s) otherwise). Compiler offload pragmas (C/C++) and directives (Fortran) control data movement to/from the coprocessor(s). This approach supports offloading regions of code potentially comprising numerous calls to Intel MKL functions, thereby amortizing the data movement over multiple computation operations.

Math libraries from other vendors, such as IMSL Numerical Libraries from Rogue Wave software and the NAG Library from The Numerical Algorithms Group Ltd. also provide support for Intel Xeon Phi coprocessors. Both of these libraries integrate portions of the Intel MKL as well to provide optimizations of highly computationally intensive functions. If your program uses any of these interfaces, or could use them, then you should definitely look at library solutions. The rest of this chapter provides further details on how to use Intel MKL for the Intel Xeon Phi coprocessor.

Intel Math Kernel Library overview

The Intel MKL includes routines and functions optimized for Intel and compatible processor-based computers running operating systems that support multiprocessing. In addition to Fortran interfaces, Intel MKL includes C-language interfaces for the BLAS[1] (called CBLAS) and LINPACK with C interfaces known as LINPACKE, Discrete Fourier transform functions, Vector Math and Vector Statistical Library functions. Intel MKL includes the following groups of routines:

- Basic Linear Algebra Subprograms (BLAS):
  - level 1 BLAS: vector operations
  - level 2 BLAS: matrix-vector operations
  - level 3 BLAS: matrix-matrix operations
- Sparse BLAS Level 1, 2, and 3 (basic operations on sparse vectors and matrices)
- LAPACK[2] routines for solving systems of linear equations, least squares problems, eigenvalue and singular value problems, Sylvester's equations and auxiliary and utility LAPACK routines
- ScaLAPACK[3] computational, driver, and auxiliary routines for solving systems of linear equations across a compute cluster
- PBLAS routines for distributed vector, matrix-vector, and matrix-matrix operation
- Direct Sparse Solver routines (PARDISO)
- Iterative Sparse Solver routines
- Vector math functions for computing core mathematical functions on vector arguments
- Vector statistical functions for generating vectors of pseudorandom numbers with different types of statistical distributions and for performing convolution and correlation computations. VSL also includes summary statistics functions. Used to accurately estimate, for example, central moments, skewness, kurtosis, variance, quantiles, and to compute variance-covariance matrices and correlation matrices.
- General Fast Fourier Transform (FFT) functions, providing fast computation of Discrete Fourier Transforms via the FFT algorithms (using the FFTW interface)
- Cluster FFT functions[4] for solving FFTs across a compute cluster
- Tools for solving partial differential equations—trigonometric transform routines and Poisson solver

[1]Basic Linear Algebra Subprograms, www.netlib.org/blas
[2]Linear Algebra PACKage
[3]supported only on Linux† and Windows† versions, not supported on Mac† OS systems
[4]supported only on Linux and Windows versions, not supported on Mac OS systems

- Optimization Solver routines for solving nonlinear least squares problems through the Trust-Region (TR) algorithms and computing Jacobi matrix by central differences
- Data Fitting functions for spline-based approximation of functions, derivatives and integrals of functions, and cell search

The *Intel Math Kernel Library Reference Manual* is the definitive resource for learning more about the many functions available in Intel MKL. A very large number of the routines have industry standard interfaces that are used to access the Intel optimized implementations.

Intel MKL provides both static and dynamic libraries for Intel Xeon Phi coprocessors. However, the Single Dynamic Library (SDL) capability is unavailable for coprocessors as the resulting library is too large for use on a coprocessor. If you are using SDL, refer to the *Intel MKL User's Guide* section "Linking on Intel Xeon Phi Coprocessors" to understand your linking options. The Intel MKL product includes a "Link Line Advisor" to help suggest the right linkage commands to meet your needs (see http://tinyurl.com/Link-MKL). The Advisor requests information about your system and on how you intend to use the library and then the tool automatically generates the appropriate link line for specified application configuration.

The focus for the remainder of this chapter is on how to use Intel MKL with an Intel Xeon Phi coprocessor, and not about the details of the functions within Intel MKL. You are encouraged to read the *Intel Math Kernel Library Reference Manual* in order to explore the many functions in Intel MKL and refer to the *Intel Math Kernel Library User's Guide* for usage details such as linking options.

Intel MKL differences on the coprocessor

In general, the Intel Math Kernel Library (Intel MKL) supports an Intel Xeon Phi coprocessor equivalently to a processor, with only one key difference:

- The addition of the ability to automatically offload from the processors to coprocessors, which is described in this chapter.

Intel MKL and Intel compiler

The Intel compiler has an option `–mkl` as a convenience option, but does not indicate dependence between the library and compiler as they can be used separately. The `mkl = lib` option indicates the part of the MKL library that the compiler should link to. Possible values are:

- `parallel`: Tells the compiler to link using the threaded part of the Intel® MKL. This is the default if the option is specified with no lib.
- `sequential`: Tells the compiler to link using the non-threaded part of the Intel® MKL.
- `cluster`: Tells the compiler to link using the cluster part and the sequential part of the Intel® MKL.

Coprocessor support overview

Intel MKL supports Intel Xeon Phi coprocessors in two major ways, from routines called on processors and versions of the routines for calling directly from code running on the coprocessor. The first way utilizes the coprocessor via offload and the second is simply native execution.

The offloading of computations to Intel Xeon Phi coprocessors can be done without requiring any change to source code with automatic offload or using pragmas or directives in the source code in what is called compiler-assisted offload.

The automatic offload capability automatically detects the presence of coprocessors and automatically offloads computations that may benefit from additional computational resources available. To use this capability, you simply link with a recent version of Intel MKL (which includes Intel Xeon Phi coprocessor support) and set an environment variable (`MKL_MIC_ENABLE=1`). Alternately, a single function call (`mkl_mic_enable`) can be inserted to activate this capability for your program as an alternative to using an environment variable. The function call takes priority over the environment variable when used.

The compiler-assisted offload offers the convenience of pragmas or directives for detailed control with the assistance of the compiler. This capability enables you to use the Intel compiler and its offload support to manage the functions and data offloaded to a coprocessor. Within an offload region, you should specify both the input and output data for the Intel MKL functions to be offloaded. Data can be reused between calls to optimize performance by reducing unnecessary back and forth data copies and allocation. After linking with the Intel MKL libraries for Intel MIC Architecture, the compiler provided runtime libraries transfer the functions along with their data to a coprocessor to carry out the computations.

In addition to offloading computations to coprocessors, you can call Intel MKL functions from an application that runs natively on a coprocessor. Native execution occurs when an application runs entirely on the coprocessor. Native mode simply uses versions of Intel MKL routines that have been tuned for Intel Xeon Phi coprocessor features including the 512-bit wide vector instructions and fused multiply add instructions. The library used on the coprocessor is identical whether invoked via offload, automatic offload, or via native usage.

Control functions for automatic offload

C and Fortran functions, and corresponding environment variable alternatives, to support the use of Intel Xeon Phi coprocessors are shown in Table 11.2 with some example usages shown in Figures 11.1 and 11.2.

The `mkl_mic_enable` function enables Intel MKL to offload computations to Intel Xeon Phi coprocessors automatically, while the `mkl_mic_disable` function disables automatic offloading.

Optional work-division control functions enable you to specify the fractional amount of work of a function to distribute between processors and the coprocessors on a single computer (node in a cluster). Work division is a fractional measure ranging from 0.0 to 1.0. For example, setting work division for processors to 0.5 means to keep half of the computational work of a function on processors and move half to the coprocessor(s). Setting work division to 0.25 for a coprocessor means to offload a quarter of the computational work to this coprocessor while leaving the rest on processors and any additional coprocessors.

Use of these support functions inside a program will take precedence over the respective environment variables. Fortran programs use include file mkl.fi, while C/C++ programs use include file mkl.h.

Table 11.2 MKL Support Functions and Environment Variables Specifically for Intel® Xeon Phi™ Coprocessors

Function {environment variable}	Description
mkl_mic_enable {MKL_MIC_ENABLE = 1}	Enables Automatic Offload mode.
mkl_mic_disable {MKL_MIC_ENABLE = 0}	Disables Automatic Offload mode.
{OFFLOAD_DEVICES}	This environment variable control offloading constructs from the compiler as well as Intel® MKL. This environment variable specifies a list of coprocessors to be used for Automatic Offload. There is no function call for this control. Should be a comma-separated list of integers, each ranging from 0 to the largest number of an Intel® Xeon Phi™ coprocessor on the system. If the list contains any non-integer data, the list is ignored completely as if the environment variable were not set at all. If this variable is not set, all the coprocessors available on the system are used for Automatic Offload.
mkl_mic_get_device_count	Returns the number of Intel Xeon Phi coprocessors on the system when called on processors.
mkl_mic_set_workdivision {MKL_MIC_WORKDIVISION or MKL_MIC_*num*_WORKDIVISION or MKL_HOST_WORKDIVISION}	For computations in the Automatic Offload mode, sets the fraction of the work for the coprocessors, all or specified by *num* to do. Values of 0.0 to 1.0, or "MKL_MIC_AUTO_WORKDIVISION" to decide the best division of work at runtime. Intel MKL interprets the values of these as guidance toward dividing work between coprocessors, but the library may choose a different work division. For LAPACK routines, setting the fraction of work to any value other than 0.0 enables the specified processor for Automatic Offload mode but does not use the value specified to divide the workload.
mkl_mic_get_workdivision	For computations in the Automatic Offload mode, retrieves the fraction of the work for the specified target (processor or coprocessor) to do.
mkl_mic_set_max_memory {MKL_MIC_MAX_MEMORY or MKL_MIC_*num*_MAX_MEMORY}	Sets the maximum amount of coprocessor memory reserved for Automatic Offload computations. Can be set for all coprocessors or a specific *num* coprocessor. Memory size in Kilobytes (K), megabytes (M), gigabytes (G), or terabytes (T). For example, a value of 4096M is the same as a value of 4G.
mkl_mic_free_memory	Frees the coprocessor memory reserved for Automatic Offload computations.
mkl_mic_set_offload_report {OFFLOAD_REPORT}	The Intel compilers and Intel MKL share the offload report capability, and reports will contain information about offload from both sources. Turns on/off reporting of Automatic Offload profiling. Values of 0 (off), 1 (essential information) or 2 (everything/verbose).

```
include 'mkl.fi'
rc = mkl_mic_enable( )
rc = mkl_mic_set_workdivision( MKL_MIC_DEFAULT_TARGET_TYPE, &
        MKL_MIC_DEFAULT_TARGET_NUMBER, 0.0D0 )
rc = mkl_mic_set_workdivision( MKL_TARGET_MIC, 0, &
        MKL_MIC_AUTO_WORKDIVISION )
rc = mkl_mic_get_workdivision( MKL_TARGET_MIC, 0, wd )
rc = mkl_mic_set_offload_report( 1 )
rc = mkl_mic_set_max_memory ( MKL_TARGET_MIC, 0, mem_size)
rc = mkl_mic_free_memory( MKL_TARGET_MIC, 0)
rc = mkl_mic_disable( )
```

FIGURE 11.1

Intel® MKL Support Function Examples for Fortran.

```
#include "mkl.h"
rc = mkl_mic_enable();
rc = mkl_mic_set_workdivision(MKL_MIC_DEFAULT_TARGET_TYPE,
                MKL_MIC_DEFAULT_TARGET_NUMBER, 0.0);
rc = mkl_mic_set_workdivision(MKL_TARGET_MIC, 0,
                MKL_MIC_AUTO_WORKDIVISION);
rc = mkl_mic_get_workdivision(MKL_TARGET_MIC, 0, &wd);
rc = mkl_mic_set_offload_report(1);
rc = mkl_mic_set_max_memory(MKL_TARGET_MIC, 0, mem_size);
rc = mkl_mic_free_memory(MKL_TARGET_MIC, 0);
rc = mkl_mic_disable();
```

FIGURE 11.2

Intel® MKL Support Function Examples for C/C++.

Examples of how to set the environment variables

The environment variables for Intel MKL need to be set precisely and exported (bash shell). Here are some actual examples to help learn the syntax properly.

For the bash shell, set the appropriate environment variable(s) as shown in Figure 11.3.

For the C shell (csh or tcsh), set the appropriate environment variable(s) as shown in Figure 11.4.

Using the coprocessor in native mode

Building to run on an Intel Xeon Phi coprocessor in native mode can be done with little or no change to source code, compiling with the `-mmic` option and simply linking with the Intel

```
export MKL_MIC_ENABLE=1

# export OFFLOAD_DEVICES=<list>
export OFFLOAD_DEVICES=1,3

# export MKL_HOST_WORKDIVISION=<value>
export MKL_HOST_WORKDIVISION=0.2

# export MKL_MIC_WORKDIVISION=<value>
# export MKL_MIC_<number>_WORKDIVISION=<value>
export MKL_MIC_2_WORKDIVISION=0.33

# export MKL_MIC_MAX_MEMORY=<value>
# export MKL_MIC_<number>_MAX_MEMORY=<value>
export MKL_MIC_0_MAX_MEMORY=2G

# export OFFLOAD_REPORT=<level>
export OFFLOAD_REPORT=2
```

FIGURE 11.3

Setting Environment Variables in the Bash Shell.

```
setenv MKL_MIC_ENABLE 1

# setenv OFFLOAD_DEVICES <list>
setenv OFFLOAD_DEVICES 1,3

# setenv MKL_HOST_WORKDIVISION <value>
setenv MKL_HOST_WORKDIVISION 0.2

# setenv MKL_MIC_WORKDIVISION <value>
# setenv MKL_MIC_<number>_WORKDIVISION <value>
setenv MKL_MIC_2_WORKDIVISION 0.33

# setenv MKL_MIC_MAX_MEMORY <value>
# setenv MKL_MIC_<number>_MAX_MEMORY <value>
setenv MKL_MIC_0_MAX_MEMORY 2G

# setenv OFFLOAD_REPORT <level>
setenv OFFLOAD_REPORT 2
```

FIGURE 11.4

Setting Environment Variables in the C Shell (csh or tcsh).

Xeon Phi coprocessor version of the library. The dynamic libraries should be transferred, along with the program, to the coprocessor. In particular, the Intel MKL libraries are available in the `<mkl directory>/lib/mic` directory and `libiomp5.so` is available in the `<Composer XE directory>/lib/mic` directory. The paths to the dynamic libraries transferred on the coprocessor should be added to the `LD_LIBRARY_PATH` environment variable. You will also likely want to set OpenMP thread affinity and the `OMP_NUM_THREADS` environment variable (as discussed in the OpenMP section of Chapter 6). You run the program just as you would on a Linux system.

Tips for using native mode

A few tips have proven valuable for many users in their usage of Intel MKL natively (without offload):

- Use all the threads to get best performance. You do not need to avoid the core where the OS resides, as you should when using offload, because the OS is much less likely to be using significant computational resources. For examples, on a 60-core Intel Xeon Phi coprocessor use the following:

  ```
  OMP_NUM_THREADS=240
  ```
- Use thread affinity to avoid thread migration. For examples, on a 60-core Intel Xeon Phi coprocessor use the following:

  ```
  KMP_AFFINITY=explicit,granularity=fine,proclist=[1-239:1,0]
  ```
- Consider enabling huge paging for memory allocation by using `libhugetlbfs.so` or using the `mmap()` system call (see Chapter 9).

Using automatic offload mode

Automatic offload is a unique feature that enables selected Intel MKL functions called in user code to take advantages of Intel Xeon Phi coprocessors automatically and transparently. With this feature, code that calls Intel MKL functions does not need any change in order to execute these functions on Intel coprocessors. There is no need to modify the process for compiling and linking your application other than to be using the latest Intel MKL. Automatic offload provides great ease-of-use for Intel MKL on coprocessor systems, allowing programmers to use the same usage model they are familiar with, while enjoying performance scaling across multicore to many core.

Automatic offload is not available for all Intel MKL functions; for those functions for which automatic offload is not an option, consider using the compiler-assisted offload, which can be used with all Intel MKL functions available for use on Intel Xeon Phi coprocessors. Consult the most recent Intel MKL documentation for a current list of functions that have automatic offload. As of the end of 2012, the list of functions with automatic offload capabilities included select routines in BLAS (`?GEMM`, `?TRSM`, and `?TRMM`) and `?GETRF`, `?GEQRF`, and `?POTRF` in LAPACK. You can check the documentation to see if this list is expanded in the future.

How to enable automatic offload

Automatic offload can be enabled using a single call of a support function (mkl_mic_enable()) or setting an environment variable (MKL_MIC_ENABLE = 1). Compiler pragmas are not needed. Users compile and link the code the usual way.

There are also environment variables that are generally needed for MKL that you should make sure are set:

```
export
MIC_LD_LIBRARY_PATH=$COMPOSER_ROOT/compiler/lib/mic:/opt/intel/mic/coi/device-
linux-release/lib:/opt/intel/mic/myo/lib:$MKLROOT/lib/mic
export
LD_LIBRARY_PATH=$COMPOSER_ROOT/compiler/lib/intel64:/opt/intel/mic/coi/host-linux-
release/lib:/opt/intel/mic/myo/lib:$MKLRO
```

In Fortran or C, the function returns zero if successful:

```
rc = mkl_mic_enable( )   ! Fortran
#include "mkl.h"          /* C */
rc = mkl_mic_enable( );
```

Alternatively, setting an environment variable MKL_MIC_ENABLE = 1 does the same thing without changing source code.

Once Automatic Offload is enabled, Intel MKL may automatically offload parts of computations within Intel MKL to one or more Intel coprocessors. Automatic offloading is transparent to the user in the sense that the Intel MKL runtime decides how much work to offload. Depending on the problem size and the current status of coprocessors, it may decide to run the whole work, part of the work, or nothing on coprocessors. It may decide to use all coprocessors available or to use only one coprocessor. For users who would like to have some control over offloading, Intel MKL provides mechanisms to fine-tune how the work should be divided between processors and coprocessors. See the "How to Control Work Division" below for the information.

Offloading is transparent also in the sense that if no coprocessor is present, the same executable still works. It simply runs all the computation on the processors as usual without any penalty.

Examples of using control work division

As we've seen, on Intel MIC architecture, Intel MKL provides a few support functions to allow users to substitute alternate guidance instead of the default work division guidance for the Intel MKL runtime as well as to query the current work division settings and the number of available coprocessors. Table 11.2 summarizes mkl_mic_set_workdivision, mkl_mic_get_workdivision, and mkl_mic_get_device_count. Note that these functions take effect only when automatic offload is enabled. Examples in Figures 11.5 and 11.6 illustrate their usage.

Tips for effective use of automatic offload

We can share a few tips to help better understand automatic offload and to get the most out of it.

```
rc = mkl_mic_enable( )
! Offload all work, i.e. no work on the host
rc = mkl_mic_set_workdivision(MKL_TARGET_HOST, &
      MIC_HOST_DEVICE, 0.0D0)
! Let MKL to decide how much to offload to the first device
rc = mkl_mic_set_workdivision(MKL_TARGET_MIC, 1, &
         MIC_AUTO_WORKDIVISION)
! Recommend that 50% of work to run on the first device
rc = mkl_mic_set_workdivision(MKL_TARGET_MIC, 0, 0.5D0 )
! Get work division specified for the first device
rc = mkl_mic_get_workdivision(MKL_TARGET_MIC, 1, wd )
```

FIGURE 11.5

Fortran: Work Division Control Using Support Functions.

```
#include "mkl.h"
rc = mkl_mic_enable( );
//Offload all work, i.e. nothing on the host
rc = mkl_mic_set_workdivision(MKL_TARGET_HOST,
        MIC_HOST_DEVICE, 0.0);
//Let MKL to decide how much to offload to the first device
rc = mkl_mic_set_workdivision(MKL_TARGET_MIC, 0,
        MIC_AUTO_WORKDIVISION);
// Recommend that 50% of work to run on the first device
rc = mkl_mic_set_workdivision(MKL_TARGET_MIC, 0, 0.5 );
// Get work division specified for the first device
rc = mkl_mic_get_workdivision(MKL_TARGET_MIC, 0, &wd );
```

FIGURE 11.6

C: Work Division Control Using Support Functions.

Automatic offload works better when matrix size is right

Matrix size is critical for automatic offload to get good performance. In fact, automatic offload does not even start when matrices are too small (generally this is when row or column size is smaller than 2048). This is because in this situation the overhead of data transferring overshadows any performance benefit offloading can bring. If matrices are sufficiently large, then the best performance is typically achieved when the matrices are square. The MKL environment variable `MKL_MIC_MAX_MEMORY` may be valuable to guide MKL on memory usage to best suit your application and system.

Debug or test by forcing execution to exit if offload fails

By default, if offload does not occur either because the runtime cannot find a coprocessor or because it cannot be properly initialized, then the runtime will automatically do all the work on the processors. This behavior is part of the transparent execution model provided by automatic offload. There is an environment variable OFFLOAD_REPORT to set to have an offloading report dumped out during runtime for seeing what is being offloaded. Users can also override the default fallback behavior by setting the environment variable (`MKL_MIC_DISABLE_HOST_FALLBACK=1`). Then, if offload cannot take place the program will exit with an error message indicating that the automatic offload could not be initialized or otherwise performed.

When not to use automatic offload

There are situations where compiler-assisted offload is more appropriate:

- When exact and precise control of offloading is needed.
- We want to reuse data for multiple operations on a coprocessor.
- We want to explicitly control memory allocation/de-allocation on a coprocessor.
- We want to force offload regardless of the type of a function or data size.

How to disable and re-enable automatic offload

Automatic offload only needs to be enabled once and its effect lasts until the end of the execution for all automatic offload-aware functions (excluding those explicitly offloaded using compiler-assisted offload). To disable automatic offload in the middle of a program, user code should call the support function `mkl_mic_disable()`. Alternatively, user code can call `mkl_mic_set_workdivision()` to set 100 percent of work to be done on the processors:

```
rc = mkl_mic_set_workdivision(MKL_TARGET_HOST, \
                              coprocessor_number, 1.0);
```

Later on, automatic offload can be re-enabled by calling `mkl_mic_enable()` or the workdivision function again to specify a different percentage for the processors or for a coprocessor. The environment variable `OFFLOAD_DEVICES` can be used to regulate the compiler and MKL library usage of devices as well.

Use automatic and compiler-assisted offload together

In addition to automatic offload, Intel MKL supports compiler-assisted offload. That is, offload can be explicitly specified using compiler pragmas provided in Intel® Fortran Compiler XE and Intel® C/C++ Compiler XE. Compiler-assisted offload requires more effort from programmers, but it provides more control and is more flexible. In sophisticated applications, cases may exist where mixing automatic offload and compiler-assisted offloading in one application is necessary. Intel MKL does allow this usage model. However, when automatic offload and compiler-assisted offload are used in the same program, and you may need to explicitly specify work division for automatic offload-aware functions using support functions but not via environment variables. The default work division setting is to run all the work on the processors.

Avoid oversubscription

To help avoid performance drops caused by oversubscribing Intel Xeon Phi coprocessors, Intel MKL limits the number of threads it uses to parallelize computations:

- For native runs on coprocessors, Intel MKL uses 4 × *Number-of-Cores* threads by default and scales down the number of threads back to this value if you request more threads and `MKL_DYNAMIC` is true.
- For runs that offload computations, Intel MKL uses 4 × (*Number-of-Cores* − 1) threads by default and scales down the number of threads back to this value if you request more threads and `MKL_DYNAMIC` is true.
- If you request fewer threads than the default number, Intel MKL will use the requested number but never more than the number in the system (MKL will not oversubscribe).

In these, *Number-of-Cores* is the number of core in an Intel Xeon Phi coprocessor.

Some tips for effective use of Intel MKL with or without offload

Optimize openMP and threading settings

To improve performance of Intel MKL routines, use the following OpenMP and threading settings:

- For BLAS, LAPACK, and Sparse BLAS, set
  `KMP_AFFINITY=compact,granularity=fine,proclist=[1-239:1,0]`
- For FFT, set `KMP_AFFINITY=balanced,...` and use a number of threads that is a power of two.

Data alignment and leading dimensions

Additionally, for data issues, to improve performance of Intel MKL you may wish to:

- For other Intel MKL function domains, use the general recommendations for data alignment.
- To improve performance of your application that calls Intel MKL, align your arrays on 64-byte boundaries and ensure that the leading dimensions of the arrays are divisible by 64.

Specifically for FFT functions, follow these additional recommendations:

- Align the first element of the input data on 64-byte boundaries.
- For two- or higher-dimensional single-precision transforms, use leading dimensions (strides) divisible by 8 but not divisible by 16.
- For two- or higher-dimensional double-precision transforms, use leading dimensions divisible by 4 but not divisible by 8.

Favor LAPACK unpacked routines

The routines with the names that contain the letters HP, OP, PP, SP, TP, or UP in the matrix type and storage position (the second and third letters respectively) operate on the matrices in the packed format (see LAPACK "Routine Naming Conventions" sections in the *Intel MKL Reference Manual*). Their functionality is equivalent to the functionality of the unpacked routines with the names containing the letters HE, OR, PO, SY, TR, or UN in the same positions, but the performance is significantly lower.

If the memory restriction is not too tight, use an unpacked routine for better performance. In this case, you need to allocate $N^2/2$ more memory than the memory required by a respective packed routine, where N is the problem size (the number of equations).

For example (Fortran code shown), to speed up solving a symmetric eigenproblem with an expert driver, use the unpacked routine:

```
call dsyevx(jobz, range, uplo, n, a, lda, vl, vu, il, iu, abstol, m, w, z, ldz, work,
lwork, iwork, ifail, info)
```

where *a* is the dimension *lda-by-N*, which is at least N^2 elements, instead of the packed routine use this:

```
call dspevx(jobz, range, uplo, n, ap, vl, vu, il, iu, abstol, m, w, z, ldz, work, iwork,
ifail, info)
```

where *ap* is an array with size of $N \times (N+1)/2$ holding the triangular part of a symmetric matrix.

Using compiler-assisted offload

Compiler-assisted offload gives more control over data movement and therefore is more powerful than automatic offload. The largest advantage is data persistence so that data can be reused on the coprocessors instead of making a round trip more often. Compiler assisted offload will require some program modifications, but the compiler offers syntax for pragmas and directives that limit the amount of work for us to do. Generally we just tell the compiler what to do and it does much of the work for us. Figures 11.7 and 11.8 have code examples showing use of compiler-assisted off-load. The offload pragmas or directives are the same as we cover in Chapter 7. All the same

```
!DEC$ ATTRIBUTES OFFLOAD: MIC :: SGEMM
!DEC$ OMP OFFLOAD TARGET( MIC ) &
!DEC$ IN( TRANSA,TRANSB,M,N,K,ALPHA,BETA,LDA,LDB,LDC ), &
!DEC$ IN( A: LENGTH( NCOLA * LDA )), &
!DEC$ IN( B: LENGTH( NCOLB * LDB )), &
!DEC$ INOUT( C: LENGTH( N * LDC ))
!$OMP PARALLEL SECTIONS
!$OMP SECTION
CALL SGEMM( TRANSA, TRANSB, M, N, K, ALPHA, &
            A, LDA, B, LDB, BETA, C, LDC )
!$OMP END PARALLEL SECTIONS
```

FIGURE 11.7

Fortran Example of Compiler-Assisted Offload.

```
__declspec(target(mic)) static float *A, *B, *C, *C1;
// Transfer matrices A, B, and C to coprocessor and do not de-allocate matrices A and B
#pragma offload target(mic) \
in(transa, transb, M, N, K, alpha, beta, LDA, LDB, LDC) \
in(A:length(NCOLA * LDA) free_if(0)) \
in(B:length(NCOLB * LDB) free_if(0)) \
inout(C:length(N * LDC))
{
   sgemm(&transa, &transb, &M, &N, &K, &alpha, A, &LDA,
         B, &LDB, &beta, C, &LDC);
}
// Transfer matrix C1 to coprocessor and reuse matrices A and B
#pragma offload target(mic) \
in(transa1, transb1, M, N, K, alpha1, beta1, LDA, LDB, LDC1) \
nocopy(A:length(NCOLA * LDA) alloc_if(0) free_if(0)) \
nocopy(B:length(NCOLB * LDB) alloc_if(0) free_if(0)) \
inout(C1:length(N * LDC1))
{
  sgemm(&transa1, &transb1, &M, &N, &K, &alpha1, A, &LDA,
        B, &LDB, &beta1, C1, &LDC1);
}
// Deallocate A and B on the coprocessor
#pragma offload target(mic) \
nocopy(A:length(NCOLA * LDA) free_if(1)) \
nocopy(B:length(NCOLB * LDB) free_if(1))
{ }
```

FIGURE 11.8

C Example of Data Persistence with Compiler-Assisted Offload.

explicit copy modifiers and modifier options are available for compiler-assisted offload with Intel MKL as are available for general code offload.

Tips for using compiler assisted offload

A few tips have proven valuable for many users in their usage of compiler assisted offload:

- Use data persistence to avoid unnecessary data copying and memory allocations and deallocations.
- Use thread affinity and avoid using the core where the OS is doing its work when using offload. For examples, on a 60-core Intel Xeon Phi coprocessor use the following:
  `MIC_KMP_AFFINITY=explicit,granularity=fine,proclist=[1-235:1,0]`
- Consider using larger pages by setting `MIC_USE_2MB_BUFFERS=64K`

Precision choices and variations

Floating point numbers have limited precision which give rise to question on both how we might speed up computation by selecting less precision or how we might make results more predictable. This section gives some of the most used options for both. The Intel compiler has many more controls for those with very precise needs, so the compiler documentation is worth reading through if you want much finer controls.

Fast transcendentals and mathematics

While a topic that is generally useful on processors and coprocessors, the existence of special 512-bit vector operations on Intel Xeon Phi coprocessors makes this topic of special interest. To use the lower accuracy vectorizable math functions with `–fp–model` precise, you would specify:

- `–fast–transcendentals` for transcendentals (`sin`, `log`, `pow`, ...)
- `–no–prec–sqrt` for square roots
- `–no–prec–div` for division
- `–fimf–precision` set desired accuracy to high, medium or low

These are compiler options, and not an MKL library capability (libraries supplied by the Intel compiler including the math library (libm) and the Short Vector Math Library, or SVML). Many algorithms find the performance of certain mathematics to be valuable and higher precision to be not required, hence the Intel compilers offers a rich set of options. Searching on these in the Intel Compiler documentation will give more details, and also links to additional related options.

Understanding the potential for floating-point arithmetic variations

The floating-point model used by the Intel® Compiler and its application to Intel® Xeon® processors is described in the online article "Consistency of Floating-Point Results using the Intel® Compiler." For a suitable choice of settings, the compiler generates code that is fully compliant with the ANSI language standards and the IEEE-754 standard for binary floating-point arithmetic. Compiler options give the user control over the tradeoffs between optimizations for performance, accuracy, reproducibility of results, and strict conformance with these standards.

The same floating-point model applies to the Intel® Xeon Phi™ coprocessor, but the architectural differences compared to Intel Xeon processors lead to a few small differences in implementation. Those differences are the subject of this section.

Basics

The Intel Xeon Phi coprocessor supports the same floating-point data types as the Intel Xeon processor. Single (32 bit) and double (64 bit) precision are supported in hardware; quadruple (128 bit) precision is supported through software. Extended (80 bit) precision is supported through the x87 instruction set. Denormalized numbers and gradual underflow are supported, but abrupt underflow is the default at all optimization levels except –O0. The same set of rounding modes is supported as for Intel Xeon processors.

Floating-point exceptions

The biggest differences arise in the treatment of floating-point exceptions. The vector floating-point unit on the Intel Xeon Phi coprocessor flags but does not support trapping of floating-point exceptions. The corresponding bit in the VXCSR register is protected; attempts to modify it result in a segmentation fault. Some compiler options such as `-fp-trap` (C/C++) or `-fpe0` (Fortran) that would unmask floating-point exceptions on Intel Xeon processors are unsupported on Intel® MIC architecture. The options `-fp-model except` or `-fp-model strict` still request strict, standard-conforming semantics for floating-point exceptions. This is achieved by generating x87 code for floating-point operations instead of code that makes use of Intel Xeon Phi coprocessor vector instructions. Because such code cannot be vectorized, this may have a substantial impact on performance. Nevertheless, these options may be useful for application debugging. For similar reasons, the options `-ansi` and `-fmath-errno` may result in calls to math functions that are implemented in x87 rather than the vector instructions.

In the Intel Fortran compiler version 13.0, the IEEE_FEATURES, IEEE_ARITHMETIC and IEEE_EXCEPTIONS modules are not yet updated for the properties of the Intel Xeon Phi coprocessor.

The –fp–model switch

The same settings of the `-fp-model` switch are supported as for Intel Xeon processors. The default setting is `-fp-model fast=1` for both. The behavior of the `-fp-model precise` option is the same, though the impact on performance may be somewhat greater for Intel Xeon Phi coprocessors, because of the larger vector width on Intel MIC architecture and larger potential performance gain from the vectorization of reduction loops and loops containing transcendental math functions, square roots or division. The impact of `-fp-model except` and `-fp-model strict` on performance may be greater, for the reasons noted above.

The setting `-fp-model fast=2` sets the `-fimf-domain-exclusion` switch and enables faster, inlined versions of some math functions for the Intel Xeon Phi Coprocessor, see the section "Precision of Math Functions" below.

The `-fp-model precise` switch enables arithmetic using denormalized numbers and disables abrupt underflow; abrupt [gradual] underflow can be enabled (but not required) explicitly using `-[no-]ftz`. This behavior is the same as on Intel Xeon processors.

Fused multiply-add

Intel Xeon processors up to and including Intel® 3rd Generation Core™ processors do not have a fused multiply-add (FMA) instruction. The FMA instruction on Intel Xeon Phi coprocessors only performs a single rounding on the final result, so can yield results that differ very slightly from separate addition and multiplication instructions.

In principle, the `-fp-model strict` switch would disable fused multiply-add (FMA) instructions. But since, as noted above, `-fp-model strict` suppresses vector instructions in favor of legacy x87 floating-point instructions, this additional behavior is moot. FMA operations are enabled by default, but may be disabled directly by the switch `-no-fma`. FMA operations are not disabled by `-fp-model precise`.

Precision of math functions

In the Intel® Composer XE 2013 product, the compiler for Intel Xeon Phi coprocessors invokes medium accuracy (< 4 ulp) transcendental functions for both scalar and vector code by default, mostly as calls to libsvml. For Intel Xeon processors, the default is libm (< 0.55 ulp) for scalar code and medium accuracy libsvml (< 4 ulp) for vector code. On Intel Xeon Phi coprocessors, division defaults to medium accuracy inlined code that uses a reciprocal instruction, whereas in the initial 13.0 compiler release, square roots call a medium accuracy SVML function by default (this will change to inlined code in a forthcoming update). An inlined version of square root may be obtained with `-fimf-domain-exclusion=15:sqrt` (double precision) or `-fimf-domain-exclusion=15:sqrtf` (single precision). See compiler documentation for details of the excluded domains. The `-fimf-domain-exclusion` switch may also be used to obtain inlined versions of certain other math functions. High accuracy (typically 0.6 ulp) vectorizable SVML versions of divide, square root, and transcendental functions may be obtained with `-fimf-precision=high`.

Using `-fp-model precise` results in high accuracy (<0.55 ulp), scalar calls to libm for transcendentals and to libsvml for square roots. For division, it results in an x87 division instruction. The switches `-no-fast-transcendentals`, `-prec-sqrt`, and `-prec-div` respectively have the same effect. In forthcoming updates, vectorizable inlined code sequences using Intel Xeon Phi coprocessor vector instructions may be used for division and square roots in preference to x87 instructions for these switches and for `-fp-model precise`. x87 instructions will continue to be generated for `-fp-model strict`.

Medium accuracy, vectorizable math functions can still be obtained in conjunction with `-fp-model precise` by specifying `-fp-model precise -fast-transcendentals -no-prec-sqrt -no-prec-div`. Higher accuracy, vectorizable versions are obtained by adding `-fimf-precision=high`.

Comparing floating-point results between Intel Xeon Phi coprocessors and Intel Xeon processors

In general, floating-point computations on an Intel Xeon Phi coprocessor may not give bit-for-bit identical results to the equivalent computations on an Intel Xeon processor, even though underlying hardware instructions conform to the same standards. Compiler optimizations may be implemented differently, math functions may be implemented differently, and so on. The fused multiply-add (FMA) instruction available on the Intel Xeon Phi coprocessor is a common source of differences. Nevertheless, the following guidelines may help to minimize differences between results obtained on different platforms, at a cost in performance:

- Build your application on both platforms using `-fp-model precise -fp-model source`
- Build your application on the Intel Xeon Phi coprocessor with `-no-fma`, to disable the use of FMA instructions. (Alternatively, for Fortran applications only, you may inhibit the use of fma instructions in individual expressions by the use of parentheses, in conjunction with the command line switch `-assume protect_parens`, for example: `X = (A+ (B*C))]`. For C or C++ applications, you may disable FMA generation for individual functions by using `#pragma fp_contract (off | on)`.
- Select high accuracy math functions on both platforms, such as using `-fimf-precision=high`.

- For OpenMP applications that perform reductions in parallel, set the environment variable KMP_DETERMINISTIC_REDUCTIONS = yes, use static scheduling, and use OMP_NUM_THREADS to set the same number of threads on each platform.
- For C++ applications making use of Intel® Threading Building Blocks, (TBB), the `parallel_deterministic_reduction()` function may help to obtain more consistent results on both platforms, even for differing numbers of threads.

These guidelines are intended to help enhance reproducibility and minimize variations in floating-point results between different platforms. The observed variations do not represent the true numerical uncertainty in your result, which may be much greater.

Summary

Automatic offload is the simplest way of using Intel MKL on Intel MIC–enabled systems and works best when calls to Intel MKL are significant and largely unrelated to each other. When data persistence is important, use of compiler-assisted offload or native mode will give more control and performance but require code changes and additional work.

In the advanced usage models of automatic offload, programmers can control work divisions between processors and coprocessors. It is also possible to use both automatic offload and compiler-assisted offload for Intel MKL functions in one application.

Intel MKL brings breakthrough performance for highly parallel applications on Intel Xeon processors and Intel Xeon Phi coprocessors.

For some complete examples to study or use as starting points, you should take a look at the example codes available in the `examples/mic_samples` directory installed with Intel MKL.

For more information

Here are some additional reading materials we recommend related to this chapter.

- Intel tools documentation including MKL reference manuals: http://software.intel.com/en-us/articles/intel-parallel-studio-xe-for-linux-documentation/
- Article titles "Consistency of Floating-Point Results using the Intel® Compiler," http://software.intel.com/en-us/articles/consistency-of-floating-point-results-using-the-intel-compiler/
- MKL Link Advisor tool, http://tinyurl.com/Link-MKL

CHAPTER

MPI

12

If you are reading this book, you likely are interested in large computational problems. But what if your problem is too big or takes too long to solve even on a system equipped with one or more Intel Xeon® Phi™ coprocessors? Frequently the answer is a cluster: multiple systems, or nodes, connected together by a fast network and used cooperatively to solve a single problem. One major difference between programming for a single system and a cluster is that each cluster node has a separate memory space. Unlike multiple threads running in a shared memory space, communication between disjoint memory spaces usually requires the programmer to make explicit communication calls. These explicit communications occur via *messages* and the Message Passing Interface (MPI) is the standard way to send and receive messages.

MPI overview

MPI is not a programming language. MPI defines a set of library routines that can be called from C and Fortran programs. MPI programs typically employ a single-program, multiple-data (SPMD) approach. Multiple instances, or MPI ranks, of the same program run concurrently. Each rank computes a different part of the larger problem and uses MPI to communicate data between ranks. From the MPI programmer's perspective, ranks may run on the same node or different nodes; the communication path may be different, but that is transparent to the MPI program.

The MPI standard contains approximately 500 function calls. However, a fully functional MPI program typically only uses 10–20 MPI functions. Every MPI program must call `MPI_Init` (or `MPI_Init_thread`) and `MPI_Finalize`. MPI provides several flavors of point-to-point communication routines as well as a set of collective communication calls to perform common communication patterns amongst groups of ranks efficiently (such as, broadcasting a value from one rank to all other ranks). MPI also provides utility routines for a rank to query its rank index (`MPI_Comm_rank`), obtain the total number of ranks (`MPI_Comm_size`), and so on.

NOTE

All the examples in this chapter use the Intel® MPI Library and the Intel® C++ Compiler. The source code of the examples is portable, but the exact usage of other tools may vary. The examples assume that the tool environment has already been setup, for example, source `mpivars.[c]sh` to establish the proper environment settings for the Intel MPI Library. Consult your documentation.

Traditionally, a "Hello World" program is used to illustrate basic syntax. The MPI version of "Hello World" is shown in Figure 12.1. Each MPI rank identifies itself by its rank and the name of the host on which it is running, as well as indicating the total number of MPI ranks.

MPI implementations typically provide compiler wrappers (for example: `mpicc`, `mpiicc`, `mpif90`) to simplify the process of building MPI programs and a utility (for example: `mpiexec`, `mpirun`) to launch MPI programs.

```
% mpiicc –o hello hello.c
% mpirun –n 4 ./hello
Hello world: rank 2 of 4 running on snode1
Hello world: rank 3 of 4 running on snode1
Hello world: rank 1 of 4 running on snode1
Hello world: rank 0 of 4 running on snode1
```

Note that the output is not ordered by rank. Each rank executes independently, and since there is no explicit MPI synchronization in this code, the output order will vary from run to run.

This chapter does not cover how to write a high performance MPI program. For instance, the essential topic of overlapping computation and communication is not discussed. Such topics are of critical importance, but they are not specific to using MPI on coprocessors. The focus of the chapter is to highlight items that are unique to using MPI on Intel Xeon Phi coprocessors. References to some good MPI programming resources are given at the end of the chapter.

```
#include <mpi.h>
#include <stdio.h>
#include <unistd.h>

int main(int argc, char *argv[]) {
  int i, namelen, rank, size;
  char name[MPI_MAX_PROCESSOR_NAME];

  MPI_Init(&argc, &argv);

  MPI_Comm_size(MPI_COMM_WORLD, &size);
  MPI_Comm_rank(MPI_COMM_WORLD, &rank);
  MPI_Get_processor_name(name, &namelen);

  printf("Hello world: rank %d of %d running on %s\n",
         rank, size, name);

  MPI_Finalize();

  return(0);
}
```

FIGURE 12.1

MPI Hello World Source Code.

Using MPI on Intel® Xeon Phi™ coprocessors

Intel Xeon Phi coprocessors run an operating system separate from the host processors, and have their own memory domain, also separate from the host processors. It is IP addressable and is capable of high performance networking via the Coprocessor Communication Link (CCL). In other words, an Intel Xeon Phi coprocessor looks very much like an independent compute node.

From this perspective, MPI is a natural fit. In principle, any existing MPI program can be run on a mixture of hosts and coprocessors without source code modification. The program execution is *symmetric*—the complete program, the main function, the computational kernel, and MPI, runs on both the host and the coprocessor. This model is only logically symmetric, however. The host and coprocessor cores do not have equivalent performance profiles and the communication performance may also be different. Dealing with this heterogeneity is a major topic of this chapter.

NOTE

By its nature, this section focuses on what is new and different with regards to MPI on Intel® Xeon Phi™ coprocessors. However, it should not be overlooked that, for the most part, MPI usage is unchanged. The full MPI API is available and an MPI rank may communicate with any other MPI rank regardless of whether the ranks are running on hosts, coprocessors, or a mixture.

Another approach to programming a cluster of hosts equipped with coprocessors is to launch MPI ranks only on the host and *offload* the computational kernel to the coprocessor. In this case, MPI is only running on the host, and MPI calls cannot be made in an offload region. A typical scenario is to launch one MPI rank per host core. Multiple MPI ranks running concurrently on the host may conflict with each other's use of the coprocessor. Avoiding this conflict will be discussed later in this chapter.

The last approach to programming a cluster equipped with coprocessors is to launch MPI on only the coprocessors. The *coprocessor-only* model avoids the complex heterogeneity of the symmetric case, but has the drawback of not taking advantage of the significant compute capacity of the host. For most workloads, this model should only be a stepping stone to get started and before moving on to the symmetric case.

The models are summarized in Table 12.1.

Heterogeneity (and why it matters)

Without a coprocessor, a modern cluster node is still heterogeneous, but it is of a relatively minor kind, such as non-uniform memory access (NUMA). MPI communication between hosts is also slightly heterogeneous in the absence of a coprocessor; ranks running on the same host will likely have a faster communication path than ranks located on different nodes using the network interface.

Adding one or more coprocessors to a node introduces a new degree of heterogeneity. Several new and unequal communication paths have been introduced with the addition of the coprocessor.

Table 12.1 Summary of the MPI Use Models

Model	Heterogeneous	Utilize all Resources	Main Function	Compute Kernel	MPI
Host-only	No	No	Host	Host	Host
Coprocessor-only	No	No	Coprocessor	Coprocessor	Coprocessor
Offload	Maybe[1]	Maybe[1]	Host	Coprocessor	Host
Symmetric	Yes	Yes	Host and coprocessor	Host and coprocessor	Host and coprocessor

[1]If the host simply waits for the coprocessor to finish the compute kernel, the offload model is homogeneous but is not utilizing the host during this time. On the other hand, if the host is working on another part of the computation concurrently with the coprocessor, then the offload model utilizes all the available resources but the execution is heterogeneous as a result.

To illustrate the new types of heterogeneity, consider the possible communication paths for a pair of MPI ranks depending on where they are located:

- Host rank (node A) to host rank (node A)
- Host rank (node A) to host rank (node B)
- Host rank (node A) to coprocessor rank (node A)—new!
- Host rank (node A) to coprocessor rank (node B)—new!
- Coprocessor rank (node A) to coprocessor rank (node A)—new!
- Coprocessor rank (node A) to coprocessor rank (node B)—new!

The "nodes" themselves, consisting of a host and a coprocessor, are also heterogeneous. The host has relatively few general purpose cores while the coprocessor has many specialized cores. A consequence of this new, highly heterogeneous environment is a large potential for load imbalance. Heterogeneity is the future—you need to embrace it to achieve good performance.

Many MPI programs were written with the implicit assumption they will run on homogeneous systems. They uniformly decompose their problem domain so that each MPI rank gets an equally sized chunk to compute (Figure 12.2). Since nearly all MPI programs must synchronize at some point, this assumption is okay as long as each MPI rank computes at the same rate. However when some ranks compute faster than others or data takes longer to communicate depending on the endpoints, the slowest rank determines the overall rate (Figure 12.3). The faster ranks wait at the synchronization for the slowest one to catch up. An MPI program may run, but without accounting for this new, highly heterogeneous environment it is unlikely to achieve good performance.

The key to good performance in a heterogeneous environment is load balance. Each MPI rank should compute for the same amount of wall time between synchronization points. One way to do this is to assign resources unequally (Figure 12.4). An existing hybrid program, one that uses MPI together with a threading model such as OpenMP, can be configured to do this by assigning the ranks different numbers of OpenMP threads. For instance, a slow rank can be augmented by

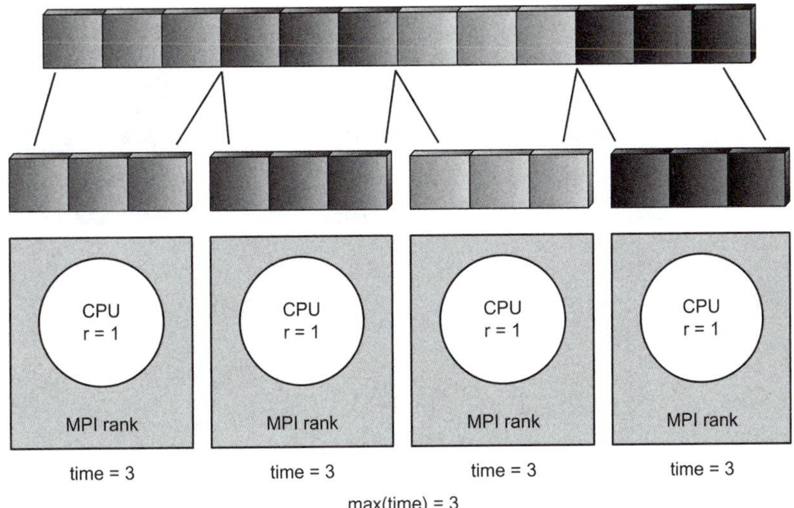

FIGURE 12.2

Uniform Parallel Decomposition of 12 Tasks onto 4 Processors; r is the Processor Execution Rate; $r = 1$ Corresponds to Computing 1 Task per Unit of Time.

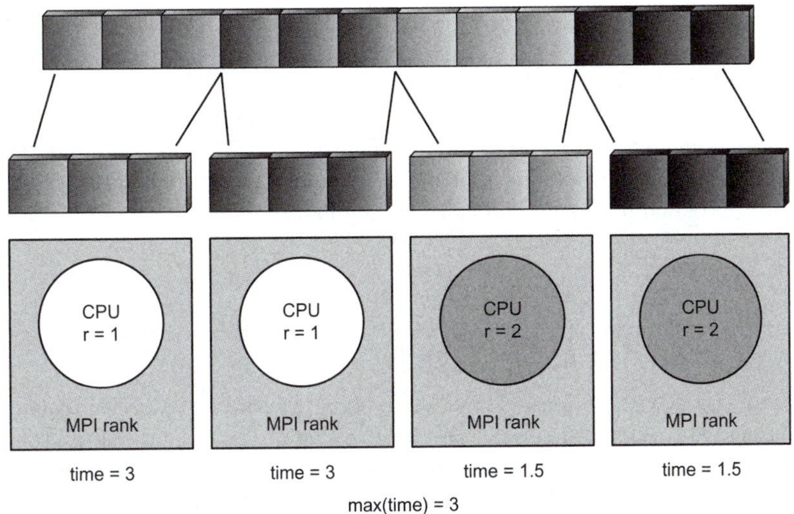

FIGURE 12.3

Load Imbalance Resulting from a Uniform Parallel Decomposition on a Heterogeneous Set of Processors.

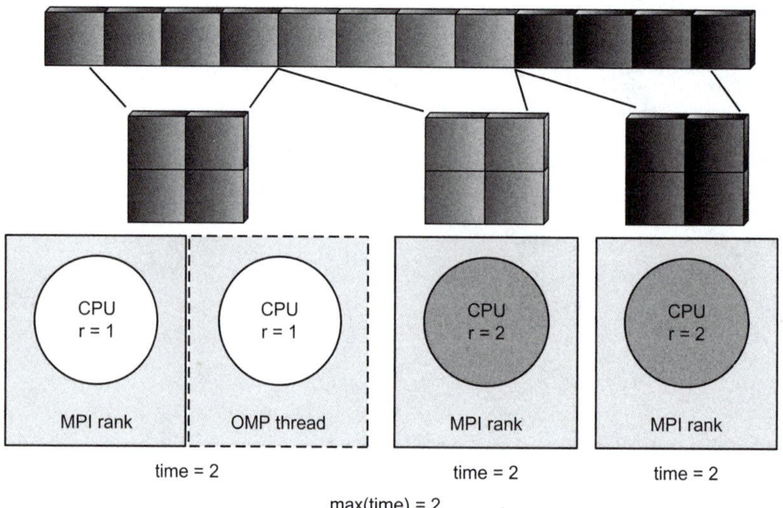

FIGURE 12.4

Unequal Resource Allocation to Achieve Optimal Performance and Load Balance on a Heterogeneous Set of Processors.

assigning it additional threads. This is only a stopgap, however. The relative balance of components will change with time, while heterogeneity is here to stay. Even within a single generation, variation exists. For instance, the optimal load balance configuration for a 2 GHz host plus a coprocessor will likely be different than for a 3 GHz host plus a coprocessor. Even worse, a program with several computational kernels may find that the optimal load balance differs for each kernel.

Another, more robust, way to use the same amount of wall time between synchronization points is to assign unequal chunks of work to each rank (Figure 12.5). The program allocates more work to faster ranks and less to slower ranks such that all ranks finish their tasks at the same time. However, an MPI program must be specifically written to do this.

Prerequisites (batteries not included)

This chapter is focused on MPI itself. However, running an MPI program depends on a properly configured cluster. For example, most clusters have a shared file system that presents a common view to all nodes. Among other things, this allows one copy of an MPI program binary and its data and also enables password-less login via shared secure shell (SSH) keys. These system configuration items are not covered in this chapter. The examples assume file system and account information are already shared between the hosts and the coprocessors, the network is properly configured, and the MPI library and other software are already installed.

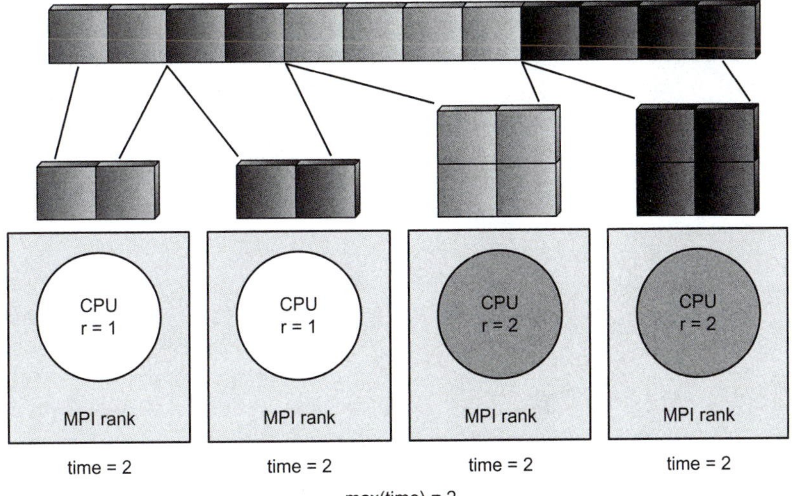

FIGURE 12.5

Unequal Parallel Decomposition to Achieve Optimal Performance and Load Balance on a Heterogeneous Set of Processors.

Offload from an MPI rank

The basic flow of an MPI program is receive some data, compute on that data, communicate the result, and repeat until the calculation is done. The key concept of MPI + Offload is to take advantage of the computational capabilities of the coprocessor by offloading the compute step. The MPI communication steps remain on the host.

From the perspective of the data, two additional communication steps are added. The data is communicated via MPI to a rank on the host as before. The offload runtime copies the data to the coprocessor, where the coprocessor performs the computation, and then the result is copied back to the host. The host communicates the result via MPI to another rank. The additional steps to copy data to and from the coprocessor must be amortized by the increased computational rate of the coprocessor compared to the host for the offload to be performance positive. MPI cannot be used inside an offload region, so these steps cannot be avoided by communicating directly from one offload instance to another (in contrast to using MPI natively on the coprocessor as discussed in the next section).

In principle, no changes need to be made to the MPI structure of the program, besides taking care to ensure that MPI calls are not used inside the offload regions. A common MPI usage model is to run one MPI rank per host core. If each rank offloads, then there may be conflicts over the shared coprocessor resource(s). Thus it may be preferable only to offload from only one rank per host.

These ideas are illustrated by two examples, an offload version of the previous Hello World program and a simple, yet representative, program to compute the value of a definite integral.

Hello world

In addition to the MPI ranks running on the host, the offloaded threads on the coprocessor should also say hello. Each thread should identify to which MPI rank on the host it corresponds, the coprocessor that it is running on, and its thread ID. The Hello World source code has been slightly modified to offload part of the program to the coprocessor (Figure 12.6).

The following example launches two MPI ranks on the host with each rank offloading four OpenMP threads.

```
% export MIC_ENV_PREFIX=MIC
% export MIC_OMP_NUM_THREADS=4
% mpirun -n 2 ./hello-offload
Hello world: rank 0 of 2 snode1
Hello world: rank 1 of 2 snode1
Hello world: rank 0 of 2 snode1, offload snode1-mic0 thread 0
Hello world: rank 0 of 2 snode1, offload snode1-mic0 thread 1
Hello world: rank 0 of 2 snode1, offload snode1-mic0 thread 3
Hello world: rank 0 of 2 snode1, offload snode1-mic0 thread 2
Hello world: rank 1 of 2 snode1, offload snode1-mic0 thread 0
Hello world: rank 1 of 2 snode1, offload snode1-mic0 thread 2
Hello world: rank 1 of 2 snode1, offload snode1-mic0 thread 3
Hello world: rank 1 of 2 snode1, offload snode1-mic0 thread 1
```

Trapezoidal rule

The next step in understanding MPI programming for the Intel Xeon Phi coprocessor is to look at a slightly more realistic example than Hello World. A simple yet illustrative case is numerical integration using the trapezoidal rule. The trapezoidal rule numerically approximates the value of a definite integral of a continuous function. The interval to be integrated is divided into smaller intervals whose area is approximated as a trapezoid. This is illustrated in Figure 12.7. Assuming a uniform interval width, the trapezoid rule can be expressed mathematically as:

$$\int_a^b f(x)dx = \lim_{N \to \infty} \frac{b-a}{2N} \sum_{k=1}^{N} (f(x_{k+1}) + f(x_k))$$

One nice property of the trapezoidal rule is that it is easily parallelized. Each MPI rank calculates a partial sum over a subset of the trapezoids and value of the integral is a reduction of the partial sums. In this version of the code (Figure 12.8), the total number of trapezoids is equally divided among the ranks and the summation calculation is offloaded to the coprocessor. The case is slightly contrived as the total number of trapezoids is much, much larger than is needed to accurately approximate the definite integral of this particular function—this was done to ensure a sufficient amount of compute to amortize the offload and MPI communication costs.

```
#include <limits.h>
#include <omp.h>
#include <mpi.h>
#include <stdio.h>
#include <unistd.h>

int main(int argc, char *argv[]) {
  int i, namelen, rank, size;
  char name[MPI_MAX_PROCESSOR_NAME];

  MPI_Init(&argc, &argv);

  MPI_Comm_size(MPI_COMM_WORLD, &size);
  MPI_Comm_rank(MPI_COMM_WORLD, &rank);
  MPI_Get_processor_name(name, &namelen);

#pragma offload target(mic) in(name, rank, size)
  {
#ifdef __INTEL_OFFLOAD
    char micname[HOST_NAME_MAX];
    gethostname(micname, HOST_NAME_MAX);
#pragma omp parallel
#pragma omp critical
    printf("Hello world: rank %d of %d %s,"
           "offload %s thread %d\n", rank, size, name,
           micname, omp_get_thread_num());
#endif
  }

  printf("Hello world: rank %d of %d running on %s\n",
         rank, size, name);

  MPI_Finalize();

  return(0);
}
```

FIGURE 12.6

MPI + Offload Hello World Source Code.

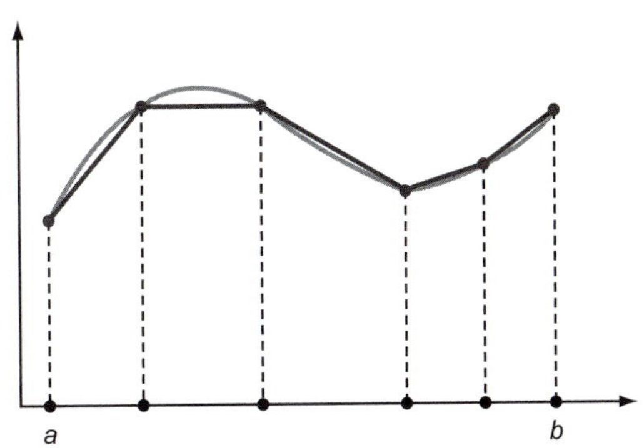

FIGURE 12.7

Illustration of the Trapezoid Rule. The Area Under the Blue Curve Is Approximated by Five Trapezoids.

```
#include <math.h>
#include <mpi.h>
#include <stdio.h>
#include <unistd.h>

#define NUM_TRAPEZOIDS 1000000000

__attribute__((target(mic))) inline double f(double x) {
  return 1.00*x*x*exp(-(x-0.0)*(x-0.0)/(2.0*0.25*0.25))
       + 0.50*x*x*exp(-(x-0.2)*(x-0.2)/(2.0*0.50*0.50))
       + 0.50*x*x*exp(-(x+0.2)*(x+0.2)/(2.0*0.50*0.50))
       + 0.25*x*x*exp(-(x-0.4)*(x-0.4)/(2.0*1.00*1.00))
       + 0.25*x*x*exp(-(x+0.4)*(x+0.4)/(2.0*1.00*1.00));
}

int main (int argc, char *argv[]) {
  int namelen, rank, size;
  char name[MPI_MAX_PROCESSOR_NAME];
  double upper_bound = 5.0, lower_bound = -5.0;
  double x0, x1, width;
  double integral = 0;
  double compute_time, total_time;
  int chunk_size;

  MPI_Init(&argc, &argv);

  MPI_Comm_size(MPI_COMM_WORLD, &size);
  MPI_Comm_rank(MPI_COMM_WORLD, &rank);
  MPI_Get_processor_name(name, &namelen);

  chunk_size = NUM_TRAPEZOIDS / size;
  x0 = lower_bound+(upper_bound-lower_bound)*rank/size;
  x1 = x0 + (upper_bound - lower_bound)/size;
  width = (x1-x0)/chunk_size;

  MPI_Barrier(MPI_COMM_WORLD);

  compute_time = total_time = MPI_Wtime();
#pragma offload target(mic)
#pragma omp parallel
#pragma omp for reduction(+:integral)
  for (int i = 0; i < chunk_size ; i++) {
    integral += 0.5*width
              *(f(x0+width*i)+f(x0+width*(i+1)));
  }
  compute_time = MPI_Wtime() - compute_time;

  MPI_Allreduce(MPI_IN_PLACE, &integral, 1, MPI_DOUBLE,
                MPI_SUM, MPI_COMM_WORLD);
  total_time = MPI_Wtime() - total_time;
```

FIGURE 12.8

MPI + Offload Trapezoidal Rule Source Code.

```
    printf("rank %d of %d on %s: %f seconds\n",
           rank, size, name, compute_time);

    if (rank == 0) {
      printf("integral = %f, time = %f\n", integral,
             total_time);
    }

    MPI_Finalize();

    return(0);
}
```

FIGURE 12.8

(Continued)

Consider the case of two MPI ranks running on the host with each rank offloading its part of the computation to the coprocessor:

```
% export MIC_ENV_PREFIX=MIC
% export MIC_KMP_AFFINITY=compact
% mpirun -n 2 ./trap-offload
rank 0 of 2 on snode4: 2.458005 seconds
rank 1 of 2 on snode4: 2.319422 seconds
integral = 1.856399, time = 2.458037 seconds
```

The time for each rank to compute its partial sum is slightly different, 2.46 versus 2.32 seconds. Since the final value of the integral can only be calculated once both ranks have finished their computation, the overall time depends on the slowest rank.

However, looking more closely, an important consideration has been overlooked. The offload runtime is not aware that multiple host processes are concurrently offloading computation. By setting `MIC_KMP_AFFINITY=compact,verbose` one can see that the two offload instances are each attempting to use the entire coprocessor, ultimately conflicting with one another. Setting `MIC_OMP_NUM_THREADS` to half the number of coprocessor cores is not a solution by itself as each instance places its threads on the same set of cores.

One solution is to manually partition the coprocessor by setting the affinity of the offloaded threads for each MPI rank using `MIC_KMP_AFFINITY=proclist[N-M],explicit`. Since the range of cores is different for each MPI rank, a method is needed to set environment variables on a per rank basis. For the Intel® MPI Library (and MPICH2 and MVAPICH), this can be done using the "argument set" syntax. The `mpirun` command line is split into sets separated by a ':' and each set can have its own settings:

```
% export MIC_ENV_PREFIX=MIC
% export MIC_OMP_NUM_THREADS=120
```

```
% mpirun -n 1 -env MIC_KMP_AFFINITY proclist=[1-120],\
> explicit,granularity=thread ./trap-offload : -n 1\
> -env MIC_KMP_AFFINITY proclist=[121-240],\
> explicit,granularity=thread ./trap-offload
rank 0 of 2 on snode1: 2.167399 seconds
rank 1 of 2 on snode1: 2.112001 seconds
integral = 1.856399, time = 2.167432 seconds
```

Note that the command line starting with `mpirun` continues for 4 lines and should be entered as one long command. When the MPI ranks are each given their own non-overlapping partition of the coprocessor, the calculation not only speeds up but there is also less variance between the two ranks.

MPI programs that offload their computational regions should avoid running many MPI ranks per node. Concurrent offload instances are initialized serially and the increased overhead may diminish the offload benefit with an increasing number of MPI rank per node. Instead, a program might only offload from one rank per node, with the other MPI ranks doing their part of the computation on the host. However, this introduces heterogeneity and thus potentially load imbalance (recall that the overall time depends on the slowest rank). A version of the trapezoidal rule program that addresses heterogeneity will be discussed in the next section.

Using MPI natively on the coprocessor

The Intel Xeon Phi coprocessor has many of the characteristics of an independent compute node. It has its own operating system, IP address, and a high performance network connection via the Coprocessor Communication Link (CCL). Programs, including MPI programs, can be run natively on the coprocessor.

The MPI standard was designed from the ground up to support a single program running on a heterogeneous set of nodes. Without any source code modification, an MPI program can be run on both the host and coprocessor. In practice, however, additional considerations such as the smaller memory per core ratio of the coprocessor may necessitate some source code changes. Program execution on the host and coprocessor is only logically symmetric though; the host and coprocessor compute at different rates, and the communication performance depends on the path connecting the MPI ranks.

Heterogeneous environments lead to load imbalance, and load imbalance leads to inefficient performance. Since MPI programs frequently synchronize, the faster ranks will idle at the synchronization point waiting for the slowest rank to finish. Load imbalance must be minimized to achieve good performance.

The examples in this section illustrate some of the ways to achieve load balance to maximize performance and the pros and cons of each method.

Hello world (again)

Let's revisit the Hello World example but with the objective of running MPI ranks natively on both the host and the coprocessor. The source code in Figure 12.1 can be reused without modification. It does, however, need to be compiled to run natively on the coprocessor. This is accomplished the same way as in previous chapters by adding the `–mmic` compiler flag; the only difference is the use of the MPI compiler wrapper.

```
% mpiicc –o hello hello.c
% mpiicc –mmic –o hello.mic hello.c
```

The second difference from the previous example is that the ranks that launch on the host need to run `hello` while the ranks on the coprocessor need to run `hello.mic`. Several methods are available to do this, three of which are discussed here.

Method 1: `mpirun` *argument sets*

Argument sets were used in the previous section to provide per rank control over the OpenMP thread affinity. They can also be used to specify different binaries depending on whether the rank is running on the host or the coprocessor. The following example launches two ranks on the host (snode1) and two ranks on the coprocessor (snode1-mic0).

```
% export I_MPI_MIC=enable
% mpirun –host snode1 –n 2 ./hello : -host snode1-mic0 –n 2 ./hello.mic
Hello world: rank 0 of 4 running on snode1
Hello world: rank 1 of 4 running on snode1
Hello world: rank 2 of 4 running on snode1-mic0
Hello world: rank 3 of 4 running on snode1-mic0
```

The advantage of this method is the precise level of control it allows. One drawback is that the command line can become very long for more than a handful of nodes. Using this method on a cluster managed by a batch queue may also require some scripting to build the command line. Setting I_MPI_MIC to "enable" overcomes the initial Intel MPI library default of "not enabled." We expect this will change in the future rendering this unnecessary but harmless.

Method 2: wrapper script

Having the Linux operating environment on the coprocessor means it is possible to use a shell script to solve the problem. A wrapper script can detect which architecture it is running on and act appropriately.

Figure 12.9 shows how one might go about writing such a wrapper script. The script takes one argument, the binary, and appends ".mic" to the end if it detects that it is running on the coprocessor. Environment settings specific to the host or the coprocessor could also be set using this method.

Using a wrapper script, one can launch a job using a hostfile containing a mixture of Intel® Xeon® and Intel Xeon Phi "nodes":

```
% export I_MPI_MIC=enable
% mpirun –n 4 –ppn 2 –f hostfile ./wrapper.sh ./hello
Hello world: rank 0 of 4 running on snode1
Hello world: rank 1 of 4 running on snode1
Hello world: rank 3 of 4 running on snode1-mic0
Hello world: rank 2 of 4 running on snode1-mic0
```

```
#!/bin/sh

EXE=$1
shift
ARCH=`uname -m`

if [ $ARCH == 'x86_64' ]; then
  # host
  exec ${EXE} $*
elif [ $ARCH == 'k1om' ]; then
  # coprocessor
  exec ${EXE}.mic $*
fi
```

FIGURE 12.9

Bourne Shell Script to Call the Correct Binary.

> **NOTE**
>
> The script shown in Figure 12.9 is not very robust and is not recommended to be used as-is in production environments. For instance, it does not perform any error checking.

Method 3: MPI implementation specific settings

Your MPI implementation may have special settings to specify the name and/or path of the binary to use if it detects that the rank is running on a coprocessor. The Intel MPI Library has several such settings. For instance, the `I_MPI_MIC_POSTFIX` setting appends a value to the binary name.

```
% export I_MPI_MIC=enable
% export I_MPI_MIC_POSTFIX=.mic
% mpirun –n 4 –ppn 2 –f hostfile ./hello
Hello world: rank 0 of 4 running on snode1
Hello world: rank 1 of 4 running on snode1
Hello world: rank 3 of 4 running on snode1-mic0
Hello world: rank 2 of 4 running on snode1-mic0
```

The behavior is very similar to the wrapper script method, but without the need for the script. The downside to this method is that the settings are not standard across all MPI implementations. Consult your MPI implementation's documentation for more information.

Trapezoidal rule (revisited)

The MPI offload implementation of the trapezoidal rule suffered from several issues. Launching MPI ranks natively on the coprocessor avoids those issues, but introduces a new issue: load imbalance. The two offload statements have been removed from the source code in Figure 12.8, but otherwise the source code is unchanged. The same source code is used for both the host and the coprocessor. Let's start by running one MPI rank on the host and one on the coprocessor.

```
% export I_MPI_MIC=enable
% export KMP_AFFINITY=compact
% mpirun -machinefile machinefile ./wrapper.sh ./trap
rank 0 of 2 on snode4: 1.214257 seconds
rank 1 of 2 on snode4-mic0: 1.015148 seconds
integral = 1.856399, time = 1.214303 seconds
```

The total time to calculate the integral is improved relative to the offload case, mostly because the host is also utilized. However, the calculation is not balanced; the host is 1.2 times slower than the coprocessor. Load imbalance is an inevitable consequence of running on a heterogeneous platform. The following sections discuss two techniques for dealing with load imbalance.

Manual load balance of hybrid workloads

The trapezoidal rule program is a hybrid of MPI and OpenMP. The amount of work is uniformly allocated per MPI rank but is independent of the number of OpenMP threads. Therefore, by experimenting with the number of MPI ranks launched on the host and the coprocessor (with the remainder of the cores available to OpenMP), load balance might be achieved.

Since the coprocessor is faster than the host in this case, the coprocessor should compute more of the trapezoids and consequently more MPI ranks should be launched on the coprocessor than the host. And since the performance ratio is 1.2, approximately 1.2 times as many ranks should be launched on the coprocessor relative to the host. Additionally, the number of ranks should be selected such that it partitions the given architecture into equally sized domains. For instance seven ranks on a 16-core host would produce OpenMP domains that either undersubscribe the system, oversubscribe the system, or unequally partition the system introducing another source of load imbalance, thus 1, 2, 4, 8, or 16 MPI ranks should be used on a 16-core host and 1, 2, 3, 4, 5, 6, 10, 12, 15, 20, 30, or 60 MPI ranks should be used on a 61-core coprocessor (assuming one core is reserved for the operating system). Together, this suggests that 5:4, 6:4, 10:8, 12:8, or 20:16 ranks on the coprocessor:host are most likely to achieve the best load balance. In this particular case, the combination that results in the best load balance is 12 MPI ranks on the coprocessor and 8 MPI ranks on the host.

```
% export I_MPI_MIC=enable
% export KMP_AFFINITY=compact
% mpirun -machinefile machinefile ./wrapper.sh ./trap
rank 0 of 20 on snode1: 0.955142 seconds
rank 1 of 20 on snode1: 0.953083 seconds
rank 3 of 20 on snode1: 0.955182 seconds
rank 4 of 20 on snode1: 0.955124 seconds
rank 5 of 20 on snode1: 0.953035 seconds
rank 6 of 20 on snode1: 0.952832 seconds
rank 2 of 20 on snode1: 0.955199 seconds
rank 7 of 20 on snode1: 0.952281 seconds
rank 8 of 20 on snode1-mic0: 0.940652 seconds
rank 9 of 20 on snode1-mic0: 0.933213 seconds
rank 11 of 20 on snode1-mic0: 0.935860 seconds
```

```
rank 16 of 20 on snodel-mic0: 0.946506 seconds
rank 17 of 20 on snodel-mic0: 0.941240 seconds
rank 19 of 20 on snodel-mic0: 0.948737 seconds
rank 10 of 20 on snodel-mic0: 0.933520 seconds
rank 12 of 20 on snodel-mic0: 0.943146 seconds
rank 13 of 20 on snodel-mic0: 0.932049 seconds
rank 14 of 20 on snodel-mic0: 0.937087 seconds
rank 15 of 20 on snodel-mic0: 0.936239 seconds
rank 18 of 20 on snodel-mic0: 0.939967 seconds
integral = 1.856399, time = 0.955248 seconds
```

With a good balance between the host and coprocessor, neither is a bottleneck and the optimum performance is achieved.

The general format for a machinefile is "<host name>:<number of MPI ranks>. For this example, the machinefile contains:

```
snodel:8
snodel-mic0:12
```

Dynamic load balance

Although load balance was achieved by experimenting with the number of MPI ranks, the combination of 12 MPI ranks on the coprocessor and 8 MPI ranks on the host is specific to this workload and the particular system it was run on. On another system with processors of different frequency, for example, the optimum load balance configuration would likely be different. A more robust way to achieve load balance in a heterogeneous environment is for the workload to dynamically allocate chunks of work; ranks that compute faster will then perform more work and load balance will automatically be achieved.

The trapezoidal rule source code was modified to implement a boss/worker model (Figure 12.10). The trapezoids are divided into many more chunks than the number of MPI ranks. Each worker rank is initially assigned one of these chunks; when the worker finishes with its chunk, it requests another from the boss rank. This continues until all the chunks have been calculated.

In this implementation, the boss rank does not do any computation. This "wastes" the cores associated with this rank with respect to computation. To minimize this impact, one MPI rank should be run per physical core, otherwise the MPI and OpenMP runtimes would devote multiple cores to the boss. The single boss may also become a bottleneck as the workload is scaled up to many nodes. A more efficient dynamic load balance scheme would be to avoid using a boss entirely. Dynamic load balance is an active area of research with multiple approaches, each with its own pros and cons. For more information about dynamic load balance see the references at the end of the chapter.

Running 16 MPI ranks on the host and 60 ranks on the coprocessor yields slightly worse performance than balancing the load by hand. This is due to losing a core to the boss rank and the overhead of sending and receiving the MPI messages. However, the advantage of automatic load balance far outweighs the slight performance cost, since this program will achieve load balance in any heterogeneous environment.

```
#include <math.h>
#include <mpi.h>
#include <stdio.h>
#include <unistd.h>

#define NUM_TRAPEZOIDS 1000000000
#define CHUNK_SIZE 100000

inline double f(double x) {
  return 1.00*x*x*exp(-(x-0.0)*(x-0.0)/(2.0*0.25*0.25))
       + 0.50*x*x*exp(-(x-0.2)*(x-0.2)/(2.0*0.50*0.50))
       + 0.50*x*x*exp(-(x+0.2)*(x+0.2)/(2.0*0.50*0.50))
       + 0.25*x*x*exp(-(x-0.4)*(x-0.4)/(2.0*1.00*1.00))
       + 0.25*x*x*exp(-(x+0.4)*(x+0.4)/(2.0*1.00*1.00));
}

int main (int argc, char *argv[]) {
  int rank, size, namelen;
  char name[MPI_MAX_PROCESSOR_NAME];
  double upper_bound = 5.0, lower_bound = -5.0;
  double x0, x1, width;
  double integral = 0;
  double compute_time, total_time;
  int chunk, N, count = 0;
  MPI_Status status;

  MPI_Init(&argc, &argv);
  MPI_Comm_size(MPI_COMM_WORLD, &size);
  MPI_Comm_rank(MPI_COMM_WORLD, &rank);
  MPI_Get_processor_name(name, &namelen);

  N = NUM_TRAPEZOIDS / CHUNK_SIZE;

  MPI_Barrier(MPI_COMM_WORLD);

  compute_time = total_time = MPI_Wtime();
  if (rank == 0) { /* boss */
    for (int i = 0 ; i < N ; i++) {
      MPI_Recv(NULL, 0, MPI_CHAR, MPI_ANY_SOURCE, 0,
               MPI_COMM_WORLD, &status);
      MPI_Send(&i, 1, MPI_INT, status.MPI_SOURCE, 0,
               MPI_COMM_WORLD);
    }
    chunk = -1;
    for (int i = 1 ; i < size ; i++) {
      MPI_Recv(NULL, 0, MPI_CHAR, MPI_ANY_SOURCE, 0,
               MPI_COMM_WORLD, &status);
      MPI_Send(&chunk, 1, MPI_INT, status.MPI_SOURCE, 0,
               MPI_COMM_WORLD);
```

FIGURE 12.10

Dynamic Load Balance Trapezoidal Rule Source Code.

```
        }
      }
      else { /* worker */
        while(chunk != -1) {
          MPI_Send(NULL, 0, MPI_CHAR, 0, 0, MPI_COMM_WORLD);
          MPI_Recv(&chunk, 1, MPI_INT, 0, 0, MPI_COMM_WORLD,
                   MPI_STATUS_IGNORE);
          if (chunk != -1) {
            count++;
            x0 = lower_bound
                 + (upper_bound-lower_bound)*chunk/N;
            x1 = x0 + (upper_bound-lower_bound)/N;
            width = (x1-x0)/CHUNK_SIZE;

#pragma omp parallel
#pragma omp for reduction(+:integral)
            for (int i = 0 ; i < CHUNK_SIZE ; i++) {
              integral += 0.5 * width *(f(x0+width*i) +
                          f(x0+width*(i+1)));
            }
          }
        }
      }
      compute_time = MPI_Wtime() - compute_time;

      MPI_Allreduce(MPI_IN_PLACE, &integral, 1, MPI_DOUBLE,
                    MPI_SUM, MPI_COMM_WORLD);
      total_time = MPI_Wtime() - total_time;

      if (rank == 0) {
        printf("integral = %f, time = %f seconds\n",
               integral, total_time);
      }
      else {
        printf("rank %d of %d on %s: %f seconds (%d)\n",
               rank, size, name, compute_time, count);
      }

      MPI_Finalize();

      return(0);
}
```

FIGURE 12.10

(Continued)

```
% export I_MPI_MIC=enable
% export KMP_AFFINITY=compact
% mpirun -machinefile machinefile ./wrapper.sh ./trap-dyn
rank 2 of 76 on snode1: 0.982912 seconds (257)
rank 4 of 76 on snode1: 0.979584 seconds (256)
```

```
rank 5 of 76 on snode1: 0.983075 seconds (257)
rank 1 of 76 on snode1: 0.983078 seconds (257)
...
rank 25 of 76 on snode1-mic0: 0.981648 seconds (101)
rank 29 of 76 on snode1-mic0: 0.983933 seconds (103)
rank 31 of 76 on snode1-mic0: 0.985047 seconds (103)
rank 59 of 76 on snode1-mic0: 0.980290 seconds (101)
rank 74 of 76 on snode1-mic0: 0.979460 seconds (101)
integral = 1.856399, time = 0.989340 seconds
```

Cluster example

The sharp eyed reader may have noticed that all the examples so far have been run on a single node. Running on a cluster only requires adding additional nodes to the file containing the list of nodes. Using the optimal configuration from the previous section with 2 nodes reduces the time by a factor of 2. No source code change or recompilation is required.

```
% export I_MPI_MIC=enable
% export KMP_AFFINITY=compact
% mpirun -machinefile machinefile ./wrapper.sh ./trap-dyn
rank 1 of 152 on snode1: 0.491094 seconds (127)
...
rank 76 of 152 on snode2: 0.489015 seconds (112)
...
rank 16 of 152 on snode1-mic0: 0.493304 seconds (52)
...
rank 92 of 152 on snode2-mic0: 0.489921 seconds (53)
...
integral = 1.856399, time = 0.497180 seconds
```

A program with dynamic load-balance is ready to take full advantage of the increased computational resources of a cluster containing Intel Xeon processors and Intel Xeon Phi coprocessors.

For this example, the machinefile contains:

```
snode1:16
snode1-mic0:60
snode2:16
snode2-mic0:60
```

Summary

The MPI programming model is a natural fit for clusters containing Intel Xeon Phi coprocessors. The programmer can accelerate individual MPI ranks by offloading the key computational kernels to the coprocessor. However, care must be taken to avoid resource conflicts and to amortize the increased amount of communication. Alternatively, the coprocessor has the characteristics of just another cluster node, albeit one with different computational capabilities than the host, and MPI ranks can run natively on the coprocessor. Either approach introduces new degrees of heterogeneity and the likelihood of load imbalance as a performance bottleneck.

The MPI programmer must adapt to this heterogeneity to take full advantage of coprocessor equipped nodes. When writing new code from scratch, dynamic load balance techniques should be adopted. While dynamic load balance is the most robust technique, few programs do that today and it may be difficult to retrofit into existing MPI programs. In those cases, hybrid programs that combine MPI with threading can achieve better performance by manually balancing the number of MPI ranks and threads.

For more information

The MPI Forum (http://www.mpi-forum.org) develops and maintains the MPI standard. MPI-3, the latest major version of the standard, was ratified in September 2012. Support for MPI-3 will start to appear in implementations in late 2012 and continue into 2013. None of the examples in this chapter use MPI-3 specific functionality.

A short list of popular and commonly available MPI implementations:

- Intel® MPI Library: http://www.intel.com/go/mpi
- MPICH2: http://www.mcs.anl.gov/research/projects/mpich2
- MVAPICH: http://mvapich.cse.ohio-state.edu
- OpenMPI: http://www.open-mpi.org

Excellent resources for more information on MPI programming:

- William Group, Ewing Lusk, and Anthony Skjellum. *Using MPI: Portable Parallel Programming with the Message-Passing Interface*, 2nd ed. Cambridge, MA: MIT Press, 1999.
- Peter S. Pacheco. *Parallel Programming with MPI*. San Francisco, CA: Morgan Kaufman, 1996.

Overviews of dynamic load balance:

- Aaron Becker, Gengbin Zheng, and Laxmikant Kale. Load Balancing, Distributed Memory. *Encyclopedia of Parallel Computing*, David Padua, Ed., New York, NY: Springer-Verlag, 2011.
- Bruce Hendrickson and Karen Devine. Dynamic load balancing in computational mechanics. *Computer Methods in Applied Mechanics and Engineering* 184(2–4):485–500, 2000.
- Vipin Kumar, Ananth Y. Grama, and Vempaty Nageshwara Rao. Scalable Load Balancing Techniques for Parallel Computers. *Journal of Parallel and Distributed Computing* 22 (1):60–79, 1994.

CHAPTER

Profiling and Timing

13

Gaining insight into what the hardware is doing can be priceless. We like to think of profiling, or performance monitoring tools, as flashlights in an otherwise dark interior of a computer system. It feels as though the more complex the internals of computers get, the darker they get without flashlights.

When we think of systems with Intel® Xeon Phi™ coprocessors, we can think about wanting insights into the activities on each thread or core or coprocessor, and wanting to understand the communication traffic between MPI ranks.

For insight into the activities of a processor or coprocessor, Intel supports event-monitoring registers. On the coprocessor these are similar to some counters on a processor, but with additional abilities for the higher core count, higher threads per core, and wider vectors. Using counters instead of more intrusive techniques (like profiling compiler time option `-pg`) is critical when dealing with high performance programs. Intrusive methods can be highly misleading because of unexpected side effects of simple profiling on the apparent performance.

We will discuss these counters and some proven formulas to compute commonly desired metrics. The premier tool for access to these counters is the Intel® VTune™ Amplifier XE product. Additionally the open source community has Performance Application Programming Interface (PAPI). PAPI provides a consistent interface and methodology for use of the performance counter hardware found in most major microprocessors including the Intel Xeon Phi coprocessor. PAPI is used by quite a number of open source tools (a list is available on the PAPI Web site, see "For More Information" at the end of this chapter) as well as come commercial products.

For insight into MPI communications between ranks regardless of whether the rank is on a processor or coprocessor, we will introduce the Intel® Trace Analyzer and Collector (ITAC).

We will not cover the actual usage of any of these tools, as each one could easily occupy an entire book. Instead, we'll highlight the key things to entice you to learn more, and focus on things specific to profiling the Intel Xeon Phi coprocessor. If you are already of a user of any of these tools, this will be sufficient to get an appreciation for the key coprocessor-specific items. If you are not a user of these tools, we will give a feel for why you should consider becoming a user. There are online tutorials and documentation available for learning; see the "For More Information" section at the end of this chapter.

Software performance optimization can occur at many levels: application tuning, system tuning, operating system tuning, and so on. Generally, a top-down approach is the most efficient: tuning of the system first, then optimizing the algorithms of the application, and then tuning at the microarchitecture level. System tuning, including tuning of the operating system, is normally done to remove hardware bottlenecks. Algorithmic tuning involves things like adding parallelism, tuning I/O, or choosing more efficient data structures or library routines. Algorithmic tuning generally relies on knowledge of the application's hotspots and familiarity with the source code, and aims to improve performance for the application in general. Tuning with a profiler can guide all these levels of optimization, but we would caution that a top-down approach is generally advisable, and therefore care should be taken to avoid optimizing at too low a level too soon. In other words, tune your kernels after you are sure that the kernels themselves are the right approaches from a "big picture" perspective.

We include information on accurate timing in this chapter, as it is related to the general topic of gaining insight into the behavior of applications. This information can enable you to collect some information about your application under program control.

Event monitoring registers on the coprocessor

The event monitoring registers on the coprocessor collect data for "activity we can count." These events will feel familiar to you if you know about event registers on processors. That's all these really are, but in a device with more cores, more threads, and wider vectors than anything before it. One of the benefits of the Intel Xeon Phi coprocessor is this familiarity and the applicability of so many existing tools.

The events are useful for microarchitectural optimizations and how to identify where optimization work may be most impactful. Microarchitectural tuning relies on knowledge of how the application is executing on the hardware such as how the pipelines, caches, and so forth are being utilized. Tuning at this level can be specific to the architecture and underlying hardware being used. For us to complete microarchitectural tuning, we need access to the real-time performance information gathered by the computing hardware itself while the application runs. This information is stored in a processing core's Performance Monitoring Unit (PMU), which can be programmed to count occurrences of particular events. Intel® VTune™ Amplifier XE 2013 gives us the ability to both collect and view sampled data from an Intel Xeon Phi coprocessor. This section offers a framework for analyzing the event data collected from an application run on the coprocessor.

We will divide our discussion of the monitoring into two considerations: Efficiency Metrics and Potential Performance Issues.

List of events used in this guide

These events, listed in Table 13.1, can be collected with VTune Amplifier XE 2013 by creating a "Custom Analysis" and then selecting "New Knights Corner Hardware Event-based Sampling Analysis" (we expect this name will be updated to Intel Xeon Phi coprocessor in a future release).

Efficiency metrics

This section lists some general measures of efficiency that can help in evaluating when to optimize a particular piece of code. The section following this one will focus on a set of metrics that are valuable for application analysis. Along with each metric and its description are a formula for calculating the metric from available events, a threshold for determining when the value for a metric *may* indicate a performance problem, and some tuning suggestions.

There are several metrics that can be used to measure general efficiency on the Intel Xeon Phi coprocessor. You should look at these metrics first, to get an idea of how well their application is

Table 13.1 Intel® Xeon Phi™ Coprocessor Events Used in This Guide

CPU_CLK_UNHALTED	The number of cycles executed by the core
INSTRUCTIONS_EXECUTED	The number of instructions executed by the thread
VPU_ELEMENTS_ACTIVE	The number of VPU operations executed by the thread
DATA_READ_OR_WRITE	The number of loads and stores seen by a thread's L1 data cache
DATA_READ_MISS_OR_WRITE_MISS	The number of demand loads or stores that miss a thread's L1 cache
L1_DATA_HIT_INFLIGHT_PF1	The number of demand loads or stores that are for a cacheline already being prefetched from L2 into L1
DATA_READ_OR_WRITE	The number of loads and stores seen by a thread's L1 data cache.
EXEC_STAGE_CYCLES	The number of cycles when the thread was executing computational operations
L2_DATA_READ/ WRITE_MISS_CACHE_FILL	Counts L2 read or read for ownership misses that were serviced by another core's L2 cache (on the same card). Includes L2 prefetches that missed the local L2 cache and so is not useful for determining demand cache fills.
L2_DATA_READ/ WRITE_MISS_MEM_FILL	Counts L2 read or read for ownership misses that were serviced by memory (on the same card). Includes L2 prefetches that missed the local L2 cache, and so is not useful for determining demand memory fills.
DATA_PAGE_WALK	The number of L1 TLB misses
LONG_DATA_PAGE_WALK	The number of L2 TLB misses
VPU_INSTRUCTIONS_EXECUTED	The number of VPU instructions executed by the thread
L2_VICTIM_REQ_WITH_DATA	The number of evictions that resulted in a memory write operation
HWP_L2MISS	The number of hardware prefetches that missed L2
SNP_HITM_L2	The number of incoming snoops that hit modified data in L2 (thus resulting in an L2 eviction)

utilizing the resources available. These metrics (except where noted) can also be used to assess the impact of various optimizations as part of an iterative tuning process.

The formulas given for each metric are meant to be calculated at the function level (using the sum of samples from all hardware threads running). The VTune Amplifier XE interface performs this summation automatically if using the "Custom Analysis" Hardware Event-based Sampling analysis type, and the "PMU events" tab with the "Function/Call stack" grouping. The summed values from this interface (per function) can be used to calculate the metrics in this guide.

CPI

CPI – events used

Event	Meaning
CPU_CLK_UNHALTED	The number of cycles executed by the core
INSTRUCTIONS_EXECUTED	The number of instructions executed by the thread

CPI – formulas and thresholds

Metric	Formula	Investigate If
Average CPI per Thread	`CPU_CLK_UNHALTED/INSTRUCTIONS_EXECUTED`	>4.0, or generally increasing
Average CPI per Core	(CPI per Thread)/Number of hardware threads used	>1.0, or generally increasing

CPI – description and usage

Cycles per instruction, or CPI, is a metric that has been a part of the VTune Amplifier XE interface for many years. It tells the average number of CPU cycles required to retire an instruction, and therefore is an indicator of how much latency in the system affected the running application. Since CPI is a ratio, it will be affected by either changes in the number of CPU cycles that an application takes (the numerator) or changes in the number of instructions executed (the denominator). For that reason, CPI is best used for comparison when only one part of the ratio is changing. For instance, changes might be made to a data structure in one part of the code that lower CPI in a (different) hotspot. "New" and "former" CPI could be compared for that hotspot as long as the code within it hasn't changed. The goal is to lower CPI, both in hotspots and for the application as a whole.

In order to make full use of the metric, it is important to understand how to interpret CPI when using multiple hardware threads. For analysis of coprocessor performance, CPI can be analyzed in two ways: "per-core" or "per-thread." Each way of analyzing CPI can be useful. The per-thread analysis is the most straightforward. It is calculated from two events: `CPU_CLK_UNHALTED` (also known as clock ticks or cycles) and `INSTRUCTIONS_EXECUTED`. `CPU_CLK_UNHALTED` counts ticks of the CPU core's clock. Since the clock is implemented in hardware on the core, all threads on a core would see the same clock. This event is counted at the core level, for a particular sample, all the threads running on the same core will have the same value. The other event used is `INSTRUCTIONS_EXECUTED`, and this event is counted at the thread level. On a sample, each thread executing on a core could have a different value for this event, depending on how many instructions from each thread have really been retired. Calculating CPI per thread is easy: it is just the result of dividing `CPU_CLK_UNHALTED` by `INSTRUCTIONS_EXECUTED`. For any given sample, this calculation will use the core's value for clock ticks and an individual hardware thread's value for instructions executed. This calculation is typically done at the function level, using the sum of all samples for each function, and so will calculate an average CPI per hardware thread, averaged across all hardware threads running for the function.

CPI per core is slightly more complex. Again, all threads running on a core share a common value for clock ticks, and they each have individual values for instructions executed. To calculate an "Aggregate" CPI, or Average CPI per core, you divide the core's `CPU_CLK_UNHALTED` value by the sum of all the threads' `INSTRUCTIONS_EXECUTED` values. For example, assume an application that is using two hardware threads per core on the Intel Xeon Phi coprocessor. One hot function in the application takes 1,200 clock ticks to complete. During those 1,200 cycles, each thread executed 600 instructions. The CPI per thread for this function would be (1200/600) or 2. The CPI per core for this function would be (1200/(600 + 600)) or 1. Now assume the application was run again using three hardware threads and the same workload. Now each thread retired 400 instructions, for a total of 1,200, in the same amount of time. Now the CPI per thread for the function would be different: (1200/400) or 3 for each thread. The CPI per core would stay the same: (1200/(400 + 400 + 400) or 1. Again, the calculation of average CPI per core is typically done at a function level using samples from all cores and threads running. Therefore an easy way to derive average CPI per core is to divide the average CPI per thread value by the number of hardware threads per core used.

The hypothetical example above illustrates how CPI per thread and CPI per core can react in different ways as the result of an application change. In the case above, after adding an additional hardware thread, CPI per thread degraded and CPI per core remained the same. In reality, the third hardware thread allowed the application to complete the same amount of work in the same time. Looking at the data gives a deeper understanding of the situation. CPI per core remained the same, indicating that the core itself was executing instructions at the same rate as before. CPI per thread degraded from 2 to 3 for each thread, revealing that each hardware thread was less efficient than before. Both of these analyses are true—the core performance remained the same running two hardware threads more efficiently or three hardware threads less efficiently. But if you were only looking at CPI per thread, it would appear that performance got worse. In typical usage scenarios on the Intel Xeon Phi coprocessor, it would be possible to make changes that affect CPI per thread and CPI per core differently, and it is important to measure and understand them both.

The Intel Xeon Phi coprocessor supports running up to four hardware threads on each physical core. However, the front-end of the pipeline can only issue up to two instructions per cycle. (This is different than traditional Intel® Xeon® processor pipelines, which currently support two hardware threads and feature front ends that can issue four instructions per cycle.) The availability of four hardware threads on the Intel Xeon Phi coprocessor can be useful for absorbing some of the latency of a workload's data access. Since the Intel Xeon Phi coprocessor pipeline operates on instructions in-order (meaning instructions must wait for previous ones to have all operands before they can execute), the support for additional hardware threading may be particularly important for some types of applications. While one hardware thread is waiting on data, another can be executing.

Another important thing to know about the front-end of the Intel Xeon Phi coprocessor pipeline is that it does not issue instructions from the same hardware thread for two clock cycles in a row, even if that hardware thread is the only one executing. So, in order to achieve the maximum issue rate, at least two hardware threads must be used. With multiple hardware threads being utilized, the front-end will switch between them in a round-robin fashion. Given these requirements and the ability to issue two instructions per clock, the minimum theoretical CPIs of any application running on Intel Xeon Phi coprocessor can be calculated, and are listed in Table 13.2.

Some applications have enough latency inherent in their data access that all four hardware threads can be utilized, with each adding performance. In this case, the addition of each thread would decrease the *per core* CPI on the same workload. It can be tricky to look at CPI when increasing or decreasing the amount of work processed, because again these changes affect the instructions executed. A general rule would be that if the amount of work completed were increasing, then in the case where each hardware thread was beneficial then CPI per core would be increasing at a rate less than the increase in work processed. CPI per core is useful in analyzing the benefit of each additional hardware thread. Even when CPI per core is decreasing (good), CPI per thread might be increasing, and this is useful to know as well, because many of the code optimizations we may apply will be addressing CPI at the thread level.

Table 13.3 shows the CPI per core and per thread for a real workload run in our lab as the number of hardware threads/core is scaled from 1 to 4. For this application, the performance of the

Table 13.2 Minimum Theoretical CPIs

Number of Hardware Threads / Core	Minimum (Best) Theoretical CPI per Core	Minimum (Best) Theoretical CPI per Thread
1	1.0	1.0
2	0.5	1.0
3	0.5	1.5
4	0.5	2.0

Table 13.3 CPI Example

Metric	1 Hardware Thread/Core	2 Hardware Threads/Core	3 Hardware Threads/Core	4 Hardware Threads/Core
CPI per Thread	5.24	8.80	11.18	13.74
CPI per Core	5.24	4.40	3.73	3.43

application was increasing with the addition of each thread, although the addition of the fourth thread did not add as much performance as did the second or third. The data shows that the CPI per thread is increasing as threads are added—meaning each is becoming less efficient—but the CPI per core is decreasing overall, as expected since each thread adds performance. For this workload, the number of instructions executed was roughly constant across all the hardware thread configurations, so the CPI directly affected execution time. When CPI per core decreased, that translated to a reduction in total execution time for the application.

NOTE

It is important to note that the thresholds for the CPI per core and CPI per thread metric are very conservative. Many applications may have higher CPI values and still be running optimally. In general, applications that are operating within the cores (doing computations on cacheable working sets) should be able to obtain CPIs at or lower than the given thresholds. Applications that need to operate at least partly across cores or utilizing memory may have higher CPIs than the thresholds given.

CPI – tuning suggestions

Any changes to an application will affect CPI, since it is likely that either the number of instructions executed or the time taken to complete them will change. The goal in general should be to reduce CPI per core (and therefore execution time), especially when compared to previous versions of the application. Most of the performance suggestions in each of the issues discussed later in the section “Potential Performance Issues” can be used to try to reduce CPI. Keep in mind that some beneficial optimizations, such as ones undertaken to increase Vectorization Intensity may actually increase CPI because the amount of work done with a single instruction increases, and thus the number of instructions executed overall can decrease. CPI is most useful as a general comparison and efficiency metric rather than as a sole determinant of performance.

Compute to data access ratio

Compute to data access ratio – events used

Event	Meaning
VPU_ELEMENTS_ACTIVE	The number of VPU[1] operations executed by the thread
DATA_READ_OR_WRITE	The number of loads and stores seen by a thread's L1 data cache
DATA_READ_MISS_OR_WRITE_MISS	The number of demand loads or stores that miss a thread's L1 cache
L1_DATA_HIT_INFLIGHT_PF1	The number of demand loads or stores that are for a cache line already being prefetched from L2 into L1

[1]*Vector processing unit, the part of the coprocessor that performs vector arithmetic.*

Compute to data access ratio – formulas and thresholds

Metric	Formula	Investigate If
L1 Compute to Data Access Ratio	VPU_ELEMENTS_ACTIVE / DATA_READ_OR_WRITE	< Vectorization Intensity
L2 Compute to Data Access Ratio	VPU_ELEMENTS_ACTIVE/ DATA_READ_MISS_OR_WRITE_MISS	< 100x L1 Compute to Data Access Ratio

Compute to data access ratio – description and usage

These metrics are a way to measure the computational density of an application, or how many computations it is performing on average for each piece of data loaded. The first, L1 Compute to Data Access Ratio, should be used to judge suitability of an application for running on the coprocessor. Applications that will perform well on the coprocessor should be vectorized, and ideally be able to perform multiple operations on the same pieces of data (or same cache lines). The L1 ratio calculates an average of the number of vectorized operations that occur for each L1 cache access. All vectorized operations, including data operations, are included in the numerator by definition of the VPU_ELEMENTS_ACTIVE event. VPU_ELEMENTS_ACTIVE was used instead of VPU_INSTRUCTIONS_EXECUTED because it gives a more accurate picture of how many operations occurred. For example, an instruction applied to a register packed with 16 floats will count as 16 operations. All demand loads and stores are included in the denominator, and no prefetches.

The threshold for the L1 metric is a guideline. Most codes that run well on the coprocessor should be able to achieve a ratio of computation to L1 access that is greater than or equal to their Vectorization Intensity. This is similar to a 1:1 ratio, one data access for one computation, except that by vectorizing each computation should be operating on multiple elements at once. An application that cannot achieve a ratio above this threshold may not be computationally dense enough to fully utilize the capabilities of the coprocessor.

Computational density at the L1 level is critical. At the L2 level, it is an indicator of whether code is operating efficiently. Again, the threshold given is a guideline. For best performance, data should be accessed from L1. This doesn't mean that data cannot be streamed from memory—the high aggregate bandwidth on Intel Xeon Phi coprocessors is advantageous for this. But, ideally, data should be streamed from memory into the caches using prefetches, and then should be available in L1 when the demand load occurs. This is even more important for the Intel Xeon Phi coprocessor than for traditional processors. Long data latency mitigates the performance benefits of vectorization, which is one of the cornerstones of coprocessor performance. The L2 Compute to Data Access Ratio shows the average number of L2 accesses that occurred for each vectorized operation. Applications that are able to block data for the L1 cache, or reduce data access in general, will have higher numbers for this ratio. As a baseline, the threshold of 100x the L1 ratio has been used, meaning there should be roughly 1 L2 data access for every 100 L1 data accesses. Like the L1 metric, it includes all vectorized operations (including data movement) in the numerator.

The denominator for the L1 metric includes all *demand*[1] loads and stores. The denominator for the L2 metric is slightly more complicated—it uses all the demanded data accesses that missed L1—only these will be requested from L2. It will be strongly related to the L1 Hit Rate discussed in later in this chapter.

Compute to data access ratio – tuning suggestions

For the L1 computational density metric, if the value is less than the Vectorization Intensity, general tunings to reduce data access should be applied. This is best accomplished by aiming to reduce the number of instructions on the critical path in general. Remove conditionals, initialization, or anything not needed in inner loops. Streamline data structures. Align data and ensure the compiler is assuming alignment in generating loads and stores. Ensure the compiler is generating good vectorized code. For example, ensure that the compiler is not register spilling. Eliminate task or thread management overhead as much as possible.

For the L2 computational density metric, try to improve data locality for the L1 cache using techniques described in later in this chapter. Restructuring code using techniques or pragmas from Intel® Cilk™ Plus can also enable the compiler to generate more efficient vectorized code, and can help improve both the L1 and L2 metrics.

Potential performance issues

This section highlights several possible performance issues that can be detected using events. For each issue, the events needed are listed along with their descriptions. Each issue is identified using metrics and thresholds. Like the metrics given in prior section, the formulas given for the metrics

[1]Demand loads and store counts do not include software or hardware prefetches in their counts.

below are meant to be calculated at the function level (using the sum of samples from all hardware threads running). The Intel VTune Amplifier XE interface performs this summation automatically if using the "Custom Analysis" Hardware Event-based Sampling analysis type, and the "PMU events" tab with the "Function/Call stack" grouping. The summed values from this interface (per function) can be used to calculate the metrics in this guide.

The value computed for each metric should then be compared to the threshold value. The thresholds given in this document are generally chosen conservatively. This means that an application is more likely to trigger the threshold criteria without having a problem than to have one of the given issues without triggering the threshold. The thresholds only indicate that you may want to investigate further. All of the metrics in this section are also designed to be used after the execution environment is fixed (will be held constant during tuning analysis work). Changes to the number of hardware threads or cores used may affect the predictability of the metrics.

General cache usage

General cache usage – events used

Event	Meaning
CPU_CLK_UNHALTED	The number of cycles in which the core was executing
DATA_READ_MISS_OR_WRITE_MISS	The number of demand loads or stores that missed the L1 data cache
L1_DATA_HIT_INFLIGHT_PF1	The number of demand loads or stores that are for a cacheline already being prefetched from L2 into L1
DATA_READ_OR_WRITE	The number of loads and stores seen by a thread's L1 data cache
EXEC_STAGE_CYCLES	The number of cycles when the thread was executing computational operations
L2_DATA_READ/ WRITE_MISS_CACHE_FILL	Counts L2 read or read for ownership misses that were serviced by another core's L2 cache (on the same card). Includes L2 prefetches that missed the local L2 cache and so is not useful for determining demand cache fills.
L2_DATA_READ/ WRITE_MISS_MEM_FILL	Counts L2 read or read for ownership misses that were serviced by memory (on the same card). Includes L2 prefetches that missed the local L2 cache, and so is not useful for determining demand memory fills.

General cache usage – formulas and thresholds

Metric	Formula	Investigate If
L1 Misses	DATA_READ_MISS_OR_WRITE_MISS + L1_DATA_HIT_INFLIGHT_PF1	<95%
L1 Hit Rate	(DATA_READ_OR_WRITE – L1 Misses) / DATA_READ_OR_WRITE	<90%
Estimated Latency Impact	(CPU_CLK_UNHALTED – EXEC_STAGE_CYCLES – DATA_READ_OR_WRITE) / DATA_READ_OR_WRITE_MISS	>145

General cache usage – description and usage

For applications running on the Intel Xeon Phi coprocessor, good data locality is critical for achieving their performance potential. In order to realize the benefit from vectorizing applications, the data must be accessible to be packed into VPU registers at as low a latency as possible. Otherwise, the time to pack the registers dominates the time to do the computation. Although being able to switch execution among four hardware threads does hide some data access latency, it can still have a significant impact on performance. Therefore, improving data locality is one of the most worthwhile optimization efforts for the Intel Xeon Phi coprocessor. Both L1 and L2 locality are important. Program changes that result in data being accessed from local L2 cache as opposed to a remote cache or memory save at least 250 cycles of access time. Under load, the savings are even greater. Accessing data from L1 as opposed to L2 saves about 20 cycles.

Traditionally, Hit Rate metrics indicate how well each level of cache is being used. It is normally calculated by dividing the number of hits by the total number of accesses for that level of cache. Hit rates also typically only apply to "demand" accesses, meaning true loads from the application as opposed to software or hardware prefetches. It is possible to determine the demand hit rate for the Data (or L1) cache, but the formula requires some explanation. Data cache accesses can be either a standard hit, a miss, or a hit to an in-flight prefetch, which is counted separately. Hits to an in-flight prefetch occur when the data was not found in the cache, and was a match for a cache line already being retrieved for the same cache level by a prefetch. These types of hits have a longer latency than a standard hit, but less than a miss. To be conservative with the hit rate, in this chapter they are treated like misses and thus subtracted in the numerator.

Unfortunately, the L2 and FILL events on the Intel Xeon Phi coprocessor are counting demand loads and stores as well as multiple types of prefetches. Not all of the prefetches are accurately counted by other events, so the formulas can't be adjusted to calculate real demand L2 hits or misses. This chapter does not recommend any metrics that depend on the L2 or FILL events, except for memory bandwidth (where including prefetches is okay). The Estimated Latency Impact metric is given in an attempt to work around the lack of L2 metrics. This metric is a rough approximation of the clock cycles devoted to each L1 cache miss. The numerator is computed by using the total CPU cycles and subtracting one for each L1 cache hit (because each L1 access should take one cycle), and one for each cycle that the `EXEC_STAGE_CYCLES` event is active. `EXEC_STAGE_CYCLES` should be active for many computations and is used to partially filter out computation cycles. What's left are considered to be cycles devoted to data access beyond the L1 cache. The denominator is L1 cache misses, giving an estimate of the number of CPU cycles spent on each L1 cache miss. It should be stressed that this is only an approximation and is not fully accurate for many reasons, including pipeline effects, un-accounted-for cycles, and overlapping memory accesses.

The Estimated Latency Impact metric can give an indication of whether the majority of L1 data misses are hitting in L2. Given that the L2 data access latency is 21 cycles, Estimated Latency Impacts that approach that number are having a high degree of L2 hits. The threshold is set at 145, as it is the average of the unloaded L2 and memory access times. The other important thing to note about the Estimated Latency Impact is that, like all ratios, it is affected by either changes in the numerator or denominator. In most cases, an optimization that positively affects data access should result in a decrease in this metric's value. However, some changes that are positive, such as a decrease in L1 misses, may result in a value for this metric that is unchanged, because it would reduce both the numerator and the denominator. This type of change would affect the L1 Hit Rate Metric instead.

Although not used in any of the metrics, the L2_DATA_READ/WRITE_MISS_CACHE_FILL and L2_DATA_READ/WRITE_MISS_MEM_FILL events can also be helpful for tuning data locality. As mentioned in the descriptions for these events, they cannot be used to compute any L2-related metrics because they include some prefetching. The quantities for these events should not be considered accurate, but the general ratio of CACHE_FILLs to MEM_FILLs may indicate that too much data was being accessed from other core's caches. Since remote cache accesses have high latency for memory accesses, they should be avoided if possible.

General cache usage – tuning suggestions

Many traditional techniques for increasing data locality apply to the Intel Xeon Phi coprocessor: cache blocking, software prefetching, data alignment, and using streaming stores can all help keep more data in cache. For issues with data residing in neighboring caches, using cache-aware data decomposition or private variables can help. Set associativity issues are another type of data locality issue that can be difficult to detect. If hit rates are low in spite of trying some of the above techniques to reduce them, conflict misses occurring from too many cachelines mapping to the same set may be the culprit. Set associativity issues (conflict misses) can occur on the Intel Xeon Phi coprocessor when an application is accessing data in L1 with a 4-KB stride or data in L2 with a 64-KB stride. Unfortunately, the specific type of miss caused by set associativity issues (conflict misses) cannot be separated from general misses detected by events. If set associativity issues are suspected, try padding data structures (while maintaining alignment) or changing the access stride.

TLB misses

TLB misses – events used

Event	Meaning
DATA_PAGE_WALK	The number of L1 TLB misses
LONG_DATA_PAGE_WALK	The number of L2 TLB misses
DATA_READ_OR_WRITE	The number of read or write operations

TLB misses – formulas and thresholds

Metric	Formula	Investigate If
L1 TLB miss ratio	DATA_PAGE_WALK/DATA_READ_OR_WRITE	>1%
L2 TLB miss ratio	LONG_DATA_PAGE_WALK/ DATA_READ_OR_WRITE	>0.1%
L1 TLB misses per L2 TLB miss	DATA_PAGE_WALK/ LONG_DATA_PAGE_WALK	Near 1

TLB misses – description and usage

The Intel Xeon Phi coprocessor has a two-level TLB[2] and at least two page sizes (4 KB and 2 MB). By default, the operating system sets up programs to use 4-KB pages. In this case, the L2 TLB acts as a page table cache and reduces the L1 TLB miss penalty (for an L2 TLB hit) to around 25 clock cycles. For large (2-MB) pages, the L2 TLB acts as a standard TLB, and the L1 miss penalty (for an L2 TLB hit) is only around 8 cycles.

The L2 TLB miss penalty is at least 100 clocks; it is impossible to hide this latency with prefetches, so it is important to try to avoid L2 TLB misses. L1 TLB misses that hit in the L2 TLB are of less concern.

Since there are 64 cache lines in a 4-KB page, the L1 TLB miss ratio for sequential access to all the cache lines in a page is 1/64. Thus any significant L1 TLB miss ratio indicates lack of spatial locality; the program is not using all the data in the page. It may also indicate thrashing; if multiple pages are accessed in the same loop, the TLB associativity or capacity may not be sufficient to hold all the TLB entries. Similar comments apply to large pages and to the L2 TLB.

If the L1 to L2 TLB miss ratio is high, then there are many more L1 TLB misses then there are L2 TLB misses. This means that the L2 TLB has the capacity to hold the program's working set, and the program may benefit from large pages.

TLB misses – tuning suggestions

For loops with multiple streams, it may be beneficial to split them into multiple loops to reduce TLB pressure (this may also help cache locality). When the addresses accessed in a loop differ by multiples of large powers of two, the effective size of the TLBs will be reduced because of associativity conflicts. Consider padding between arrays by one 4-KB page.

If the L1 to L2 ratio is high then consider using large pages.

In general, any program transformation that improves spatial locality will benefit both cache utilization and TLB utilization. The TLB is just another kind of cache.

VPU usage

VPU usage – events used

Event	Meaning
VPU_INSTRUCTIONS_EXECUTED	The number of VPU instructions executed by the thread
VPU_ELEMENTS_ACTIVE	The number of vector elements active for a VPU instruction

VPU usage – formula and threshold

Metric	Formula	Investigate If
Vectorization Intensity	VPU_ELEMENTS_ACTIVE / VPU_INSTRUCTIONS_EXECUTED	<8 (DP), <16(SP)

[2]Translation look-aside buffer, hardware for accelerating translation of virtual addresses to physical addresses by caching translations in a buffer.

Vectorization intensity cannot exceed 8 for double-precision code and 16 for single-precision code. Small values probably indicated poor vectorization; for example, lots of scalar operations or lots of gathers and scatters. The compiler vectorization report should be examined.

VPU usage – description and usage

We would like to be able to measure efficiency in terms of floating-point operations per second, as that can easily be compared to the peak floating-point performance of the machine. However, the Intel Xeon Phi coprocessor does not have events to count floating-point operations. An alternative is to measure the number of vector instructions executed.

Vector instructions include instructions that perform floating-point operations, instructions that load vector registers from memory and store them to memory, instructions to manipulate vector mask registers, and other special purpose instructions such as vector shuffle.

Vector operations that operate on full vectors use the hardware's "all-ones" mask register %k0. Thus when a vector operation on two full vectors is performed, the `VPU_ELEMENTS_ACTIVE` event is incremented by 16 (for single precision) or 8 (for double precision). Scalar FP operations are generally implemented by the compiler using the vector registers, but with a mask indicating that they apply to only one vector element.

So a reasonable rule of thumb to see how well a loop is vectorized is to add up the values of `VPU_ELEMENTS_ACTIVE` and `VPU_INSTRUCTIONS_EXECUTED` for every assembly instruction in the loop and take the ratio. If this number approaches 8 or 16 then there's a good chance that the loop is well vectorized. If the number is much smaller, then the loop was not well vectorized.

This method should be used in conjunction with the compiler's vectorization report to get a more complete understanding.

Care should be taken when attempting to apply this method to larger pieces of code. Various vagaries in code generation and the fact that mask manipulation instructions count as vector instructions can skew the ratio and lead to incorrect conclusions.

VPU usage – tuning suggestions

Low vectorization intensity may indicate that the compiler failed to vectorize a particular loop, or that the vectorization was inefficient. Examination of the vectorization report may provide insight into the problems. Problems are typically one or more of:

1. Unknown data dependences. #pragma simd and #pragma ivdep can be used to tell the compiler to ignore unknown dependences or to tell it that dependences are of a certain type, such as a reduction.
2. Non–unit-stride accesses. These can be due to indexing in multidimensional arrays, or due to accessing fields in arrays of structures. Loop interchange and data structure transformations can eliminate some of these.
3. True indirection (indexing an array with a subscript that is also an array element). These are typically algorithmic in nature and may require major data structure reorganization to eliminate.

Memory bandwidth

Memory bandwidth – events used

Event	Meaning
L2_DATA_READ_MISS_MEM_FILL	The number of read operations that resulted in a memory read (includes prefetches).
L2_DATA_WRITE_MISS_MEM_FILL	The number of write operations that resulted in a memory read. Writes are implemented using a memory Read for Ownership (RFO) transaction to maintain coherency. Includes prefetches.
L2_VICTIM_REQ_WITH_DATA	The number of evictions that resulted in a memory write operation
HWP_L2MISS	The number of hardware prefetches that missed L2
SNP_HITM_L2	The number of incoming snoops that hit modified data in L2 (thus resulting in an L2 eviction)
CPU_CLK_UNHALTED	The number of cycles

Memory bandwidth – formulas and threshold

Metric	Formula	Investigate If
Read bandwidth (bytes/clock)	(L2_DATA_READ_MISS_MEM_FILL + L2_DATA_MISS_MEM_FILL + HWP_L2MISS) * 64 / CPU_CLK_UNHALTED	
Write bandwidth (bytes/clock)	(L2_VICTIM_REQ_WITH_DATA + SNP_HITM_L2) * 64 / CPU_CLK_UNHALTED	
Bandwidth (GB/Sec)	(Read bandwidth + Write bandwidth) × frequency (in GHz)	<80 GB/Sec

Memory bandwidth – description and usage

This formula computes bandwidth by summing up the data transfers from all the different types of events that cause memory reads or writes. It does not take into account streaming stores. For an application using streaming stores, bandwidth will be underestimated.

When the core executes an instruction that reads memory, it must fill both the L2 and the L1 cache with the data. If the data is in neither cache, the core will read the data from either another core's cache or from memory. The latter case results in an L2_DATA_READ_MISS_MEM_FILL event. When the core executes an instruction that writes memory, it must first execute a Read for Ownership (RFO) to bring the data into the cache hierarchy. If that data is fulfilled from memory the write operation results in an L2_DATA_WRITE_MISS_MEM_FILL event. As noted previously, the FILL events include some types of prefetches. Although this makes them inappropriate for use in calculating Hit Rates, which assume demand data only, they can still be used in bandwidth calculations, as a prefetch does use real bandwidth.

When an L2 entry is required to hold a datum and there are no available lines, the core must evict a line; if that line has been modified then it must be written to memory. This results in an L2_VICTIM_REQ_WITH_DATA event. If data has been modified in one core's cache and another core needs that data, the first core receives a snoop Hit Modified (HITM) event which causes it to evict that data. This results in an SNP_HITM_L2 event. Normally the snoop would result in a cache-to-cache transfer to the second core but if the core is using the `clevict`[3] instructions then they appear as incoming snoops even though they were generated by the same core. It is usually safe to ignore this event but there are some cases in which the compiler or runtime will use `clevict` instructions. If there is a lot of modified data shared between two cores, including this event can result in overestimation of memory bandwidth (by including cache-to-cache transfers).

This method of calculating bandwidth uses core events. An alternate method exists which collects samples from uncore events found on the memory controllers. The VTune Amplifier XE "Bandwidth" profile uses the uncore sampling method. Both methods should result in approximately the same values for memory bandwidth in most cases.

Memory bandwidth – tuning suggestions

The user must know how much memory bandwidth their application should be using. If data sets fit entirely in a core's L2 cache, then the memory bandwidth numbers will be small. If the application is expected to use a lot of memory bandwidth (for example by streaming through long vectors) then this method provides a way to estimate how much of the theoretical bandwidth is achieved.

In practice achieved bandwidth of >140 GB/sec is near the maximum that an application is likely to see. If the achieved bandwidth is substantially less than this it is probably due to poor spatial locality in the caches, possibly because of set associativity conflicts, or because of insufficient prefetching. In the extreme case (random access to memory), many TLB misses will be observed as well.

Intel® VTune™ Amplifier XE product

The most widely used tool for collecting and analyzing the event monitoring registers on the coprocessor is the Intel VTune Amplifier XE. The current process for using VTune Amplifier XE to collect and view data from an Intel Xeon Phi coprocessor is detailed in several documents listed in the "For More Information" section at the end of this chapter. If you do not yet use VTune, you should consider learning it from one the fine documents or tutorials online.

Data may need to be collected over multiple runs, and metrics will need to be calculated outside of VTune Amplifier XE. Support within VTune Amplifier XE for the Intel Xeon Phi coprocessor will certainly continue to evolve and improve.

Although looking at the individual counts of various events can be useful, in this document most events will be used within the context of metrics covered in earlier sections. The general method to follow for performance analysis with VTune is:

1. Select a hotspot (a function with a large percentage of the application's total computational cycles).
2. Evaluate the efficiency of that hotspot using the metrics in prior section titled "Efficiency Metrics."
3. If inefficient, check each applicable metric in the prior section titles "Potential Performance Issues." If a value of a metric is below the suggested threshold, or unacceptable by other standards, use the additional information in this guide to find and fix the problem.
4. Repeat until all significant hotspots have been evaluated.

[3]CLEVICT0 and CLEVICT1 instructions cause eviction of L1 or L2 cache lines, respectively. Full documentation of these instructions can be found in the Intel® Xeon Phi™ Coprocessor Instruction Set Architecture Reference Manual, http://intel.com/software/mic.

When following this method, it is important to carefully select a representative workload. Many of the metrics involve collecting several events, and this may require running the workload multiple times to collect data. An ideal workload should have some steady state phase(s), where behavior is constant for a duration longer than the data collection interval. The workload should also give consistent, repeatable results, and be the only application consuming a significant portion of computational time during data collection. If the workload is being run multiple times to collect data, ensure that there are no warm-cache effects or other factors that affect performance. Finally, before beginning analysis, a sanity check with basic coprocessor and instruction events is encouraged—ensure the event counts are constant run-to-run and fall within expectations.

Avoid simple profiling

Instrumenting for profiling using the `-pg` option will generally diminish or stop optimizations, thereby reduce performance from what the real "release" build would create. Better profiling can be done using the less intrusive Intel VTune Amplifier XE because the "release" build should be used with VTune Amplifier.

Performance application programming interface

Another way to use the event monitoring registers on the coprocessor is through the Performance Application Programming Interface (PAPI) and tools that use PAPI. The Intel® Trace Analyzer and Collector supports PAPI as well. The PAPI API is a popular project to access hardware counters in a consistent manner to allow use of the performance counter hardware found in most major microprocessors including the Intel Xeon Phi coprocessor. There are pointers to more information in the "For More Information" at the end of this chapter.

MPI analysis: Intel Trace Analyzer and Collector

In order to help you analyze the performance of an MPI-based application, the Intel Trace Collector gathers information from running programs into a trace file, and the Intel Trace Analyzer allows the collected data to be viewed and analyzed after a run. The Intel Trace Analyzer and Collector support processors and coprocessors. The Trace Collector can integrate information from multiple sources including an instrumented Intel® MPI Library and PAPI. If you do not yet use the Intel Trace Analyzer and Collector, you should consider learning it.

The support for the Intel Xeon Phi coprocessor is a straightforward extension of the processor support that takes into consideration the existence of coprocessors in a system.

Because trace files need to be collected to disk, the tool assumes that you have set up NFS properly on the host processors and the coprocessors (documentation is online, see "For More Information" at the end of this chapter). It is important to save the traces to an NFS mounted drive to avoid competing with the application for limited memory.

Be sure to set the environment variable `VT_TIMER` to `CPU_Norm` is needed get correct traces from the applications running on the coprocessor alone. The release notes and documentation will have up-to-date changes as needed and more information on available timers.

Generating a trace file: coprocessor only application

To generate a trace file from an MPI application running on a coprocessor, you need to use the MPI libraries, Trace Collector libraries, and a compiler that can generate an executable file compatible with the targeted coprocessor. Do the following steps to complete these tasks:

1. Source `mpivars.sh` and `itacvars.sh` from the `mic/bin` directories.
2. Compile the application using the statically linked Intel Trace Collector libraries:
   ```
   host$ mpiicc -mmic -trace myApp.c -o myApp_mic
   ```
3. Run this binary with `-wdir` option. Ideally, save the trace files to an NFS mounted file system:
   ```
   host$ mpiexec.hydra -host host1-mic0 -wdir /mnt/nfs/traces -n 4 myApp_mic
   ```
4. If everything is correct, you get a message that a trace file has been written into the `/mnt/nfs/traces` directory.

Generating a trace file: processor + coprocessor application

To generate a trace file from an application running on the host system and coprocessor simultaneously, compile one part for the host system and another part for the coprocessor:

1. Set the compiler, MPI, and Intel Trace Analyzer and Collector variables for the Intel® MIC Architecture.
2. Source `itacvars.sh` from the `<itac_installdir>/mic/bin` directory and compile the application:
   ```
   host$ mpiicc -mmic -trace myApp.c -o myApp_mic
   ```
3. Set the MPI and Intel Trace Analyzer and Collector variables for the host system.
4. Source `itacvars.sh` from the `<itac_installdir>/intel64/bin` directory and compile the same application for the host:
   ```
   host$ mpiicc -trace myApp.c -o myApp_host
   ```
5. Run the application:
   ```
   host$ mpiexec.hydra -wdir /mnt/nfs/traces -genv I_MPI_FABRICS shm:tcp -
     host localhost -n 4 myApp_host : -host host1-mic0 -env LD_LIBRARY_PATH $MPI_ROOT/mic/
     lib -n 16 myApp_mic
   ```

To generate a trace file from an application not linked with Trace Collector library you need to do the following:

1. Source `mpivars.sh` and `itacvars.sh` from the `intel64/bin` directories.
2. Make sure that `libelf.so`, `libdwarf.so`, and `libvtunwind.so` are available either through `LD_LIBRARY_PATH` environment variable or in a system library directory.
3. Run the application:
   ```
   host$ mpiexec.hydra -trace -wdir /mnt/nfs/traces -genv I_MPI_FABRICS shm:tcp -host
     localhost -n 4 myApp_host : -host host1-mic0 -env LD_LIBRARY_PATH $MPI_ROOT/mic/lib:
     $VT_ROOT/mic/slib -n 16 myApp_mic
   ```
4. The trace file will be generated on the host in the `/mnt/nfs/traces directory`.

NOTE

Note: If your application requires a shared library it may be required to add the path to that library to the `LD_LIBRARY_PATH` variable.

Timing

The Intel Xeon Phi coprocessor inherits from the Intel Xeon processor family a well-established architecture and programming concepts that allow us to re-use highly parallel applications. Unlike the Intel Xeon server family, timer hardware devices including the programmable interval timer (PIT), the CMOS real time clock (RTC), the advanced configuration and power interface (ACPI) timer, and the high precision event timer (HPET) are absent on the coprocessor.

Clocksources on the coprocessor

There are two clock generators that can generate clock signals. At the system level is the PCIe clock generator; the second is the ICC PLL. From the programmers point of view there are two clock sources accessible on the coprocessor: MIC Elapsed Time Counter (`micetc`) and the Time Stamp Counter (`tsc`).

MIC elapsed time counter (micetc)

The default clock source on the coprocessor has been micetc. There is now a mechanism to use TSC as the clocksource, we may post additional information on http://lotsofcores.com on this topic. This counter is located in the System BOX (SBOX); therefore there is just one per coprocessor. The frequency of this clock is spread within a 0.5 percent following a 30-KHz triangular profile to reduce EMC emissions as shown in Figure 13.1. An additional mechanism is implemented on software to compensate for this spread.

The `micetc clocksource` is also compensated for power management events delivering a very stable `clocksource`.

Time stamp counter (tsc)

Each core has a 64-bit counter that monotonically increments the time-stamp counter every clock cycle and reset to 0 whenever the processor is reset. Having multiple counters in the coprocessor increases the complexity to synchronize all of them when time measurements are required on different cores.

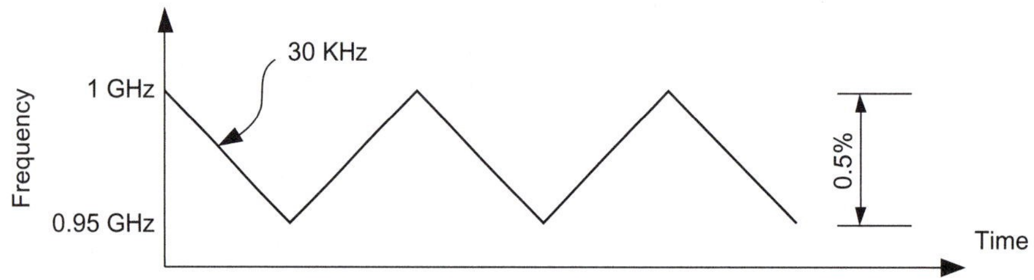

FIGURE 13.1

Spread-Spectrum Frequency for ETC.

The Read Time-Stamp Counter instruction `RDTSC` allows to load the content of the core's time-stamp counter into the `EDX:EAX` registers.

The slow-down factor can be calculated by the area under the frequency curve. Since the spread-spectrum profile is triangular, the effective area is simply half of the height, more specifically ½ × 0.5 % = 0.25 %. In addition, although this `clocksource` is low overhead, it is greatly affected by changes in power management therefore it is not possible to assure that the timestamp on multiple cores will be synchronized. When a thermal event occurs, a change in the frequency is performed to allow cooling, but this marks the clock as unstable hence it is deleted from `available_clocksource` and `current_clocksource` is switched to `micetc`.

For this reason the `tsc clocksource` is limited to cases where it is required to time very tight loops or just counting cycles will suffice.

Setting the clocksource

Setting the clocksource can be done with the following procedure. First, ssh into the Xeon Phi card as root:

1. Verify your current clocksource with:
   `cat /sys/devices/system/clocksource/clocksource0/current_clocksource`
2. Verify the available clocksources with:
   `cat /sys/devices/system/clocksource/clocksource0/available_clocksource`
3. Change to tsc with:
   `echo tsc > /sys/devices/system/clocksource/clocksource0/current_clocksource`
4. Verify it "worked" (same command as step 2)

Time structures

C programmers have had access to functions to get a point in time for time now. These libraries have been progressing with ever increasing precision, from seconds to nanoseconds. Each change in precision comes with a new interface and structural representation.

The first function to measure time is time and uses the following structure:

```
time_t time (time_t*);
time_t is used to time in seconds. A function that returns the time duration between two
points in time
double difftime(time_t t1, time_t t2);
Increasing in precision is the function ftime, now marked as legacy.
struct timeb
{
    time_t time;          // seconds
    unsigned short millitm;   // milliseconds
};
int ftime(struct timeb *tp);
```

The following two functions are widely in used today: `gettimeofday` and `clock_gettime`.

```
struct timeval
{
    time_t tv_sec;         // seconds
    int_least20_t tv_usec;   // microseconds
};
int gettimeofday(struct timeval *tv, struct timezone *tz);
struct timespec
{
    time_t tv_sec;         // seconds
    long tv_nsec;        // nanoseconds
};
int clock_gettime(clockid_t clk_id, struct timespec *tp);
```

`clk_id` identifies a particular clock. A clock may be system-wide (`micetc`) and thus visible to all processes, or per-process (`tsc`) if it measures time only within a single process. The values supported are (man `clock_gettime`):

CLOCK_REALTIME	System-wide real-time clock. Setting this clock requires appropriate privileges.
CLOCK_MONOTONIC	Clock that cannot be set and represents monotonic time since some unspecified starting point.
CLOCK_PROCESS_CPUTIME_ID	High-resolution per-process timer from the CPU.
CLOCK_THREAD_CPUTIME_ID	Thread-specific CPU-time clock.
CLOCK_REALTIME_HR	High-resolution version of CLOCK_REALTIME
CLOCK_MONOTONIC_HR	High-resolution version of CLOCK_MONOTONIC

Time penalty

When measuring code sections using `gettimeofday` or `clock_gettime` there is a time penalty that needs to be taken into consideration. A series of experiments were run on a preproduction Intel Xeon Phi coprocessor with a frequency of 1.2 GHz and can be summarized in Table 13.4.

Table 13.4 Time Penalty Incurred by the Clocksources micetc and tsc (Nanoseconds) When Called from a Single Thread

	micetc		tsc	
	clock_gettime	**gettimeofday**	**clock_gettime**	**gettimeofday**
Avg	1550.46	1612.81	200.25	291.44
Stddev	304.19	239.45	1.61	4.40
MIN	1370.15	1470.21	198.03	281.58
MAX	2665.89	2399.03	202.83	300.76

The average penalty of using `micetc` for `clock_gettime` is 1550.46 nanoseconds and 1612.81 nanoseconds for `gettimeofday`. In the case of `tsc clock_gettime` is 200.25 nanoseconds and 291.44 nanoseconds for `gettimeofday`. Both cases when called from a single thread. There is a difference between `clock_gettime` and `gettimeofday` of ~62 nanoseconds (4.02 percent) when the `clocksource` is `micetc` and ~91 nanoseconds (45.53 percent) for `tsc`. The penalty of using `tsc` to `micetc` is 1:7.74 for `clock_gettime` and 1:5.53 for `gettimeofday`.

Measuring timing and data in offload regions

You can measure both the amount of time it takes to execute an offload region of code, as well as the amount of data transferred during the execution of the offload region. This is described in Chapter 7 in a section titled "Measuring Timing and Data in Offload Regions."

Summary

Profiling a program is a critical element in gaining accurate insights into how a program is running, and therefore in how to tune an application. It is important to use a top-down approach to optimization to avoid optimizing a small portion of a code embodied in a nonoptimal high-level approach. Some profiling tools can give insight based on event counters built into the coprocessor. Other profiling tools specialize in analysis of communication traffic when using MPI. Both can yield critical insights that may lead to breakthroughs in performance of an application.

The coprocessor has two `clocksources` available; `micetc` incurs a higher time penalty in exchange of system-wide clock with a stable measurement in presence of power management events. The use of the `tsc clocksource` is useful for needs where timing of tight loops is required or just the counting of cycles is enough.

For more information

- Compiler Methodology (including performance optimization) for Intel Many Integrated Core architecture, http://software.intel.com/en-us/articles/programming-and-compiling-for-intel-many-integrated-core-architecture
- How To: NFS Mounting with Intel Many Integrated Core Architecture, http://intel.com/software/mic
- Intel VTune Amplifier XE 2013 Evaluation Center, http://software.intel.com/en-us/intel-vtune-amplifier-xe-2013-evaluation-options/
- Intel VTune Amplifier XE 2013 Product Page, http://software.intel.com/en-us/intel-vtune-amplifier-xe/
- Intel Xeon Phi coprocessor developer portal, http://intel.com/software/mic-developer
- Intel Xeon Phi Coprocessor Performance Monitoring Units documentation, separately or as part of the Software Developers Guide, http://intel.com/software/mic

- "Optimization and Performance Tuning for Intel® Xeon Phi™ Coprocessors, Part 2: Understanding and Using Hardware Events," http://software.intel.com/en-us/articles/optimization-and-performance-tuning-for-intel-xeon-phi-coprocessors-part-2-understanding
- PAPI Web site, http://icl.cs.utk.edu/papi/index.html
- Trace Analyzer and Collector for Linux OS Documentation, http://software.intel.com/en-us/intel-trace-analyzer/
- Updates on topics from this or other chapters, see http://lotsofcores.com/errata/

CHAPTER

Summary

14

In this book, we worked to demystify the Intel® Xeon Phi™ coprocessor and provide the foundational information that would fit in one book. The most challenging part of using such highly parallel device is parallel programming itself. That is a topic unto itself that we have only touched on a little in this book. The better understanding of parallel programming one has, the more sophisticated a programmer can be at eliminating nonparallel computations from an application.

If you are seeking to learn more about parallel programming, we recommend *Structured Parallel Programming* that was coauthored by James Reinders along with Michael McCool and Arch Robison. In that book, the authors work to explain common algorithms or patterns and how to implement them to utilize parallel programming. Perhaps most importantly, they do it without having to devote a lot of attention and learning to detailed computer architecture. The book examples are all using shared memory programming, so the important topic of MPI is not discussed. The reasoning is that parallelism is a fundamental notion that needs to be intuitive, and the models one uses should come second.

However, in the real world, you may be most interested in retrofitting a program for parallelism, in which case a solid understanding of MPI and a threading model may be a better starting point. Threading models would include OpenMP†, Intel® Threading Building Blocks (TBB) and Intel® Cilk™ Plus. There are good books on MPI, OpenMP, and TBB, and we recommend reading to learn at least MPI and a threading model. *Structured Parallel Programming* does explain and use TBB and Cilk Plus well.

Advice

In this book we covered many topics, so now we can summarize how to put it all to work:

- Focus on adding effective parallelism to your program, which will serve both processors and coprocessors. Use of standards languages, portable parallelism models, and standard tools so as to avoid hardware-specific coding will generally lead to this.
- Think about libraries first, such as the Intel® Math Kernel Library (MKL). Chapter 11 covers this.
- Pay attention to exposing vector operations so as to get good vectorization. Chapter 5 covers this.
- Pay attention to exposing tasks so as to get scaling through use of many core and hardware threads. Chapter 6 covers this.
- Consider offload and/or message passing.

  - Offload using Intel's extensions, or the coming OpenMP directives for offload. Chapter 7 covers this.
  - Using MPI to connect ranks spread across a system. Chapter 12 covers this.
- Use tuning tools to better understand bottlenecks and address them. Chapter 13 covers this.

Additional resources

- Intel Cilk Plus Language Specification and Intel Cilk Plus Application Binary Interface Specification documents, available from http://cilkplus.org.
- Intel® Threading Building Blocks, http://threadingbuildingblocks.org
- Intel tools, http://intel.com/software/products
- Online information from Intel, http://intel.com/software/mic
- OpenMP, http://openmp.org
- *Structured Parallel Programming: Patterns for Efficient Computation,* Michael McCool, Arch Robison, James Reinders; Morgan Kaufmann Publishers Inc., San Francisco, CA, USA, 2012.

Another book coming?

We could not fit everything in this book. As we finish this volume, we are considering a "Volume 2" perhaps with a title like "Experts Only." If you've read this book, you'll be plenty expert enough. We hope to dive into some topics more deeply and discuss additional opportunities. Look for something by late 2013.

Feedback appreciated

We would enjoy receiving feedback. We encourage you to join us at http://lotsofcores.com to find out how to direct feedback to us most effectively. Thank you, in advance, for anything you share with us!

Glossary

Advisor Intel® Advisor XE, analysis tool for determining potential benefits from various approached to adding parallelism without having to write, debug, and test code in order to study the benefits.

affinity Specification of methods to associate a particular software thread to a particular hardware thread usually with the objective of getting better or more predictable performance. Affinity specifications include the concept of being maximally spread apart to reduce contention, or to pack tightly (compact) to minimize distances for communication. OpenMP supports a rich set of affinity controls at various levels from abstract to full manual control. Fortran 2008 does not specify controls, but Intel reuses the OpenMP controls for "do concurrent." Intel Threading Building Blocks (TBB) provides an abstract loop-to-loop affinity biasing capability. Intel Cilk™ Plus relies only on fully automatic mechanisms with no user controls or overrides.

aliasing When two distinct program identifiers or expressions refer to overlapping memory locations. For example, if two pointers p and q point to the same location, then $p[x]$ and $q[x]$ are said to alias each other. The potential for aliasing can severely restrict a compiler's ability to optimize a program, even when there is no actual aliasing.

Amdahl's law Speedup is limited by the nonparallelizable serial portion of the work. A program where two thirds of the program can be run in parallel and one third of the original nonparallel program cannot be sped up by parallelism will find that speedup can only approach 3X and never exceed it assuming the same work is done. If scaling the problem size places more demands on the parallel portions of the program, then Amdahl's law is not as bad as it may seem—see **Gustafson's law**.

Amplifier See **VTune**.

application programming interface (API) An interface (set of function calls, operators, variables, and/or classes) used by an application developer to use a module. The implementation details of a module are ideally hidden from the application developer and the functionality is only defined through the API.

atomic operation An operation that is guaranteed to appear as if it occurred indivisibly without interference from other threads. For example, a processor might provide a memory increment operation. This operation needs to read a value from memory, increment it, and write it back to memory. An atomic increment guarantees that the final memory value is the same as would have occurred if no other operations on that memory location were allowed to happen between the read and the write.

automatic offload (AO) A generic library feature that automatically redirects some computation to use a specialty device for data parallelism, such as a coprocessor (MIC). AO is supported by the Intel® Math Kernel Library (Intel MKL). When desired, AO can also be controlled more finely with more complex parameters through additional options within Intel MKL. A key concept is that offloading will occur when it will benefit the computation. The other key concept in AO is that the computation will be performed by processor(s) if offloading is not available. Put another way, if you ignore all AO-related extensions in the program, it will do the same computation but without use of the coprocessor(s). See Chapter 11.

bandwidth The rate at which information is transferred, either from memory or over a communications channel. This term is used when the process being measured can be given a frequency-domain interpretation. When applied to computation, it can be seen as being equivalent to throughput.

barrier When a computation is broken into phases, it is often necessary to ensure that all threads complete all the work in one phase before any thread moves onto another phase. A barrier is a form of synchronization that ensures this: threads arriving at a barrier wait there until the last thread arrives, then all threads continue. A barrier can be implemented using atomic operations. For example, all threads might try to increment a shared variable, then block if the value of that variable does not equal the number of threads that need to synchronize at the barrier. The last thread to arrive can then reset the barrier to zero and release all the blocked threads.

Basic Linear Algebra Subprograms See BLAS.

Berkeley Lab Checkpoint Restore See BLCR.

bitwise copyable A characteristic of a data structure that allows a simple bit-by-bit copy (sometimes called a "shallow" copy) operation to work properly. This term is used in the C++ standard. A bitwise copyable data structure will not contain pointers and does not invoke constructors or destructors.

BLAS The BLAS (Basic Linear Algebra Subprograms) are routines that provide standard building blocks for basic vector and matrix operations. The Level 1 BLAS perform scalar, vector, and vector-vector operations, the Level 2 BLAS perform matrix-vector operations, and the Level 3 BLAS perform matrix-matrix operations. Because the BLAS are efficient, portable, and widely available, they are commonly used in the development of high quality linear algebra software, LAPACK for example. A sophisticated and generic implementation of BLAS has been maintained for decades at http://netlib.org/blas. Vendor-specific implementations of BLAS are common, including the Intel Math Kernel Library (Intel MKL) that is a highly efficient version of BLAS and other standard routines for Intel architecture.

BLCR Berkeley Lab Checkpoint Restore allows one or more processes to be saved to a file and later restarted from that file. This can be used for scheduling, process migration, or failure recovery. The latter is often considered very important when running jobs that may go for multiple days or weeks so as to do a checkpoint periodically to limit how much time is wasted in the event of a system shutdown for any reason. BLCR is supported by the Intel MPSS for Intel Xeon Phi coprocessors.

block Block can be used in two senses: (1) a state in which a thread is unable to proceed while it waits for some synchronization event, or (2) a region of memory. The second meaning is also used in the sense of dividing a loop into a set of parallel tasks of a suitable granularity. To avoid confusion in this book the term *tile* is generally used for the second meaning, and likewise the term *tiling* is preferred over *blocking*.

C++ Composer Intel® C++ Composer XE, Intel C/C++ Compiler plus libraries. Supports both processors and coprocessors.

C-state Core idle state, a power savings capability on processors and coprocessors with a tradeoff being lower power but higher latency to do the next real work when available. Deeper sleep states offer lower power but take longer to revive to full performance.

cache A part of memory system that stores copies of data temporarily in a fast memory so that future uses for that data can be handled more quickly than if the request had to be fetched again from a more distant storage. Caches are generally automatic and are designed to enhance programs with temporal locality and/or spatial locality. Caching systems in modern computers are usually multileveled.

cache line The units in which data are retrieved and held by a cache, which in order to exploit spatial locality are generally larger than a word. The general trend is for increasing cache line sizes, which are generally large enough to hold at least two double-precision floating-point numbers, but unlikely to hold more than eight on any current design. Larger cache lines allow for more efficient bulk transfers from main memory but worsen certain issues including false sharing, which generally degrades performance.

CCL See Coprocessor Communication Link.

Cilk Plus: Intel® Cilk™ Plus (Cilk Plus) A parallel programming model for C and C++ with support for task, data and vector parallelism. Cilk Plus is an open specification from Intel, based on decades of research and publications from M.I.T. The Cilk Plus specification has been implemented by the Intel compilers for Windows, Linux, and OS X, as well as an experimental feature in a branch of the Gnu C++ compiler.

cluster A set of computers with distributed memory communicating over a high-speed interconnect. The individual computers are often called **nodes**.

Cluster Ready A compliance program for cluster systems and cluster software to reduce cost through higher degrees of hardware and software compliance to a defined set of APIs and configurations.

Cluster Studio Intel® Cluster Studio XE, suite of tools from Intel consisting of Intel® Parallel Studio XE plus Intel tools for MPI including Intel® MPI Library and Intel® Trace Analyzer and Collector. Supports both processors and coprocessors.

COI See Coprocessor Offload Infrastructure.

communication Any exchange of data or **synchronization** between software tasks or threads. Understanding that communication costs are often a limiting factor in scaling is a critical concept for parallel programming.

composability The ability to use two components in concert with each other without causing failure or unreasonable conflict (ideally no conflict). Limitations on composability, if they exist, are best when completely diagnosed at build time instead of requiring any testing. Composability problems that manifest only at runtime are the biggest problem with non-composable systems. Can refer to system features, programming models, or software components.

Composer Intel compilers plus libraries.

concurrent Logically happening simultaneously. Two tasks that are both logically active at some point in time are considered to be concurrent. Contrast with **parallel**.

coprocessor A separate processor, often on an add-in card (such as a PCIe card), usually with its own physical memory, which may or may not be in a separate address space from the host processor. Often also known as an accelerator (although it may only accelerate specific workloads). In the case of Intel Xeon Phi coprocessors, a coprocessor is a computing device that cannot be the only computing device in a system design. In other words, a computing device that also requires a processor in a system design.

Coprocessor Communication Link Intel® Xeon Phi™ Coprocessor Communication Link (CCL).

Coprocessor Offload Infrastructure Intel® Coprocessor Offload Infrastructure (COI), a middleware layer written by Intel with an API that supports the asynchronous delivery and management of code and data buffers between an Intel Xeon® host processor and an Intel Xeon Phi coprocessor(s). COI is primarily targeted for providing programmatic control for development tools and higher level interfaces such as compiler runtimes, system management tools, and OpenCL. Some applications may benefit from directly using the finer control COI provides but will likely require a greater development investment than using a compiler or other run-time. COI is an advanced topic, generally not of use to application developers, and is not discussed in this book.

core A separate sub-processor on a multicore processor. A core should be able to support (at least one) separate and divergent flow of control from other cores on the same processor. Note: there is some inconsistency in the use of this term. For example, some graphic processor vendors use the term as well for SIMD **lanes** supporting fibers. However, the separate flows of control in fibers are simulated with masking on these devices, so there is a performance penalty for divergence. We will restrict the use of the term **core** to the case where control flow divergence can be done without penalty.

DAPL Direct Access Programming Library is a transport-independent, platform-independent, high-performance API for accessing the remote direct memory access (RDMA) capabilities of interconnects. The Intel MPI library provides high performance support for many interconnects by hooking into their DAPL API.

data parallelism An attempt to an approach to parallelism that is more oriented around data rather than tasks. However, in reality, successful strategies in parallel algorithm development tend to focus on exploiting the parallelism in data, because data decomposition (generating tasks for different units of data) scales, but functional decomposition (generation of heterogeneous tasks for different functions) does not. See Amdahl's law and Gustafson-Barsis' law.

deadlock A programming error. Deadlock occurs when at least two tasks wait for each other and each will not resume until the other task proceeds. This happens easily when code requires locking multiple mutexes. For example, each task can be holding a mutex required by the other task.

deterministic A deterministic algorithm is an algorithm that behaves predictably. Given a particular input, a deterministic algorithm will always produce the same output. The definition of what is the "same" may be important due to limited precision in mathematical operations and the likelihood that optimizations including parallelization will rearrange the order of operations. These are often referred to as "rounding" differences, which result when the order of mathematical operations to compute answer differ between the original program and the final concurrent program. Concurrency is not the only factor that can lead to **non-deterministic** algorithms but in practice it is often the cause. Use of programming models with sequential semantics and eliminating data races with proper access controls will generally eliminate the major effects of concurrency other than the "rounding" differences.

Direct Access Programming Library See DAPL.

distributed memory Memory that is physically located in separate computers. An indirect interface, such as message passing, is required to access memory on remote computers, while local memory can be accessed directly. Distributed memory is typically supported by clusters which, for purposes of this definition, we are considering to be a collection of computers. Since the memory on attached coprocessors also cannot typically be addressed directly from the host, it can be considered, for functional purposes, to be a form of distributed memory.

ECC Error Correction Code, a method to increase reliability by correcting transient errors on a device. Used extensively on Intel Xeon processors and Intel Xeon Phi coprocessors to offer high degrees of reliability.

embarrassing parallelism An algorithm has **embarrassing parallelism** if it can be decomposed into a large number of independent tasks with little or no synchronization or communication required.

EMON Event monitoring: counting of events such as cache misses on a processor or coprocessor. See Chapter 13.

ETC Elapsed Time Counter. The default clock source on the coprocessor is micetc. The micetc clocksource is also compensated for power management events delivering a very stable clocksource. See Chapter 13.

false sharing Two separate tasks in two separate cores may write to separate locations in memory, but if those memory locations happened to be allocated in the same cache line, the cache coherence hardware will attempt to keep the cache lines coherent, resulting in extra interprocessor communication and reduced performance, even though the tasks are not actually sharing data.

FMA Fused Multiply and Add, a capability to request a multiply and an add operation in one instruction while maintaining precision thereby potentially doubling the computational throughput of a device.

Fortran Programming language used primarily for scientific and engineering problem solving. Originally spelled FORTRAN as an abbreviation for FORmula TRANslation.

Fortran Composer Intel® Fortran Composer XE, Intel Fortran Compiler plus libraries. Supports both processors and coprocessors.

forward scaling The concept of having a program or algorithm scalable already in threads and/or vectors so as to be ready to take advantage of growth of parallelism in future hardware with a simple recompile with a new compiler or relink to a new library. Using the right abstractions to express parallelism is normally a key to enabling forward scaling when writing a parallel program.

future-proofed A computer program written in a manner so it will survive future computer architecture changes without requiring significant changes to the program itself. Generally, the more abstract a programming method is, the more **future-proof** that program is. Lower level programming methods that in some way mirror computer architectural details will be less able to survive the future without change. Writing in an abstract, more **future-proof** fashion may involve tradeoffs in efficiency, however.

gather Gather-scatter is a type of memory access pattern that often arises when addressing vectors in sparse linear algebra operations. A gather utilizes indexed reads and a scatter utilizes indexed writes. Special vector instructions provide gather-scatter operations to assist.

GDDR5 Graphics Double Data Rate, version 5, the memory type used by Intel Xeon Phi coprocessors. Use of ECC is not directly supported by GDDR5, and activation of ECC (at coprocessor boot time) requires 12.5 percent of memory be used for error correction bits but with only a small performance overhead.

Gustafson-Barsis' law A different view on **Amdahl's law** that factors in the fact that as problem sizes grow, the serial portion of computations tend to shrink as a percentage of the total work to be done. Compare with other attempts to characterize the bounds of parallelism **Amdahl's law** and **span complexity**.

hardware thread A hardware implementation of a task with a separate flow of control. Multiple hardware threads can be implemented using multiple cores, or can run concurrently or simultaneously on one core in order to hide latency using methods such as hyper-threading of a processor core. Intel Xeon Phi coprocessors do have four hardware threads per core, and they are not hyper-threads.

host processor The main control processor in a system, as opposed to any graphics processors or coprocessors. The host processor is responsible for booting and running the operating system.

HPC High performance computing. HPC refers to the highest performance computing available at a point in time, which today generally means at least a teraFLOP/s of computational capability. The term HPC is occasionally used as a synonym for supercomputing, although supercomputing is probably more specific to even higher performance systems (today, at least ten teraFLOP/s). While the use of HPC is spreading to more industries, it is general associated with solution of the most challenging problems in science and engineering.

hyperobjects A mechanism in Cilk Plus to support operations such as reduction that combine multiple objects.

Hyper-threading Multithreading on a single processor core with the purpose of more fully utilizing the functional units in an out-of-order core by bringing together more instructions from than one software thread. With hyper-threading, multiple hardware threads may run on one core and share resources, but some benefit is still obtained from parallelism or concurrency. Typically each hyper-thread has, at least, its own register file and program counter, so that switching between hyper-threads is relatively lightweight. Intel Xeon Phi coprocessors do have four threads per core, but they are not hyper-threads as they are utilized with an in-order core to hide latencies inherent in an in-order design.

IA A commonly used abbreviation for Intel architecture, also referred to as x86 in reference to Intel's original 8088 and 8086 processors that implemented Intel architecture.

IMCI Intel® Initial Many Core Instructions is the official name for the new instructions available in the Intel® Xeon Phi™ coprocessor codenamed Knights Corner. The Intel® Xeon Phi™ coprocessor codenamed Knights Corner is the first device to offer 512-bit wide SIMD instructions. Intel has published a disclaimer that it does not guarantee these will be supported in future processors. One could guess that feedback will be critical to their future.

Inlining Inlining is an optimization that replaces a call to a subroutine or function with the actual code from the subroutine or function. This can be done by a compiler or done by hand in the source code. This optimization has to be weighed against the disadvantages of increasing the size of the program. Some sophisticated compilers can do partial inlining to somewhat address this. A subroutine or function may be inlined by a compiler at the call site to improve performance by two methods: (1) remove the call overhead, (2) enable optimizations by bringing the code together instead of having code separated by a call.

Inspector Intel® Inspector XE, analysis tool specializing in finding threading and memory related errors in a program. Can detect latent threading bugs (ones that are no causing program failure).

intrinsics Intrinsics appear to be functions in a language, but are supported by the compiler directly. In the case of SSE or vector intrinsics, the intrinsic function may map directly to a small number, often one, of machine instructions, which the compiler inserts without the overhead of a real function call.

ISA Instruction Set Architecture.

lambda function A lambda function, for programmers, is an anonymous function. Long a staple of languages such as LISP, it was only recently supported for C++ per the C++11 standard. A lambda function enables a fragment of code to be passed to another function without having to write a separate named function or functor. This ability is particularly handy for using TBB.

lane An element of a SIMD register file and associated functional unit, considered as a unit of hardware for performing parallel computation. SIMD instructions execute computations across multiple lanes.

Language Extensions for Offloading (LEO) A feature of the Intel compiler to specify offloading regions and data movement. Predated standardization of target directives by OpenMP. Intel compilers, supporting C, C++ and Fortran, support unofficial OpenMP extensions (see Chapter 7) to support Intel Xeon Phi coprocessors by allowing a number of additional features to offload select computations to coprocessors and assist in the data movement between processor and coprocessor memories. This capability is available to software developers through several extensions to the C, C++, and Fortran language. A key concept in LEO is that the computation will be performed by host processor(s) if offloading is not available. Put another way, if you ignore all LEO related extensions in the program it will do the same computation but without use of the coprocessor(s). LEO consists of pragma-based (directives) compiler feature that allows a program to select computations to available to offload to run on coprocessors such as the Intel Xeon Phi coprocessors and assist in the data movement between processor and coprocessor memories. Intel's C, C11, and Fortran compilers support LEO. LEO will be rendered obsolete by OpenMP target directives. One can expect a migration path and legacy support.

latency The time it takes to complete a task; that is, the time between when the task begins and when it ends. Latency has units of time. The scale can be anywhere from nanoseconds to days. Lower latency is better in general.

latency hiding Latency hiding schedules computations on a processing element while other tasks using that core are waiting for long-latency operations to complete, such as memory or disk transfers. The latency is not actually hidden, since each task still takes the same time to complete, but more tasks can be completed in a given time since resources are shared more efficiently, so throughput is improved.

load balancing Assigning tasks to resources while handling uneven sizes of tasks.

locality Locality refers to utilizing memory locations that are closer, rather than further, apart. This will maximize reuse of cache lines, memory pages, and so on. Maintaining a high degree of locality of reference is a key to scaling.

lock A mechanism for implementing **mutual exclusion**. Before entering a mutual exclusion region, a thread must first try to acquire a lock on that region. If the lock has already been acquired by another thread, the current thread must **block**, which it may do by either suspending operation or spinning. When the lock is released, then the current thread is free to acquire it. Locks can be implemented using **atomic operations**, which are themselves a form of mutual exclusion on basic operations, implemented in hardware.

many-core processor A **multicore** processor with so many cores that in practice we do not enumerate them; there are just "lots." The term has been generally used with processors with 32 or more cores, but there is no precise definition.

Many-core Platform Software Stack Intel® Many-core Platform Software Stack (MPSS), the stack of software supplied by Intel in binaries and open source to support the Intel Xeon Phi coprocessor. It includes drivers, Intel COI, SCIF, plus mods for Linux OS, gcc, and gdb. Available freely from http://intel.com/software/mic.

Math Kernel Library Intel® Math Kernel Library (Intel MKL), includes numerous routines to provide a high level of performance from this hand-optimized library. Intel MKL includes highly vectorized and threaded linear algebra, fast Fourier transforms (FFTs), vector math and statistics functions. Through a

single C or Fortran API call, these functions automatically scale across previous, current, and future processor architectures by selecting the best code path for each. See Chapter 11.

megahertz era A historical period of time during which processors doubled clock rates at a rate similar to the doubling of transistors in a design, roughly every two years. Such rapid rise in processor clock speeds ceased at just under 4 GHz (four thousand megahertz) in 2004. Designs shifted toward adding more cores marking the shift to the **multicore era**.

memory hierarchy See **memory subsystem**.

memory subsystem The portion of a computer system responsible for moving code and data between the main system memory and the computational units. The memory subsystem may include additional connections to I/O devices including graphics cards, disk drives, and network interfaces. A modern memory subsystem will generally have many levels including some levels of caching both on and off the processor die. Coherent memory subsystems, which are used in most computers, provide for a single view of the contents of the main system memory despite temporary copies in caches and concurrency in the system.

Message Passing Interface (MPI) An industry-standard approach to distributed computing. Can be used between and within multicore processor and MIC coprocessor network nodes. Can be used for native, offload, and reverse offload approaches.

MIC Stands for "Intel Many Integrated Core Architecture." Architecture from Intel designed for highly parallel workloads. The architecture emphasizes higher core counts on a single die, and simpler more efficient cores, than on a traditional CPU. See also Xeon Phi.

MIC Elapsed Time Counter (micetc or ETC) See ETC.

MKL See Math Kernel Library.

MPI See Message Passing Interface.

MPSS See Many-core Platform Software Stack.

multicore A processor with multiple sub-processors, each sub-processor (known as a **core**) supporting at least one hardware thread.

multicore era Time after which processor designs shifted away from rapidly rising clock rates and shifted toward adding more cores. This era began roughly in 2005.

mutual exclusion A mechanism for protecting a set of data values so that while they are manipulated by one parallel thread, they cannot be manipulated by another.

MYO A software shared memory capability supplied by Intel for use with Intel Xeon Phi coprocessors. Stands for Mine-Yours-Ours in recognition of the three states in which data can be shared between the host and a coprocessor. In MYO, data can have the same virtual address on both host and coprocessors so that pointers are valid on both and can be exchanged. This is not normally the case for data since the memories are not shared. The Intel compiler supports MYO through the _Cilk_Shared type as part of Intel **Cilk Plus** support for Intel Xeon Phi coprocessors.

node (in a cluster) A shared memory computer, often on a single board with multiple processors, that is connected with other nodes to form a **cluster** computer or supercomputer.

nondeterministic Exhibiting a lack of deterministic behavior, so results can vary from run to run of an algorithm. Concurrency is not the only factor that can lead to nondeterministic algorithms but in practice it is often the cause. See more in the definition for **deterministic**.

NTS Stands for "No Thermal Solution" referring to coprocessors shipped by Intel where the OEM is responsible for installing a thermal solution to keep the coprocessor cooled. Contrasts with actively cooled (fan) and passively cooled (heat sink) solutions that may be available on some coprocessor models.

OFA Open Fabrics Alliance develops, tests, licenses, supports and distributes OpenFabrics Enterprise Distribution (OFED) open source software to deliver high-efficiency computing, wire-speed messaging, ultra-low microsecond latencies and fast I/O. The Alliance seeks to deliver a unified, cross-platform, transport-independent software stack for RDMA and kernel bypass so that users can utilize the same

OpenFabrics RDMA and kernel bypass API and run their applications agnostically over various inconnects.

OFED Open Fabrics Enterprise Distribution. See OFA.

offload Placing part of a computation on an attached device such as a GPU or coprocessor. See also LEO, OpenMP and OpenACC.

OpenACC nVidia's OpenACC is a specification formulated by four companies (nVidia, PGI, Cray, and CAPS) to provide pragma-based offload for nVidia GPUs. OpenACC will be rendered obsolete by OpenMP target directives. One can expect a migration path and legacy support.

OpenCL Open Compute Language, initiated by Apple Corporation, OpenCL is now a standard defined by the Khronos group for graphics processors and coprocessors. However, OpenCL can also be used to specify parallel and vectorized computations on multicore host processors. Supported by the Intel® SDK for OpenCL Applications.

OpenMP an API that supports multi-platform shared memory multiprocessing programming in C, C++, and Fortran, on most processor architectures and operating systems. It is made up of a set of compiler directives, library routines, and environment variables that influence runtime behavior. OpenMP is managed by the nonprofit technology consortium OpenMP Architecture Review Board and is jointly defined by a group of major computer hardware and software vendors (http://openmp.org). See Chapter 6.

page The granularity at which virtual to physical address mapping is done. Within a page, the mapping of virtual to physical memory addresses is continuous.

parallel Physically happening simultaneously. Two tasks that are both actually doing work at some point in time are considered to be operating in parallel. When a distinction is made between concurrent and parallel, the key is whether work can ever be done simultaneously. Multiplexing of a single processor core, by multitasking operating systems, has allowed concurrency for decades even when simultaneous execution was impossible because there was only one processing core.

Parallel Studio Intel® Parallel Studio XE, suite of tools for node level programming (no MPI support included). Consists of C/C++ and Fortran compilers, libraries, debugging and analysis tools. Supports both processors and coprocessors.

parallelism Doing more than one thing at a time. Attempts to classify types of parallelism are numerous.

parallelization The act of transforming code to enable simultaneous activities. The parallelization of a program allows at least parts of it to execute in parallel.

peel loop A loop, usually compiler generated, created to go before a highly efficient (main) loop to set up conditions needed for the efficient loop. This is commonly needed with the efficient loop assumes N aligned elements per iterations, usually for vectorization, and the peel loop has to do any iterations that precede the required alignment. See also remainder loop.

PMON Performance monitoring. See Chapter 13.

PMU Performance Monitoring Unit, programmable portion of Intel Xeon Phi coprocessor for monitoring performance counters. See Chapter 13.

pragma A pragma is used to give a hint to a compiler, but not change the semantics of a program. OpenMP consists entirely of pragmas. Cilk Plus includes some pragmas in its definition. Also called a "compiler directive."

process A application-level unit of parallel work. A process has its own thread of control and is managed by the operating system. Usually, unless special provisions are made for shared memory, a process cannot access the memory of another process.

race condition Nondeterministic behavior in a parallel program that is generally a programming error. A race condition occurs when concurrent tasks perform operations on the same memory location without proper synchronization, and one of the memory operations is a write. Code with a race may operate correctly sometimes, and fail other times.

recursion Recursion is the act of a function being reentered while an instance of the function is still active in the same thread of execution. In the simplest and most common case, a function directly calls itself, although recursion can also occur between multiple functions. Recursion is supported by storing the state for the continuations of partially completed functions in dynamically allocated memory, such as on a stack, although if higher-order functions are supported a more complex memory allocation scheme may be required. Bounding the amount of recursion can be important to prevent excessive use of memory.

relaxed sequential semantics See **sequential semantics** for an explanation.

remainder loop A loop, usually compiler generated, created to go after a highly efficient (main) loop to clean up any remaining iterations that did not fit within the scope of the efficient loop. This is commonly needed with the efficient loop assumes N elements per iterations, usually for vectorization, and the remainder loop has to finish less than N iterations that are left over. See also peel loop.

Reverse offload (RO) This is a concept of running a program on coprocessor and doing offload to Intel Xeon processor(s). It is a concept only, and not supported directly by the Intel development tools (although programs can be written to do this with some manual effort).

ring level Protection rings are mechanisms to protect data and programs from faults and malicious attacks. Intel Architecture has a four ring capability, which is generally used simply as user (ring 3, most restricted) and kernel (ring 0, least restricted).

SAE Suppress All Exceptions: the Intel® Xeon Phi™ coprocessor introduces the SAE attribute feature. An instruction with SAE set will not raise any kind of floating-point exception flags, independent of the inputs.

scalability Scalability is a measure of the increase in performance as a function of the availability of more hardware to use in parallel.

scalable An application is **scalable** if its performance increases when additional parallel hardware resources are added. See **scalability**.

scatter See gather.

SCI See Symmetric Communications Interface.

SCIF See Symmetric Communications Interface.

sequential consistency Sequential consistency is a relaxed memory consistency model where it is assumed that every task in a concurrent system should see memory writes (updates) in the exact order issued by the original task, but that the knowledge of the relative ordering of writes issued by multiple tasks, or among any reads, is unimportant. If such ordering is important it would require further program control to ensure. Strict consistency models, although generally consider impractical, require that all tasks observe the activities of all tasks in the order they actually occurred in real time.

sequential semantics Sequential semantics means that a (parallel) program can be executed using a single thread of control as an ordinary sequential program without changing the semantics of the program. Parallel programming with sequential semantics has many advantages over programming in a manner that precludes serial execution, and is therefore strongly encouraged. Such programs are considered easier to understand, easier to debug, more efficient on sequential machines and better at supporting nested parallelism. Sequential semantics casts parallelism as an accelerator and not as mandatory for correctness. This means that one does not need a conceptual parallel model to understand or execute a program with sequential semantics. Examples of **mandatory parallelism** include producer-consumer relationships with bounded buffers (hence the producer cannot necessarily be completely executed before the consumer because the producer can become blocked) and message passing (for example, MPI) programs with cyclic message passing. Due to timing, precision, and other sources of inexactness the results of a sequential execution may differ from the concurrent invocation of the same program. Sequential semantics solely means that any such variation is not due to the semantics of the program. The term "relaxed sequential semantics" is sometimes used to explicitly acknowledge the variations possible due to non-semantic differences in serial vs. concurrent executions.

serial Neither concurrent nor parallel.

serial elision The serial elision of a Cilk Plus program is generated by erasing occurrences of the cilk_spawn and cilk_sync keywords and replacing cilk_for with for. Cilk Plus is a faithful extension of C/C++ in the sense that the serial elision of any Cilk Plus program is both a serial C/C++ program *and* a semantically valid implementation of the Cilk Plus program. The term **elision** arose from earlier versions of Cilk that lacked cilk_for, and hence eliding (omitting) the two other keywords sufficed. The term "C elision" is sometimes used too, harking back to when Cilk was an extension of C but not C++.

serial illusion The apparent serial execution order of machine language instructions in a computer. In fact, hardware is naturally parallel and many low-level optimizations and high-performance implementation techniques can reorder operations.

serial semantics Same as **sequential semantics**.

serial traps A serial trap is a programming construct that semantically requires serial execution for proper results in general even though common cases may be over-constrained with regards to concurrency by such semantics. The term "trap" acknowledges how such constructs can easily escape attention as barriers to parallelism, in part because they are so common and were not intentionally designed to preclude parallelism. For instance, for, in the C language, has semantics that dictate the order of iterations by allowing an iteration to assume that all prior iterations have been executed. Many loops do not rely upon side effects of prior iterations, and would be natural candidates for parallel execution, but require analysis in order for a system to determine that parallel execution would not violate the program semantics. Use of cilk_for, for instance, has no such serial semantic and therefore is not a serial trap.

serialization When the tasks in a potentially parallel algorithm are executed in a specific serial order, typically due to resource constraints. The opposite of parallelization.

shared address space Even if units of parallel work do not share a physical memory, they may agree on conventions that allow a single unified set of addresses to be used. For example, one range of addresses could refer to memory on the host, while another range could refer to memory on a specific coprocessor. The use of unified addresses simplifies memory management.

shared memory When two units of parallel work can access data in the same location. Normally doing this safely requires synchronization. The units of parallel work, processes, threads, tasks, and fibers can all share data this way, if the physical memory system allows it. However, processes do not share memory by default and special calls to the operating system are required to set it up.

SIMD Single-instruction-multiple-data referring to the ability to process multiple pieces of data (such as elements of an array) with all the same operation. SIMD is a computer architecture within a widely used classification system known as Flynn's taxonomy, first proposed in 1966.

software thread A software thread is a virtual hardware thread; in other words, a single flow of execution in software intended to map one for one to a hardware thread. An operating system typically enables many more software threads to exist than there are actual hardware threads, by mapping software threads to hardware threads as necessary.

spatial locality Nearby when measured in terms of distance (in memory address). Compare with temporal locality. Spatial locality refers to a program behavior where the use of one data element indicates that data nearby, often the next data element, will probably be used soon. Algorithms exhibiting good spatial locality in data usage can benefit from cache lines structures and prefetching hardware, both common components in modern computers.

spawn Generically, the creation of a new task. In terms of Cilk Plus, cilk_spawn creates a spawn, but the new task created is actually the continuation and not the statement that is the target of the spawn keyword.

spawning block The function, try block, or cilk_for body that contains the spawn. A sync (cilk_sync) waits only for spawns that have occurred in the same spawning block and have no effect on spawns done by other tasks, threads, nor those done prior to entering the current spawning block. A sync is always done, if there have been spawns, when exiting the enclosing spawning block.

speedup Speedup is the ratio between the latency for solving a problem with one processing unit versus the latency for solving the same problem with multiple processing units in parallel.

SPMD Single-program-multiple-data referring to the ability to process multiple pieces of data (such as elements of an array) with the same program, in contrast with a more restrictive SIMD architecture. SPMD most often refers to message passing programming on distributed memory computer architectures (See Chapter 12). SPMD is a subcategory of MIMD computer architectures within a widely used classification system known as Flynn's taxonomy, first proposed in 1966.

Stampede The first announced computer system using Intel Xeon Phi coprocessors (outside Intel). It is located at the Texas Advanced Computing Center in Austin Texas and deployed in January 2013. Stampede will have a peak performance of more than 2 petaFLOP/sec from the base cluster of Intel Xeon processors and more than 7 petaFLOP/sec from the Intel® Xeon® Phi™ coprocessors. See also http://www.tacc.utexas.edu/stampede.

strangled scaling A programming error in which the performance of parallel code is poor due to high contention or overhead, so much so that it may underperform the nonparallel (serial) code.

Symmetric Communications Interface Intel® Symmetric Communications Interface (SCI). SCIF provides a mechanism for inter-node communications within a single platform. A node, for SCIF purposes, is defined as either an Intel Xeon Phi coprocessor or the Intel Xeon processor. In particular, SCIF abstracts the details of communicating over the PCI Express bus. The SCIF APIs are callable from both user space (uSCIF) and kernel-space (kSCIF). SCIF provides only data transfer services. Code control is provided by COI or other operating system services. SCIF exposes a distributed communication software interface very similar to sockets programming. The same programmer interface is exposed whether the implementation is running on an Intel Xeon host or a MIC card, therefore making it "symmetric" as far as functionality and code development is concerned. This enables other communications layers such as TCP/IP, OFED, and standard sockets to be more easily built upon SCIF. Implementing these standard communication interfaces on top SCIF allows a MIC card such as an Intel® Xeon Phi™ coprocessor to be assigned a standard IP address, enabling the card to be logically viewed as an independent computing node in a network or cluster. Familiar distributed usages and access models such as rsh, ssh, Network File System (NFS) mounting are all made possible through SCIF, standard communications layers, and the MIC cards' on-board Linux operating system. Some applications may benefit from direct access to SCIF but may require a significantly higher development investment versus using other standard data transfer and communication mechanisms. SCIF is an advanced topic, not often used directly in application code, and is not covered in this book.

sync In terms of Cilk Plus, cilk_sync creates a sync point. The program flow executing the sync will not progress until all spawns have occurred in the same spawning block. A sync is not affected by spawns done by other tasks, threads, nor those done prior to entering the current spawning block. A sync is always done when exiting a spawning block that contained any spawns. This is required for program **composability**.

synchronization The coordination, of tasks or threads, in order to obtain the desired runtime order. Commonly used to avoid undesired race conditions.

task A lightweight unit of potential parallelism with its own control flow. Unlike threads, tasks are usually serialized on a single core and run to completion. When contrasted with "thread" the distinction is made that tasks are pieces of work without any assumptions about where they will run, while threads have a one-to-one mapping of software threads to hardware threads. Threads are a mechanism for executing tasks in parallel, while tasks are units of work that merely provide the *opportunity* for parallel execution; tasks are not themselves a mechanism of parallel execution.

task parallelism An attempt to classify parallelism as more oriented around tasks than data. We deliberately avoid this term, task parallelism, because its meaning varies. In particular, elsewhere "task parallelism" can refer to tasks generated by functional decomposition *or* to irregular tasks that still generated by data decomposition. In this book, any parallelism generated by data decomposition, regular or irregular, is considered data parallelism.

TBB See **Threading Building Blocks (TBB).**

temporal locality Nearby when measured in terms of time. Compare with spatial locality. Temporal locality refers to a program behavior in which data is likely to be reused relatively soon. Algorithms exhibiting good temporal locality in data usage can benefit from data caching, which is common in modern computers. It is not unusual to be able to achieve both temporal and spatial locality in data usage. Computer systems are generally more able to achieve optimal performance when both are achieved hence the interest in algorithm design to do so.

thread In general, a "software thread" is any software unit of parallel work with an independent flow of control, and a "hardware thread" is any hardware unit capable of executing a single flow of control (in particular, a hardware unit that maintains a single program counter). When "thread" is compared with "task" the distinction is made that tasks are pieces of work without any assumptions about where they will run, while threads have a one-to-one mapping of software threads to hardware threads. Threads are a mechanism for implementing tasks. A multitasking or multithreading operating system will multiplex multiple software threads onto a single hardware thread by interleaving execution via software created time slices. A multicore or many-core processor consists of multiple cores to execute at least one independent software thread per core through duplication of hardware. A multithreaded or hyper-threaded processor core will multiplex a single core to execute multiple software threads through interleaving of software threads via hardware mechanisms.

thread parallelism A mechanism for implementing parallelism in hardware using a separate flow of control for each task.

Threading Building Blocks Intel® Threading Building Blocks (TBB) is the most popular abstract solution for parallel programming in C++. TBB is an open source project created by Intel that has been ported to a very wide range of operating systems and processors from many vendors. OpenMP and TBB seldom compete for developers in reality. While more popular than OpenMP in terms of the number of developers using it, TBB is popular with C++ programmers whereas OpenMP is most used by Fortran and C programmers.

throughput Given a set of tasks to be performed, the rate at which those tasks are completed. Throughput measures the rate of computation, and it is given in units of tasks per unit time. See **bandwidth** and **latency**.

tiling Dividing a loop into a set of parallel tasks of a suitable granularity. In general, tiling consists of applying multiple steps on a smaller part of a problem instead of running each step on the whole problem one after the other. The purpose of tiling is to increase reuse of data in caches. Tiling can lead to dramatic performance increases when a whole problem does not fit in cache. We prefer the term "tiling" instead of "blocking" and "tile" instead of "block." Tiling and tile have become the more common term in recent times.

TLB An abbreviation for Translation Lookaside Buffer. A TLB is a specialized cache that is used to hold translations of virtual to physical page addresses. The number of elements in the TLB determines how many pages of memory can be accessed simultaneously with good efficiency. Accessing a page not in the TLB will cause a TLB miss. A TLB miss typically causes a trap to the operating system so that the page table can be referenced and the TLB updated.

Trace Analyzer and Collector Intel® Trace Analyzer and Collector, a tool for analyzing MPI communication traffic in order to detect opportunities for improvement. See Chapter 13.

Translation Lookaside Buffer See **TLB**.

trip count The number of times a given loop will execute ("trip"); same as "iteration count."

TSC Timestamp Counter, standard counter in modern x86 processors including the Intel Xeon Phi coprocessor. Each core has a 64-bit counter that monotonically increments the timestamp counter every clock cycle and reset to 0 whenever the processor is reset. Having multiple counters in the coprocessor increases the complexity to synchronize all of them when time measurements are required on different cores. The Read Time-Stamp Counter instruction RDTSC allows the loading of the content of the core's timestamp counter into the EDX:EAX registers. Although this clocksource is low overhead, it is greatly affected by changes in power management therefore it is not possible to assure that the timestamp on multiple cores will be synchronized. See Chapter 13.

vector operation A low-level operation that can act on multiple data elements at once in SIMD fashion.

unroll Complete unrolling of a loop is accomplished by duplicating the body of the loop, for each iteration, into straight code so no loop is needed. For instance: for (i = 0;i < 3;i++) a[i] = i; can be unrolled to a[0] = 0; a[1] = 1; a[2] = 2; partial unrolling retains the loop but expands the loop body to do multiple iterations each time through the loop. This is commonly done to enable vectorization. Unrolling is a common compiler optimization and has been common in source code in the past although it is a bad idea these days (see Section "Avoid manual loop unrolling" in Chapter 5).

vector parallelism A mechanism for implementing parallelism in hardware using the same flow of control on multiple data elements.

vector processing unit (VPU) The portion of the coprocessor dedicated to processing vector operations. See Chapter 5.

vectorization The act of transforming code to enable simultaneous computations using vector hardware. Instructions such as MMX, SSE, and AVX instructions utilize vector hardware. The vectorization of code tends to enhance performance because more data is processed per instruction than would be done otherwise. See also **vectorize**.

vectorize Converting a program from a scalar implementation to a vectorized implementation to utilize vector hardware such as SIMD instructions (MMX, SSE, AVX, and so on). Vectorization is a specialized form of parallelism.

virtual memory Virtual memory decouples the address used by software from the physical addresses of real memory. The translation from virtual addresses to physical addresses is done in hardware that is initialized and controlled by the operating system.

VPU Vector Processing Unit. The portion of the coprocessor dedicated to processing vector operations. See Chapter 5.

VTune Intel® VTune™ Amplifier XE, analysis tool specializing in use of EMON counters to profile activity on processors and coprocessor. See Chapter 13.

Xeon Phi Intel® Xeon Phi™ coprocessors based on Intel® Many Integrated Core (MIC) Architecture. A prototype with up to 32 cores and based on 45nm process technology, known as Knight Ferry, was made available, but not sold, by Intel in 2010 and 2011. A product, known as the Intel® Xeon Phi™ coprocessor, built on 22nm process technology with up to 61 cores, started shipping in late 2012 and was announced in November 2012 at the conference known as "SC12" (Supercomputing 2012 in Salt Lake City Utah). The SC12 announcement coincided with seven machines using the Intel® Xeon Phi™ coprocessor appearing on the "Top 500 List" and the most energy efficient computer in the world (#1 spot on "Green 500") utilized Intel® Xeon Phi™ coprocessors. See also **MIC**.

Index

Note: Page numbers followed by "*f*" and "*t*" refer to figures and tables, respectively.

D

E

F

J

K

L

P

Q

R

U

V

W

X